ON HUMAN RIGHTS

This book is prompted by the widespread belief that we do not yet have a clear enough idea of what human rights are. The term 'natural right', in its modern sense of an entitlement that a person has, first appeared in the late Middle Ages. When during the seventeenth and eighteenth centuries the theological content of the idea was abandoned in stages, nothing was put in its place. The secularized notion that we were left with at the end of the Enlightenment is still our notion today, in this respect. Its intension has not changed since then: *a right that we have simply in virtue of being human.* During the twentieth century international law has contributed to settling its extension, but its contribution has its limits.

The notion of a human right that we have inherited suffers from no small indeterminateness of sense. The term has been left with so few criteria for determining when it is used correctly that we often have a plainly inadequate grasp on what is at issue. We today need to remedy its indeterminateness; we need to complete the incomplete idea. That is the aim of this book.

Its argument is of concern, and is accessible, to philosophers, jurisprudents, political theorists, international lawyers, civil servants, and rights activists.

James Griffin is White's Professor of Moral Philosophy Emeritus at the University of Oxford; Visiting Professor of Philosophy at Rutgers University; and Adjunct Professor at the Centre for Applied Philosophy and Public Ethics, Canberra.

On Human Rights

JAMES GRIFFIN

OXFORD
UNIVERSITY PRESS

OXFORD

UNIVERSITY PRESS

Great Clarendon Street, Oxford OX2 6DP
United Kingdom

Oxford University Press is a department of the University of Oxford.
It furthers the University's objective of excellence in research, scholarship,
and education by publishing worldwide. Oxford is a registered trade mark of
Oxford University Press in the UK and in certain other countries

British Library Cataloguing in Publication Data
Data available

Library of Congress Cataloging in Publication Data
Data available

ISBN 978-0-19-957310-3

For

Nico and Julia

Jess and John

Acknowledgements

I owe special thanks to three colleagues. When I first contemplated this book, I gave a seminar on the subject with my Oxford colleague Joseph Raz, who obligingly subjected my developing views, then and since, to his powerful scepticism. My Rutgers colleague Ruth Chang read the whole of two drafts. I postponed handing over the typescript to the Press when a chance arose of giving a seminar with her on my typescript in the autumn of 2006. I owe a lot to her skill at keeping her eye firmly on the main point while not missing a single minor lapse. Another Oxford colleague, John Tasioulas, has over many years brought to my work his broad knowledge and fine judgement. He generously organized a workshop on the first draft of the whole book, and I am grateful to those who responded to his invitation to show me what still needed to be done: Roger Crisp, John Gardner, David Miller, Hillel Steiner, Leif Wenar, and Jo Woolf.

I have also been helped by conversations with my Rutgers colleagues: Douglas Husak, Larry Temkin, and Jeff McMahan, and with my colleagues at the Centre for Applied Philosophy and Public Ethics in Canberra: Seumas Miller, Tom Campbell, and Thomas Pogge.

Carl Wellman and I have talked about rights over very many years, and I have benefited from his incomparable knowledge of the subject and his generosity in imparting it.

James Nickel was a reader of my typescript for the Press who chose not to remain anonymous. I thank him for bringing to that task an ideal combination: warm encouragement and cool criticism.

In 2003 I gave an earlier version of this book as the José Gaos Lectures at the Universidad Nacional Autónoma de México. The audience gave me much help, though I should single out Mark Platts for special thanks.

Then there are the unsung ranks of bright graduate students, who not infrequently taught me as much as I taught them—a process for which, none the less, I got paid.

Jo Cartmell spent about as many years working on this book as I have. She put my original manuscript on disk and then incorporated change after change.

Earlier drafts of some of my chapters have appeared previously in print:

Chapter 1 in *Anales de la Cátedra Francisco Suarez* 38 (2004).

Chapter 2 in *European Journal of Philosophy* 9 (2001).

Chapter 3 in M. Friedman, L. May, *et al.* (eds.), *Rights and Reasons* (Dordrecht: Kluwer, 2000).

Chapter 4 in D. Archard and C. M. Macleod (eds.), *The Moral and Political Status of Children* (Oxford: Oxford University Press, 2002).

Chapter 5 in T. Campbell and S. Miller (eds.), *Human Rights and the Moral Responsibilities of Corporate and Public Sector Organizations* (Dordrecht: Kluwer, 2004).

Chapter 10 in *Journal of Ethics* 4 (2000).

Chapter 11, Presidential Address, in *Proceedings of the Aristotelian Society*, 101 (2000–1).

Chapter 12 in *Telos* 8 (1998).

Chapter 15 in Lukas Meyer, Stanley Paulson, and Thomas Pogge (eds.), *Rights, Culture, and the Law: Themes from the Legal and Political Philosophy of Joseph Raz* (Oxford: Oxford University Press, 2003).

J.P.G.

July 2007

Contents

Introduction   1

PART I: AN ACCOUNT OF HUMAN RIGHTS

1. Human Rights: The Incomplete Idea   9

    1.1   The Enlightenment project on human rights   9

    1.2   The indeterminateness of the term 'human right'   14

    1.3   Remedies for the indeterminateness   18

    1.4   Different approaches to explaining rights: substantive and structural accounts   20

    1.5   A different kind of substantive account   22

    1.6   How should we go about completing the idea?   27

2. First Steps in an Account of Human Rights   29

    2.1   Top-down and bottom-up accounts   29

    2.2   The human rights tradition   30

    2.3   A proposal of a substantive account   32

    2.4   One ground for human rights: personhood   33

    2.5   A second ground: practicalities   37

    2.6   Is there a third ground?: equality   39

    2.7   How we should understand 'agency'?   44

    2.8   In what sense are human rights 'universal'?   48

    2.9   Do we need a more pluralist account?   51

3. When Human Rights Conflict   57

    3.1   One of the central questions of ethics   57

    3.2   Conflicts between human rights themselves   58

    3.3   Are human rights co-possible?   60

3.4 Conflicts between a human right and other kinds of moral
    consideration   63
3.5 A proposal and a qualification   66
3.6 A step beyond intuition   76
3.7 Some ways in which human rights resist trade-offs   79
3.8 Reprise   81

4. **Whose Rights?**   83

4.1 The scope of the question   83
4.2 Potential agents   83
4.3 The inference from moral weight to human rights   86
4.4 Need accounts of human rights   88
4.5 A class of rights on their own?   90
4.6 A role for stipulation   91
4.7 Coming into rights in stages   94

5. **My Rights: But Whose Duties?**   96

5.1 Introduction   96
5.2 What duties?   97
5.3 Whose duties?   101
5.4 Primary and secondary duties   104
5.5 AIDS in Africa   105
5.6 Can there be rights without indentifiable duty-bearers?   107

6. **The Metaphysics of Human Rights**   111

6.1 Two models of value judgement   111
6.2 Human interests and the natural world   116
6.3 The test of the best explanation   121
6.4 The metaphysics of human rights   124

7. **The Relativity and Ethnocentricity of Human Rights**   129

7.1 Ethical relativity   129
7.2 The relativity of human rights   133
7.3 What is the problem of ethnocentricity?   137
7.4 Tolerance   142

PART II: HIGHEST-LEVEL HUMAN RIGHTS

8. **Autonomy**   149

  8.1 The three highest-level human rights   149
  8.2 The distinction between autonomy and liberty   149
  8.3 The value of autonomy   151
  8.4 The content of the right to autonomy   152
  8.5 Autonomy and free will: what if we are not autonomous?   157

9. **Liberty**   159

  9.1 Highest-level rights   159
  9.2 Broad and narrow interpretations of liberty   159
  9.3 'Pursuit'   160
  9.4 Negative and positive sides of liberty   166
  9.5 How demanding is the right?   167
  9.6 Mill's 'one very simple principle' of liberty   169
  9.7 Generalizing the results   174

10. **Welfare**   176

  10.1 The historical growth of rights   176
  10.2 Welfare: a civil, not a human, right?   177
  10.3 A case for a human right to welfare   179
  10.4 Is the proposed right too demanding?   182
  10.5 The undeserving poor   184
  10.6 Human rights, legal rights, and rights in the United
      Nations   186

PART III: APPLICATIONS

11. **Human Rights: Discrepancies Between Philosophy and
International Law**   191

  11.1 Applications of the personhood account   191
  11.2 Bringing philosophical theory and legal practice together   191

11.3 The list of human rights that emerges from the personhood
       account   192
11.4 Current legal lists: civil and political rights   193
11.5 Interlude on the aims and status of international law   202
11.6 Current legal lists: economic, social, and cultural rights   206
11.7 The future of international lists of human rights   209

12. A Right to Life, a Right to Death   212

12.1 The scope of the right to life   212
12.2 Locke on the scope of the right   213
12.3 Personhood as the ground of the right   215
12.4 From a right to life to a right to death   216
12.5 Is there a right to death?   221
12.6 Is it a positive or a negative right?   223

13. Privacy   225

13.1 Personhood and the content of a human right to privacy   225
13.2 Legal approaches to the right to privacy   227
13.3 How broad is the right? : (*i*) privacy of information, (*ii*)
       privacy of space and life, and (*iii*) the privacy of liberty 234
13.4 A proposal about the right to privacy   238
13.5 Privacy versus freedom of expression and the right to
       information   239

14. Do Human Rights Require Democracy?   242

14.1 Two plausible lines of thought   242
14.2 Autonomy and liberty   243
14.3 Democracy   243
14.4 Do human rights require democracy?   247
14.5 In modern conditions?   251

15. Group Rights   256

15.1 Three generations of rights   256
15.2 No quick way of dismissing group rights   256
15.3 A case for group rights: the good-based argument   258

15.4 Another case for group rights: the justice-based argument   265

15.5 Exclusion   271

15.6 Reduction   273

15.7 What is left?   275

Notes   277
Index   331

Introduction

This book is prompted by the not uncommon belief that we do not yet have a clear enough idea of what human rights are. But this belief needs more focus. Human rights as used in ethics? In the law? In politics? If in ethics, in an abstract framework such as deontology or teleology? In ethical judgements applied to our societies? If in the law, the law as it is? As it should be? The law where? If in politics, in its history? In empirical explanation? In setting standards?

My focus is ethics. And I prefer to start with ethical judgements as applied to the assessment of our societies—the judgements not just of philosophers but also of political theorists, politicians, international lawyers, and civil servants. The term 'natural right' (*ius naturale*), in its modern sense of an entitlement that a person has, first appeared in the late Middle Ages. God was thought to have placed in us natural dispositions towards the good, dispositions giving rise to action-guiding precepts. These precepts expressed natural laws, from which natural rights could be derived. The theological content of the idea of a natural right was abandoned in stages during the seventeenth and eighteenth centuries, when thinkers increasingly accepted that human rights were available to human reason alone, without belief in God. The idea moved out of the library on to the barricades in the eighteenth century with the American and French revolutions, and the French marked the secularization of the concept by changing its name from 'natural rights' to 'human rights' (*les droits de l'homme*). In its secular form at the end of the Enlightenment it was often still thought to be derived from natural law, but natural law by then widely reduced to no more than a moral principle independent of law and convention. It went into partial eclipse in the nineteenth century, in no small measure in reaction to the bloodiness of the French Revolution. It was brought back into full light by, among others, Franklin Roosevelt at the start of the Second World War and, even more so, by the United Nations at its end. The secularized notion that we were left with at the end of the

Enlightenment is still our notion today, at least in this way. Its intension has not changed since then: *a right that we have simply in virtue of being human.* It is not that there have been no changes at all. An important one is the growth of the international law of human rights in the twentieth century. This has brought about changes in the extension of the term, and changes in extension can constitute changes in meaning—a matter I shall return to shortly.

There is a continuous, developing notion of human rights running through this history—call it the 'historical notion'. That is the notion with which I want to start. Start, but most likely not finish. I am looking for the notion of human rights that fits into the best ethics that we can establish, and it is unlikely that the notion that history has yielded is already in perfect form for its place in ethics. One of the first things that one notices about the historical notion is that it suffers from no small indeterminateness of sense. When during the seventeenth and eighteenth centuries the theological content of the idea was abandoned, nothing was put in its place. The term was left with so few criteria for determining when it is used correctly, and when incorrectly, that we often have only a tenuous, and sometimes a plainly inadequate, grasp on what is at issue. Its indeterminateness of sense is not something characteristic of ethical terms in general; it is a problem specifically, though perhaps not uniquely, with the term 'human right'. We today need to remedy its indeterminateness; we need to complete the incomplete notion, and thereby most likely change it.

How may we remedy the indeterminateness? Although the theological content of the term was abandoned, the ethical content was not. From time to time in the course of the history one encounters the idea that human rights are protections of our human status and that the human status in question is our rational or, more specifically, normative agency. In my attempt to make the sense of the term 'human rights' more determinate, I suggest that we adopt this part of the tradition, that we see human rights as protections of our normative agency.

I prefer, I say, to start with the historical notion. Where else might someone whose focus is ethics start? In philosophy the most common approach to rights is to derive them from one, or a few, highest-level moral principles. There are well-known examples of this procedure. Kant derives human rights (his 'natural rights') from one of the most abstract principles of his ethics—what he calls 'The Universal Principle of Right', which goes: 'any action is right if it can coexist with everyone's freedom in accordance with a universal law'. From this principle he derives the single innate right: the 'right belonging to every man by virtue of his humanity', the content of which is the same as that of the Universal Principle of Right. So this one innate right, and the rights derivable from it, cover much of morality—not quite all (not, for example, duties arising from the Doctrine of Virtue), but a large part of it, far more than is covered by the human rights in the Enlightenment and onwards. And John Stuart Mill, in the final chapter of *Utilitarianism*, introduces 'rights' as claims on specifiable others, ultimately derivable from the Principle of Utility, taking into account the disutilities of a society's formulating rules, promulgating them, punishing their disobedience, and so on—a notion of rights that also covers much more of morality than do the human rights of the political life of the last few centuries.

Neither Kant nor Mill was trying to explore the notion of human rights as it appears in that historical tradition. They were just commandeering the term 'human rights' (or 'natural rights' or, in Mill's case, just plain 'rights') to do service in the exposition of their own general moral theory. There is nothing wrong with that so long as we are not misled by it. The extension of their term 'rights' is so substantially different from the extension of the Enlightenment notion that we may well think that Kant and Mill are introducing a different concept, that they are, in effect, changing the subject. And in our day John Rawls has followed in Kant's and Mill's footsteps, in this respect: he too commandeers the term 'human right' for service in his overall account of political justice between peoples, also with a marked difference in extension from the Enlightenment notion, though in his case narrower.

Why do I not do the same as Kant and Mill, only try to do better? If their highest-level moral principles were the wrong ones to start with, why do I not start with the right ones? And if what comes out of my attempt at derivation is, as it was in Kant's and Mill's case, a considerably different extension, so be it. But that, as we saw, could change the subject, which I am reluctant to do. The historical notion is the one that is now so powerful in our political life and that, to my mind, has generally been a force for the good. And it is, at the same time, a key idea in ethics. It is an idea that many of us connect with the notion of 'the dignity of the human person', on some interpretation of that phrase. We see human rights as protections of that dignity, and so as potentially having connections with familiar philosophical concerns about respect for persons, the inviolability of the person, and limits on the pursuit of the common good. Indeed, it confronts us with that key choice in ethics between deontology and teleology. It has a foot in both politics and ethics, and in both theoretical and applied ethics. The bottom-up approach that

I prefer may eventually meet the top-down approach of Kant and Mill. In remedying the indeterminateness of sense, in determining the content of human rights, especially in seeing how to resolve conflict between them, the bottom-up approach will have to rise considerably in theoretical abstraction. Whether it must rise quite to the level of abstraction of the Categorical Imperative or the Principle of Utility we can wait to see. There are merits in starting with the historical notion.

I propose, as I have said, that we see human rights as protections of our normative agency. That is not a *derivation* of human rights from normative agency; it is a *proposal* based on a hunch that this way of remedying the indeterminateness of the term will best suit its role in ethics. The requirement that it suit ethics holds out prospects—realized, I should say—of supplying standards for determining whether an account of human rights is 'right' or 'wrong'. What I do is distant from what Kant and Mill did. It is also distant from what Alan Gewirth did recently, in seeking to establish human rights by appeal to certain logical necessities. That he too makes human agency central to his project does not make his project close to mine. His first step is to derive rights from agency in the prudential case: every agent, even the purely self-interested, must accept, on pain of contradiction, that 'I have rights to the proximate necessary conditions of my action'. His next step is from the prudential case to the universal: the agent must accept, because of the logical principle of universalizability, and again on pain of contradiction, that 'all other agents equally have these rights', thus establishing them as *human* rights. In contrast, I claim no logical necessity for my proposal that we see human rights as protections of normative agency. Indeed, some of my colleagues not only reject it but also make plausible, contradiction-free counter-proposals that must in some way be seriously assessed.

How would one go about assessing my proposal? Ultimately, by deciding whether it gives us human rights that fit into the best ethics overall. More immediately, by working out its consequences, especially its consequences for supposed human rights that we find contentious or unclear. And by assessing my proposal against counter-proposals: for example, the counter-proposal that the ground of human rights is not solely normative agency but certain other values as well, or that the ground is not normative agency but basic human needs, and so on. And even by answering largely empirical questions such as how determinate we must make the sense of the term 'human right' to avoid creating serious practical problems for ourselves. Such assessments cannot be made quickly; they take a fairly long book.

It may look as though, in *proposing* a sense for the term 'human rights', I am just stipulating its sense. If so, then it is in the way that the writers in the late Middle Ages who first introduced our modern notion of a 'human right' stipulated its sense. They by no means stipulated arbitrarily. They were trying to get at something that, if not morally foundational, was at least morally important.

My remedy for the indeterminateness is by no means the only one on offer. My remedy is to add to the evaluative content of the notion. Not only are there possible evaluative additions other than mine, there are also non-evaluative remedies. Some think that international law has already remedied the indeterminateness in its own quite different way. International law, some think, has by now authoritatively settled the extension of the term 'human right', and in settling its extension has thereby adequately determined its sense.

Has international law settled the extension? No matter who we are, we cannot establish the existence of a human right just by declaring it to be one. We can get it wrong, and we owe attention, therefore, to what are the criteria for right and wrong here. For example, the Universal Declaration contains a right to periodic holidays with pay, to which the overwhelming and cheering reaction has been that, whatever that supposed entitlement is, it is certainly not a human right. The Universal Declaration also includes a right to democratic participation, but it is possible to argue in an intellectually responsible way about whether it really is a human right. Again, we owe attention to how we would settle that argument. And there are widespread doubts about welfare rights—for instance, whether they are human or only civil rights, or whether some of them have not been drawn too lavishly. We quite reasonably want to know how strong the case is for considering them human rights. Again, how would the case be made? And we need far more than a *list* of human rights. We need more than just their *names*. We must also know their content. But how do we decide it? And we need to know how to resolve conflicts between them. A judge on an international bench cannot resolve conflicts by *fiat*. The resolution must be reasoned. But what are to count as good reasons? Even if the list of human rights in current international law were authoritative, which I see no reason to believe, it would not give us all we need. We also need answers to these questions.

To get those answers, I suggest, we should search for a satisfactory interpretation of 'dignity' in the phrase 'the dignity of the human person' when used as the ground of human rights, because obviously not all kinds of dignity are. A better understanding will increase the intension of the term 'human right'.

As for a sufficiently determinate sense for the term, we do not have it yet. The law contributes to greater determinateness. It is especially good at moving from particular cases to more general understanding of what is at issue. Not all increases in determinateness are increases in determinateness of *sense*. The latter has to do specifically with determinateness in the criteria for correct and incorrect use of the term. But to the extent that the law makes clearer what is at issue it also contributes to determinateness of sense. My argument is that ethics must make a contribution too, not that it alone will do the job. We will not reach sufficient determinateness of sense without contribution from ethics. That I do not say much about international law is simply because I do not know much about it.

Those, summarily rehearsed, are the thoughts that give my book its direction and will, I hope, make its direction clear to readers. I shall return to all of these matters in a more dialectical spirit and with some scholarly apparatus in what follows.

PART I

AN ACCOUNT OF HUMAN RIGHTS

1

Human Rights: The Incomplete Idea

1.1 THE ENLIGHTENMENT PROJECT ON HUMAN RIGHTS

Use of the term 'human rights' began at the end of the eighteenth century (for example, in the French Declaration of the Rights of Man and of the Citizen (1789)—'les droits de l'homme'), but it gained wide currency only in the middle of the twentieth century. Before the end of the eighteenth century, the talk was instead of 'natural rights'. The two terms come from the same continuous tradition; they have largely the same extension,[1] though different intensions. 'Natural rights' were generally seen as derived from 'natural laws'. As we shall see, it is altogether harder to say from what 'human rights' are supposed to be derived.

Although the doctrine of natural law has ramified roots deep in Greek and Roman antiquity, it was given its most influential statement by Thomas Aquinas. God has placed in all things various innate natural dispositions, but only in human beings has he further placed a disposition to reason: that is, a disposition issuing in various precepts to guide action—for example, that we are to preserve ourselves in being; to propagate our kind; to seek knowledge of, and to worship, God; and to live peacefully in society.[2] These and other precepts constitute the natural law, and the natural law serves as the measure of the natural right. But Aquinas's reference here to 'right' is by no means our modern sense of 'a right', which is an entitlement that a person *has*. Rather, the 'right' that Aquinas here wrote of is a property of a state of affairs: namely, that the state of affairs is right or just or fair. Aquinas had much to say about natural law and the natural right, but it is a matter of dispute whether he had our modern concept of a natural right.[3]

Indeed, the term 'natural right', in our modern sense, though it first appeared in the late Middle Ages, did not itself gain wide use until the seventeenth and eighteenth centuries. Let me retrace some of the steps on the route from Aquinas to the Enlightenment. Clearly one major natural disposition leading human beings to the good is rationality, which issues in the precept: follow practical rationality. That precept largely lacks moral content; it is more a directive for arriving at that content, indeed so comprehensive a directive that it threatens to displace all other precepts. And if human reason is sufficient to identify natural law, can God be necessary to it? Francisco Suarez, the most influential writer in the Thomist tradition in the seventeenth century,[4] had an answer. Although their reason gives human beings a certain independence of God, that independence has its limits. Human beings can, unaided, understand the content of natural laws, but what they understand has the status of law—that is, of a command with force—only because of God's will.

The Protestant Hugo Grotius earned his reputation as the founder of the modern secular theory of natural law by taking the further step of arguing that God is not needed even to explain the obligatoriness of natural law. He wrote that 'what we have been saying [namely, that there are natural laws and that they obligate] would have a certain degree of validity even if we should concede that which cannot be conceded without the utmost wickedness, that there is no God, or that the affairs of men are of no concern to him'.[5] Grotius, a pious Christian, never himself made the 'wicked concession'. None the less, he thought that we can establish natural laws through the kind of understanding open to all of us, whatever we believe about religion: namely, that we must act in accord with our rational nature, and that we must do the various things necessary to maintain a society both consonant with reason and composed of inconsistently motivated members such as us—by nature desirous of society yet by nature so self-interested as to undermine society.

Like Grotius, Samuel Pufendorf thought that although divine revelation may help us to know natural law, 'it can still be investigated and definitely proved, even without such aid, by the power of reason'.[6] What particularly needs empirical investigation, he thought, is which precepts are needed to produce a rationally stable society out of the unsocially social creatures that human beings are.[7]

With these steps we arrive at the Enlightenment, which I shall take as running from the last fifteen years or so of the seventeenth century to the end of the eighteenth.[8] In the *Two Treatises of Civil Government* John Locke still gave central place in his argument to both natural law and natural rights; the latter he too thought derivable from the former.[9]

However, he paid little attention to how the derivation was supposed to work; he used the language of natural law as a well-established, relatively unproblematic way of speaking.[10] Reason alone, he thought, can establish fundamental moral principles—indeed, can establish them with certainty. At the core of this reasoning, as Pufendorf said before him, will be empirical investigation into the laws needed to enable unsocially social individuals to become members of a properly ordered society. In the course of this reasoning, we need not—indeed, cannot successfully—appeal to any views about the ends of human life; rational persons, he thought, will disagree about them, so a belief about the *summum bonum*, though at the heart of classical and medieval thought, is at best of peripheral interest here, because it is incapable of commanding universal assent and thus of effectively guiding the heterogeneous members of a society.[11] Locke does from time to time refer to God, but it is the God of the Deists: the designer who set the great machine going and then departed from the scene—no intervention, no revelation. Locke's primary interest in the *Two Treatises* was moral constraints on the arbitrary acts of rulers. So it is not surprising that the natural rights that he focused on were the taking of a person's life, liberty, or property without due process, the three most common ways for monarchs to keep their subjects under their thumb.

I referred at the start to 'the Enlightenment project on human rights'. I should now explain what I mean. Why *the* project? Rights were hardly the only concern of Enlightenment writers. What is more, there was no single conception of 'natural law' or 'natural right' that all Enlightenment thinkers shared; indeed, some of them contemptuously repudiated the entire discourse.[12] Yet there was a general movement of thought in the course of the Enlightenment. There was the continued secularization of the doctrines of natural law and natural rights, following the expanding role of human reason. There was the closely related abandonment of much in the way of metaphysical or epistemological background for them. Admittedly, this was not entirely true of Locke, who appealed to God in order to establish the now sometimes overlooked principle of equality at the base of his political thought; but it was true of many of his successors in the eighteenth century. By the end of the Enlightenment, acceptance of natural law seems to have become compatible with just about any metaphysical and epistemological view. In the universe, as conceived by Aquinas, everything has its divinely assigned end. One could therefore see human ends as part of, and readable off, nature. This view, developed in a certain way, can support a strong form of natural law. It can support, for instance, a form of moral realism—that is, the view that human goods and perhaps even moral principles are not human constructs, but part of a reality that is independent of human thought and attitude. And this sort of moral realism can, in turn, support the epistemic view that judgements about human good and moral principles are capable of truth and falsity in the strong sense that more familiar kinds of reports about nature are. That would be the strongest interpretation of the naturalness of natural law, and there are progressively weaker ones. For instance, we might require of judgements about natural law only that they be objective—that is, that they not be merely expressions of human attitudes. In the course of the seventeenth and eighteenth centuries the claim that there are natural laws became weaker still; it was commonly reduced to no more than the claim that there are moral principles independent of positive law and social convention. It became much like the use in our day of the notion of 'natural justice', which in the mouths of lawyers nowadays commits one to no more than the existence of a standard of justice independent of positive law and convention. And this very weak claim is compatible with virtually all conceptions of ethics—including, for example, Hume's subjectivism—except for ethical relativism, which in any case was a rare view in those days.

So the general movement of thought about rights in the course of the Enlightenment was not just a matter of secularization. Indeed, the secularization was well launched by philosophers who preceded the Enlightenment. In the course of the Enlightenment, though, there were two further developments. Writers aimed at comprehensive lists of *natural* or *human* rights.[13] Lists of rights, of course, were drawn up long before then, but they were lists of positive rights, already or then being granted. The Emperor Constantine, in the Edict of Milan (313), did not claim that Christians already and everywhere had religious freedom; he granted it to them, and others, in the Roman Empire: 'no one whatsoever should be denied the opportunity to give his heart to the observance of the Christian religion, or of that religion which he should think best'. In England, Magna Carta (1215) concerned the rights of certain social classes and institutions: earls, barons, and their widows and heirs; the English Church; the City of London; the clergy; merchants; free men; and so on. It was concerned with establishing a *modus vivendi* for those who had to share power. The rights were not based on human nature; they did not apply to *all* men and only indirectly to women, as wives. Over time, though, the rights and privileges on the lists began to be applied to increasingly broader groups. The English Bill of Rights (1688) was concerned with 'vindicating and asserting their ancient rights and liberties', 'they' being 'the lords spiritual and temporal, and commons', and though some of the rights—for example, to fair procedure in courts—actually applied to a still larger group, none were derived simply from being human. This was true, too, of virtually all of the charters that poured forth from the sometimes restive British Colonies in North America in the course of the seventeenth and eighteenth centuries; they laid claim only to 'the rights of Englishmen', rights already established in the common law of the mother country. They laid claim, as the Virginia Charter (1606) put it, to 'all liberties, franchises and immunities ... to all intents and purposes as if they had been abiding and born within England'.[14] The American colonists no doubt thought that they were on more promising ground claiming rights that had already been granted, but when that strategy got nowhere, their eventual Declaration of Independence (1776) fell back on *natural* rights. The eighteenth century came to an end with comprehensive lists of what were meant to be the most basic or important natural or human rights[15]—namely, the French *Declaration of the Rights of Man and of the Citizen* (1789) and the United States Bill of Rights (1791). And along with these codes of human rights there came a second development. These lists took centre-stage in political life. They justified rebellion—in a detached, retrospective way in the case of Locke's defence of the Glorious Revolution of 1688,[16] but in an altogether more engaged way in the case of the American and French revolutions. Natural or human rights became a popular political force.[17]

The notion of human rights that emerged by the end of the Enlightenment—what can reasonably be called the Enlightenment notion—is the notion we have today. There has been no theoretical development of the idea itself since then. It is not, of course, that there have been no developments of any sort. The League of Nations developed, through treaties, basic mechanisms for the international protection of human rights. The United Nations, through the Universal Declaration and subsequent instruments, created a largely agreed list of human rights, which has had wide ramifications in political life. International law now embodies human rights and has developed complex institutions of adjudication.[18] And so on. But despite the many changes, none has been to the idea itself. The idea is still that of a right we have simply in virtue of being human, with no further explanation of what 'human' means here. Settling the extension of the term, it is true, is one way of determining its sense, and international law is sometimes seen as having settled the extension of 'human right'. But it has not done anything so decisive. International law has, or should have, ambitions to incorporate human rights determined, at least in part, by ethical considerations independent of law or convention. I shall come back to the aims of international law later.[19]

Natural law began as part of a teleological metaphysics capable of supporting strong interpretations of how morality is rooted in nature, and it ended up at the close of the eighteenth century in something approaching vacuity.[20] It is not that the strong, non-vacuous conceptions of natural law do not have their own considerable problems.[21] Still, many scholastic conceptions of natural law gave us at least *something* to go on in deciding what natural rights there are. Once the metaphysical and epistemological background that they provided is abandoned, as it was in the course of the Enlightenment, what is left? Is enough left?

1.2 THE INDETERMINATENESS OF THE TERM 'HUMAN RIGHT'

In what state is the discourse of human rights today? Take two examples, the first from the United Nations. Thirty world leaders, in a statement issued through the Secretary-General of the United Nations, claimed that 'the opportunity to decide the number and spacing of their children is a basic human right' of parents.[22] Does China's one-child policy then really infringe a human right? Would a five- or a ten-child policy do so too? Next, an example from philosophy, where the scene is not much brighter. In the course of a well-known article about abortion, a distinguished American philosopher builds her case on a presumed right to determine what happens in and to one's body.[23] But do we have such a broad right? If the government were to prohibit us from selling our body parts, as many governments are thinking of doing, would our human rights be infringed? This proposed right is not dissimilar to a widely accepted human right—a right to security of person. But one's person's being secure is considerably different from one's body's being in all respects under one's own determination. How are we to tell whether we have such a strong right?

We do not know. The term 'human right' is nearly criterionless. There are unusually few criteria for determining when the term is used correctly and when incorrectly—and not just among politicians, but among philosophers, political theorists, and jurisprudents as well. The language of human rights has, in this way, become debased.

Others need not agree with me on the particular lack I see in the term 'human right' for my project to be of use. Nearly everyone accepts that the idea is incomplete in some serious way or other, that it needs more explanation before its use will have the rationality it should have. And my project should go some way towards meeting this widely felt need. Still, I see a specific lack, centring on determinateness of sense.

Determinateness of sense is, admittedly, a matter of degree; one can live with some indeterminateness. It is a rare common noun that has criteria allowing us to determine in all cases whether it is being correctly or incorrectly used; there are usually at least borderline cases. But if, quite apart from the generally recognized borderline cases, there are very many other cases in which nothing is available to us to settle whether a term is being correctly or incorrectly used, then the term is seriously defective. The term 'human right' is far less determinate than most common nouns—even than most ethical terms. We have a range of quite specific ethical terms which clearly do not suffer from unacceptable indeterminateness of sense. We know perfectly well what makes an act 'courageous' or 'considerate'. And the far broader term 'justice' does not suffer from it either. A trouble with the idea of 'justice' is that it is so elastic: it is sometimes used to cover the whole of morality, and sometimes a specific part of it, and it is used of several different specific parts (distributive justice, retributive justice, procedural justice, and so on). It is, in this way, equivocal. But to be equivocal or ambiguous or vague is not to be indeterminate in the way I have in mind. Rather, on each occasion we have to work out in which of its perhaps tolerably determinate senses 'justice' is being used.

It is false, too, that the term 'human rights' is no worse off than very broad and not especially contentful ethical notions such as 'wrong', which we manage to get on with well enough. If you and I were to disagree as to whether a certain action is (morally) wrong, there would be considerable, perhaps complete, agreement between us about what bears on the matter. There might also, of course, be disagreements. You might cite a prohibition about which I had doubts—say, a near absolute prohibition against deliberately taking an innocent person's life without that person's consent. I would not for a moment, though, doubt the relevance of that prohibition to the issue; human life is of great value, which will translate into a stringent moral prohibition. I might disagree with you over the best way to express the value of human life as a norm of action, or over how many exceptions the norm permits. We may, in the end, be unable to agree whether a certain action is wrong, because we are unable to agree how to express the moral norm—perhaps because you get your norm from religious belief and I am not a believer. Although we are unable to agree, we are, none the less, still able to see what is at issue—perhaps, in the case I have described, whether there is a God or whether we can know what he wants. Contrast this case with the case of our disagreeing about whether there is a broad human right to determine whatever happens in and to our bodies. In this case there is practically no agreement about what is at issue. We agree that human rights are derived from 'human standing' or 'human nature', but have virtually no agreement about the relevant sense of these two supposedly criteria-providing terms.

Do I exaggerate the trouble with the term 'human rights'? It is not that it is entirely unusable. There are at least *some* criteria for determining when the term is used correctly and when incorrectly. I have said that there is an Enlightenment notion of human rights, that it has an element of intension—namely, that a human right is a right that we have simply in virtue of being human—and an extension—roughly, the rights found in the United States Bill of Rights, in the French Declaration of the Rights of Man, and in certain key United Nations instruments. Thin though its intension is, and challengeable though its extension is, the Enlightenment notion is not completely empty. So we often can, and do, make negative judgements. The Universal Declaration of 1948, the most restrained of United Nations' lists of human rights, blunders at one point in asserting a right to periodic holidays with pay, which, as I mentioned in the introduction, is widely rejected. What is more, we all agree on several paradigms: freedom of expression, freedom of worship, and so on. We must be able to settle some harder cases by extrapolation from these paradigm cases. But the resources here are still too meagre. The few criteria attaching to the term 'human rights' would still leave very many cases of its use, far more than borderline cases, undetermined. And the paradigms on which we agree are all civil and political rights, which would leave us with too many unanswered questions. Do we have a human right to determine how many children we have? Do we have a human right to determine whatever happens in and to our bodies?

But do I not exaggerate at least the rarity of the lack I find in the term 'human rights'? Is not the progress that I desiderate in the case of 'human rights' simply the progress sought for in very many other moral ideas: namely, the progress from 'concept' to 'conception', as that distinction is drawn by John Rawls in *A Theory of Justice*? [24] We have a common concept of, say, justice, and what more is needed is to fill it out into a particular conception, such as Rawls's justice as fairness. What I am maintaining is that in the case of the term 'human rights' there is a serious lack on the *concept* side, which has no parallel in the case of, say, justice.

The cases of 'justice' and 'human rights', I have admitted, differ only in degree. In the case of 'human rights' there are so few criteria to determine when the term is used correctly or incorrectly that we are largely in the dark even as to what considerations are to be taken as relevant. In contrast, we largely agree about what is relevant to correct and incorrect use of the word 'justice'. The words 'just' and 'fair', as we have them in ordinary speech, are such that, so long as the context or the speaker makes clear what sort of justice is under discussion—distributive, retributive, procedural, or so on—we largely agree on what is at issue. Agreement of that degree is not available to us in the case of the term 'human right'. Do we have a human right to determine how many children we have? Can we even tell what is relevant to the question? Well, the fragment of intension we have—namely, a claim that we have on others simply in virtue of our being human—holds of moral claims in general, and not all moral claims are rights-generated. For example, the claim that one has on others that they not gratuitously cause one pain is not. Either a claim arising from a human right is a special sort of claim, not merely a moral claim, or the human status from which the claim arises is something more specific than that human beings are the subject of moral obligations. Until we have agreement on some such matters as these, the concept of a 'human right' will remain, among moral terms, unusually thin.

This indeterminateness of sense mattered less in the seventeenth and eighteenth centuries, when there was wide agreement on examples. As the problem commanding urgent attention at the time was autocratic rulers, the solution naturally focused on a range of civil and political rights. [25] By the twentieth century, however, the general agreement on examples had vanished. Constitutions and international instruments began including hotly resisted welfare rights, [26] as well as such suspect items as rights to peace, [27] to inherit, [28] and to freedom of residence within the borders of one's own country. [29] These too, it was asserted, are human rights. But are they? The runaway growth of the extension of the term in our time makes having some grasp of its intension the more urgent, and its intension is what is so especially thin.

It is not that we must now come up with a definition of the term 'human right'—some form of words more or less synonymous with the term, or a list of essential features.[30] It is not clear, even, that the component term 'right' is definable in that sense, although several contemporary philosophers offer a definition or something close to it.[31] Many terms have satisfactorily determinate senses, not because they can be defined, but simply in virtue of having a fairly well settled use. But the term 'human rights' has a largely unsettled use. It is a theoretical term, introduced as the successor to another highly theoretical term, 'natural rights'—introduced, though, without much in the way of necessary background. We may not need definition, but we certainly need more in the way of explanation.

The job of philosophers and jurisprudents and political theorists in our time is to remedy the indeterminateness—to do what the Enlightenment failed to do.

1.3 REMEDIES FOR THE INDETERMINATENESS

One drastic remedy is simply to abandon human rights discourse. If it is so unsatisfactory, why not jettison it?

But, despite what Bentham says, it is not that the term is nonsense. And there is no shortage of ways to remedy its indeterminateness. If human rights were basic in the whole moral structure, then we could not do without the term. But human rights are not, I think, basic; they appear on a low-to-middle level in the whole structure, though my reasons for saying so will have to wait.[32]

There is, though, a question that we can answer now. If, as I think, our ethical vocabulary is ample enough for us to drop the term 'human right' and carry on instead with a more circuitous way of saying the same thing, would anything important be lost? One may think that mankind has already been in that position. There has been a fair amount of discussion recently as to whether the ancient Greeks and Romans had the concept of a human right—not a term with roughly the same meaning but the concept.[33] This raises the general question of what it is to have a concept, and whether a high degree of circuitousness is not itself prima facie ground to doubt its possession. And we cannot tell whether the ancients had our modern concept of human rights, unless we know what that is, about which more later. To my mind, the circuitous formulae that the ancients assembled always fell short of our modern concept.

But would something be lost simply by not having a single word or simple term for human rights? Having a simple term serves several practical purposes. It highlights a certain consideration, attracts our attention to it, marks its importance in our culture, makes its discussion easier, increases the chances of its having certain social effects such as ease of transmission and potency in political action. It can facilitate deep moral shifts, such as the emergence of individualism at the end of the Middle Ages. It lends itself to political slogans and provides the centrepiece of popular movements. It allows lists of 'human rights', and so checklists for the sort of monitoring done by Amnesty International and Human Rights Watch.[34] It can empower individuals. I was told recently[35] of a woman in Senegal whose husband had left her and taken the children, which he was legally entitled to do, and the land they lived on, which she had brought into marriage. The term 'human rights' had entered their language only a few years before, but the woman was spurred by its possession to complain forcefully and publicly: she had a right, she said, to some of the land and to see her children. She had no hope that the elders would help her, but they were eventually moved by the confidence and persistence of her complaints to allow that, despite their customs, she had a case.

Ethics should be concerned not just with identifying right and wrong, but also with realizing the right and preventing the wrong. Having the simple term 'human right' is important to the latter. Strictly speaking, though, that is a case for having a simple term, not necessarily for the term's being 'human rights'. It could instead be 'constitutional rights' or 'basic rights' or 'entrenched rights', to which we could attach a satisfactorily determinate sense, say of a positive nature: a 'constitutional right', we could say, is one chosen by a certain sort of convention of citizens and given a certain sort of foundational place in the legal system. Of course, what would be lost by taking this route would be the idea that certain rights have their foundational status in society not because of conventions or place in the legal system but because of their moral status. And that is something that we need not, and should not, lose.

In any case, we philosophers, jurisprudents, and political theorists could not undermine 'human rights' discourse, with its large ambitions to regulate the world, even if we tried. It is much too well established for that. Our only realistic option, quite optimistic enough, is to influence it, to develop it, to complete it.[36]

1.4 DIFFERENT APPROACHES TO EXPLAINING RIGHTS: SUBSTANTIVE AND STRUCTURAL ACCOUNTS

We need an account of 'human rights' with at least enough content to tell us, for any such proposed right, difficult borderline cases aside, whether it really is one and to what it is a right.

There are several accounts of rights that, however much they give us, do not give us what we need here. Several modern philosophers try to characterize rights largely by their structural features. For instance, Joel Feinberg's account of rights is largely structural. A right, he says, is a claim with two features: it is a claim, first, *against* specifiable individuals and, second, *to* their action or omission on one's behalf. Or, more strictly, it is such a claim when it is sufficiently backed by laws or moral principles and therefore valid.[37] But this is intended as an account of rights in general, not of human rights in particular. An obvious way to get an account of human rights out of Feinberg's framework is to add a contentful specification of one or more of the moral principles that Feinberg has in mind—a principle that, perhaps, expresses the value of our human standing. But that, of course, is to add some substantial evaluation, as Feinberg would doubtless agree.

Ronald Dworkin's view that rights are 'trumps' is another highly structural one.[38] But the point of rights, even the basic legal rights that Dworkin has primarily in mind, cannot be, as he claims, to act as trumps over appeals to the general welfare. The consequence of that claim would be that rights have no point in restraining most of the agents whom in the course of history they have been used to restrain: overreaching popes, absolute monarchs, dictatorships of the proletariat, murderous thugs who seize political power, not all of whom (to put it no higher) had the general welfare as their goal. Nor is the claim much more plausible if we reinterpret Dworkin more sympathetically to be referring only to ideal political conditions, when the state is committed to pursuing the impartial maximization of welfare, or whatever the best conception of promoting a people's good turns out to be.[39] The point of rights in those ideal conditions, we can understand Dworkin to be saying, is as trumps over the best policy of promoting the good of all. But that cannot be right either. It does nothing to lessen the implausibility of denying human rights the role they have played throughout their history. Besides, justice and fairness are likely also sometimes to trump the promotion of the good of all, and, as we shall see later,[40] the domain of justice and the domain of human rights are only overlapping, not congruent. If more than rights are trumps, one cannot use trumping to characterize rights. In any case, rights are not, strictly speaking, trumps. There is some, perhaps especially high, level of the general good at which it would override a right, as Dworkin himself accepts.[41] At what level? To answer that, we need to know how to attach moral weight both to rights and to different levels of the general good. If the weight we attach to rights is not to be arbitrary, we must have a sufficiently rich understanding of the value that rights represent—for *human* rights that would most likely require a sufficiently rich understanding of the dignity, or worth, of the human person, whatever the proper understanding of that now widely used phrase is.[42] A satisfactory account of *human* rights, therefore, must contain some adumbration of that exceedingly vague term 'human dignity', again not in all of its varied uses but in its role as a ground for human rights. So the account must have more substantive evaluative elements than Dworkin supplies.[43]

Robert Nozick's account of rights as 'side-constraints' has a little more ethical content than Dworkin's, but is still largely structural: rights set limits on the permissible pursuit of personal or the common good; these side-constraints, though, may be overridden in the extremely rare case of a 'catastrophe'.[44] But Nozick's proposal is not helpful without a gloss on the word 'catastrophe'. It is something on the order of a nuclear holocaust, he has explained. But all that this example does is to set the level of resistance to trade-offs extraordinarily high, without saying exactly how high, and without supplying any reason why that is where to set it. For example, would the threat of a repetition of the terrorist attack on Manhattan of 11 September 2001, though this time with a primitive nuclear bomb capable of destroying the southern half of the island, constitute a 'catastrophe' in the relevant sense? Destruction of the southern half of Manhattan, for all its terribleness, is well short of nuclear holocaust. Still, would this lesser threat justify, for example, the detention without trial introduced subsequently by the United States government with just this sort of possibility in mind? We do not know; the word 'catastrophe' gives far too little help. In any case, Nozick does not regard being overrideable only by a catastrophe as a characterization of what a human right *is*, or of the very point of such rights. If it were such a characterization, then anyone adopting a less demanding standard for the overriding conditions, even if the standard still required much more than a simple surplus of the general good over the right, would be making a mistake about what a human right is, which is clearly not so. On the contrary, Nozick introduces an element of ethical substance: rights represent the moral significance of the separateness of persons. But it is also highly unclear what that significance is, and Nozick says nothing in its further explanation. What we need in order to make progress with these matters is, among other things, further explanation of the idea of the separateness of persons. Despite the ethical substance that Nozick has given us, we need more.

   In general, what we need is a more ethically substantive account of human rights than Feinberg's or Dworkin's or Nozick's. I say '*more* substantive' because no plausible account of human rights will be purely structural or substantive; it will be a mixture of the two. The more ethically substantive account that we need will itself have structural implications. I have no general argument that, in order to explain human rights, structural accounts must become more substantive. Besides the fact that the class of structural accounts is not well defined, I have found no one failing in the three particular cases I have looked at. My remarks are, at best, suggestive—suggestive that an account of human rights should have more substantive evaluation than that offered by any of the well-known, predominantly structural accounts we now have.

1.5 A DIFFERENT KIND OF SUBSTANTIVE ACCOUNT

Still, I do not now mean to imply that the only way to make an account of human rights more ethically substantive is to ground the rights directly in substantive *values*, a belief that John Rawls has recently challenged.[45] He is right that one can also make the account more substantive by spelling out the role that human rights play in a larger theory—in Rawls's case, in a theory of political justice between peoples. What we need in order to establish a law of peoples, he thinks, is a set of notions and principles usable in a practical political context in which what he calls 'well-ordered' peoples with, it may be, considerably different religious, philosophical, and moral beliefs will come to agree, without coercion, on rules to govern their behaviour to one another. The class of well-ordered peoples includes, besides liberal democracies, what Rawls labels 'hierarchical' peoples who are not aggressive, respect human rights, have a legal system that their members take to impose bona fide moral duties on them, follow a common-good idea of justice, and have a basic political structure that, while not democratic, contains at least a certain minimal 'consultation hierarchy'.[46] None the less, Rawls's case for his version of the law of peoples is, by design, deeply rooted in the perspective of a politically liberal society; it works outward from that in two stages. He argues, first, that a group of liberal democratic peoples, wishing to arrive at just rules for behaviour among themselves, will settle on his version of the law of peoples. He then argues that a group of liberal democratic peoples, similarly wishing to establish just rules for their dealings with decent hierarchical societies, would reach agreement with them on the same version of the law of peoples. This version, he concludes, is thereby established as the law of peoples for all well-ordered peoples.

Now, persons exercising reason under free institutions, Rawls plausibly believes, will typically arrive at differing comprehensive religious, philosophical, and moral views; in short, freedom fosters this sort of pluralism.[47] To reach agreement between well-ordered peoples at either stage of the argument, one must appeal, Rawls says, to public reasons: reasons that do not derive from any particular comprehensive view and will be accepted as authoritative by all parties to the agreement. This is all the more to the point when the agreement at stake is between liberal peoples and decent hierarchical peoples. Then we have to avoid ethnocentricity. As Rawls puts it, we should avoid saying 'that human beings are moral persons and have equal worth in the eyes of God; or that they have certain moral and intellectual powers that entitle them to the rights'; we do not want to ground rights directly in such evaluative notions, he thinks, because decent hierarchical peoples might reject the notions 'as liberal or democratic, or as in some way distinctive of Western political tradition and prejudicial to other cultures'.[48] Instead, the principles behind the law of peoples, Rawls says, 'are expressed solely in terms of a political conception and its political values'.[49] These restrictions lead to a markedly shorter list of human rights than the lists common in liberal democracies.[50] Rawls's own shorter list omits such typical human rights as freedom of expression, freedom of association (except what is needed for freedom of conscience and of religious observance), the right to democratic political participation, and any economic rights that go beyond our right to mere subsistence.[51] And the role of human rights, on Rawls's conception of them, is quite restricted: it is to provide the justifying reasons for war and its conduct, and to set conditions for when one state may coercively intervene in another.[52]

So much for Rawls's proposal. In the course of history, there have been many different lists of rights: Rawls's shortened list for the law of peoples is an example, as is the longer list adopted by certain constitutional liberal democracies, and the still longer list that emerges from a compilation of United Nations documents, and the lists derived from comprehensive moral views such as a Thomist or Kantian or Utilitarian view, and so on. If we step back for a moment and ask which of the items on these lists almost universally attracts the label 'human rights', it is clearly those on the second (certain liberal democracies) or third (the United Nations). Rawls's shorter list is, he says, a proper subset of the second or third sort of list.[53] Why, then, does Rawls adopt the label 'human rights' for his shorter list? For no sufficient reason. Even if Rawls is correct that the law of peoples needs a shortened list, which I doubt for reasons I shall come to later,[54] that is no reason why he should consider it a list of 'human' rights. He gives no reason to think that this is what human rights really are, or are now best thought of as being. He makes no effort to show that it is only the rights on his list that human beings have simply as human beings, or however else he wants to interpret 'human'. He says that his list contains 'a special class of urgent rights',[55] without telling us how they are urgent while the excluded rights on the liberal democratic lists are not. To establish that Rawls's shorter list is what human rights are best thought of as being would take a much stronger argument—say, an argument to the effect that all versions of the liberal democratic list are incorrigibly flawed. There are such arguments,[56] but none that I know of establishes anything approaching such a strong conclusion. And Rawls's characterization of the *role* of human rights—briefly, that their role is to establish rules of war between nations and conditions for one nation's being allowed to intervene in another—is similarly under-motivated. The point of human rights, on the almost universally accepted conception of them, is far wider than that. For example, they quite obviously have point intra-nationally: to justify rebellion, to establish a case for peaceful reform, to curb an autocratic ruler, to criticize a majority's treatment of racial or ethnic minorities. And they are used by the United Nations and by non-governmental agencies to issue periodic reports on the human rights record of individual countries, seen from an internal point of view. They are also used to criticize institutions within a single society. Many hospitals are still condemned for denying patients really informed consent. And some parents can reasonably be criticized for violating their mature children's autonomy and liberty.

Of course, when seeking agreement between well-ordered nations on a law of peoples, we should, when possible, use language that will cross cultures. Rawls says, more strongly, that we should use a 'public reason'; it is, he claims, our best hope for reaching agreement. But that is an empirical claim, which he never tries to justify. He treats it as obvious; but it is, on the contrary, quite doubtful. To my mind, Rawls's views about ethnocentricity are fast going out of date.[57]

Shirin Ebadi, the winner of the Nobel Peace Prize for 2003, said in an interview following the announcement of her prize that the human-rights-based reform movement in Iran 'cannot be stopped. In every society there comes a time when people want to be free. That time has come in Iran.'[58] This view is widespread among educated Iranians, as has been manifested by large student demonstrations. Much the same is true of China and South-East Asia. And unforced agreement between nations does not require every member to adopt the language of human rights; it is enough if the more politically alert and active do so. Admittedly, some of the tribal societies of the Middle East are not yet ripe for freedom. Still, if one wants a *practical* route to a law of peoples, if one wants the ideal society of peoples also to be *realistic*, as Rawls does, then one would promote, perhaps with minor amendments, the United Nations list of human rights—or so I shall shortly argue.

In any case, international discourse needs a largely agreed list of human rights; whether it needs an agreed justification of the list is another matter. We have had a fairly largely agreed list for the last fifty years. When in 1947 the United Nations set up a committee to draft a declaration of human rights, the newly created UNESCO set up a parallel commission of philosophers to advise the drafting commission. Philosophers were assembled from all major cultures; even more were polled. They had no trouble agreeing on a list of human rights, much like the list that eventually appeared in the Universal Declaration of 1948. Jacques Maritain, the French Thomist, a member of the UNESCO committee, reported that when a visitor to their proceedings expressed amazement that such a culturally diverse group was able to agree on a list of human rights, he was told, 'we agree about the rights but on condition no one asks us why'.[59] This sensible silence on the part of the philosophers is like the silence of the law on the justification of many of its norms. For instance, in the criminal law members of a society have no trouble agreeing on a list of major crimes, while often substantially disagreeing about what makes them crimes.[60]

None the less, having agreement only on a list of human rights, and not on any reasons behind it, has major drawbacks. A greater measure of convergence on the justification of the list might produce more wholehearted promotion of human rights, fewer disagreements over their content, fewer disputes about priorities between them, and more rational and more uniform resolution of their conflicts—all much to be desired.

But what are the most likely ways for this to come about? This is the empirical question Rawls raises. There are, I should say, two most likely ways. The first is the continued spread of the largely Western-inspired discourse of human rights that we have witnessed over the last sixty years. At its core is the idea that human beings are unique, that we are made in God's image (Genesis 1: 27), that we too are creators—creators of ourselves, and by our actions, of part of the world around us, on which we shall be judged. Genesis is common to 'the people of the book': Jews, Christians, and Muslims. But the egalitarian and individualist implications of the idea that we are made in God's image lay dormant in Christianity until the late Middle Ages. Then the authoritarian strand in the Church gave some ground to the view that we cannot earn reward or punishment unless we are responsible for our acts, that we cannot be responsible unless we are autonomous, and that we cannot be autonomous unless we can exercise our individual consciences. There is no dignity in mere submission to authority. And human rights are to be seen as protections of this elevated status of human beings, although there are many different accounts of how, in detail, this justification of rights works. The transition of thought from merit to individual conscience is not particularly Western; it is essential to one's seeing oneself as a moral agent among other moral agents. Admittedly, the final step—the step from moral agency to the adoption of the discourse of human rights—need not be taken; but the idea that one's moral agency is to be protected is integral to the idea of one's moral agency's being of particularly high value. The latter idea is such a deep component of the moral point of view that there is reasonable expectation that its appeal extends well beyond the bounds of the Western world. There is the view among some Western writers that it would be 'intolerant' of us to tie the idea of human rights to our peculiar Western conception of them;[61] but it is hardly intolerant of us to be reluctant to give up the moral point of view, as we understand it, in which our idea of human rights, though separable, is deeply rooted.

The second of the most likely ways in which we might reach greater convergence on justification is by finding justifying ideas present, even if only latently, in non-Western cultures. Several writers have lately been searching non-Western cultures for such ideas.[62] And the ones that they have found have often shown striking overlap with those used in the West: individual responsibility, autonomy, freedom, and human dignity.[63]

This second way may look less ethnocentric, and so more promising, than the first. I shall argue later[64] that, despite appearances, it is, rather, the first approach that is the more promising.

Neither of these two ways, however, is the contractualist way. Neither appeals to the sort of public reason that Rawls thinks necessary. Instead, they involve an agreement directly on values—not on a comprehensive moral view, it is true, but on a particularly deep conception of agency that figures, or can without daunting difficulty come to figure, in all of them. Human rights can, therefore, be directly grounded in values without becoming culturally limited. What Rawls says about the law of peoples should not leave us any less interested than before in pursuing the liberal understanding of human rights or in developing an ethically substantive account by grounding them directly in values.[65]

1.6 HOW SHOULD WE GO ABOUT COMPLETING THE IDEA?

Why have recent writers (for example, Feinberg, Dworkin, Nozick) so favoured structural or (Rawls, Beitz) legal-functional accounts of rights? Most writers long ago abandoned all but the weakest natural law accounts. Today most would also like to avoid accounts with any sort of broad ethical commitment: that way, they think, lies mere sentiment and endless disagreement. No substantive account but the very vaguest has achieved currency: for example, the United Nations' claim that human rights derive from 'the dignity of the human person'. If an account becomes much less vague, it is thought, we get entangled in our own incompatible comprehensive ethical beliefs. That was Locke's point about not appealing to a *summum bonum*; it was Hume's point, so dominant in the twentieth century, about ethical judgements' being expressions of sentiment. Still, we feel that the idea of rights, especially the idea of human rights, needs something more in the way of explanation. Lacking a substantive account that is well worked out and congenial to the modern mind, we naturally look elsewhere.

But, as we have seen, the largely structural or legal-functional accounts that many looked to are short on explanatory power. A couple of centuries ago philosophers showed no reluctance to produce richer substantive accounts—for example, by incorporating rights into their comprehensive ethical views. Kant did that for 'natural rights' in his late work *The Metaphysics of Morals*, and Mill did it for 'rights' in the last chapter of *Utilitarianism*. Neither of these stipulations, though, has done anything to solve the problem of the indeterminateness of the idea of 'human rights'. There is no good reason, I just said, to accept Rawls's stipulation. The case with Kant and Mill is different; their stipulations have been around long enough for us to be able to conclude that not enough speakers or writers have accepted them—in contrast to some philosophers accepting their larger theories—for them to have become a broadly accepted part of the criteria for the correct and incorrect use of the term 'right' or 'human right'.

Kant's, Mill's, and Rawls's stipulations all yield extensions for the term substantially different from that in the Enlightenment tradition: in Rawls's case, as we have seen, markedly smaller, and in Kant's and Mill's very much larger.[66] And if a stipulation for the term 'human right' yields a very different extension from that in the Enlightenment, why think that it is the *best* stipulation? Why think even that it explains the term we set out to explain in the first place? Does it not just change the subject?

Still, we cannot decide instead just to adumbrate the Enlightenment idea of a 'human right'. That is the seriously incomplete idea. To gain a satisfactory notion of human rights, we need not adumbration of this idea but its completion.

Meanwhile, my immediate question stands: what content should we add to the notion of a human right?

2

First Steps in an Account of Human Rights

2.1 TOP-DOWN AND BOTTOM-UP ACCOUNTS

At the end of the last chapter we met two general ways for philosophy to supply a more substantive account of human rights. There is a top-down approach: one starts with an overarching principle, or principles, or an authoritative decision procedure—say, the principle of utility or the Categorical Imperative or the model of parties to a contract reaching agreement—from which human rights can then be derived. Most accounts of rights in philosophy these days are top-down. Then there is a bottom-up approach: one starts with human rights as used in our actual social life by politicians, lawyers, social campaigners, as well as theorists of various sorts, and then sees what higher principles one must resort to in order to explain their moral weight, when one thinks they have it, and to resolve conflicts between them.

We should welcome both approaches, and see what help each can give us. I prefer the bottom-up approach. We may not have to rise all the way to the highly abstract moral principles used in the top-down approach in order to explain what needs explaining. And we shall not then have to assume, at least initially, the correctness of any of these contentious abstract moral principles, or indeed even the possibility of large-scale system in ethics. In any case, the top-down approach cannot do without some explanation of how the notion of human rights is used in our social life. We need it to test whether what is derivable from these highly abstract moral principles *are* human rights and *all* human rights. We need not treat the use of the term in present social life as beyond revision, but we need some understanding of what human rights are independent of the principle or principles from which they are said to be derivable, and their social use is the most likely source.

What content, then, should we attach to the notion of a human right? If we adopt the bottom-up approach, there are two parts to the job. Clearly the content will be determined to some degree by the criteria for use, insufficient as they are, that the notion of 'human rights' already has attaching to it. So the first part of our job is to consult the long tradition from which the notion comes and to discover the content already there. Although the notion is incomplete, it is not completely empty.

Still, the seventeenth- and eighteenth-century accounts, which remain for us the last major development of the idea itself, left much for us to add. Because that is our job, we today are, to a surprising extent, in at the creation both of a substantive account and therefore, to some extent, of human rights themselves. The account that we need will, as we shall see, turn out to have a measure of stipulation. That gives us freedom, though freedom under constraints. There is the constraint of the tradition and the constraints of meeting practical needs and of fitting well with the rest of our ethical thought.

2.2 THE HUMAN RIGHTS TRADITION

Let me now give, in summary form, what seems to me the most plausible history of the idea of a right.[1]

As I mentioned in the Introduction, a term with our modern sense of a 'right' emerged in the late Middle Ages, probably first in Bologna, in the work of the canonists, who glossed, commented on, and to some extent brought harmony to the many, not always consistent, norms of canon law and, on the civil side, Roman law. In the course of the twelfth and thirteenth centuries the use of the Latin word *ius* expanded from meaning what is fair to include also our modern sense of a 'right'—that is, an entitlement that a person possesses to control or claim something. Modern writers have come to refer to these two senses of natural right (*ius naturale*) as the 'objective' and the 'subjective'. Aquinas, for instance, wrote often of 'the natural right,' but never used a term translatable as 'a natural right', though some believe he had the concept.[2] In the 1280s, Geoffrey of Fontaines used the modern subjective idea of a right in mounting a case against papal power.[3] But a more sustained use came in the course of the curious poverty debates. After the death of Francis of Assisi, the Franciscans themselves began disputing what exactly their vow of poverty implied. And soon the popes, understandably unnerved by the teaching that the ideal Christian life required the renunciation of property and power, joined in. One argument to command attention—a preposterous one—went like this: when someone gives a Franciscan meat and bread for his supper, it is clearly not a loan; a loan requires care and eventual return of the goods; the goods given to the Franciscan, however, are meant to be consumed; so, once in receipt of them, the Franciscan must own them and has not therefore truly renounced property.[4] Another argument, in this case Ockham's, went like this: Franciscans have not renounced property. Each of us has an inalienable natural right to goods when in extreme need. To alienate it is not allowed, because it would be, in effect, to commit suicide.[5] Behind the various arguments in the poverty debates was a certain view of property. God gave the riches of the world to us all in common. But unless particular persons have responsibility for particular goods, they will not be preserved or usefully exploited. So, not God, but human beings introduce schemes of property. But ownership of property is only stewardship; the goods may be taken back into a common stock as needed. In these debates one finds the transition from the form of words that it is a natural law (*ius*) that all things are held in common, and so a person in mortal need who takes from a person in surplus does not steal, to the newly emergent form of words that a person in need has a right (*ius*) to take from a person in surplus and so does not steal. And twelfth- and thirteenth-century commentators began using the word *ius* of a faculty or power, reinforcing the subjective sense: a faculty or power, such as rational agency, is something an individual has.[6] Two world-changing events of the twelfth century were the recovery of the entire corpus of Roman Law and the appearance of a critically ordered edition of some of the mass of canon law texts, in the *Decretum* of Gratian (*c*.1140). And it is plausible that the subjective sense of 'natural right' appeared not too much later,[7] in the struggle of commentators to bring a greater measure of order and understanding to these two sets of laws.

William of Ockham (*c*.1285–1349), following a tradition going back to the early canonists, saw reason as giving us freedom, and freedom as giving us dignity. Pico della Mirandola, an early Renaissance philosopher who studied canon law in Bologna in 1477, gave an influential account of the link between our freedom and the dignity of our status. God fixed the nature of all other things, but left man alone free to determine his own nature. In this he is God-like. Man too is a creator—a creator of himself. It is given to man 'to have that which he chooses and be that which he wills'.[8] This freedom constitutes, as it is put in the title of Pico's best-known work, 'the dignity of man'.

This same link between freedom and dignity was at the centre of the early sixteenth-century Indian debates about the Spanish enslavement of the natives of the New World. Many canonists argued emphatically that the American natives were undeniably agents and, therefore, should not be deprived of their autonomy and liberty, which the Spanish commanders were everywhere doing. The same notion of dignity was also central to political thought in the seventeenth and eighteenth centuries, when it received its most powerful development at the hands of Rousseau and Kant. But I shall stop here; these last remarks take us well into the modern period, with which my historical comments in Chapter 1 began.

What I have sketched is the dominant conception of natural rights in the late Middle Ages and Renaissance. Of course, there were also deviant conceptions. At one time, for example, a theory was developed that cut the link between natural rights and agency, allowing rights-bearers also to include animals and inanimate objects.[9] But this deviant interpretation did not endure. Shortly thereafter, Francisco de Vitoria (1492–1546) was again asserting the link between our bearing rights and our being made in God's image.

2.3 A PROPOSAL OF A SUBSTANTIVE ACCOUNT

The human rights tradition does not lead us inescapably to any particular substantive account. There can be reasons to take a tradition in a new direction or to break with it altogether. Still, the best substantive account is, to my mind, in the spirit of the tradition and goes like this. Human life is different from the life of other animals. We human beings have a conception of ourselves and of our past and future. We reflect and assess. We form pictures of what a good life would be—often, it is true, only on a small scale, but occasionally also on a large scale. And we try to realize these pictures. This is what we mean by a distinctively *human* existence—distinctive so far as we know. Perhaps Great Apes share more of our nature than we used to think, though we have no evidence that any species but *Homo sapiens* can form and pursue conceptions of a worthwhile life. But there might be intelligent creatures elsewhere in the universe also capable of such deliberation and action. If so, we should have to consider how *human* rights would have to be adapted to fit them. So long as we do not ignore this possibility, there is no harm in continuing to speak of a distinctively 'human' existence. And we value our status as human beings especially highly, often more highly than even our happiness. This status centres on our being agents—deliberating, assessing, choosing, and acting to make what we see as a good life for ourselves.

Human rights can then be seen as protections of our human standing or, as I shall put it, our personhood. And one can break down the notion of personhood into clearer components by breaking down the notion of agency. To be an agent, in the fullest sense of which we are capable, one must (first) choose one's own path through life—that is, not be dominated or controlled by someone or something else (call it 'autonomy'). And (second) one's choice must be real; one must have at least a certain minimum education and information. And having chosen, one must then be able to act; that is, one must have at least the minimum provision of resources and capabilities that it takes (call all of this 'minimum provision'). And none of this is any good if someone then blocks one; so (third) others must also not forcibly stop one from pursuing what one sees as a worthwhile life (call this 'liberty'). Because we attach such high value to our individual personhood, we see its domain of exercise as privileged and protected.

That is the central intuitive idea. In this chapter I want to sketch, in quick broad strokes, my proposed substantive account of human rights, and then return in later chapters to elaboration and fuller argument.

2.4 ONE GROUND FOR HUMAN RIGHTS: PERSONHOOD

In what should we say that human rights are grounded? Well, primarily in personhood. Out of the notion of personhood we can generate most of the conventional list of human rights. We have a right to life (without it, personhood is impossible), to security of person (for the same reason), to a voice in political decision (a key exercise of autonomy), to free expression, to assembly, and to a free press (without them, exercise of autonomy would be hollow), to worship (a key exercise of what one takes to be the point of life). It also generates, I should say (though this is hotly disputed), a positive freedom: namely, a right to basic education and minimum provision needed for existence as a person—something more, that is, than mere physical survival. It also generates a right not to be tortured, because, among its several evils, torture destroys one's capacity to decide and to stick to the decision. And so on. It should already be clear that the generative capacities of the notion of personhood are quite great.

My making personhood central helps explain further the way in which my account is substantive. Some of the structural accounts that I mentioned earlier also aim to provide existence conditions. But substantive accounts go further; my account, for instance, grounds human rights not in formal features or a role in a larger moral structure, but directly in a central range of substantive values, the values of personhood.

Grounding human rights in personhood imposes an obvious constraint on their content: they are rights not to anything that promotes human *good* or *flourishing*, but merely to what is needed for human *status*. They are protections of that somewhat austere state, a characteristically human life, not of a good or happy or perfected or flourishing human life. For one thing, it seems that the more austere notion is what the tradition of human rights supports. For another, it seems to be the proper stipulation to make. If we had rights to all that is needed for a good or happy life, then the language of rights would become redundant. We already have a perfectly adequate way of speaking about individual well-being and any obligations there might be to promote it. At most, we have a right to the *pursuit* of happiness, to the base on which one might oneself construct a happy life, not to happiness itself.

What does this tell us about how we should understand the key word 'human' in 'human rights'? 'Human' cannot there mean simply being a member of the species *Homo sapiens*. Infants, the severely mentally retarded, people in an irreversible coma, are all members of the species, but are not agents. It is tempting, then, to identify 'human beings' with 'agents' and to abstract from biological species entirely. More than just *Homo sapiens* can be agents: aliens emerging from a spaceship would be. But this line of thought is dangerous. It turns the holder of rights into a highly spare, abstract entity, characterized solely by rationality and intentionality. To my mind, this goes too far. One of the features of the spare, abstract agent would be autonomy; that would have to be a feature if the concept of agency were to yield any rights at all. Kant thought that one would be autonomous only if one's actions came from a purely rational, intentional centre, undetermined by anything outside it—undetermined, for instance, by one's biology or one's society. Kant contrasted this noumenal self, of course, with the familiar phenomenal self, which is part of the causal network, shaped by nature and nurture. But rationality requires thought; thought—at least thought about how to live one's life—requires language; and language is a cultural artefact, deeply influenced by the form of life lived by animals like us. If one peels away everything about us that is shaped by nature or nurture, not enough is left.

Autonomy should be explained, therefore, as we find it in the phenomenal world, and we find it there deeply embedded in the causal network. So the kind of autonomy we are interested in will reflect the peculiarly human way of experiencing and conceptualizing the world; it will be shaped by characteristic human concerns and sense of importance. We do not know what it is like to be Martian or Venusian. Our aim must be the more modest one of understanding not the autonomy of a spare, abstract self, but the autonomy of *Homo sapiens*. So by the word 'human' in the phrase 'human rights' we should mean, roughly, a functioning human agent. And human rights cannot therefore be entirely ahistorical.

But just how deeply embedded in a particular history must human rights therefore be? Statements about human nature could most easily lay claim to cross-cultural standards of correctness if they could be seen, as some classical natural law theorists saw them, as observations of the constitution and workings of part of the natural world.[10] But, on the face of it, this looks like trying to derive values (human rights) from facts (human nature), which generations of philosophers have been taught cannot be done. But it cannot be done only on a certain conception of nature: namely, the conception that sees nature as what the natural sciences, especially the physical sciences, describe. As such, nature excludes values. On this narrow conception of the natural, the conception of the 'human' that I am proposing is not natural. I single out functioning human agents via notions such as their autonomy and liberty, and I choose those features precisely because they are especially important human interests. It is only because they are especially important interests that rights can be derived from them; rights are strong protections, and so require something especially valuable to attract protection. So my notions of 'human nature' and 'human agent' are already well within the normative circle, and there is no obvious fallacy involved in deriving rights from notions as evaluatively rich as they are.

Still, that defence of the derivation, by drawing the notions of 'human nature' and 'human agency' inside the normative circle, seems to sacrifice a central feature of the human rights tradition: namely, that human rights are derived from something objective and factual, and so demand universal acknowledgement. It is, though, much too quick to think that what is evaluative cannot also be objective. It is too quick to think that it cannot also be natural. David Hume's dichotomy of fact and value depended upon his narrow conception of fact. But, to my mind, there is a weighty case for thinking that basic human interests are features of the world, and that these interests' being met or not met are goings-on in the world. One of our basic interests is in avoiding pain. In fact, our concept of pain is made up both of how pains feel and how those feelings characteristically figure in human life—that we want to avoid them, to have them alleviated, and suchlike. So, if I say that I am in pain, I make both a statement of fact and an evaluative statement. The most plausible interpretation of the notion of 'nature', I should say, is not Hume's but a more expansive one, including both features such as basic human interests and also events such as their being met or not met. All of this needs much more investigation, some of which I have tried to provide in a book I published some years ago[11] and which I shall revisit later in this book.[12] But if this expansive naturalism is, as I think, borne out, it gives hope of restoring a form of that central feature of the human rights tradition: namely, that these rights are grounded in natural facts about human beings.

There are, at the heart of ethics, different ways of understanding the weight of personhood. One might, as Kant does, contrast 'persons' with mere 'things': 'things' have 'price' and so have equivalents (the loss of one thing can be compensated by the gain of another of the same value). 'Persons', however, have 'dignity'; they are of unique value; they have no equivalents.[13] One might want to endow human rights, therefore, with something akin to the power of trumps over all aggregates of other moral considerations. Morality, in any case, is not just a matter of promoting the ends that make a human life good; personhood has a value independent of their promotion. This helps to explain why so many philosophers regard human rights, especially on the personhood account, as essentially deontological. →right or wrong

But that is only one way to understand personhood. Another way is to see our exercise of our personhood—that is, our autonomously and, no doubt, repeatedly choosing paths through life and being at liberty to pursue them—as in itself an end the realization of which characteristically enhances the quality of life. They would clearly be highly important such features, but none the less not, in principle, immune to trade-off with other elements of a good life, such as accomplishment, certain kinds of understanding, deep personal relations, enjoyment, and so on. It is because of the special importance, though by no means necessarily uniquely great importance, of these particular human interests that, on this understanding, we ring-fence them with the notion of human rights. This would explain how we might see human rights within a teleological morality, where 'teleological' is a broader term than either 'consequentialist' or 'utilitarian'.

The choice between these two understandings of personhood is crucial. It settles the source and degree of the resistance of human rights to trade-offs with other values. The best account of human rights will make them resistant to trade-offs, but not too resistant. That, of course, is a mere truism, but one surprisingly hard to satisfy. It is not altogether problem-free whichever understanding of personhood one chooses. I shall return to this choice later.[14]

2.5 A SECOND GROUND: PRACTICALITIES

Could personhood be the only ground needed for human rights? I think not. It leaves many human rights still too indeterminate. Personhood tells us that each of us has a right to security of person. But that just raises the question that I asked earlier about a supposed right to determine what happens in and to our bodies. It struck me that the right would not be quite as wide as that, and the personhood ground gives us some idea of why it may be narrower. The right is only to what is necessary for living a *human* existence, and the extensive power to determine everything that happens in and to our bodies goes far beyond that. If my blood had some marvellous factor and a few drops painlessly extracted from my finger in a minute's time could save scores of lives, then, on the face of it, the personhood ground yields no right that needs to be outweighed. Pricking my finger would hardly destroy my personhood. But what happens if we up the stakes? Does my right to security of person not protect me against, say, the health authority that wants one of my kidneys? After all, the few weeks that it would take me to recover from a kidney extraction would not prevent me from living a recognizably human life either. Where is the line to be drawn? What is clear is that, on its own, the personhood consideration is often not up to fixing anything approaching a determinate enough line for practice. We have also to think about society. There are practical considerations: to be effective, the line has to be clear and so not take too many complicated bends; given our proneness to stretch a point, we should probably have to leave a generous safety margin. So to make the content of the right to security of person determinate enough to be an effective guide to behaviour, we need a further ground—call it 'practicalities'. We need also to consult human nature, the nature of society, and so on, in drawing the line.

Sometimes we do not need to consult practicalities; personhood alone can fix the content of rights. The right not to be tortured is, I think, one such.[15] But in most cases we do. In those cases, without a more determinate line, we shall be reluctant to say that a right yet exists. What we are after are the existence conditions for a human right. Its existence must depend, to some extent, upon the concept's being determinate enough in sense to yield human rights with enough content for them to be an effective, socially manageable claim on others. This requirement of social manageability may seem to threaten the universality of human rights. More than just determinateness of sense is likely also to be necessary for human rights to be socially manageable claims on others. Might not certain social institutions such as the police and courts also be necessary? And might not what is necessary vary from one time or place to another, thereby undermining the universality of human rights?[16] But those worries misunderstand what I am claiming. What I claim is that the term 'human right' must be determinate enough *in sense* for it to serve as the *conceptually* adequate part of an effective, socially manageable claim on others—that is, effective and manageable so far as the term goes. What a philosophical account of human rights can reasonably be expected to do is to identify a sense for the term 'human right', through their existence conditions, which will allow us to decide tolerably fully the content of individual human rights—not only *that* they are such rights but also what they are rights *to*. And for that, I suggest, we need to introduce features of human nature and of the nature of human societies as a second ground. Those features are 'practicalities', as I am using the term. And the fact that pure values, such as the values of personhood, unsupplemented by what I mean by practicalities, often yield only highly indeterminate norms is true not just of human rights but of moral norms generally.

Practicalities, as I use the term, are not tied to particular times or places. They are universal, as any existence condition for rights that one has simply in virtue of being human must be. Practicalities will be empirical information about, as I say, human nature and human societies, prominently about the limits of human understanding and motivation. Still, that a requirement of universality is built into the idea of human rights does not imply that the content of a human right cannot make reference to particular times and places. I shall later talk about both basic, universal human rights—for example, freedom of expression—and derived, non-universal human rights got by applying basic rights to particular circumstances—for example, freedom of the press.[17] To this day there are societies in which presses do not exist, perhaps a few in which not even the concept of a press exists, and the human right to freedom of the press therefore has no relevance.

The practicalities ground gives us a further reason to confine human rights to normal *human* agents, not agents generally. Practicalities are needed to determine the content of many human rights, and the considerations they introduce may well be special to human life.

But is it reasonable to expect that solely universal features, both person-hood and those practicalities with universal scope, will give us sufficient determinateness of sense? The best way to answer that question is to look at several human rights and see what is actually needed to achieve the required determinateness, which I shall do later, especially in Parts II and III. And this question raises the further question of the sense in which human rights must be 'universal', to which I shall return shortly.

2.6 IS THERE A THIRD GROUND?: EQUALITY

Is there a third ground? The most likely further ground is equality. The idea of human rights emerged with the growth of egalitarianism, and it is an obvious thought that equality is *a*, or even at a deep level *the*, ground for those rights.

The trouble that we face in thinking about equality is that there are very many ethically important principles of equality, easily confused. There is moral standing itself, the moral point of view: we are all moral persons and so command some sort of equal respect—call it, for short, the principle of equal respect. This is different from, and may not even imply, a principle of equal distribution of goods, which, in turn, is different from a principle of equal opportunity, and so on.

It is obvious that on one interpretation of 'equality'—namely, equal respect—and on one interpretation of 'grounds', equality is indeed a ground for human rights. Equal respect expresses the moral point of view itself, and human rights, being moral standards, must likewise be expressions of it. Some philosophers have seen equal respect as itself a human right, indeed the one absolute right—a right, for instance, to equal respect in the procedures that determine the compromises and adjustments between all the other non-absolute rights.[18] It is absolute because it is moral standing itself, and morality can never recommend suspending the moral point of view. But it is doubtful that equal respect, being the whole of morality, should be seen as anything so specific as one human right among others. In any case, it cannot be a *ground* for human rights in the sense that I have been using the term here. Ronald Dworkin has spoken of a 'favoured form of argument for political rights': namely, their derivation from 'the abstract right to [equal] concern and respect, taken to be fundamental and axiomatic'.[19] Let me concentrate on his invocation of equal respect; the fact that he also speaks of equal concern does not affect what I shall say. The principle of equal respect is extremely vague; it needs content built into it through further notions, such as the Ideal Observer or the Ideal Contractor, though even those particular notions suffer from no small vagueness themselves. But, on its own, the notion of equal respect is far too empty for us to be able to derive from it anything as contentful as a list of human rights. And it is not that we must build more content into the notion of equal respect before we try deriving the list, because the way we shall put more content into it is precisely by settling such less abstract matters as what human rights there are. Morality is built at many different levels of generality at the same time. It does not display the sort of priorities that allow much in the way of what we can call 'derivation' of lower-level ideas from highest-level, axiomatic ones. So what we are after now, in looking for the *grounds* for human rights, are the sorts of ideas that will substantially help to settle what human rights exist and what their content actually is. Those ideas will, therefore, have to have a lot of content themselves, and so are likely to be on more or less the same level of abstraction as human rights.

But surely equality must be somewhere among the grounds for human rights, someone might say, if only because human rights grew out of the egalitarianism of the late Middle Ages. Before then, one's important powers and privileges were derived from one's social status: lord, freeman, slave, and so on. In the late Middle Ages, important powers and privileges, it was claimed, were to be derived simply from one's human status. We differ in social status; we are equal in human status. In that sense, it is undeniable that human rights are based on our equal human status. Still, if one wants to identify the existence conditions for human rights, one would not look to the equality of our human status but to the human status itself, and the personhood ground already captures that. There is no guarantee in late medieval egalitarianism of other forms of equality, as important as they often are—for example, of equal distribution of material goods. To say that we are all equally endowed with rights is not to say that we are all endowed with a right to equality, where that means other forms of equality.

Still, someone might persist, do we not have a human right to *some* other forms of equality? And would they not have to be grounded in some background principle of equality? Imagine this case. You and I are seventeenth-century settlers in the New World. As our boat beaches, you jump off before me and claim the lush, fertile half of the island, leaving the rocky, barren half to me. When I protest, you point out that my half, if tended, would yield at least the minimum resources necessary for a recognizably human existence, which is all that, on my own account, I have a right to. You can be sure that I would protest, echoing John Locke, that you could claim no more than what left as much and as good for me, that we are moral equals, that my life matters equally as much as yours, that I have a claim to as much of the available resources as you. The word 'equality' would come tumbling from my lips, and rightly so. Part of what I am claiming for myself is equal respect and all that follows from it, such as justice and fairness.

But a human right is a quite particular moral consideration. Human rights do not exhaust the whole moral domain; they do not exhaust even the whole domain of justice and fairness.[20] If you free-ride on the bus, you do not violate my rights, even though you act unfairly. That explains why the Enlightenment tradition regards procedural justice in courts as a matter of human rights, but not, at least in general, distributive or retributive justice. Procedural justice protects our life, liberty, and property. There are forms of distributive justice, for all their importance, that do not bear on our personhood—so long, that is, as the human right to minimum provision is respected. Human rights themselves have distributive implications, but ones limited to the protection of personhood. In fact, as most people in most societies never attract the attention of police or courts, their interests are likely to be far more affected by matters of distributive justice than of procedural justice. But matters of justice can be highly important in our lives without being matters of human rights.

Just as there are many different, morally important considerations of equality, so there are of fairness. Some of these considerations of fairness are internal to human rights. If a society respects men's human rights but not women's, then women are being denied their equal rights. A person is a bearer of human rights in virtue of being a normative agent, and women are equal to men in normative agency. Their being denied their rights is therefore unfair. Another form of fairness included in human rights is, as we have seen, a fair trial. But there are also forms of fairness that are not the concern of human rights: for example, the unfairness of free-riding and cheating at cards. My point is that the domains of human rights and fairness overlap but are not congruent.

Because objectionable forms of discrimination have violations of equality and fairness at their base, they too overlap, but are not congruent with, human rights. Some objectionable forms of discrimination clearly violate human rights, as when the thuggish organs of a government randomly round up members of a hated racial minority and subject them to painful physical abuse. It might seem initially that this periodic abuse need not destroy its victims' autonomous agency, but it usually would. Simply to be a member of a hated—or even a merely scorned or belittled—group would be likely to undermine one's life as an agent. A member of a hated minority would be inhibited from speaking out on unpopular issues, and from acting in a way that would attract the majority's attention. And members of a hated group living in a community with police given to physical abuse would be all the more constrained. And it is hard to maintain self-esteem, hard not to sink into passivity, when one's society as a whole gives one such a demeaning picture of oneself. None the less, even though this is a case of violation of human rights, the most obvious thing to say about it is something different: namely, that it is a monstrous injustice, a flagrant violation of equal respect.

Then there are cases of objectionable discrimination that are not matters of human rights. Two top executives of a multinational firm, equally competent and with equal responsibilities, may receive unequal pay merely because one of them is the CEO's brother. The lower-paid, though still handsomely paid, of the two does not have his human rights violated; what is objectionable about this case is the unfairness, the inequality with no good reason. The cases of discrimination that exercise us seriously nowadays, mainly racism[21] and sexism, range between these two extremes. In this middle ground it is often hard to tell objectionable from unobjectionable discrimination, the sorts of discrimination that violate human rights and the sorts that do not. I think that, in general, racism and sexism are likely to violate human rights because of their potentially destructive effect on an agent's self-image. However, the case of ageism—say, a compulsory retirement age—is much less clear. I shall return to these matters later.[22]

I remarked a moment ago that the domain of human rights includes procedural justice in courts, but not many forms of distributive or retributive justice. But this is speaking roughly. As we saw, human rights include at least one distributive requirement, minimum provision, because it is required by personhood. And for the same reason, human rights include some retributive requirements, such as proportionality in punishment and a ban on cruel and unusual punishment—proportionality because it is a protection of liberty, and the ban because it is a protection of agency generally. Torture, for instance, which I shall come to shortly, characteristically undermines agency, which is indeed its purpose. But what amount of punishment fits a certain crime, and whether desert alone can justify punishment, are matters of retributive justice, not of human rights.

To return now to my example, when I complain to you that I should have an equal share of the resources of the island, I am citing a principle of equal distribution, which is a principle of justice, which we can see, as our imagined conversation shows, as involved in equal respect. I am sure that you *ought* to divide the riches of the island equally with me. But to make it a matter of rights would create substantial problems. Where would we draw the line between the moral demands of equal respect, or of justice, that are rights and those that are not, other than where the personhood account has already drawn it? What rationale would we have for drawing it elsewhere? Would the line be clear enough?

My proposal to exclude certain, but not all, forms of justice and fairness from the domain of human rights goes against a not uncommon current belief that the domains of human rights and of justice are identical. But that belief is at striking variance with the extension of the term 'human right' as it has stood since the Enlightenment. I acknowledge that I shall sometimes later make appeal to equality, fairness, and justice in arguing for my conclusions about human rights, but they will often be the equality, fairness, and justice internal to the notion of a human right. For example, I claim, as do many others, that our human right to liberty is confined to liberty compatible with equal liberty for all—an equality that arises from our all equally being normative agents.[23] Sometimes, though, I shall appeal to a fairness that is not internal to the notion of a human right. I think that, in assigning the duties correlative to certain human rights to welfare, an appeal to our general ideal of fairness is indispensable.[24] It would be surprising if, in working out the implications of human rights, fairness and justice in general did not put in an appearance. But it is a non sequitur to move from a value's being indispensable in working out these implications of human rights to its being foundational to the notion of a human right itself. It should not matter to us that the exclusion of some forms of justice from the domain of human rights means that some of the most heavyweight moral obligations have no connection to these rights (e.g. my entirely justified claim to an equal share of the fertile land on that island). It is a great, but now common, mistake to think that, because we see rights as especially important in morality, we must make everything especially important in morality into a right. I shall return to the non-congruence of the domains of justice and fairness several times later.[25]

I propose, therefore, only two grounds for human rights: personhood and practicalities. The existence conditions for a human right would, then, be these. One establishes the existence of such a right by showing, first, that it protects an essential feature of human standing and, second, that its determinate content results from the sorts of practical considerations that I roughly sketched earlier.

2.7 HOW WE SHOULD UNDERSTAND 'AGENCY'?

If we adopt the personhood approach, we shall have to sharpen considerably the notion of 'agency' that is at its heart.

Agency can quite reasonably be seen as appearing in degrees. Children become agents in stages. Some adults are better than others at reflecting about values, or more effective at achieving them. Must a personhood account, then, imply that human rights come in proportionate degrees? Does it justify, in the end, less an egalitarian than a Platonic vision of society, with different classes having rights appropriate to their different reflective and executive capacities?[26]

This worry arises from using a different conception of 'agency' from the one that an account of human rights should employ. As we saw a while ago, our concept of rights emerged at the historic stage when belief in human equality started to supplant belief in a natural social hierarchy. Up to a point, egalitarianism is a bundle of factual claims (though usually laced with evaluations). One is the claim that many striking differences between social groups—for example, the far cruder taste and judgement of some—are not ordained by nature but are the brutalizing effect of social deprivation or the accidental effect of cultural development. Another of the factual claims is that among normal human beings there is not much correlation between IQ and a sense of what matters in life. And these, and many other factual claims in the bundle, are defensible on empirical grounds. Even if differences in taste and judgement persist because deprivation too persists, the overriding moral interest is not in giving them weight but in removing the deprivation. Of course, egalitarianism is an ethical thesis too. What we attach value to, what we regard as giving dignity to human life, is our capacity to choose and to pursue our conception of a worthwhile life. Mental defectives present difficult borderline problems here, and there is, of course, the question of when a child becomes an agent. But the vast majority of adult mankind are capable of reaching (a factual claim) this valuable state (an evaluative claim). Anyone who crosses the borderline, anyone who rises any degree above the threshold, is equally inside the class of agents, because everyone in the class thereby possesses the status to which we attach high value.[27] It is true that, above the threshold, certain differences in degree persist: for example, differences in IQ, in sensitivity to and skill in characterizing good-making features of life, in knowing how to realize these values, and so on. But none of these continuing differences in degree prevent there being a status entered just by passing the threshold, and a status that does not come in degrees. One might call it, as the United Nations does, 'the dignity of the human person'. Any further differences in sensitivity to values or skill in realizing them, and so on, will no longer matter to being a normative agent or a bearer of human rights—in short, to possessing this dignity.[28]

I say that what we attach value to, in this account of human rights, is specifically our capacity to choose and to pursue our conception of a worthwhile life. So the word 'agency' alone is not enough; there is an acceptable sense in which higher animals are agents. The term 'rational agents' is not specific enough. What we are concerned with is the agency involved in living a worthwhile life. Call it 'normative agency'.

This now leads us to the view that normative agency is the typical human condition. But is not having a conception of a worthwhile life, on the contrary, an exceedingly rare achievement? We must not, though, confuse having 'a conception of a worthwhile life', as I am using the term, with having 'a plan of life'. Having a plan of life is indeed exceedingly rare, and also questionably desirable. Why live by a plan of life when we are constantly learning more about the ways of the world, our values continually mature, and any plan of life is bound, to a fairly large degree, to be wrong? If one should adopt a plan of life, one should, at least, always be prepared to revise it. Even then, we should not aim to have highly detailed plans. One cannot predict what opportunities or mishaps will come one's way; one cannot know how one's emotional attachments will develop or how other persons will behave; and one cannot get one's mind around all the circumstances that would have to enter the rational calculation of even a fairly rudimentary plan of life. And the rough, incomplete plan of life that one might rationally formulate would amount to no more than a few policies—such as to spend more time with one's family, to go to concerts more often, and so on. Then having set oneself such goals, some planning would no doubt be sensible—say, planning one's weekly schedule so that one can indeed fit in these activities. This is as much planning as most of us ever do, or should try to do, and a weekly schedule is well short of a plan of life.

Nor should we confuse having 'a conception of a worthwhile life' with living 'an examined life', in Socrates' sense, when he famously declared that 'an unexamined life is not worth living'. Socrates regarded virtue as a matter of knowledge and vice as a matter of ignorance. We reach virtue through a long process of dialectic: doubting, challenging, recognizing our ignorance, and slowly working our way to an understanding of the good. One might regard this arduous dialectic as necessary to human life either because its very exercise is itself the peak of human excellence or because it is the only means to a good life. But neither is true. It is not the exercise of rationality that is the peak of excellence; the peak is, at most, what the use of reason might lead us to. And it is not true that an unexamined life, in the Socratic sense, is not worth living. Autonomously achieving a good life does not require periods of rational deliberation. Some persons are just by nature good at distinguishing true values from false; they simply have a good nose for these matters. Anyone who has the capacity to identify the good, whatever the extent of the capacity and whatever its source, has what I mean by 'a conception of a worthwhile life'; they have ideas, some of them reliable, about what makes a life better or worse. The ideas are not, and should not be, about the whole shape of one's life; they are piecemeal and, to varying degrees, incomplete. And it is the mere possession of this common capacity to identify the good that guarantees persons the protection of human rights.

There is another worry about the notion of 'agency'. An obvious objection to a personhood account is that a person can be denied religious freedom, even be cruelly persecuted, without ceasing to be an agent. Could anyone plausibly deny that at least some of the martyred saints were agents? On the contrary, there is a sense in which persecution can even enhance agency. When Alexander Solzhenitsyn was sent to a gulag, he seems to have become a more focused and determined agent than ever. But that is not the picture of agency at the heart of my account of human rights. My somewhat ampler picture is of a self-decider (i.e. someone autonomous) who, within limits, is not blocked from pursuing his or her conception of a worthwhile life (i.e. someone also at liberty). If either autonomy or liberty is missing, one's agency, on this ampler interpretation, is deficient. What we need is a normative picture of agency: autonomy and liberty are of special value to us, and thus attract the special protection of rights. Further, it is characteristic of human beings that they do not choose their goals once and for all. People mature; their values change. Liberty is freedom to live this sort of continually evolving life.

These last remarks help to answer another question about agency. By 'agency' we must mean not just having certain capacities (autonomous thought, executive action) but also exercising them. One can trample on a good many of a person's human rights (e.g. Solzhenitsyn's) without in the least damaging these *capacities*. In general, all that a person needs in order to *have* human rights is these capacities, but what human rights *protect* is something more: their exercise as well. I said earlier that on the personhood account we have a human right to education. But is not an illiterate peasant with no education still an agent in the sense we mean? So education it seems, is not necessary for this sort of agency; if basic literacy is not necessary, then neither is primary or secondary or university education. How, then, can education be a human right? It is a human right because it is necessary for the *exercise* of this sort of agency. The value behind human rights is not just the dignity of being able to be this sort of agent but also of being one. This sort, however, centres on our being able to form a conception of a worthwhile life and then pursue it; that is the source of its dignity. And that requires more than a life entirely devoted to the struggle to keep body and soul together. One's horizons must not be so low. We must know something about the options the world offers, or could offer with change that is well within human capacity to bring about. Otherwise, in our ignorance, we shall suffer from a kind of paucity of options that, as I shall argue later,[29] can violate our liberty. Our choices must meet certain standards for being informed. And literacy is an important means to being informed. We need also to be able to pursue our aims, and that requires more than mere literacy: for example, some skills and some knowledge of the world, including the world beyond the edges of our direct experience. And we need knowledge not only to protect autonomy and liberty but to protect other rights too: for example, in many developing countries the best way to reduce mortality, say from AIDS, is to increase literacy. Of course, we face the task of determining the level of education guaranteed by human rights, which requires more of the line of thought we have just begun. But, in one way or another, we face the task of fixing the level with most human rights, and we face it not just on the personhood account but on any plausible understanding of human rights.[30]

A last clarification of 'agency'. I say that 'agency', as used in the personhood account, includes both having certain capacities and exercising them. I want now to add that 'exercising' in this context must also include succeeding, within limits, in realizing the aim of the exercise. Suppose our governors wish us to live a simple life and, to that end, keep our society poorer than it need be, thus closing off options that many of us would find much more choice-worthy. At first glance, it may seem that the personhood account would have no complaint. After all, our governors leave us still able to form a conception of a worthwhile life and to pursue it; it is merely that in many cases we should have almost no chance of achieving it. But what our governors have done amounts to coercion—a violation of our liberty. What is valuable in normative agency must also include actually being able to make something good of our lives. If normative agency did not often make possible that final stage of realization of our aims, it would lose a large part of its value. Of course, the right to liberty offers no guarantee of success; the right to the pursuit of happiness is not a right to happiness. Still, the right to 'pursuit' is not limited to a right merely to expend effort; it is, at the very least, a right to expend effort without certain deliberate impediments, still to be specified. Indeed, much more about 'pursuit' needs to be specified, so much that I shall have to leave it until later when I come to liberty.[31]

The word 'agency' is used more or less broadly within the spectrum from deliberation to choice to action to outcome. In the personhood account it is used broadly—to cover all of these stages. If one of those parts is missing, we do not have the values that, according to the account, are the ground of human rights.

2.8 IN WHAT SENSE ARE HUMAN RIGHTS 'UNIVERSAL'?

Human rights, it seems, must be universal, because they are possessed by human agents simply in virtue of their normative agency.

But there is the following sceptical line of thought.[32] Virtually all, perhaps all, examples we cite of human rights are not in fact universal, so not true human rights. If there are *any* true human rights, any that are indeed universal in the class of human agents, they are not especially important to us. And what are important to us are the merely supposed human rights—such as freedom of expression—which, not being universal, are not true human rights.

The argument goes like this. Freedom of expression, for example, is highly important in certain social settings and quite unimportant in others. Anyone who lives, as we do, in a society with democratic political institutions, culturally heterodox citizens, a complex economy needing mobility of labour and having to absorb fast-developing science and technology, vitally needs freedom of expression. It is sufficiently important to us in this setting to justify promulgating the right and imposing the correlative duties. But anyone who lived in a traditional medieval hamlet, with static technology and an unchallenged social tradition, and where necessary skills were acquired just by growing up in the place, quite rightly had a relatively minor interest in freedom of expression—an interest too minor to justify the burdensome apparatus of a right. So whatever freedom of expression is, it is not a human right because it is not universal.

But this argument misunderstands what the right to free expression protects. True, we may not need it for the economy of the medieval hamlet to flourish. True, if I am terribly shy and have no wish to speak, I may mind much less that I am not allowed to. But the ground for freedom of expression lies in a normative notion of agency: we are self-deciders; that is part of the dignity of human standing. To be a tolerably successful self-decider typically requires an ability to ask questions, hear what others think, and so on. It would not matter to my having the right that I am shy and may not exercise it. Others can ask or offer answers, and that itself would help me. Medieval hamlets too can be grossly oppressive. One might well have wanted to question the sort of life that the local lord or the abbot of the monastery imposed upon one, discover whether others too were discontent, and decide with them what to do. And the lord or the abbot might have wanted to stifle free speech to protect orthodoxy. One's status as a self-determiner is vulnerable in any social setting. Applying the right in the setting of the medieval hamlet might produce different derived principles from the ones that it would produce in a large, modern, industrialized society. But there would still be a robust enough sense of the identity of the right through the various applications of it needed in different social settings.

One's status as a self-determiner, I just said, is vulnerable in any *social* setting. Is that not a problem? What of non-social settings—say, hunter-gatherers in family units with no social structure to speak of between them? Would human rights apply even to them? Well, why not? There would be vulnerability even there: one could still be murdered, enslaved, or oppressed by others. But even if human rights were not to apply to hunter-gatherers, they could still have a qualified, though quite good enough, form of universality. One could just gloss the claim: human rights, one could say, are rights that we all have simply in virtue of being *human agents in society*. That must be, in any case, all the universality that the original advocates of human rights ever dreamt of. Besides, human rights, on the personhood account, are not universal in the class of human beings; they are restricted to the sub-class of human normative agents. It would not be a revolutionary step to restrict them further to the class of human normative agents in society. Not even morality, to my mind, applies universally to moral agents regardless of conditions: for example, it does not apply if conditions get desperate enough—*sauve qui peut* situations. Despite that, it is perfectly reasonable to go on saying that moral principles apply universally, that is, to us all simply in virtue of our being moral agents (i.e. given that morality applies at all).

Of course, there are human rights that clearly do not apply even in all societies—say, freedom of the press. There are a few present, and many past, societies with no press, or even the concept of one. Such apparent failures in universality have been used as a reason for us to abandon the idea that human rights are grounded in universal human nature itself and to adopt a different ground and possibly, as a consequence, a much revised list of rights[33] —say, Rawls's much shortened list.[34] But we must keep in mind the distinction between basic rights and applied or derived rights. Rights may be expressed at different levels of abstraction. The highest level would emerge when we articulate the values that we attach to agency: as I listed them earlier, autonomy, minimum provision, and liberty. Then less abstract characterizations would come about as a result of the application of these highest-level considerations with increasing attention to circumstances. Freedom of expression is derived from, as a necessary condition of, autonomy and liberty. Freedom of the press is derived, in certain social circumstances, from freedom of expression. We should expect abstractly formulated rights, when applied to the conditions of a particular society, to be formulated in the language of its time and place and actual concerns, and we should expect no one particularly to notice when the move down the scale of abstraction passes from global to local vocabulary. We should claim only that universality is there at the higher levels.

Still, is it not a consequence of saying that we have these rights simply in virtue of being human that we should have them even in the state of nature? Yes. How, then, may I so easily allow that it would be possible for human rights to have point only in society? The claim that we should have human rights even in the state of nature should be taken to mean that we have human rights solely in virtue of features of our humanity, not because of any social status or relation. Our normative agency may need protection only in society (though I doubt that), but it is a status we have independently of society.

But what of the whole range of welfare rights, now generally accepted as human rights? Do they not violate the universality requirement? Classical liberty rights are doubly universal: all human agents have them, and all owe the correlative duties. But welfare rights, it seems, are doubly particular: only members of a particular society can claim them, and they can claim them only from their own society. And in the case of classical liberty rights one can read off the duty-bearer from the content of the right: the right not to be interfered with imposes a duty not to interfere upon all others. But the content of a welfare right, being a claim of the needy to be helped, does not indicate who of all those able to help has the duty to do so. Indeed, Kant thought that duties to help, being 'imperfect' duties—that is, not perfectly (fully) specified—lack correlative rights. That is the strongest doubt: not only are so-called welfare rights not really human rights, they are not any kind of moral right either. And, one might go on, as welfare rights do not themselves specify the correlative duty-bearers, they can be specified only by an authoritative social institution, and therefore welfare rights cannot be, as they are supposed to be, independent of society.[35] To my mind, these lines of reasoning fail; some welfare rights are human rights and they, like all human rights, are universal—indeed, doubly universal. But the arguments for this conclusion involve many further issues and will have to wait till later.[36]

2.9 DO WE NEED A MORE PLURALIST ACCOUNT?

My personhood account can be seen as trinist (if I may coin a word to come next in the sequence 'monist', 'dualist'). Human rights, I propose, have their ground in the three values of personhood: autonomy, liberty, and minimum provision. My confining the ground to these three values is, of course, at the centre of my attempt to give the term 'human right' a sufficiently determinate sense—an attempt that everyone interested in making the term part of serious thought about morality must, in some form or other, make. An obvious worry, though, is whether all human rights can be derived from such a relatively slender base. Personhood, sceptics may allow, is an important part of the story, but not the whole story. Human rights, they may say, both need and can have a broader base.[37]

Take an example. The long-established right not to be tortured does not seem to be derived just from the values of normative agency. True, torture typically renders us unable to decide for ourselves or to stick to our decision. What is wrong with torture, though, is not just that it thus undermines normative agency, but also, and far more obviously, that it involves excruciating pain. So it seems more plausible, and certainly more straightforward, to say that the basic human interest in avoiding pain is weighty enough on its own to justify promulgating a right against torture and imposing the correlative duty on others. Think, too, of our right to education. No doubt it is based partly on education's being a necessary condition for effective agency. But another obvious ground for the right is simply our considerable interest in achieving certain forms of understanding. And so on.

We cannot finally settle the issues between my account and this more expansive pluralist account now, but we can make a start on them.

If we were asked what is wrong about torture, of course the most obvious thing to say would be that it causes great pain. But the question that concerns us now is not nearly so broad. Our question is: Why is torture a matter of a human right? And the answer to that could not be, Because it causes great pain. There are many cases of one person's gratuitously inflicting great pain on another that are not a matter of human rights. One partner in an unsuccessful marriage, for example, might treat the other coldly and callously, and the suffering caused the second partner over the years might mount up into something much worse than a short period of physical torture. The first partner, however, simply by being cruel, does not thereby violate the second's human rights. Or an older sibling might beat a younger sibling about the head from time to time, out of the common resentment that a displaced older child feels of a younger, but, even if painful, it would be hard to call it 'torture' — except in the extended sense in which any considerable pain (bad sunburn, say) may be called 'torture'.

Torture has characteristic aims. It is used to make someone recant a belief, reveal a secret, 'confess' a crime whether guilty or not, abandon a cause, or do someone else's bidding. All of these characteristic purposes involve undermining someone else's will, getting them to do what they do not want to do, or are even resolved not to do.[38] In one way or an other, they all involve an attack on normative agency. If the older sibling were to beat the younger about the head in order to extract a secret, the word 'torture' would fit much better. As we can have infliction of great pain without the intention to destroy normative agency, we can also have intentional destruction of normative agency without infliction of great pain. People use torture to undermine agency usually because they have no better way. Now sometimes we do: there are truth drugs that sometimes help in extracting secrets, and with time there may be far more successful painless techniques for imposing one's own will upon others or discovering what they think.[39] We could not call this 'torture' because it is essential to 'torture' that the infliction of great pain be the means. But what concerns us here is whether the painless chemical destruction of another person's will raises any issues of human rights. And it does. It does so because painless domination is still a gross undermining of personhood.

The same approach suits the other example I just mentioned, the right to education. There is a difference between the varied benefits that make education valuable and what makes it a human right. There is a minimalist character to human rights, which different writers will explain in different ways. I explain it as coming from human rights' being protections not of a fully flourishing life but only of the more austere life of a normative agent. But we should all agree that there are highly valuable forms of education that lie beyond what is required by human rights. This is a common phenomenon. There are levels of health,[40] and forms of privacy,[41] and of several other human interests of which it is also true. On their own, the examples fall short of demonstrating a need for a more pluralist account.

There are, as well, theoretical problems facing a more pluralist account. Clearly, not any human interest will be a ground of a human right. How, then, will the more pluralist account identify the interests that are a ground? And how will it meet our pressing initial problem: that the sense of the term 'human right' must be made much more determinate?[42] And, faced with a choice between my personhood account and a more pluralist account, there is the question, Which is the better way to speak about human rights? Nearly all of us want to see a less free-wheeling, more criteria-governed use of the discourse of 'human rights'. Unless the more pluralist account can reduce its considerable vagueness, the likelihood of its having the desired effects will be low. What is lacking, I have admitted, is not a verbal definition of the term 'human right'; a determinate sense for the term could come about simply by its having a settled use, even a quite complex one. And might not authoritative institutions, such as international law, be just the agency to bring this about? As I said earlier,[43] I think not. When it comes to human rights, it is not enough for the appropriate international institutions, following the proper procedures, to reach and declare agreement. International law, being positive law, can certainly create positive rights. But the international law of human rights aims, or should aim, at least in part, to incorporate certain extra-legal ethical standards. The creators of international law do not, and cannot plausibly, say that what they deem to be a human right *is* a human right, that on this subject they are infallible. And as human rights in international law should incorporate something ethical, why should we let the use settle down without influence from ethical thought? More must be said, and I shall return to international law later.[44] It may seem that the answer to the question, Which is the better way to speak about human rights?, is: As their moral content requires, independent of practical effects. I think not, and shall return to the question later.[45]

An advocate of a more pluralist account might respond to these challenges along the following lines. There are various constraints on the human interests that can serve as a ground of human rights. They are, first of all, restricted to the interests of human beings as human beings; that follows from the sort of universality that human rights have. But well-being, even at high levels, qualifies as such a human interest. An obvious further constraint, then, would be that the human interests be *important* or *major* or *urgent*. But not all important (or major or urgent) interests can plausibly be a ground for a human right. Things can be of great importance to our lives—indeed, greater than a lot of issues of human rights—without themselves thereby becoming grounds for human rights. I touched on this earlier. According to the rights tradition, procedural justice is a matter of human rights, but not many forms of distributive justice, although distributive justice may well be more important in most people's lives than procedural justice. Recall too the example of the cold and callous spouse: the cold and callous treatment may well be worse than the infringement of certain of the unfortunate spouse's human rights (say, a minor infringement of the unfortunate spouse's right to privacy).

Now, the advocate of a more pluralist account might appeal, as I did a moment ago in stating the account, to the highly influential explanation of a 'right' that we owe to Joseph Raz. Applied to the case of human rights, it would go like this: a human right arises when there are universal human interests sufficient to justify imposing the correlative duties on others.[46] This definition has the advantage of allowing more human interests to serve as grounds for human rights than just autonomy, liberty, and minimum provision, yet imposes the constraint on the additional interests that they be able to justify the imposition of duties on others. This is still not enough, though. The suffering of the spouse with the cold and callous partner is surely enough to justify imposing a duty on the partner to stop this treatment. This case is only one instance of a general worry: human rights must not expand to fill most of the domain of well-being. We have an important interest, for example, in there being a rich array of options in life from which we may choose. The benefits of our having such a rich array are so considerable that they would justify imposing on certain agents—perhaps on our fellow citizens—the burden of promoting them. The trouble with this is that it is likely to justify a human right to even quite high levels of well-being. It would justify any level, no matter how high, at which the benefits are great enough to justify imposing the burden. The benefits of a flourishing life—for example, of having a rich array of options from which to build one's life—are characteristically so enormous that they are likely to justify imposing a burden on others, particularly as the burden would not be so great. To have a rich array of options would require having a fairly high level of social wealth and a fairly advanced culture, which most of us are already independently motivated to produce. But this undermines our belief that we have a human right to material and cultural resources only up to a minimum acceptable level beyond which they are *not* a matter of right.

Let me follow the theoretical problems facing more pluralist accounts through just one more twist. One might say, as Raz himself does, that the benefit must be great enough to justify imposing not any duty but a particular kind of duty—namely, a duty that supplies an 'exclusionary reason'.[47] An exclusionary reason is the kind of reason that excludes a certain range of other reasons from being taken into consideration. Promising is a paradigm case. The fact that one has promised excludes one's then giving weight to every consideration of one's own convenience that in other circumstances would quite properly have weight. But I doubt that the introduction of exclusionary reasons is enough. It is not at all easy to see how this particular deontic notion—a duty with this exclusionary effect—is supposed to work in ethical thought, nor when it is present. Where on the spectrum from one spouse's minor unpleasantness to the other, at one end, to the spouse's most damagingly callous behaviour, at the other, do we reach interests that produce an exclusionary duty? And where on the spectrum of levels of well-being, or of flourishing life, do we reach that point? It is hard to say. These cases have none of the clarity of the case of promising. We do not understand what a human right is until we understand roughly where along such spectra we are to make the break. It is not that there are no ways of explaining that. One can say, as I propose we do, that in the case of the spouse's cruelty, for example, the break comes when the cruelty starts to undermine the other's ability to function as an agent, which at some point it certainly will. But that simply takes us back to the personhood account. My belief is that Raz's account does not supply a sufficient condition for the existence of a right, and that therefore there will be many cases in which the interests at stake are sufficient to justify imposing on others whatever the appropriate sort of duty is, yet are not matters of human rights. It would, at least, take radical revision to our intuitions for us to accept them as human rights.

This chapter has been a preliminary canter across our terrain. I shall return to many parts of it later on.

3

When Human Rights Conflict

3.1 ONE OF THE CENTRAL QUESTIONS OF ETHICS

There is no better test of an account of human rights than the plausibility of what it has to say about rights in conflict. There is no better way to force thought about human rights to a deeper level than to try to say something about how to resolve conflicts involving them. If one human right conflicts with another, or with some other moral consideration, then we try to resolve the conflict by somehow or other weighing the conflicting items. To weigh them, we have to decide what gives them their weight in the first place. If we favour the personhood account, for example, then we are forced to decide between a deontological and a teleological understanding of the value of personhood. That abruptly brings us to the heart of normative ethics.

I spoke earlier of two different ways of understanding the value of personhood.[1] One might, following Kant, contrast 'persons' with mere 'things'. 'Things' have 'price', and so have equivalents. 'Persons', however, have 'dignity'; they are of unique value; they have no equivalents. One might want to endow human rights, therefore, with something akin to the power of trumps over all aggregates of other moral considerations. Or one might want to make a somewhat weaker claim: that the value of personhood cannot be outweighed by a mere surplus of other values also to be promoted; it can be outweighed, rather, only by a substantial surplus. Personhood, that is, has a value independent of promoting the ends that make a human life good.

The second way to understand the value of personhood is to see the exercise of our personhood as an end the realization of which enhances the value of life. It would clearly be a highly important such feature, but none the less not, in principle, immune to trade-off with other things that make a life good, such as accomplishment, certain kinds of understanding, deep personal relations, and so on. It is because of the special importance, though by no means necessarily uniquely great importance, of these particular human interests that, on this understanding, we ring-fence them with the notion of human rights. This would explain how we might place human rights within a teleological morality.

The way to resolve conflicts of human rights should not come as an afterthought, or as a matter of merely spelling out the consequences of an account of human rights already decided independently. It should occupy centre-stage when one is trying to settle the most important issue: the existence conditions for human rights.

3.2 CONFLICTS BETWEEN HUMAN RIGHTS THEMSELVES

Some apparent conflicts between human rights themselves turn out to be merely pseudo-conflicts. Once the content of each of the apparently conflicting human rights is spelt out sufficiently, one often finds that there is no conflict after all. For example, it is widely thought that one person's liberty can all too easily conflict with another's. Freedom for the pike, the saying goes, is death for the minnows. There are, however, constraints on the content of the right to liberty. The ground for my liberty is a ground for your equal liberty; the ground cannot justify my being more at liberty than you are. That identifies a formal constraint on the content of the right: each person's liberty must be compatible with the same liberty for all. If that is so, then instead of conflict, a degree of harmony is built into people's liberties. There is also a material constraint on the right to liberty: according to the personhood account, what makes liberty an important value demanding protection by something as strong as a human right is its being a constituent of our personhood. My being able to gratify a passing whim (e.g. driving the wrong way down a one-way street) would certainly not be that, while my being able to pursue central features of what I regard as a worthwhile life would be. My apparent human right to drive the wrong way down a one-way street does not conflict with your apparent human right to efficiently regulated traffic. Neither is a human right. With this further clarity about the content of the right, many supposed conflicts disappear. Much more will have to be said in defence of this understanding of liberty, of course, and I shall come to it later.[2]

That outcome prompts the thought: might we find, when we understand the content of all human rights fully enough, that there are no conflicts between them? One can see how one might come to think so. I distinguished earlier top-down and bottom-up approaches to explaining human rights.[3] We can see how certain top-down approaches might imply harmony between human rights. Consequentialists might be able to show (though I doubt that their calculations would be nearly reliable enough to be taken seriously) that a set of human rights framed so that, fully articulated, they did not conflict had best consequences overall. But the more promising approach is Kant's. What Kant calls 'The Universal Principle of Right' can be stated as a principle for distribution of freedom: 'Any action is *right*', the Principle says, 'if it can coexist with everyone's freedom in accordance with a universal law, or if on its maxim the freedom of choice of each can coexist with everyone's freedom in accordance with a universal law.'[4] The formal constraint on liberty that I adopted a moment ago has some similarity to Kant's constraint on the distribution of freedom: one person's liberty must be compatible with equal liberty for all. Does Kant's constraint ensure that one person's exercise of a human right must be co-possible with another's?[5]

For the moment, however, I want to carry on with my preferred bottom-up approach and not assume the correctness of any highly abstract, systematic moral view. Once I develop the personhood account further, though, it soon brings us up against the Kantian view and the question of co-possibility.

On my bottom-up approach, there may still be arguments for the harmony of human rights—for example, further piecemeal arguments of the sort that I just deployed to dissolve certain apparent conflicts of liberties. Even if the class of pseudo-conflicts can, as I suspect, thus be enlarged considerably further, I want to claim that there remain conflicts of rights that resist such dissolution. It is widely, perhaps nearly universally, accepted that if a threat to the survival of the nation is great enough, if its ability to protect the life and liberty of its citizens is in sufficient peril—in short, in a grave emergency—a government may set aside certain human rights. In the first days of the US Civil War, just after the fall of Fort Sumter, Lincoln suspended *habeas corpus* in federal areas where enemy troops were operating, and asked rhetorically, and in powerful justification of his decision, 'Are all the laws *but one* [viz. *habeas corpus*] to go unexecuted, and the government itself go to pieces, lest that one be violated?'[6] Once in the 1970s, and once again in the 1980s, at the height of terrorism in Northern Ireland, the British government introduced arbitrary detention. After the terrorist attacks on New York and Washington on 11 September 2001, both the United States and Britain introduced detention without trial. Explicit exemptions at times of emergency are distributed throughout the basic twentieth-century human rights documents.[7] The Universal Declaration of Human Rights (1948), Article 29. 9, is particularly generous, perhaps too generous, in that respect:[8]

In the exercise of his rights and freedoms, everyone shall be subject only to such limitations as are determined by law solely for the purpose of securing due recognition and respect of the rights of others and of meeting the just requirements of morality, public order and the general welfare in a democratic society.

We may dispute whether the threat in the three cases I just mentioned was great enough to justify detention without trial; all that I want to claim is that *if* the threat is indeed great enough, we may detain suspects without trial.[9] We can admit the likelihood of our having thereby detained, along with the real terrorists, say, some innocent people. We should certainly be violating *their* liberty. The liberty of the real terrorists is unlikely to extend to bombing innocent civilians, but the liberty of the innocent detainees certainly extends to their going about their perfectly innocent business. But what we think justifies the violation of their true liberty is that only by detention without trial can we save many civilian lives. We should be all the more willing to accept this exchange if the detention were fairly brief. Is this not a conflict of human rights: the liberty of the innocent detainees in conflict with the rights to life and to personal security of the civilians?[10]

3.3 ARE HUMAN RIGHTS CO-POSSIBLE?

Perhaps not all of morality is by nature free of conflict, but only a part of it, including, in some strict sense, our exercise of our human rights. Several writers think so. Robert Nozick, for instance, says, though without explanation, 'Individual rights are co-possible: each person may exercise his rights as he chooses.'[11] Perhaps the counter-examples I just offered do not fall into this central class.

I have suggested that the best case for co-possibility is Kant's. What does Kant think 'natural rights' (to use his term for them) are? His fullest account is found in Part I of his late work *The Metaphysics of Morals* and is part of his much broader 'Doctrine of Right'. He speaks variously of 'right' (*Recht*), 'the right' (*das Recht*), and 'a right' (*ein Recht*): 'right' is the adjectival notion of being right; 'the right' is the set of principles that determine what is right and wrong; and 'a right' is our modern notion of an entitlement that an individual has.[12] He goes on to distinguish *innate* from *acquired* rights. An 'innate' right belongs 'to everyone by nature independently of any act that would establish a right', while 'acquired' rights are those that require such an act.[13] There is only one innate right: namely, '*freedom* (independence of constraint by another's choice) insofar as it can coexist with the freedom of every other in accordance with a universal law'; it is 'the only original right belonging to every man by virtue of his humanity'.[14] Kant has made here a fateful move: the content of the one overarching right is the same as what Kant calls 'The Universal Principle of Right',[15] which I stated a moment ago, suggesting that the one innate right and the rights that follow from it cover much of morality. It is not that Kant thinks that rights cover all of morality; they omit, for example, duties arising from the Doctrine of Virtue (Part II of *The Metaphysics of Morals*) and those duties arising from a mix of the a priori and a posteriori.[16] 'Natural' rights, in contrast to 'positive' rights, rest only on a priori principles, specifically on The Universal Principle of Right.[17] More fully, a 'natural right', Kant says, 'is one derived from *a priori* principles for a civil constitution'.[18] Of the several natural rights Kant derives from the one innate right, he mentions, among others, rights to procedural and distributive justice,[19] to retributive justice (a right exercised on our behalf by the sovereign power),[20] to grant clemency (also the sovereign's exercise),[21] to have one's reputation defended against unjust charges even after one's death,[22] to marriage if one's partner wishes to use one's 'sexual attributes',[23] to help in dire need,[24] and perhaps also not to be subjected to gratuitous suffering (I can find no explicit mention of this final right in the texts, but it is a negative right; it can be publicly commanded and enforced).

There is much overlap between what Kant says of 'natural rights' and my personhood account of 'human rights', because they are both centred on the idea of respect for persons. But there is also a great difference. What I mean by 'liberty' is freedom to pursue one's conception of a worthwhile life; liberty is one among other rights, the other ones on the same high level of abstraction being autonomy and minimum provision.[25] These rights are protections of something quite specific: our status as normative agents. What Kant means by 'freedom' is much broader than this: it is the area of action left to us after excluding what we are required to do and prohibited from doing by the Doctrine of Right. So what I called Kant's fateful move does indeed result in a list of rights considerably longer than the ones in the Enlightenment tradition. As I pointed out earlier,[26] although that tradition includes procedural justice (fair procedure in law) among human rights, it strikingly does not include many forms of distributive or retributive justice or a right to grant clemency, highly important moral matters though these be. Nor does it include a right to marriage to one's sexual partner, although there might be a moral case for it, though the feeble one that Kant himself mounts is not it.[27] And if Kant believed there to be a natural right not to be made gratuitously to suffer, that does not count as a right in the Enlightenment tradition either. Recall my earlier example of one spouse's subjecting the other to relentless unpleasantness, which causes the other spouse greatly to suffer but not so much, or in such a way, as to lose personhood.[28] Again, most persons raised in the use of the language of the Enlightenment tradition of natural rights would find it counter-intuitive to say that the first spouse thereby violated the second's human rights. The first spouse does the second a serious moral wrong, but that is different. In Kant's hands, natural rights cover not only more ground than those in the Enlightenment tradition; they also have a different moral weight. For Kant, natural rights are absolute. In the tradition, they are not.

What should we make of these differences? Are they so great, especially in the extensions they yield, that we should doubt that Kant's account is, after all, an account of 'natural rights'? Or is his high-level Doctrine of Right, in association with the Categorical Imperative, so compelling that we should be willing to abandon the tradition, including our linguistic intuitions arising from it. It is clear from Part I of the *Metaphysics of Morals* that Kant's interest is in spelling out what can be derived from the Categorical Imperative, in particular from the Doctrine of Right, and not at all in accommodating how those around him at the height of the Enlightenment were using the term 'natural right'. Kant simply commandeers the term to do service in his grand theory.

To return now to our question: does Kant's account of natural rights establish their co-possibility? I think not. I am not persuaded by Kant's case for the Categorical Imperative and the Doctrine of Right. But suppose that one were so persuaded, and furthermore accepted his notion of natural rights. That would still leave the Enlightenment notion, with its considerably different extension. The only way that the Enlightenment notion would disappear is if it were to be shown to be so flawed that it would be better abandoned. I said earlier that, though arguments to that effect have occasionally been advanced, none has succeeded in establishing anything approaching such a strong conclusion,[29] and the last chapter offered my reasons.[30] In any case, it is the Enlightenment notion that virtually all of us, Kantians or not, understand by 'human rights' and have in mind when we ask whether human rights are co-possible. So let us, for now, answer the questions so understood.

The example of detention without trial that I gave a short while ago used a government as one of the agents involved, because that is the form in which we actually encounter this sort of case. But the presence of a government is an unnecessary complication—a complication because the government's duty to act here may be thought to arise from more than just the rights to self-defence of the citizens for whom it acts. It might, for instance, be thought to arise from a contract-like relation between the government and its citizens. But the example can be simplified. The members of a certain group, let us say, have a human right to defend themselves against a clear and present danger to their lives, and the only effective way for them to exercise it is to round up those members of another group threatening them, knowing that it is likely that some of those rounded up will be innocent. Their exercising their right to self-defence, derived from their right to life, conflicts with the innocent detainees' exercising their legitimate right to liberty. This, then, is a simpler counter-example: a case of some persons' exercise of a human right conflicting with other persons' exercise of a human right.

If there are absolute rights, they must be co-possible. But it is false that, on the Enlightenment notion, natural rights are co-possible. So, by *modus tollens*, not all of them are absolute. On my personhood account everyone has maximum liberty compatible with equal liberty for all, 'equal liberty' here meaning that all persons possess the same right to liberty, where the content of the right is not so full, nor capable of being made so full, that it guarantees harmony in the exercise of all human rights.

3.4 CONFLICTS BETWEEN A HUMAN RIGHT AND OTHER KINDS OF MORAL CONSIDERATION

Do human rights sometimes conflict with welfare? There are abundant pseudo-conflicts here too. Many writers regard any restriction on one's doing what one wants as an infringement, no doubt often justified, of one's liberty. Liberty, they say, conflicts with efficiency. The one-way traffic restriction infringes my liberty, but this minor liberty is outweighed by the increase in efficiency. But, as we saw earlier, liberty does not protect one in doing whatever one wants. Liberty, the moral and political value that is the ground of the right, is not even at stake in this case. There is no conflict.

Still, there are genuine conflicts here as well. A country, let us say, decides to hold a referendum on whether to devote a percentage of its GDP to foreign aid and, if so, what percentage it should be. In a democracy, the right to autonomy, at least in modern conditions, requires consulting citizens on certain major decisions affecting what is done to them and for them. A crisis arises in a neighbouring country, causing great suffering (but not deaths, let us suppose, in order to simplify things) and needing quick remedy. The government announces that, as there is not time to await the results of the referendum, it will send aid. The suffering is widespread and severe, it explains, the neighbours have long-standing ties to us of friendship and mutual help, and the autonomy denied our own citizens is not of a particularly high order (after all, it is a one-off action on the part of the government, and if the coming referendum goes against further foreign aid, it will not be repeated). There must be some level of suffering and some level of importance of an exercise of autonomy at which the suffering outweighs the loss of autonomy.

That is an example of the most widely discussed sort of conflict: a right–welfare conflict. But there are kinds of moral consideration besides human rights and welfare. There are, for example, considerations of justice, and though some parts of justice overlap with human rights, not all do. Let me briefly remind you of my earlier argument, which was an appeal to strong and widespread linguistic intuitions.[31] Justice has many departments: retributive justice, distributive justice, procedural justice, fairness (there are reasons, I should say, for thinking that fairness is not exhausted by those departments already mentioned), and still more. Now, if you free-ride on the bus because you know that no harm will come, as the rest of us are paying our fare, you do not infringe my human rights, though you do, clearly, act unfairly. That helps to explain why the tradition regards the whole of procedural justice in courts as a matter of human rights, but not the whole of distributive justice. It regards the requirements of procedural justice in courts as human rights because, to put it briefly, they are important protections of life, liberty, and supporting goods—all necessary conditions for agency. Of course, human rights have their own distributive consequences, say the right to the minimum material resources needed to function as an agent. On distributive matters above that level, however—say, whether resources or welfare should be distributed equally, or whether deviations from equality that make the worst off better off should be allowed—human rights are silent.

If the domain of rights does not exhaust the domain of justice, then there may be right–justice conflicts. For example, think of a properly convicted criminal who is imprisoned or executed. One is supposed to have human rights simply in virtue of being human. The criminal, in virtue of the crime, does not cease being human in the relevant sense—namely, a normative agent—so the criminal, it seems, retains all human rights, including rights to life and liberty. If one thinks that what justifies punishment is its good consequences, then one has here a potential right–welfare conflict. But many people would insist that what justifies punishment is, or is also, desert. Would we have here, if that were so, a right–justice conflict?

It would, of course, be a grotesque theoretical embarrassment if human rights were to prove an obstacle to fair punishment. The embarrassment was meant to have been avoided by a doctrine of forfeit.[32] A criminal forfeits human rights. If that were so, then this case too would thereby become another pseudo-conflict. The doctrine of forfeit, however, is a factitious measure, never deeply worked out. What exactly, according to the doctrine, does a murderer or a thief forfeit? Rights generally? The right to life? The right to liberty? The right to security of person (e.g. the right not to have one's hand cut off, as it might be under Shariah law)? The appropriate way to answer those questions is by appeal to desert: what punishment would fit the crime? Punishment involves taking away something typically valuable to human beings—for example, life, liberty, or property. What, and how much, good is to be taken is determined by the offender's desert. What the offender might be thought to forfeit is not a right *simpliciter*; the 'forfeit' is whatever punishment turns out to be just. There are cases in which different punishments are all equally just: the guilty party, let us say, might appropriately be given either six months in jail or a £20,000 fine or three years' community service. So, in the language of 'forfeits', the offender would forfeit either the right to liberty to the extent of six months or the right to property to the extent of £20,000 or occasional liberty to the extent of three years. But what are important here are the judgements about desert, from which one can derive, if one should care to, judgements about what is forfeited. But why should one care to? To speak of 'forfeit' suggests that the right in some way disappears from the scene. But it does not disappear. On the contrary, we have just seen that the personhood account leaves no space for forfeits; an offender is still a person. That is why an offender retains, among others, a right not to be tortured. It is more perspicuous to say that the demands of justice can sometimes, and to some appropriate degree, outweigh the protection of human rights. That is why it is indeed reasonable to talk here in terms of conflict—a conflict between human rights and justice.

Might justice, then, not only outweigh a human right but also upset the calculations that I say go into the resolution of conflicts? Might the resolution of a right–right conflict, for instance, based as it is on degrees of loss of personhood, be altered by considerations of distributive justice—say, maxi–min? In principle, yes; but rarely. We can apply the principle of maxi–min only if we know the welfare levels of those involved, either individually or as a group. Think of cases of temporary arbitrary detention. We typically do not know the welfare levels of those involved, either individually or as a group. Even if we did, it would be unlikely to make a difference, because so many lives are at stake.

To summarize: there are, then, right–right conflicts, right–welfare conflicts, right–justice conflicts, and possibly more. I think that there are indeed more, some of which are neither dissoluble nor resolvable.[33]

3.5 A PROPOSAL AND A QUALIFICATION

There is a general requirement on the resolution of conflicts of values: if it is not to be arbitrary, one must know what values are at stake and how to attach weight to them. No matter how basic in the whole moral structure human rights may be, there is still language available that allows us to articulate, at least in part, why they are so valuable. It need not be the language of ends. It could be the language of duties. Kant, as we saw, speaks of persons' having 'dignity' in virtue of their freedom, and of their dignity's giving them inviolability. Non-Kantians can make a similar point. We all need to understand why persons are regarded as especially valuable. Since the late Middle Ages many writers have explained it by pointing to the special feature of humanity that I have been stressing: our capacity for normative agency. We can easily understand why the term 'dignity' was attached to our status as normative agents, and why other forms of animal life were thought to lack that dignity. It is not that the direction of explanation need run solely from 'dignity' to 'human right'; it might be that adumbrating human rights is an indispensable way of understanding that particularly vague term 'dignity'.

Our agency is far from simple. It has parts: autonomy, liberty, and minimum provision. One can lose one part and not others. And each part itself can be at stake in different degrees. There are, for example, minor liberties and major ones, minor exercises of autonomy and major ones. The ground for our drawing this difference between liberties and exercises of autonomy is their degree of centrality to personhood. For instance, we are at liberty to visit other countries, other cultures, other political systems, and people with other attitudes. The United States government's prohibition of its citizens' visiting Castro's Cuba was an infringement of their liberty, but less drastic than a prohibition on all foreign travel would have been, which in turn would have been a less serious infringement than a prohibition of all foreign contact. So behind the idea of major and minor infringements of rights is the idea of an attack on something nearer to or further from the centre of one's agency. More or less of one's liberty, more or less of one's autonomy, can be at stake at different times. What is more, there is the temporal dimension; the loss can be for a short or a long time.[34]

Is my talk here of degrees of agency inconsistent with what I said earlier? I say now that a person can lose one component of agency but not others, and each component to different degrees. Yet I said earlier that personhood is a threshold concept: once inside the class of persons, there are no degrees of being a person. There are two senses of agency that chiefly concern us. There is the sort of agency that makes us bearers of human rights—namely, our capacities for autonomy and liberty—and there is the sort of agency that human rights are meant to protect—that is, not only the possession of these capacities but also their exercise. It can happen, either through the action of other agents or, more commonly, through illness (polio, say, or motor neurone disease) or accident that one loses one's natural capacity to exercise liberty. One can no longer pursue various parts of one's conception of a worthwhile life because one has insufficient control over one's body. Is this a loss of agency? And of one's human rights? It is clear to me that, however one explains personhood and the possession of rights, such an alert person trapped inside a non-functioning body must be classed as a *person* and as a *bearer of rights*. This is uncontroversial. It can also be accommodated within the personhood account. Because of the value of personhood, we have a duty, correlative to human rights, to restore that person's capacity to act. We think so, for instance, in the case of the crippled; we build special access for them to schools, museums, concert halls, and so on. And we can similarly help persons trapped in non-functioning bodies; we can, for instance, become their surrogate arms and legs; we can become the executors of their rational conceptions of a worthwhile life—perhaps even including a merciful death. I shall come back to that last issue later.[35]

Look now at the idea that human rights are absolute. We have seen that human rights can conflict—both one with another and one with other kinds of moral considerations. Therefore they cannot be absolute. There are, it is true, intuitions that seem to support absolutism. Some pairs of values are such that, no matter how much one of them increases, it can never reach the level of the other. Elsewhere I have called this sort of relation 'discontinuity'.[36] We constantly meet welfare–welfare conflicts, and we all believe that utilitarian calculation is usually the appropriate way to resolve them. For instance, we weigh up how many airplane passengers are convenienced, and how much, by there being early morning and late night flights, and then weigh up how many people living under the flight path of the airport are disturbed (assuming that it is no worse than disturbance), and how much. But certain other cases seem radically different. Suppose that, if I were to live the only sort of life that I regard as worth living, my neighbours would be upset and distressed. But, unlike in the airport case, we do not think we should now count heads. We do not, because upset and distress, so long as they remain ordinary upset and distress, can never add up to anything as important as one's being able to live out what one regards as a worthwhile life—not if there were a hundred neighbours upset and distressed, or a hundred thousand, or a million. Upset and distress are not the kind of thing that could ever match the centre of a person's liberty.

But the existence of discontinuities does nothing to support the existence of absolute human rights. On the contrary, the admission of discontinuities is compatible with utilitarianism; it does not even introduce an incomparability; it is indeed an especially emphatic comparison. And the example I have just used constitutes a discontinuity only because the two conflicting values come in degrees. It matters that it is my most *central* liberty at stake, and *wholly* at stake. It matters that my neighbours do not experience anything worse than upset and distress. If, on the contrary, they were caused considerable suffering, and I lost only briefly a relatively minor liberty, we should think again.

There are, I have proposed, right–right conflicts. Virtually everyone would agree that an important part of their resolution comes by determining the degrees of the values constitutive of personhood at stake. The innocent detainees have their liberty violated for the period of their arbitrary detention — not totally violated, because they ought still to retain several liberties while in detention. The innocent victims of terrorism, however, lose their liberty, and all other freedoms and protections, totally, if they lose their lives. Now, comparisons need a bridging notion: that is, some conceptual background that supplies the terms in which the conflicting items are compared.[37] The bridging notion need not itself be a substantive value; it could be the notion of 'value' itself: 'the relief of this suffering is more valuable than the temporary loss of this element of autonomy'. Or it could be, say, the notion of a 'reason': 'this is a stronger reason than that'. A bridging notion in the resolution of right–right conflicts is protection of personhood. Saving the lives of twenty or thirty innocent bystanders is more protective of personhood than detaining a handful of innocent suspects for six months is destructive of it.

Much the same can be said about right–welfare conflicts. Once we understand the value of human rights, we see how their value admits of degrees. One might not be prepared to accept the denial of many people's very status as agents to relieve a certain suffering, but one might, if the suffering were great enough, accept some partial, short-term surrender of autonomy to avoid it. In this case one is making a relative judgement about importance to life. That broader notion, importance to life, is a bridging notion in right–welfare conflicts.

We have now reached a point in the argument at which the bottom-up approach must rise appreciably in abstraction. It may not have to rise as high as some top-down approaches, but it must move in that direction. Both of the proposals for resolution of conflict that I have just sketched would command wide acceptance, as far as they go. Virtually everyone would agree that the considerations they make central are indeed central. But, as they stand now, the proposals look consequentialist. Can we not then resolve all conflicts involving human rights by calculating consequences for the quality of lives? And if so, are not human rights co-possible after all, now on a consequentialist basis? Many writers would deny it. The resolution of conflict, they would insist, is more complicated than that. We must take account of certain deontological elements, some would say; or we have still to introduce certain teleological but non-consequentialist elements; or we have yet to accommodate the foundational role of the virtues.

This, as forecast, brings us to the heart of normative ethics. The heart of normative ethics is a large subject to be introducing into my argument in what will have to be a fairly summary way, but anyone wishing to understand human rights must at this point, willy-nilly, face several questions. It is important, at the very least, to mark out what these questions are. I have said something in answer to them elsewhere;[38] but more still is needed, although it will have to wait for another occasion. I think that many readers will have accepted the claims I have made so far about human rights—in effect, the personhood account. They are likely to agree that personhood, at least, is a large part of the explanation of human rights. But one cannot expect wide agreement about the heart of normative ethics. Anyone who disagrees with what I shall now go on to say must find something else to put in its place. So it is worth marking out what that place is.

There are limits to our capacity to calculate consequences. We do not, of course, need our calculations to be certain; we generally live by probabilities. But we do need the probabilities to be high enough for us to be prepared to stake our lives on them. Clearly, sometimes our calculations have a high enough probability, and sometimes not. The crucial question, then, is how often they do not, and how central to moral life these failures are. If, as I think, the most plausible form of consequentialism is highly indirect, then a consequentialist must be able to answer some such question as: which set of rules and dispositions, if they were the dominant ones in our society, would have best consequences in the society at large and in the long run? No one has ever come even close to answering that question. The closest we have come is certain cost–benefit analyses, but they have gaping holes. They have trouble finding adequate expression in their formalization for certain key values—famously, for the value of human life and the value of the environment (especially those environmental values that cannot be reduced to good and bad outcomes for human beings). The assumptions on which the calculations in cost–benefit analysis are based are often so oversimplified that we are rightly hesitant to act on them. And an indirect consequentialist would have to calculate on a vastly greater scale than any cost–benefit analyst has yet attempted.

Some will think that this worry can be met by what Bernard Williams called 'the early days reply'. Purely secular ethics, the reply goes, is in its youth—a little over two centuries old, at most—and our modern ethical 'theories' have been developed as yet only in the roughest terms. But this reply, though consisting of two true claims, is reassuring only if the obstacles we face in calculating consequences are the sort that will yield to more time. But that is an extraordinarily strong assumption. It is an assumption that many philosophers today indeed make, largely because they assume that if an ethical 'theory' needs agents to have certain powers of intellect or will, agents have them. But that assumption has only to be articulated to be seen to be ridiculous.

One of the greatest under-discussed questions of ethics is: what, in fact, are the capacities of the agents whom ethics seeks to regulate? We are able *sometimes* to calculate, fairly reliably, the good and bad consequences of very large-scale, long-term social arrangements. If the arrangements being contemplated are extreme enough, we clearly can. For example, if we were to consider moving to a world without the rule of law or fair means of resolving conflict, we could make a fairly safe guess that we should be worse off in it. But the cases that we think of as live options, worth taking seriously, are not the extreme ones. And when they are not extreme, we flounder. Take a realistic case: suppose that our rules and dispositions concerning respect for innocent human life become less strict; we start deliberately killing non-combatants in time of war (Shock and Awe tactics); we use terrorism widely as a political instrument; we make troublesome political opponents 'disappear'; surgeons begin to kill one patient on the sly to save several others; and so on. They are all cases that, if justified, are justified on grounds of better consequences overall. But are they better? I doubt that anyone can answer that question to a reliable degree of probability. And it is hard to see how 'early days' could matter. We know the great problem we face: identifying and collecting all the relevant information and then expressing it in a form that will allow reliable reduction to a single answer. How will later days make that any easier?

This example of lessening respect for innocent human life suggests something further. Perhaps most people would agree that, if what we are comparing are not very different possible worlds, we cannot now, nor can we in a likely future, do the consequentialist calculation to a reliable degree of probability. But some persons say that all that consequentialism needs is a smaller-scale, more manageable calculation about certain changes from the *status quo*. But the case of lessening respect for innocent human life is a change from the *status quo*, and not more manageable for that.

A fairly common defence of consequentialism is that any relevant limitation in human understanding and will for which there is adequate empirical evidence can simply be incorporated into the calculus. We should ask: which dispositions, rules, and principles would, if they were dominant in our society, have best consequences, given agents with such-and-such limitations in understanding and will, over society as a whole and in the long run? But this is no answer to the doubts. It just makes the already dubious calculation even more difficult to do.

Another common reply is to cite the distinction between a decision procedure (the way we should actually decide what to do) and a criterion of right and wrong (what in the end settles what is the right thing to do). It does not matter, the reply goes, that we often cannot calculate consequences to a sufficient degree of probability in deciding what to do; we do not have to; instead, we are right to follow ingrained dispositions or well-established rules or the like. But that is too weak a defence of consequentialist calculation. There are epistemic constraints on a criterion of right and wrong too: a 'criterion' largely beyond our capacity to apply cannot serve as a criterion; it will not perform its function of sanctioning our decision procedure.

There are several other ethics-shaping human limitations.[39] Let me mention just one more. Not every action is within normal human motivational capacity. If persons are, as surely we should want them to be, capable of love, affection, and deep commitment to particular persons, institutions, careers, and causes, then certain actions will be beyond their motivational reach. One cannot enter into and exit from these commitments at will—say, as calculations of consequences might demand. When the ship goes down, I shall save my own child rather than a larger number of unknown children. On the most plausible interpretation of '*ought* implies *can*', I cannot ignore my own child and save the others, so it is not the case that I ought to do so. Many philosophers believe that my lack of obligation to save the other children is grounded not in motivation but in morality: I am duty-bound to give each person his or her due, and much more care is due from me to my own child than to other children. We are dealing here, they say, with a moral limit, not a motivational one. But we are also dealing with a motivational limit. Motivational limits are a reality, and, because '*ought* implies *can*', these limits have moral consequences.

There are, of course, weighty replies to what I have claimed about the limits of human motivation. Let me give just a sample of them. Human motivation, it will correctly be said, is plastic. For one thing, motivation can be enlarged by knowledge. Charities know that a single photograph that brings home the reality of a famine can spur many of us to reach for our cheque-books. Still, greater knowledge does not render characteristic human agents able to meet any demand that any ethics might impose. Famine relief workers in the field, well motivated and with ample understanding of the suffering they see all around them, do not generally sacrifice themselves and those they love to the point where a further sacrifice would exceed a further benefit to the starving. It is true that there are often good impartial-maximizing reasons for those aiding to have more than those aided—for one thing, they must be able to carry on helping—but relief workers generally do not sacrifice themselves to that point either.

Perhaps, then, the need is for a more inspiring ethics. There certainly are dreary, narrow, depressing ethics. An exciting ethics—perhaps certain religious ethics or the Platonic vision of the Good that Iris Murdoch thought could inspire a prisoner in a concentration camp to take a stranger's place in the queue for the gas chamber—would help us to rise to ethics' greatest demands. The trouble, to my mind, is that the sorts of ethics that can so revolutionize motivation are not plausible, and the sorts that are plausible cannot so revolutionize motivation. But cannot unreachable goals still play an important ethical role? They stretch us, and most of us are undeniably less benevolent than we could and should be. But it is an oxymoron to speak of my adopting what I accept is an 'unreachable goal'. Whatever grunts and groans you come upon me making, I cannot seriously tell you that I am *trying* to jump unaided a hundred metres into the air.

But cannot the right education or rigorous training enlarge motivation? Do we not regularly see how military training can turn quite ordinary persons into ones willing to die for their country? During the Cultural Revolution, the Chinese government managed to produce the Red Guard, some of whom became free enough from earlier patterns of behaviour to turn their dissident or bourgeois or merely learned parents over to the police. But this sort of training does not succeed widely or for long. The fanatical personality of the Red Guard and their most ardent collaborators was unstable. Some of the young among them turned up years later in the tents in Tiananmen Square.

We cannot understand much about human rights until we know a fair amount about moral norms in general. I have only most roughly sketched a normative ethics that is teleological but not consequentialist. It is teleological somewhat in the way that Aristotle's ethics is: the only values used in the derivation of moral principles are the ends of human life, but more enters the derivation than simply these ends. Besides the personhood ground for human rights, there is also the practicalities ground, and although some practicalities come down to consideration of quality of life, not all do. For example, we have to fix boundaries for the right to security of person. The boundaries that any particular society chooses will be to some degree arbitrary. They will not be chosen because we can calculate to a sufficient degree of probability that *this* would be the maximizing place to fix them; we can eliminate extreme options, but there will remain very many alternatives in a large middle range which we simply cannot rank reliably. What is more, the rule 'Don't deliberately kill the innocent' is based on the great value that we attach to human life, but not only on that. It is a rule shaped considerably by human limitations. We adopt the rule, which, given the high value of human life, we regard as demanding *strict* respect. The strictness of that respect will manifest itself in various ways, importantly in our demanding that any exception to the rule have an exceptionally strong justification, as perhaps there is for carefully circumscribed euthanasia. The justification in the case of euthanasia would probably be in terms of good consequences, or largely in those terms: the benefit to those in need of a good death would outweigh the costs elsewhere in society. But good consequences do not capture the element of *policy* in the rule 'Don't deliberately kill the innocent'—the policy of making an exception only when it is especially strongly justified. And the package made up of the rule and its exceptions does not get its authority from its maximizing good consequences. We do not know whether it does. There are very many other packages made up of a rule about respect for life and its exceptions that we cannot rank as to good outcomes. At times, the only moral life open to us involves *respecting* values, not *promoting* them. By 'respecting' the value of human life, for example, I mean primarily, but not solely, not oneself taking innocent life; by 'promoting' life, I mean bringing about its preservation as much as possible by any means open to one.[40] We must come to terms with how certain limits to human nature determine limits to moral obligation.

From the eighteenth century to the present, most philosophers, dazzled by the success of natural scientists, pre-eminently Newton, went in search of highly systematic theory. Moral philosophers sought the reduction of all our varied moral thought to one principle, or to a small number of them. Kant, consciously inspired by Newton, stopped there: moral obligation, he thought, could be reduced to a single a priori principle, the Categorical Imperative. Hume, Adam Smith, and the Utilitarians went further; they looked not just for high system but for empirical system. And that is roughly where we are now: committed to moral 'theories' at a Newtonian level of abstraction, and proposing to assess them with a coherence or reflective equilibrium test that is effective in the natural sciences only because of the presence of features that are absent in ethics.[41]

I think that we have no choice but to take a highly practical turn in ethics, not just to ensure that our abstract principles are adequate to our practice, but also to accommodate the ways in which our practice—our human nature with all its limitations and the needs of our actual societies—determine the content of our principles. My proposed turn to the practical makes central to ethics both following rules and training dispositions—for example, turning to rules of the nature of 'Don't deliberately kill the innocent'. This rule is little like a Newtonian principle; it has major elements of policy in it. We follow it not because doing so is best for everyone impartially considered; we just follow it. It is practical not just because it guides practice, but also because it is shaped by the sort of practice possible for agents like us. We live the kind of moral life open to us. I say 'my proposed turn', but it is a turn taken a long time ago by common-sense ethics and the law, neither of which has needed a highly abstract, systematic morality behind it in order to be authoritative and effective. What I approve of here is not the present content of common-sense ethics, which leaves a lot to be desired, but its lack of pretension to system.

To return to our subject: these human limitations inevitably shape human rights. The rule 'Don't deliberately kill the innocent', was, historically, the first component of the right to life. In the seventeenth century, indeed, the right to life was largely seen as little more than the supposedly negative right not to have one's life taken without due process. If thousands of citizens in Argentina and Chile would feel more secure if a radical reformer were made to 'disappear', the conflict between their welfare and the reformer's right to life cannot be settled just by consulting effects on quality of life. We are unlikely to be able to calculate them well enough, and, in any case, they would not adequately capture the rule. We simply must not deliberately kill the innocent unless the case before us falls under an especially strongly justified exception, and that some middle-class Argentines or Chileans, rightly or not, would feel somewhat more secure is certainly not one of them.

That there are such moral rules complicates the resolution of conflicts. Sometimes we can resolve conflicts involving human rights by deciding the severity of effects on personhood, or on the quality of life. But when a moral rule derived not only from the quality of life enters consideration, then we cannot. Moral deliberation must then take place largely on the common-sense level at which it occurs in ordinary life. We usually think in terms of 'murder' (i.e. 'deliberately killing the innocent'), 'the parent–child relation', 'a right to life', 'a right to free expression', and so on. And although the resolution of conflict puts pressure on us to rise to language of greater abstraction, not all of this everyday vocabulary can be left behind.

3.6 A STEP BEYOND INTUITION

Human rights are resistant to trade-offs, but not completely so. The strongest version of this non-absolutist view is that only something on the order of a catastrophe, such as a nuclear holocaust, can outweigh a human right. This, as we have seen, is Robert Nozick's view.[42] I have proposed various considerations that should enter the resolution of conflicts. My proposal makes it seem that the detention of a smallish number of suspected terrorists for only a few months would be justified if it were to avert a serious threat of the nuclear destruction of half of Manhattan. Yet the destruction of half of Manhattan, for all its terribleness, is well short of nuclear holocaust. On my proposal, exceptions to human rights are unlikely to be quite so exceedingly rare. But near-absolutists are likely to complain that I have simply failed to introduce into the scales precisely the crucial consideration: respect for persons. But I have not failed to introduce it: I have spelled out the values that the long human rights tradition attaches to our status as persons. What have I, or the tradition, left out? One possible answer is that, though I have included *an* interpretation of respect for persons, I have not included the Kant-like one that most deontologists have in mind. I say 'Kant-like', because Kant is an absolutist, and we are now addressing strong forms of non-absolutism. The near-absolutist, Kant-like interpretation must therefore have sufficient richness to show where the turning point is and why it is where they put it. I cannot find a plausible one. My response is short of conclusive, and I shall return to it presently.

The near-absolutist view is a special case of what I shall call the 'common' version of the non-absolutist view. That version holds that an exception is justified, not by a simple surplus of value over a human right, but only by a sufficiently great surplus, where sufficiency may be fixed at catastrophe or somewhere short of it. But what are the two scales appealed to in this common version? We have, it appears, to be able to tell when the competing value *just* exceeds the human right, and then, on a new scale, when the excess is enough. Where is the conceptual complexity that will allow the construction of those two scales? Our dim and undeveloped idea here is, I should guess, that the first comparison appeals to a scale of well-being, and the second to a scale of moral importance—the first to quality of life, the second to normative weight. But that cannot be right. Take an example. We decide that the relief of such-and-such a degree of suffering justifies the loss of thus-and-so aspects of autonomy. If earlier I described our thoughts about this case accurately, the bridging notion here is gain and loss to the quality of human life: the gain of the relief is greater, in the case I described, than the loss of the fairly minor elements of autonomy. This makes it seem to be the first of the two supposed measurements. In terms of quality of life, we judge that the relief of suffering just exceeds the loss of autonomy. But it just exceeds it in terms that constitute justification: this is a gain that justifies the loss. But to be justified is (simply) to be justified. The idea of a *sufficient* surplus of justification is nonsense.

So this makes it seem that, contrary to our first impression, we must have here not the first but the second of the two supposed measurements. Are there any materials, then, out of which to construct the first scale? It might be suspected that my reintroducing the example of the conflict between autonomy and suffering, along with my earlier remarks about it, is question-begging. My earlier explanation of this conflict, it might be thought, already revealed my teleological drift; quality of life comparisons are relatively well understood and the mark of the modern economic mind. But to go along with the teleological drift may be simply to assume that deontology is wrong. So let us keep looking a little longer for that other scale. A judgement to the effect that the relief of suffering justifies the partial loss of autonomy, we are now hypothesizing, must be employing the final scale, the scale on which the welfare consideration overrides the right. We need, then, the materials for constructing the initial scale, the scale on which the welfare *just* exceeds the right. But there are none.

Let me, therefore, drop this two-point model of the non-absolutist view; it may be obscuring the central point in deontology: that the right is often prior to the good. Is not the requirement of a *sufficient* surplus of good simply a representation of this independent weight of the right, and can this not be done without the two points? On this suggestion, a deontologist's judgements of when we reach sufficiency may be ground-floor and intuitive, but I am in no position to object to that feature of them. So may be the judgements that I have to make to resolve conflict. But think again of the example of conflict between autonomy and suffering. Suppose we weigh solely the good at stake for the persons involved, leaving the independent deontological weight of the human right aside for the moment. On the one hand there is the suffering of the people in the neighbouring country, and on the other our loss of autonomy in our not having a say in the decision.

One can imagine being able intuitively to judge in this particular case that the relief of suffering just exceeds the loss of autonomy, again basing one's decision solely on the goods for the persons involved. But there still seems to be no need for a further judgement; we already have here the justification of the trade-off.

To try to avoid this conclusion, we might say instead that the judgement that I have just imagined already incorporates the independent deontological weight of our right to autonomy. But this would make the trade-off point using this Kant-like interpretation of respect for persons the same in this case as the trade-off point using my interpretation of it. It would not, though, show that the points will be the same in all cases; whether they will be the same depends upon what the Kant-like interpretation actually says. I cannot claim unproblematic clarity for my interpretation of what is at stake, but deontology has always had to struggle with the obscurity of the idea 'respect for persons' when it must give us reasons not just about right and wrong but also, as in our present cases, about when the consideration 'respect for persons' is just outweighed, in action-justifying terms, by quality of life. We hope for more content to the Kant-like idea of 'respect for persons' so that we can know what is going on in this judgement. The mere fact that people are prepared to make these rankings hardly shows that the rankings are rational; the human psyche finds paths to rankings apart from rationality.

Perhaps one might get this more Kant-like interpretation that we are looking for from contemporary Kant-inspired contractualism. But there is Judith Jarvis Thomson's powerful challenge to contractualism to contend with:

For my own part, I cannot bring myself to believe that what *makes* it wrong to torture babies to death for fun (for example) is that doing this 'would be disallowed by any system of rules for the general regulation of behaviour which no one could reasonably reject as a basis for informed, unforced general agreement.' My impression is that explanation goes in the opposite direction—that it is the patent wrongfulness of the conduct that explains why there would be general agreement to disallow it.[43]

T. M. Scanlon, at whose version of contractualism this objection was aimed, responds:[44]

The contractualist formula that Thomson quotes is intended as an account of what it is for an act to be wrong. What *makes* an act wrong are the properties that would make any principle that allows it one that it would be reasonable to reject (in this case, the needless suffering and death of the baby).

Scanlon reasonably distinguishes here what it *is* for an act to be wrong from what *makes* it wrong. This leaves a great deal of moral thought to be conducted in terms of particular right-making and wrong-making features of acts (e.g. suffering and death) and not by pondering whether the act fits the criterion of what wrongness *is*.

In the case we are considering, what make the act right or wrong are our loss of autonomy and the suffering of the people in the neighbouring country. They are also what make it right or wrong to a particular degree. In thinking about this case, we would consider how intense and widespread the suffering is and how large-scale or small-scale, and long-term or short-term, the loss of autonomy is. This suggests that the non-absolutist deontologist following this contractualist interpretation of respect for persons and an agent following my interpretation would not only arrive at the same conclusion, but arrive at it for the same reasons.

It is a commonplace that human rights are particularly hard for utilitarianism to explain. I agree, but would want to add, what is not a commonplace, that they are no less hard for deontology to explain. And we need an explanation not just of right–welfare conflicts, which is what I have been discussing and which the model of two scales was, I believe, designed to fit. We also need explanation of right–right conflicts, right–justice conflicts, and probably yet more.

3.7 SOME WAYS IN WHICH HUMAN RIGHTS RESIST TRADE-OFFS

Teleology can fairly readily explain why human rights are not *too* resistant to trade-offs. But can it explain why, in the first place, they are *resistant*?

I have suggested that in different situations a human right can be under threat to different degrees. So clearly can welfare. To resolve conflicts between them, we look for how much under threat each is. Once one deliberates in terms of 'how much', we are well on the way to wanting to minimize loss of personhood or maximize its protection. And once on the way to minimization and maximization, the fear understandably arises that we are on the way to the sort of moral mathematics that will justify, say, killing one person to save five.

What I have suggested, though, is not any kind of utilitarianism or consequentialism, but a kind of teleology. Although utilitarianism and consequentialism are forms of teleology, they restrict the test of right and wrong to the production of as much good as rationality requires—maximizing, say, or, on a different view of rationality, satisficing. Teleology allows yet other ways of basing the right on the good.[45] To explain this further, let me turn to various ways in which, consistently with teleology, human rights can be resistant to trade-offs.

One way comes from the great value we attach to our personhood. That we attach such great value to it, especially once we are above a minimum acceptable level of material provision, which virtually all people in the First World are, means that it has a general resistance to trade-offs with welfare. Once above the minimum acceptable level, it takes some unusually large amount of welfare to outweigh personhood. This remark echoes talk about a 'sufficient surplus', but it does not require two scales.

A second, particularly striking way that personhood resists trade-offs is through discontinuities. Some values—an obvious case being our status as persons—are such that no amount of certain other values can ever equal or surpass them. The value that we attach to personhood is unchallengeable by these other values. This remark echoes what is sometimes said in support of there being absolute human rights; but it does not really support it.

A third way I discussed a short while ago. I appealed to a distinction between 'respecting' and 'promoting' goods.[46] Respecting goods, as well as promoting them, can be a teleological position; both positions can hold that the good is basic in the moral structure and the right derived from it. My example earlier was that life must be respected, and that one must simply follow the norm, 'Don't deliberately kill the innocent'—follow it because that is the only moral life available to the likes of us, though one might also adopt the policy that exceptions will be allowed only so long as the case for them is especially convincing. This talk of requiring an *especially* convincing case echoes the talk of a *sufficient* surplus of value, but it is not the same point. Talk of an especially convincing case introduces an epistemic scale, not another moral one. It is the statement of a policy—an openly conservative policy—for what to do when something as important as human life is at stake and our calculations of the goods at stake are altogether too shaky and incomplete and badly conceptualized for us to be willing to live by.

3.8 REPRISE

As my argument in this chapter, more than most in philosophy, moves step by step, it may be helpful to summarize it in that form.

1. We need to supply existence conditions for human rights.
2. The existence conditions for human rights in particular will have to have some substantive evaluative elements, in order to express the value to be attached to human status.
3. Those substantive evaluative elements then impose material constraints on the content of human rights: for example, the personhood account says that human rights protect not just anything that we rationally desire or that benefits us, but rather our status as normative agents.
4. Normative agency can be divided into parts: namely, autonomy, minimum provision, and liberty.
5. Each part of normative agency can be threatened by other persons, and threatened to different degrees: one can lose a little, or a lot, of one's autonomy, material provision, or liberty.
6. These degrees are determined by effect on one's personhood: for example, a minor liberty is one the loss of which detracts from one's personhood to a fairly small extent; a major liberty is one the loss of which detracts from one's personhood substantially.
7. When we can resolve conflicts involving human rights, we do so in the case of right–right conflicts by appeal to their effects on one's personhood; in the case of right–welfare conflicts, to those and to effects on welfare; in the case of right–justice conflicts, to those and to the weight of justice involved; and so on — though sometimes, in all of these cases, by appeal to a moral rule.
8. These resolutions need a bridging concept, or concepts, in order to allow us to determine the weight of conflicting considerations in sufficiently similar terms for us to be able to decide which is the weightier. The bridging concept need not itself be a substantive value; it could, for example, be the concept of prudential value itself. In the case of some conflicts there may be no bridging concept.
9. In the case of right–right conflicts, the bridging notion is loss/gain in personhood. In the case of right–welfare conflicts, the bridging notion must be broader: loss/gain in quality of life.

10. In both cases, the loss/gain has to be interpersonally comparable.

11. All of these loss/gain considerations are relevant to the resolution of the conflicts involving human rights that I have in particular considered, viz. right–right and right–welfare conflicts; so too are certain moral rules. There are no other relevant considerations.

12. Near-absolutists have no adequate explanation of the turning point they must posit. The more moderate (and more common) deontologists have no adequate explanation of how we can identify the two points they posit: a *simple* surplus of good and a *sufficient* surplus to override a human right.

4

Whose Rights?

4.1 THE SCOPE OF THE QUESTION

Human infants are not normative agents. Neither are human foetuses, nor the severely mentally handicapped, nor sufferers from advanced dementia. Do none of them, then, have human rights?[1] Perhaps we should not be so fixated on the award of the label 'human rights'. Do none of them at least have certain general moral rights simply in virtue of being human—only analogous to human rights, it may be, but for all practical purposes just as good?

4.2 POTENTIAL AGENTS

I shall concentrate on the case of children. My conclusion about them can, I believe, be extended to the other difficult marginal cases, which I shall return to at the end of the chapter.

Normal human adults have a kind of natural equality: they are all equally normative agents; they all cross the threshold into the class of such agents. This means that, when it comes to human rights, distinctions between man and woman, black and white, highly educated and little educated—in fact, all distinctions but for agent and non-agent[2]—are irrelevant. But it is not clear how to regard the distinction between infant and adult. As John Locke succinctly puts it, '*Children*, I confess are not born in this full state of *Equality*, though they are born to it.'[3] That the normal natural destiny of infants is to become agents must itself be a reason for an especially high concern for them. What makes infanticide in general a great wrong? A major part of the answer, but not all, must be that to deny an infant the whole of a possibly happy, productive, and rewarding life is an enormous deprivation. The mere potential of an infant must confer moral weight on it.

How much weight? And is it the kind of weight that allows an inference to human rights? A potential agent is a being having the power to become an agent, a being whose agency is in a latent or undeveloped state (*in posse*).[4] There is the obvious difficulty that, on this meaning, a foetus, a zygote, an embryo, even a sperm and an egg on course for fertilization would all then be potential agents, and so would all have moral weight and perhaps even a right to life. Many persons find this—I think correctly—close to a *reductio ad absurdum*. Another difficulty is that this definition does not capture our strong intuition that an infant has moral weight simply in virtue of its potential. But our intuition is nothing so simple as that all agents *in posse* have moral weight. That would include too much: a sperm and egg on course for fertilization and the rest. Our intuition is that the potential of an infant, in particular, to become an agent gives *it* moral significance. That intuition is widespread, and often accompanied by the intuition that a late foetus too has moral significance, though perhaps less than an infant but more than an early foetus or embryo. So, if we want to capture these intuitions, we should have to narrow the sort of potential that we see as conferring moral significance. It would be the potential of, particularly, an infant, or a late foetus, or ... (wherever we thought the line should come). The moral significance of potentiality, then, would depend upon not only what it is potential for, but also what it is the potential of. We must therefore be able to tell the moral weight of an infant, a late foetus, an early foetus, and so on. Without these further restrictions, potentiality for agency does not confer anything even approaching a right to life. So, at least, these strong intuitions go, and I shall assume that they are sound.

There are further restrictions needed on potentiality. A new-born baby with a certain serious cerebral deficit will not develop into an agent, let us say, unless stem cells are planted in the brain to remedy the deficit, a treatment not yet available.[5] Would such a baby have anything akin to the moral weight of a person or an agent just because it has the potential to become one? If not, we should add to this 'potentiality' the requirement that it be realizable with resources available at the time needed.

We also have a strong intuition that an infant is morally significant just by being a member of a species, *Homo sapiens*, a characteristic example of which is an agent. It is a belief I share. This acknowledges the moral significance of a severely mentally handicapped infant or an infant with *spina bifida* who will die within a few months of birth. Think of an extreme case of those thereby accorded moral significance: an anencephalic baby. Though there is good reason to accord anencephalic babies great respect, a reason having to do precisely with our common membership of the species, it is not a reason to accord them, despite their condition, the value attaching to normative agency or even to potential agency on the restricted interpretation just sketched.

The United Nations, in its Convention on the Rights of the Child (1989), stresses not children's potentiality, but their vulnerability.[6] It attributes a raft of rights to children, but the only ones that it makes sense to attribute to infants, as distinct from children, are the well-established right to life and two less well-established, more questionable rights proposed in the Convention: namely, a right to the protection and care necessary for well-being and a right to development 'to the maximum extent possible'.[7] Certainly children's vulnerability imposes substantial obligations on us not imposed by those able to look after themselves. But one must not run together a justification of an obligation and a justification of a right. There are obligations, including highly important ones, that are not correlative to a human right. Also one must be alert to the difference between moral human rights and legal human rights—the first established on moral grounds, the second established on the broader grounds that concern the law, among which morality may well figure. United Nations agencies tend to speak of 'rights', not explicitly of 'human rights', and their aim is to draw up standards of treatment—in this case, of children—that they think all governments should guarantee. There is no gainsaying that aim, despite the doubts one may have about certain of their proposed rights. Do we really want to recognize a duty to ensure a child's development to the maximum extent possible? That would mean developing to the last degree every single potential talent and ability a child has, which seems a thoroughly dubious policy for raising sane and healthy children, let alone a duty we have to a child, let alone a claim that a child can make on us by right.[8]

Their vulnerability of itself does not establish that children are bearers of human rights. Too many things are vulnerable: plants, sperm, foetuses, and so on. And, as with potentiality, we have to have independent understanding of the value of plants, sperm, foetuses, and so on, before we can reach any moral conclusion. If a thing is not itself worth preserving, its vulnerability gives us no reason to protect it. So neither the idea of 'potentiality' nor that of 'vulnerability' on its own helps us much, though, to my mind, the strong intuitions behind them must still, in some form or other, be accommodated by an adequate ethics.

4.3 THE INFERENCE FROM MORAL WEIGHT
TO HUMAN RIGHTS

How should we now proceed? Should we first determine the moral significance of infants, late foetuses, early foetuses, and so on, and then decide, on that basis, whether the significance of any of them is such as to justify their having human rights? Fortunately, it is not necessary.

As I remarked a moment ago, there is no inference from something's being morally significant to its bearing human rights. There are grounds for something's being morally significant, even for being highly so, that are not grounds for its bearing human rights—grounds such as being persons requiring justice, or being animals capable of great suffering.[9]

Nor is there an inference from an infant's being a 'person', if that is what we should in the end decide it is, to an infant's bearing human rights. There are several senses in which 'person' may be used, and not all of them allow the inference. We should still have to decide whether the sense in which a being is a person would figure centrally in the best account of the ground of a human right. For instance, there is the following argument that an infant is a person.[10] A normal fully developed human being is of considerable moral weight, perhaps for several reasons, but one of them is simply that the human being is a *person*. What sort of being are we persons essentially? We are embodied minds—that is, something with the capacity to support consciousness. So when did I, a being of this sort, begin to exist? It must be that I began to exist when my brain first acquired the capacity to support consciousness. So I am the *same* person as only entities that are also persons. I may say that I am the same person as the new-born baby in that photograph over there, because a new-born baby has in fact acquired the capacity in question and so is a person. I am not, however, the same person as the early foetus or embryo that was a previous biological stage of that baby, because embryos and early foetuses lack the capacity. I may, however, be the same person as the late foetus that preceded that baby, some say,[11] because the brain of late foetuses may already have developed the capacity. In any case, this account of personal identity provides a stop to the temporally backward proliferation that I spoke of earlier—from baby to foetus to embryo to sperm and egg on course for fertilization.

But we now have two quite different contexts in which we are employing the word 'person': we are employing it in an account of what constitutes personal identity, and we are employing it in characterizing an especially valued status, the dignity of the human person, or, as it was captured in an earlier period, the worth that comes of being made in God's image. It is doubtful that we may infer from the fact that a particular person is morally significant that anything identical to it is also morally significant. But we certainly may not infer from the fact that a particular person is morally significant that anything identical to it, on this criterion of identity, is just *as* morally significant. For example, it would be the plainest of non sequiturs to argue that because a normal adult person has human rights, anything that is the same person as it has human rights.

There is a response to this last claim. One might reply that the idea of a person that appears in the criteria of personal identity is the idea of something with moral weight. We value a being that has risen to the level of a capacity to support consciousness. It thereby becomes an entity of *our* kind, with the same essence as us. It is *one of us*, and that is an important status. Well, it is 'one of us' at least in this sense: we share characteristics with it. Not human consciousness, however. An infant has highly limited consciousness; it responds to hunger, pain, light, and noise, but the new-born baby of many other species is far more conscious of the world than the human baby. That, no doubt, is why the proposal about identity, as I formulated it, claimed only that human babies have the *capacity to support* consciousness, and, one may add, to strengthen the importance of the status, to support the peculiarly *human* form of consciousness. But the human infant does not have that consciousness yet. It has no sense of 'self' and 'other', of 'future', of 'objects'. It is not just that the infant has not yet had time to learn these things; its brain has to go on developing physically before it can begin to acquire them. The sense in which the infant's brain has the capacity to support consciousness is that all the parts of the brain that bring about consciousness are present, though in a stage of physical development that will not yet actually yield typical human consciousness. So the infant and, still more, the late foetus have only a *potential* for such consciousness, in a sense similar to that in which an early foetus has a potential for typical human consciousness: with favourable conditions it will in time acquire such consciousness. If that is all that it means to be 'one of us', then it is hard to see what value to attach to that status.

To sum up: we want to decide whether or not infants have human rights. Knowing the moral significance of infants will not tell us whether they do; we need also to know the kind of moral significance required to be a bearer of human rights. Also, and more to our point, knowing whether an infant is a person will not tell us; we need to know what kind of personhood supports human rights, and nothing in these views about personal identity settles it.[12]

On my personhood account, the decision about infant rights could go either way. It could be elaborated so as to include infants or to exclude them. Which way it goes is, in some measure, a matter of stipulation. I shall come to that shortly.

4.4 NEED ACCOUNTS OF HUMAN RIGHTS

This is the place to pause and reflect upon another major alternative to the personhood account.[13] If one believes that infants have human rights, then one might well wish to explore the idea that these rights are based, not on personhood, but on some especially fundamental needs. Infants (and human beings in an irreversible coma and so on) certainly have needs.

Statements of need are always of the form: x needs a in order to ϕ. An element needs a free electron to conduct electricity; a terrorist needs cool nerves to plant a bomb.[14] The first task for a need account of human rights is to specify the kind of need that will serve as a ground for them. The plausible proposal is that human rights are grounded in 'basic' human needs. The idea of a 'basic' human need is generally explained like this. One can distinguish adventitious needs that persons acquire in virtue of their choosing one particular goal rather than another (if I were to decide to plant a bomb, I should need cool nerves) from needs that arise from goals that, in a sense, are not chosen but are characteristic of human life generally. As human beings, we need food simply in order to survive. Although in special circumstances survival can become subject to choice, in normal circumstances it is not; survival is, rather, what human life characteristically aims at. Human beings, as such, need air, food, water, shelter, rest, health, companionship, and so on. A basic human need, we might say as a first attempt at definition, is what human beings need in order to avoid ailment, harm, or malfunction—or, to put it positively, what they need to function normally.[15]

We should obviously have to go well beyond this initial definition to make the notion of a basic need determinate enough to provide a satisfactory explanation of human rights. Is interesting work a basic need? Well, without it, alienation, a kind of social pathology, results. Is education? Well, without it, one's intellect will atrophy. And how much education is a basic need?

This is not to make an objection to the need account, but merely to point out work that still has to be done. But there are reasons to doubt that this further work can be carried out. The need account seems to be pointed in the wrong direction. Its central notion is that of normal functioning. The paradigm case would be the normal functioning of the human body and mind. To that idea of normal functioning we could add a description of characteristic human roles or tasks in order to give content to the notion of 'function'. Now, as an account of basic needs, this is an attractive, if still fairly primitive, proposal. But basic needs, so understood, do not make a promising ground for human rights. My human rights would be violated if on some occasion I were to be denied freedom of religious observance. But is it at all plausible to think that I should then be ailing, that my body or mind would be malfunctioning? That puts the malfunction in the wrong place. What is functioning badly is my society. The idea of health, mental and physical, may be central to a useful notion of basic needs, but it is the wrong place to be looking for an explanation of human rights. It is too narrow. One could stretch it, but, as I think the example of freedom of religion shows, we should have in the end effectively to abandon the central idea of health or normal functioning and replace it with a quite different one.

There is a closely related point. If we were to have a human right to anything needed to avoid ailment and malfunction, then human rights would be in danger of becoming implausibly lavish. I could then demand by right that society devote resources, if it had them, to curing any ailment I had, however slight, and to correcting any malfunction I experienced, however unimportant. But nearly everyone accepts that, on the contrary, there comes a point where ailments and malfunctions become minor enough that they do not create, by right, a demand upon others to remedy them. When we have a cold, we ail. We all have minor psychological hang-ups that sometimes cause us to malfunction, such as the hang-up that causes some of us to be irritatingly late for appointments. But it is deeply counter-intuitive that ailments such as those give us a right, even an easily overrideable one, to a cure. Perhaps, if a society were well off and a cold or these minor hang-ups could be cured by a cheap pill, then the National Health Service ought to provide it. It is hard to find in the need account resources to draw the line we want here.[16]

So far I have mentioned ailment and malfunction, which are only two of the three terms that I used earlier to define 'basic' human need. The third term is 'harm', which has more breadth, so perhaps more promise, than the first two terms. A basic human need, one could say, is what is needed to avoid harm.[17] But that, too, is not enough. Foetuses, embryos *in vitro*, and so on can also be harmed. And harm specifically to human beings extends far beyond any plausible ground for human rights. One can harm someone by being continually nasty to them; in fact, one can often do more harm that way, which is no violation of their rights, than one can by denying them some minor liberty, which would be. What a need account has to explain is what kinds of harms violate rights. The explanation cannot simply be that they are great harms, as the last example shows. It is a quality of harm that we are after, not a quantity.[18]

All of that said, I must not exaggerate the difference between the need account and my personhood account. The personhood account generates a positive right to the minimum provision necessary to support life as a normative agent, which is substantially more than just subsistence. So my personhood account too faces the difficulties of compiling and justifying a list of basic needs. My account can therefore be seen as a kind of need account: what is needed to function as a normative agent. What is needed will be air, food, water, shelter, rest, health, companionship, education, and so on. There will clearly be great overlap between the lists that emerge from these two accounts. And if the need account spells out the notion of 'normal functioning' by appeal to the especially basic roles in a characteristic human life—say, parent, householder, worker, and citizen[19] —then the convergence of the two lists will be still greater. But the lists will not be the same. The personhood account is more focused and exclusive in the role it specifies: what is needed to function as a normative agent.

4.5 A CLASS OF RIGHTS ON THEIR OWN?

Perhaps it is wrong to treat children's rights, if they have them, as a species of human rights. I mentioned at the start that they might instead form a class of rights on their own, general moral rights that children have simply in virtue of being children—only analogous to human rights, but perhaps none the worse for that.

If a child had these rights simply in virtue of being a child, then we should need some grasp of what it is about children that attracts this strong protection. That is, we should need to know the existence conditions of this class of general moral rights. The United Nations, as we know, cites children's vulnerability. But zygotes, embryos, foetuses, and indeed many forms of animal life are vulnerable; yet we do not regard that feature as sufficient for their having rights.

A better proposal is that the existence condition is their being potential persons. That they have such potentiality and such vulnerability fully justifies the especially strong obligations we feel to them. But for the reasons I gave earlier, they do not seem to be the existence conditions for a narrow enough class of moral rights.

4.6 A ROLE FOR STIPULATION

I said earlier that the grounds for infants' having stringent moral protections are not necessarily also grounds for their having human rights. For instance, reasons for bringing, or not bringing, infants under protection of the prohibition of murder are not identical with reasons for regarding, or not regarding, them as bearers of human rights. What shows this is that there is something more at issue in the second matter than the first. There is an element of stipulation in the second matter, and even if there is also some stipulation in the first, it is a different one, needing its own justification.

If any conclusion about infants' rights is even partly stipulative, why not make a different stipulation from the one I favour? Stipulation gives one freedom. Why not stipulate that infants, though only potential agents, be deemed 'persons' in the sense relevant to grounding human rights? Why not also, in order to exclude foetuses, further stipulate, as we do for murder, that a person in the relevant sense must already be born? If this proposed stipulation were to catch on, the word 'person' in the relevant sense might eventually have a settled use, and the stipulation might eventually produce a satisfactorily determinate sense.

As the personhood account can accommodate either the stipulation that infants be regarded as holders of human rights or the stipulation that they not be, the personhood account is not at stake here. But the first stipulation would, I think, be the wrong one to make. My argument for that is empirical, and the relevant facts, I admit, are not easy to determine. One criterion for a successful stipulation is that it improves our ethical vocabulary overall—makes it fuller, more perspicuous, or more user-friendly. Another criterion is feasibility; there is no point in making a stipulation that will be almost entirely ignored. Of course, a stipulation might commend itself to a small coterie of theorists; they may find that it helps clarify their ethical thought or makes discussion between them less confused. But they might also be willing to trade off that improvement in their small circle for a stipulation that would be accepted by the much wider circle of, say, all educated persons who want to take human rights seriously. In any case, at present, educated opinion on whether infants have human rights is divided, with many on both sides. There is therefore some point in asking which the better stipulation here would be.

Our ultimate aim is to make the sense of the term 'human right' satisfactorily determinate. There are strong inflationary pressures on the term that have brought about its debasement (as I called it earlier), and they are still at work. The belief is widespread that human rights mark what is most important in morality; so whatever any group in society regards as most important, it will be strongly tempted to declare to be a human right. The group will be out to annexe the force of the term for its own keenest concerns. It is now also a common, and not unjustified, belief that getting something widely accepted as a human right is a good first step to getting it made a legal right; so there is a great temptation to assert that anything to which one wants to have a legal guarantee is a human right. And getting something accepted as a human right transforms one's case. One is transformed from beggar ('you ought to help me') to chooser ('it is mine by right'). If one can claim by right, one is not dependent upon the grace or kindness or charity of others. These features of the discourse of human rights are responsible both for great good and great bad, the bad being the ballooning of the discourse itself.

My belief is that we have a better chance of improving the discourse of human rights if we stipulate that only normative agents bear human rights— *no exceptions*: not infants, not the seriously mentally disabled, not those in a permanent vegetative state, and so on. For the discourse to be improved, the criteria for correct and incorrect use of the term must be fairly widely agreed. They would not have to be anything like universally agreed, but there would have to be fairly wide agreement among those who take human rights seriously: moral and political philosophers, jurisprudents, international lawyers, drafters of relevant legislation and documents generally, human rights activists, and journalists. If a good number of the members of those groups came to agree on the criteria, the rest of the members would be likely in time to follow, and the general public would themselves to some extent eventually fall in line.

That sequence of events is what we should need for an appreciable improvement in the discourse. What, then, should we need to set off that favourable sequence of events? The start would be the appearance of a substantive account of human rights—some not too complicated, fairly sharp-edged normative intension for the term—which commended itself to a growing number of those who take human rights seriously. There is no mechanism available that would be likely to lead us to agree a very few, but not more, exceptions to the proposed new intension. Even if there were, the inflationary pressures are all still with us and all still very strong; there would soon be too many exceptions for the criteria for correct and incorrect use to remain sharp-edged enough to produce the needed improvement.

I should stress again that what moves me is not the wish to reverse the proliferation of rights. I have no views about how many human rights there are. Nor, given the different levels of abstraction in their formulation, do I know how to enumerate them. We speak of 'proliferation', in a pejorative sense, only because we suspect that some of the declared rights are not true rights. What moves me is the wish to end the damaging indeterminateness of sense of the term 'human right'.

Once one thus admits elements of stipulation into the grounds of human rights, does one not abandon a central claim of the natural rights/human rights tradition: that human rights are grounded in human nature? I think not. On the contrary, the decision embodied in the stipulation is the decision to derive human rights solely from certain values constitutive of human nature. That element of stipulation does not make the constituent values of normative agency, autonomy and liberty, any less able to be considered 'objective' or 'natural' or even in a sense 'real'. I shall come to the metaphysics of human rights shortly.[20] Still, one cannot deny that there are several feasible alternatives to adopting the restriction to normative agency that I recommend. For example, there is the personhood account expanded to include certain potential persons such as infants; there is the basic need account; there is, as I mentioned earlier,[21] a more pluralist account than mine that includes other elements of well-being besides the goods of normative agency; and so on. Any of these further accounts could be adopted, though, I am claiming, with less benefit. I may not simply insist that human rights *are* derived solely from normative agency; that belief would need a great deal in the way of justification. Although some of the alternative accounts (e.g. the need account) can be faulted for not adequately explaining human rights, others of them (the account that includes certain potential persons or the more pluralist account) cannot be. The objection to them is practical: they do not give us the beneficial determinateness of sense available to us. That is why the sort of stipulation I am making is not arbitrary. It has to be justified.

There are different kinds of stipulation. Many, of course, *are* arbitrary: for instance, announcing at the start of a book, 'By "rich" I shall mean "having more than 2.5 million pounds in personal assets".' With that common sort of stipulation, one can pretty much do as one pleases. But some stipulations are part of a disciplined project—for example, looking for the best language in which to think and on which to base one's action. Indeed, the whole language of human rights itself is such a project. We saw earlier that the idea of a human right grew out of a transmutation of the discourse of *what is* actually right into the discourse of *having* a natural right.[22] Ethics, I maintained, could do without the discourse of natural rights and still say all that is necessary to it.[23] Still, the discourse has distinct merits. It focuses and gives prominence to obligations that arise, not from social status or special talents or skills, but from the dignity of human status itself. The dignity of human status itself is not the only, or the most, important moral status that human beings have. The case for singling it out is largely practical. Ring-fencing this particular status gives it prominence, ease of transmission, enhanced effectiveness in our social life, and indeed in our moral life, and so on. My stipulation here is of this kind.

4.7 COMING INTO RIGHTS IN STAGES

For these reasons, it seems to me best to reserve the term 'human rights' for normative agents. That then leaves us the large problem of settling the boundary disputes about when a human being is a normative agent. In the natural development of a child, the capacity for autonomy and liberty appears in stages, and therefore respect for the child's personhood should (ideally) increase in parallel stages. But parents and schools and governments face all of these difficult definitional problems already—for instance, in deciding when, and to what degree, paternalism is justified (say, in determining how much weight to put on a child's wishes in a custody decision in a divorce).

What seems to me clear is that many children, as opposed to infants, are capable of normative agency. So my scepticism about infants' rights does not extend in any wholesale way to children's rights. I should certainly have no doubts about many children's having rights on the definition of a 'child' employed in the United Nations' Convention on the Rights of the Child: namely, anyone under legal majority (so in most countries anyone under

18). Indeed, children are capable of some degree of agency much younger than that. The autonomy of children of only a few years has sometimes to be respected, and they rightly think that their dignity is affronted if it is not. We should see children as acquiring rights in stages—the stages in which they acquire agency.[24]

So I am inclined to conclude that human rights should not be extended to infants, to patients in an irreversible coma or with advanced dementia, or to the severely mentally defective. And if they do not extend to them, it is hard to find a case for extending them to foetuses.

This conclusion is compatible with our none the less having the weightiest obligations to members of all these classes. We have constantly to remind ourselves of the destructive modern tendency to turn all important moral matters into matters of rights, especially of human rights. We have to recover our sense of the power of the rest of our moral vocabulary—for example, the language of justice and fairness. We have to feel again the power of the term 'murder'. We should be better off if we reserved talk about 'human rights' to a more restricted sense—and in that way gave it tolerably clear criteria for correct and incorrect use. It is, or should be, quite enough to say that wantonly to take an infant's life is murder, and one of the most grievous kinds of murder. To deny an infant the chance to reach and exercise and enjoy maturity is a far more horrendous wrong than most infringements of human rights. Once we recover a sense of the full range of our moral vocabulary, we shall no longer feel the need to turn all important moral claims into claims of rights. My personhood account is deflationary in three related ways. It supplies a ground for rejecting certain actual declarations of human rights. It tends to narrow the content of individual human rights. And it reduces the importance of human rights. None of these deflationary effects seems to me regrettable. Human rights cover only one special part of morality; there are very many highly important moral domains outside the domain of human rights: for example, certain considerations of justice and fairness, some forms of equality, and many cases of one person's cruelty to another. In addition, human rights can be at stake in ways that are not especially important: a pretty minor liberty might be at stake, or a minor exercise of autonomy. If so much of such very great moral importance falls outside the domain of human rights, can infants, the severely mentally handicapped, and sufferers from advanced dementia not find the protection they deserve there?

5

My Rights: But Whose Duties?

5.1 INTRODUCTION

Who bears the duty correlative to a human right? Many Kantians have a ready answer. There are, they say, three kinds of obligations. Some are universal (owed by all agents to all others, so doubly universal) and perfect (those who owe and those who are owed are perfectly—i.e. fully—specified). Some obligations are perfect but not universal, because the classes of those who owe and those who are owed are less than universal; a promise is a clear example. The two kinds of perfect obligations just described have correlative rights—universal (human) rights in the first case, special rights in the second. Finally, some obligations are imperfect and non-universal: for example, obligations to be kind, helpful, or charitable to others. They are deficient not as obligations but, rather, in their specification of the persons owed the duty. There is no specification; the duty-bearer may use discretion in choosing upon whom to discharge the obligation. Imperfect obligations, therefore, cannot have correlative rights. Who could come forward as a rights-bearer? This Kantian schema[1] is, I suspect, largely responsible for the belief that the identification of the duty-bearer correlative to human rights is not the problem that it seems to me to be.

This Kantian trichotomy is undermined if human rights are not entirely negative: that is, if either some positive rights, such as a right to basic welfare, are also human rights, or if the apparently negative rights, such as a right to liberty, are not purely negative but, upon closer examination, are found to contain positive elements, such as provision of courts, competent judges, and police to prevent intimidation. Human rights fail to be entirely negative in both of these ways.[2]

5.2 WHAT DUTIES?

Let us start with the question, What duties? Here the answer is indeed straightforward. The content of a human right is also the content of the corresponding duty. What one party may demand, as of human right, another party has some sort of obligation to supply. We have only to know the content of human rights. But deciding that, of course, is not always easy.

Take, for example, the right to life. On the personhood ground, the intuitive case for it would go roughly like this. We attach a high value to our living as normative agents. Then it is not surprising that we should include among human rights, as the tradition has long done, not only rights to autonomy and liberty (which the tradition has generally lumped together under the word 'freedom' or 'liberty'), but also a right to life. Can we value living in a characteristically human way without valuing the living as well as the autonomy and liberty that make it characteristically human? If human rights are protections of that form of life, they should protect the life as well as that form of it. The case for the existence of a right to life is, as these things go, fairly clear.

One can thus be satisfied that a certain human right exists without being clear what it is a right to. In the seventeenth century most of the proponents of a right to life seem to have conceived of it negatively—as a right not to be deprived of life without due process. But since then, the supposed content of the right has broadened, and lately has positively ballooned: from a right against the arbitrary termination of life, to a right to rescue, to a right to protection of anything deemed to be covered by the term 'sanctity of life', including a right against the prevention of life (so against euthanasia, abortion, sterilization, etc.—a use of the right made by many 'pro-life' campaigners), to a right to a fairly modest basic welfare provision, all the way up to a right to a fully flourishing life.[3] And that last extension clearly goes too far.

What is the content of the right to life? To my mind, the personhood ground supports a right to life with positive as well as negative elements. For present purposes I shall give just a quick intuitive case for these positive elements and leave the argument for later.[4] The rationale for human rights, on the personhood account, is centred on the high value attaching to certain features that we sum up under the heading 'personhood'. One attacks the value of life if one wantonly discards it. And it would seem to be possible to discard it wantonly by more than just murder—for instance, by my not bothering to throw a life-belt to you when you are drowning, or, in general, by failure to save life when one can do so at little cost to oneself.

If we accept that the right to life implies positive as well as negative duties, then we face the great problem of precisely how far the positive duties go. One plausible limit is this. The right is only to life as a normative agent—that is, to characteristic human existence. It is not a right to that ultimate human goal: a good, fulfilled, flourishing life. The ultimate goal—a fully flourishing life—would make enormous demands upon others, and it is not the subject of *any* human right. The right to life is merely to survival as an agent.

Still, that leaves the right quite demanding enough. You have a right to rescue and to aid in mortal distress. So does everyone else—the millions starving in the Third World, potential victims of genocide, anyone with a fatal illness that might yield to a crash research programme.

Rescue or aid at what cost to oneself? Locke attaches the obvious proviso that one does not have to save another person's life at the cost of one's own. But that is a weak proviso; surely the cost can be somewhat lower, and one still not have to pay it. I have mentioned another conventional proviso: provided that the cost to oneself is slight. But that is doubtless too weak in the opposite direction; surely the cost can be somewhat more than slight, and one would still have to pay it. In any case, these provisos need a rationale.

I think that there is a rationale for them—extremely rough and ready, I admit, but a rationale all the same. And it goes a long way towards meeting the objection that many positive duties are too demanding to be plausible. I discussed this earlier;[5] the principle *'ought' implies 'can'* enters here. There are limits both to human understanding and to human motivation. Sometimes we are able to calculate fairly reliably the good and bad consequences of large-scale, long-term social arrangements, but sometimes we are not. And our failures in understanding are often not peripheral to morality but at its centre and great enough to leave us with no belief upon which we should be willing to base our lives. Moreover, not all action is within human motivational capacity. We are by nature partial, and cannot enter into and exit from all our particular commitments at will. Both of these limitations help shape the content of our obligations.[6]

There are limits, therefore, to what one may demand of the sort of persons we are and have no sufficient reason not to be. Such persons will sacrifice themselves and their families for others, perhaps more than common-sense ethics now demands, but still only up to a point. That point will be difficult to place exactly, and anyone who tries to place it will have to put up with roughness and arbitrariness. But these are, or at any rate should be, familiar features of ethical life. This implies that there are limits to what any redistributive welfare programme may require. Its demands must stay within the capacities of the sort of people that society seeks to regulate. We should do what, with present resources, we can to raise the destitute to the minimum acceptable level. But do so at what cost to ourselves? The answer to that question is inevitably rough, but it is along these lines: at a cost within the capacities of the sort of persons we are. There are other restrictions as well, but this is a major one. It still leaves open the possibility of hefty claims on governments and, through taxation and charities, on individual citizens to help the needy. And it by no means implies that our current common-sense ethics has drawn the line in the right place.

Let me now make my example more concrete. If the right to life includes the positive elements I have mentioned, then it includes a right to health, at least to the degree of health needed for life as a normative agent. And, indeed, the United Nations includes on its list of human rights a right to health. How much is that a right to? I shall respond more fully later on,[7] but for now let me quickly sketch an answer.

A human right to health cannot be a right, literally, to health. We have only limited control over health. If I am struck down by an unpreventable and incurable cancer, my rights are not violated. 'Ought' implies 'can': in many cases we cannot do anything to preserve health. Nor is the right to health, instead, a right just to health care. Health is often best promoted by action well outside the bounds of health care, as normally understood. For example, in many countries the best way to reduce infant mortality is to raise female literacy. The right to health is a welfare right: it is a right to the sorts of welfare provision that support health: antibiotics and other medicines, of course, but also sewers, education of women, or advice to change one's diet.

But a right to how much health support? The International Covenant on Economic, Social and Cultural Rights of the United Nations, followed by many other international documents, announces that we have a human right to 'the highest attainable standard of physical and mental health'.[8] But that cannot be so. The highest attainable standard of physical and mental health is not even a reasonable social aim, let alone a right. Rich societies could mount crash programmes, on the model of the Manhattan Project, in the case of illnesses for which cures are attainable, but they often do not. They regard themselves as free to decide when they have spent enough on health, even if they fall short of the highest attainable standards, and may instead devote their inevitably limited resources to education, preservation of the environment, and other major social goods.

The United Nations Committee on Economic, Social and Cultural Rights, in a session in 2000,[9] spelt out what a violation of the right to health would be. The 'highest attainable' level of health, it said, requires each state party merely to attain the level it can 'to the maximum of its available resources'. But no current state, no matter how rich, spends 'the maximum of its available resources' on health. Nor should it.

Of course, the phrase 'available resources' was meant to be concessive: a state need not spend more than is available to it. That concessive spirit suggests a rather different interpretation from the one I have just adopted. Perhaps when the drafters wrote of 'the highest attainable standard' and 'the maximum of its available resources', they meant to take account of just the realities I have pointed out in criticism. Perhaps they meant 'highest attainable standard, given the other standards that a state should also meet'; and perhaps by 'maximum available resources' they meant 'available after proper allocation to other important social goals'. If they did mean this, one would be justified to ask why they did not say so. In any case, this interpretation is no better. A right to health must specify, at least roughly, the level of health we have a right to; otherwise the right is too indeterminate to be a useful social claim. To say that one has a right to the level of health support possible given expenditure on other worthy social goals, with no account of which other social goals are worthy, or of their worthiness relative to health, is to say far too little. The first interpretation makes the right ridiculously lavish; the second makes it next to empty.

On the personhood account, we have a right to life, because life is a necessary condition of normative agency. And on the personhood account we also have a right to the health support necessary for our functioning as normative agents. These statements of the right to life and the right to health are still very loose, and much work has to be put into making them determinate enough for political life. But I should say that there is nothing in the personhood account that implies that life must be extended as long as possible or that health must be as rude as possible. And that seems intuitively right.

So, to repeat, what is the right to health a right to? There are many forms of ill health that do not jeopardize normative agency. We all get sniffles from time to time. The sniffles are pathological; they are illnesses. But they do not stop us from being agents. According to the United Nations, we have a human right to have these sniffles treated; according to the personhood account, we do not. All the same, it is compatible with the personhood account that, if there were cheap pills that would cure these sniffles, and if our society were sufficiently well off, then we should have them. There would be a perfectly good reason for that, only not a human right: namely, that it would increase the quality of our lives. But 'health' is not equivalent to 'well-being', although the World Health Organization, in the Preamble to its Constitution, in effect declares that it is.

On the personhood account, our main project in the case of the right to health is to specify what is needed—some sort of basic kit of capacities and opportunities—for life as an agent. The sketch would inevitably be very rough and, at points, arbitrary. But roughness and arbitrariness run through nearly all moral principles.

Here is a start on describing the basic kit. Protecting normative agency requires protecting certain human capacities: namely, those without which one's options in life shrink so drastically that life as a normative agent is undermined. Life as a normative agent requires a reasonable span of life and level of health. Children become agents only with time, and one requires a good run of adult years to form mature aims and to have time to realize some of the most major ones. And many people in old age naturally lose some of the powers of agency, and often the major achievements in their lives are already behind them. This hardly means that there is no longer a moral case for caring for the elderly, but agency may play a smaller part in it. So a right to health requires high priority being given to a fair span of life, but its demands in old age can decline in strength—for example, in determining allocation of scarce medical resources.

5.3 WHOSE DUTIES?

With those preliminaries over, we may now turn to our main question: Whose duties?

As I mentioned at the start, a human right is widely thought to be doubly universal. But welfare rights in general, and a right to health in particular, seem to be doubly particular. We think that only members of a particular group—say, citizens of a certain country—can claim welfare, and can claim it, say, from only their own government. If human rights have to be doubly universal, then welfare rights are not human rights.

But I am just assuming—what I think is correct and shall come to later—that rights to certain forms of welfare are indeed *human* rights.[10] In any case, classical liberty rights are not entirely negative; they too sometimes give rise to duties of implementation, often costly implementation (think of the cost of an effective system of justice), and with them too there can be the problem of identifying the correlative duty-ower. And I think that there is a solution to the problem of identifying a less than universal duty-ower in the case of welfare rights generally, and the right to health in particular, without thereby undermining their status as human rights.

In ethics, we accept a general obligation to help those in distress, at least if the benefit we can confer is great and the cost to us is small. That is almost universally agreed upon. If I see a child fall into a pond, and I can save it just by wading in, and no one else is about, why must *I* do it? The right to rescue is doubly universal; it is a claim that all of us make upon all the rest of us. Why, then, should it fall upon *me* in particular? Well, obviously because I happen to be the only one on the scene. Accidental facts such as being in a position to help can impose moral responsibilities—and nothing more special to the situation than that may bring the responsibility. Of course, in many cases of need, it is one's own family, or local community, or central government that has the ability to help. At different periods in history, different agencies have had that ability. And, of course, the families of the needy have additional reasons to help them. Central governments may too, but simple ability, apart from any of the reasons arising from special relations, itself remains at least one reason-generating consideration. And ability provides a ground in the world as it is to distribute the burden to help along membership lines: a family to its members, a central government to its citizens.

Ability also explains why, over time, the burden has shifted from one group to another.[11] In the late Middle Ages and early modern period in England the Church had the resources and the highly developed organization, the central government playing a much smaller role in society than it does now, and it fell to the clergy to provide almshouses and the like. With the dissolution of the monasteries and religious confraternities, a new source of welfare had to be found. The Poor Law of 1572 secularized support for the indigent: the burden shifted from the Church to local civil entities ('every city, borough, town, village, hamlet'), and money was raised through a local tax. By the eighteenth century, after both agricultural and industrial revolutions, local welfare provision no longer met the problem. The Poor Law assumed a static workforce, and the new economy needed a mobile one. The shift to national welfare provision fitfully began. In 1834, the Benthamite Chief Commissioner for the Poor Law, Edwin Chadwick, promoted the Poor Law Amendment Act, which left funding as a local responsibility but introduced central control through a board of Poor Law commissioners. Chadwick also designed beneficial schemes to improve water supplies, sewers, and housing. The Liberal government of 1906 introduced a wide range of centrally funded welfare benefits; the Labour government of 1945 created a 'welfare state'. There are perfectly good reasons for assigning the responsibility for welfare to one agency rather than another. And recently, as we shall come to shortly, there have been signs of a globalization of the burden of aid.

I said a moment ago that simple ability is one reason-generating consideration in cases of aid. But moral life is more complicated than that. Many other considerations also shape moral norms, for instance, the one I glanced at earlier: that a good life is a life of deep commitments to particular persons, causes, careers, and institutions; that deep commitments limit our wills in major ways; and that our powers of large-scale calculation about what maximizes good outcomes are also limited. Unless one stresses these other reason-generating considerations, my proposal that ability can fix who should give aid might look odd. A Bill Gates or a John Paul Getty has a great ability to help the needy. That ability, no doubt, means that they have above-average obligations to help. But the obligation upon them does not go on until their marginal loss equals the marginal gain of the needy; nor does it with us. The ethical story is far more complicated than that. The Gateses and the Gettys—and we—are allowed substantially to honour our own commitments and follow our own interests, and these permissions limit our obligations. All that I wish to claim is that mere ability is *one* consideration in fixing where to place the duty to help.

As with identifying the content of a human right, so also with identifying the related duty-ower: my remarks are only a start. It is characteristic of the work involved in identifying duty-owers that it, too, can be long, hard, and contentious. I think that sometimes it will prove impossible to make a clearly successful case for holding anyone in particular the appropriate duty-ower. Sometimes the identification will have elements of arbitrariness and convention in it. Sometimes it will be subject to negotiation in a particular place or time. We can know that there is a moral burden, without yet knowing who should shoulder it.

Still, in the case of the human right to welfare it seems to me justified, in these times of concentration of wealth and power in central governments, to place the burden to a large extent on them. And if poor central governments are unable to shoulder the burden, then perhaps the time has come for us to consider whether the burden should not also be placed on a group of rich nations—although a lot of work would have to go into deciding which nations count as 'rich' for this purpose, how great a demand can be made on them, and what a fair distribution of the burden between them would be. To test whether the right to welfare, at a deep moral level, is doubly universal, one should look at what happens when the duty-bearers specified at a particular time cannot discharge the duty. That the right to welfare is a human right is compatible with there also being other sorts of rights to welfare—say, a special right to welfare in circumstances of social contract, settled expectations, or agreed definition of the functions of government.

5.4 PRIMARY AND SECONDARY DUTIES

So far I have been talking about the primary duties correlative to a human right, defined as the duties with the same content as the related rights. But there are also duties more loosely connected to human rights—call them 'secondary' duties.

For example, who is to *promote* human rights? Rights will be largely ineffectual unless someone declares and publicizes them, and educates people in them, and gives them weight in society. One might give them weight by turning them into domestic or international law: one might give them further weight by entrenching a bill of rights into a constitution—though whether bills of rights are, all things considered, good for a society is properly a subject of active debate. All of these promotional attempts are meant to give human rights their proper place in our action. During the twentieth century the duty of promotion was accepted by organizations whose object was to bring about respect for human rights: mainly the United Nations but also non-governmental organizations such as Amnesty International.

Then, who is to *monitor* the observance of human rights? Even when human rights have been incorporated into international law, there has been as yet only limited prosecution and punishment of offending nations. In this situation it is important to monitor compliance. If, for whatever reason, legal sanction is not available, the sanction of shame should take its place.

Most importantly, who is to *ensure compliance*, when that is indeed feasible? For instance, who is to protect our liberty from its enemies, domestic and foreign? Who is to detect, prosecute, and punish violators of human rights? Here we need legislators, judges, lawyers, police, army, and so on—complex and costly institutions. Now, a small group of people on a remote seventeenth-century frontier who have to dispense justice to one of their number might do so faultlessly; they might act justly by nature, even down to the finest points of procedure. But such a society, while not impossible, is highly unusual. In our actual societies we need institutions to make laws, to keep track of and publicize them, to lay down procedures for dealing with the accused, to defend participants in these procedures from intimidation, and so on. Although this duty to create and sustain a legal system is not strictly identical to the primary duty, as the frontier example shows, in our actual social conditions the two duties are so close as to be treatable, for all practical purposes, as one.

Some secondary duties are at a considerable remove from their related primary duties. But it would be artificial to regard a right to procedural justice and a right to the social institutions needed for any realistic chance of procedural justice as other than the same human right. Similarly, the primary duty to respect people's liberty is, in our circumstances, indistinguishable from the secondary duty effectively to protect people's liberty—with institutions such as police or army. Not all secondary duties merge in this way with their primary duty, but some do.

5.5 AIDS IN AFRICA

Let me take an example, if only to acknowledge further how hard it can sometimes be to identify the duty-ower. With the right to health, the duty in an emergency now falls, in the first instance, on the right-holder's government. But the present AIDS epidemic in the developing world is so extensive, and the really effective treatment (the anti-retroviral 'cocktail' of drugs introduced in 1996) so costly, that some governments cannot afford it. For example, recently the adult rate of infection was 35.8 per cent in Botswana and 19.94 per cent in South Africa, and the cost in the West for the anti-retroviral treatment was US$10,000 to $15,000 per person per year.[12] To use the word I put stress on earlier, these governments lack the *ability*. But other agencies are able: to mention two, some rich countries and some pharmaceutical firms. Should we conclude that the duty now shifts to another agency? And how do we decide which agency? And as there are fatal diseases other than AIDS in countries unable to buy the effective medicines or technology, how far must these other agencies go? Or, to step back for a moment, do these questions show that I must be wrong about where the duty lies?

One problem is that, on my account, the duties threaten to become exceedingly burdensome. I have already given part of a solution to that threat: there are limits to the moral obligation; there are, for example, permitted areas of partiality. The problem of the excessive demandingness of ethics is one that we in the First World already face as individuals, given the present poverty in the Third World. The place where we fix the limits on these demands is not easy either to decide or to defend. But, again, this is not a problem special to human rights.

Now, if in the circumstances I described a moment ago the duty to help many of the AIDS victims in Africa shifts away from their governments, where does it go? To the extent that ability to help is our guide, it is natural to think of rich First World governments. If we were to follow this line of thought, then we should have to put a lot of work into deciding what a fair distribution of the burden between the 'rich' nations would be. Even without that, there have been moves towards the globalization of help. In May 2004 President Bush promised 15 billion US dollars to treat HIV in developing countries over five years.[13] Of course, there was self-interest in the decision. Poor nations are poor trading partners; poverty can produce political instability, hostility, and in the worst case terrorism. The motive behind charity has always been so. The Poor Law of 1572 in England, in making aid local, aimed at preventing the formation of large bands of the poor roaming the countryside menacing the better-off. But the motives behind aid are often not solely self-interested.

But it has already occurred to some that the demand might also appropriately be addressed to pharmaceutical firms. The anti-retroviral drugs are still under patent, but the firms that produce them have already made huge profits from them. As pharmaceutical firms can now decide between life and death, and as there is a human right to life, these firms are in a special moral position. If the present death rate from AIDS in southern Africa continues in the most productive age group, then several future generations seem destined for deep poverty. These firms are the ones who have already profited greatly from the near-monopoly position that patents give them, and it is the international community that has granted them this privileged position by establishing the laws of patent. It is true that nations could change the patent laws—say, change the present twenty-year duration of patents on the anti-retroviral medicines—but there is a limit to the fine-tuning possible in legislation. And perhaps the remedy for some crises, such as AIDS in Africa, should not be delayed until new laws of patent can be put in place. The scene is changing: national emergency is now seen as justifying special commercial arrangements, and some governments are now allowed, under special license, to use cheaper generic versions of the drugs.[14]

If we were to follow this second line of thought, then we should have to decide how much profit from the development of a new drug is 'sufficient', for present purposes. And we might speed up the decision if we were to develop institutions to decide when First World governments and when pharmaceutical firms had to shoulder the burden. We should also have to decide which other businesses might be subject to a similar obligation. And, of course, we should have to decide whether this complicated scheme is either feasible or fair. If it is not, that would suggest that we think again about First World governments, or some combination of the two agencies.

I shall leave the matter here. If my example of the AIDS crisis has done no more than to highlight how hard it can sometimes be to identify the duty-ower, then, in the present state of our understanding of human rights, that is some advance.

5.6 CAN THERE BE RIGHTS WITHOUT IDENTIFIABLE DUTY-BEARERS?

Would we not have a right unless the correlative duty-bearers were identifiable? Must rights be, in this sense, claimable? Some writers think so.[15]

Some of them use this requirement of claimability to argue that welfare rights cannot be human rights. The duties correlative to a right to welfare, they say, fall upon what we can describe no more specifically than '*some* agents', thus failing to identify any actual agents against whom to make the claim. A right to welfare therefore will not meet the requirement of claimability until certain social institutions, such as governments, are on the scene to decide on both the content and the bearers of such duties.[16] Rights of this sort, accordingly, can be civil but not human rights.[17] It is not that *all* rights with correlative positive duties depend upon the existence of certain social institutions. When a baby falls into a pond, we can often identify the bearer of the duty of rescue without the help of institutions. Perhaps the strongest claim that should be made is that for the great majority of rights with positive duties, institutions are necessary for claimability.[18]

But that is not so. My example of the AIDS epidemic is a typical case of a right to help, and the deliberation necessary to identify the extent of the duty and its bearer, as we have just seen, does not require any special institution. What instead is needed is deliberation about ability, responsibility, fairness of burden, speed with which help can be delivered, and so on. In any case, there are as yet no international institutions with the role of settling these questions. Yet we can manage all the same. We can get together a new *ad hoc* group, perhaps composed of representatives of rich nations, of pharmaceutical firms, and of the countries badly stricken with AIDS, and there is no impossibility to their reaching agreement on who should do what—especially if there is an ex-President of the United States around (Bill Clinton), anxious to redeem his reputation by helping to broker a deal. But their reaching agreement is no more evidence of the existence of an institution than would be the bystanders' agreeing on who should do what when a baby falls into a pond.

It is doubtful, too, that claimability is anything as strong as an existence condition of a right, though the requirement treats it as such. If one knows the content of a right, one thereby knows the content of the correlative duties, even if one does not know against whom to make the claim. One has all that is needed to settle the existence of a human right without knowing the duty-bearers. One will also have all that one needs to determine the content of a human right, and thereby the content of the correlative primary duties. This is because such a substantive account gives human rights a rich evaluative content in terms of human interests. The mode of reasoning then proceeds from interests to rights to duties. Of course, anyone who believes that the relevant duties can be prior to considerations of the human good will resist this mode of reasoning, and will wish to make duty independently, normatively rich. But why must that greater normative richness have to include the identity of the duty-bearers? Why could the duty-bearers not be specified, as in the case of the bystanders when the child falls into the pond, with the not fully identifying formula 'one or more of us must save the child'?

We saw earlier how the statement of a human right can vary in abstraction, from a universal form (e.g. a right to life) to a more particular form relevant to certain circumstances (e.g. a right of AIDS sufferers to anti-retroviral drugs).[19] Given that the content of a human right tells us the content of the correlative duty, the latter can also vary in degree of abstraction. And the more particular the content of the duty becomes, the more will specific potential duty-bearers come into focus. If the right in question is stated as the right of AIDS sufferers, then First World governments, pharmaceutical firms, the capitalist system, patent law, and so on enter the frame, and we can at last start the difficult process of identifying specific duty-bearers. According to the claimability requirement, though, it is only at this level of particularity, or some roughly similar one, that a right exists. The more common view is that the right of AIDS sufferers arises from the application to their situation of more abstract rights, such as the right to life or the right to health. According to this common view, the same right, with perfectly coherent criteria of identity, appears at many different levels of abstraction and in many different situations of application. To the extent that the common model is plausible, the requirement of claimability is not.[20]

It ought to be acknowledged that the intention behind the claimability requirement (and also behind the stronger, less plausible, enforceability requirement)[21] is a sympathetic one: namely, to curb the recent uncontrolled multiplication of rights. There must be much stiffer existence conditions for a human right than that it would be beneficial, even very beneficial, even important, for us to have it. But the best way to get these stiffer conditions is to remedy the great indeterminateness of sense of the term 'human right'; stiffer conditions will come with an adequate understanding of what a human right is.

All the same, there is a form of claimability requirement on human rights, weaker than the earlier ones, that it seems to me we must accept. There cannot be a right with *no* specifiable duty-bearers. A right is most commonly a claim, and one cannot have a claim that is a claim on no one identifiable in thought. We should not have created a legal claim, for instance, if the law stated merely that we all had the right to live in peace but made no one responsible for achieving it (compare the United Nations' human right to peace). No moral claim at all emerges from the mere fact that such-and-such would increase someone's well-being. What would arise would be, at best, an admirable aspiration. The strongest defensible requirement is that a claim generated by a human right must be a claim on someone specifiable in words, though not necessarily confrontable in flesh and blood.

How weak can the requirements on the duty side get? Is it possible for the correlative duties not even, in aggregate, to meet the claims? That there are duties correlative to claim rights does not imply that whatever rights demand, there will be duties sufficient to supply it. I see no reason why there cannot be a shortfall on the supply side. Suppose the rich nations of the world were not so rich that they could eliminate all starvation without a heavy cost to themselves. Everyone has a right to life, including a right to rescue when in dire enough straits. But are there not also limits to what may be morally demanded of us? Are we not permitted certain sorts of partiality—partiality in the pursuit of our own central ends in life and partiality in promoting the well-being of those close to us? There is a sound line of thought leading us to an acceptance of human rights to life and to minimum provision. But there is also a sound line of thought leading us to acceptance of a domain of permitted partiality. Might not the former line of thought lead to a level of demand that the latter line of thought does not require that we supply? Whether that is possible depends partly upon what kind of system, if any, ethics can aspire to. Can ethics have the kind of system that will ensure that the conclusion of one correct line of thought will always be in harmony with the conclusion of another? Or might it be that the most plausible ethics is not like that?

The acceptable requirement of claimability is that the duty-bearers be specifiable, not that they exist. It is possible, in certain states of the world, for the duty to fall on specifiable bearers but for no one actually to meet the specification. Even then, there would still be a point in publicly announcing and justifying the description of the duty-bearers, if there might eventually be some. I can find no case for a stronger claimability requirement than that.

6

The Metaphysics of Human Rights

6.1 TWO MODELS OF VALUE JUDGEMENT

There is a 'taste model' of value judgement, given its classic statement by Hume, still highly influential in philosophy, all but dominant in the social sciences, and now widely absorbed into common sense.[1] According to it, value judgements are a matter of taste or attitude: you have your opinion; I have mine. Each of our opinions can be corrected for factual or logical error, but once that is done, there is no further ground for regarding one value judgement as better than another. Factual judgements can be true or false; value judgements are neither. Factual judgements are objective; value judgements are subjective—subjective in both of the two most common senses. They are, first of all, merely expressions of taste or attitude. And, second, values are not part of the furniture of the world; the world contains physical objects, properties, events, minds, but it does not also contain values. When philosophers thought they were deriving natural rights from human nature—that is, from empirical facts about human beings—they were really deriving them from human interests, using the word 'interest' to mean what is in one's interest or to one's advantage. That is, they were deriving human rights from value judgements that other cultures might not share.

The taste model is obviously appealing, as attested by its current popularity. But it seems to me to collapse, in the end, from its own explanatory inadequacy. According to the taste model, our preference fixes on an object, which thereby becomes valuable. But value cannot be explained so simply. There is no reliable correlation between our *actual* preferences and what is *valuable* to us. It is a discouraging, and not uncommon, fact of life that one can get what one actually wants, even sometimes what one most wants in life, only to find that one is no better off.

So we might, as many philosophers and social scientists do, drop *actual* preferences in favour of *rational* preferences. We can accept, as surely we must, that a thing does not become valuable just by being desired; our desires can be based on false or incomplete information. We must understand more fully or more accurately what the natural world is like, and only then, in this enhanced state of knowledge, might our reactions of desire be directed at what can count as a value. This 'rational preference account' is much the more plausible, and among philosophers now the more common form of the taste model. But what standard does 'rational' represent? We might say, as Richard Brandt proposes, that a desire is rational if it persists when I have become aware of all the relevant natural facts and when I have purged my thought of logical error.[2] But is this enough? Take an instructive example that we owe to John Rawls.[3] A man has a particularly crazy aim in life—say, counting the blades of grass in various lawns. He knows that no one is interested in the results, that the information is of no use, and so on; he commits no logical error. But we should be hard put to it to see the fulfilment of this obsessive desire as enhancing his life—apart, that is, from preventing anxieties and tensions that might be set up by frustrating his desire, but that is to introduce other values. What we should be hard put to see is the fulfilment of his desire as, in itself, improving the quality of his life. Or, if Rawls's example is thought doubtful because the man does not exhibit normal human rationality, take a woman with a sadistic streak who, after years of psychotherapy, knows full well how much her sadistic behaviour harms herself but finds it too intensely pleasurable to give it up. As she is a normally reasonable person, she will most likely have two desires: to give up her sadism and not to give it up. The first is for her the most sensible desire; the second is the motivationally more powerful desire. But both desires pass the test set by the taste model: they survive confrontation with all relevant facts and logic. The mere persistence of a desire does not make its object good for us. The first desire is the rational one; her sadism does her more harm than good. But that is a form of rationality that the taste model has trouble accommodating.

What these examples suggest is that our standard for 'rational' has not become strong enough yet. The way to make it stronger, though, is to make desires 'rational' in some such sense as 'formed in appropriate appreciation of the nature of their object'. But though this seems to handle the counter-examples, it seems also to undermine the preference account of value. It stresses an *appropriate* reaction of desire, and so suggests that there is an element here of getting things right. Once the idea of the 'appropriateness' of a response enters, standards of correctness and incorrectness enter. The taste model has no ready answer to the question, When is a response appropriate? The mere fact that the term 'rational preference' retains the word 'preference' does not show that much of the taste model is surviving. One cannot answer that the appropriate response is to be understood as the 'natural' or 'normal' one. If 'normal' here is taken to introduce some sort of statistical standard such as 'most common', then we may well find that most of us, even when informed, go on wanting certain things—say, to assert ourselves—too much; it may just be an unfortunate tendency in human nature that we have to struggle to keep in check. If 'normal' is taken to mean something closer to 'correct', then that is just the stronger standard that we are trying to explain.

We have more critical resources than the taste model recognizes. We can ask more searching questions about our aims, and resort to more radical criticism in answering them, than the taste model allows.

First, there is what has to be in place for language even to be possible. A word has meaning only in virtue of there being rules for its use, rules that settle whether or not the word is used correctly. Wittgenstein has argued that these rules cannot, in the end, be satisfactorily understood as a template that we carry in our heads—an image, say, or a list of defining properties—but only as part of shared practices in a community. And these shared practices are possible only because of the human beliefs, interests, dispositions, sense of importance, and so on that go to make up what he called 'a form of life'.[4] Our form of life provides the setting in which our language develops and only within which it is intelligible. And a form of life seems to consist in part in a shared set of beliefs and values. It is because, and only because, we see others as, like us, understanding the world in a certain way, caring about certain things, regarding certain things as important, that we can communicate with one another. So, among other things, shared values are needed: such things as that we feel pain and ordinarily dislike it and want to avoid it or have it alleviated, that we aim at certain kinds of things and can be gratified or frustrated. Donald Davidson has a similar argument.[5] We cannot, he thinks, interpret the language that others use without assuming that we have certain beliefs and attitudes in common with them—that, for instance, many of our aims, interests, desires, and concerns are the same. If that is right, then general scepticism about basic common-sense values is self-defeating. Certain values are part of the necessary conditions for our language, which sets for us the bounds of intelligibility. These arguments of Wittgenstein and Davidson seem to me persuasive; the difficulty is to say how far they take us. How many such basic beliefs are there? They will be confined, I think, to a few of the most basic human interests, the interests that I have already mentioned: that we want to avoid pain and anxiety, that we have goals and attach importance to their being fulfilled (and perhaps also a few moral norms closely connected to these interests, such as that cruelty is wrong). But in any case, what Wittgenstein and Davidson say is a start in finding the various sources of our beliefs about human interests, still using 'interests' in the sense I explained a short while ago.

Then there are interests outside the central core needed for intelligibility. Suppose that one day I am struck by the thought that your life seems, in some way, better than mine. I have a sense that I am frittering away my life in trivia, and you strike me as accomplishing things with your life that give it weight or point. My thought might initially be quite ill-focused, and I should have to try to sharpen it. Not just any achievement of yours would contribute much weight—say, walking the length of Broad Street in Oxford on your hands. It will have to be the achievement of something that is itself valuable. But that is not enough either. Some values are just too small-scale to give one's life weight or point. I should have to go on in this vein, trying to isolate what it is that I think so valuable in your life. I should be driven to use value-rich vocabulary to bring this possible value into focus: 'accomplishment' (if I may simply commandeer this word for what I am after) is roughly the sort of achievement that gives life weight or point. Then, having isolated it, having distinguished it from other values and from the valueless, I should have to decide whether what is left really is valuable—or rather, as the search for the definition already brings in value-rich language, these two processes, definition of the possible value and decision about its value, go hand in hand. And one decides about its value not by appeal to one's own subjective set of desires. There is nothing there to appeal to, except the vacuous desire to have a good life, which does not do the job, because the present job is to decide specifically whether accomplishment, so defined, makes a life good. What seems to be playing a big role here is not my subjective set of desires, but my understanding what accomplishment is. This sort of understanding, which has its own standards of success, might therefore introduce a new value into my life, in a way that the taste model fails to explain. Call this second model 'the perception model'.

For me to see anything as enhancing my life, I must see it as enhancing life in a generally intelligible way, in a way that pertains to *human* life and not just to my particular life. Why should this be so? It runs counter to widespread belief. One reason why we resist this conclusion is that we tend to overlook the constraints that are part of the constitution of desires: desires of the sort we are interested in—that is, the ones that have links to values—are not just brute psychological responses to objects that we can delineate in purely natural terms. To think that they are is to overlook the fact that we must also see the object as in some way good. There are, of course, different sorts of desires. Some desires are, in effect, afflictions: for instance, cravings, obsessions, compulsions, post-hypnotic suggestions, addictions, habits. We passively observe their occurrence in us. But there are also desires that are part of normal intentional action, part of the sort of behaviour that makes up the vast bulk of human life. We have options; we reflect, choose, and act—none of it necessarily very consciously. Desires of this sort aim at the good. An agent's normal behaviour is to recognize interests and to act to meet them. This sort of desire is the sort that concerns us in an account of values, and it fails on its own terms if it does not aim at something that we take to be good. It essentially involves a judgement of good, even if only a primitive form of one.

Another reason why we resist this conclusion is that it seems to fly in the face of the plain fact that people are very different from one another and get very different things out of life. I may greatly value playing the piano well; you may value expert rock climbing; and neither of us may care a fig for what the other cares about. But merely caring about something does not make it valuable. For anyone to see anything as valuable, from any point of view, requires being able to see it as worth wanting. This is a perfectly general requirement on values; it is the basis of the distinction between mere wanting and the sort of wanting that connects with values. One way to see something as worth wanting is to see it under the heading of some general human interest. Anyone who thinks that not all values are like that must then explain in what further way we can see them as worth wanting. What could make playing the piano well something worth wanting is that it would be in some way rewarding: I should enjoy it, or it would be an accomplishment, and so on. And you will have to do the same with your rock climbing. To see anything as making life better, we must see it as an instance of something generally intelligible as valuable and, furthermore, as valuable for any normal human being.

Deliberation about human interests ends up, I think, with a list of values. I am less concerned with precisely what is on the list than I am with the conclusion that deliberation ends with a general profile of values, a chart of the various high points that human life can rise to. My own list (no doubt incomplete) is this: accomplishment, enjoyment, deep personal relations, certain kinds of understanding, and—the interests that are most immediately relevant to human rights—the components of personhood. I shall return to the last item on the list shortly.

6.2 HUMAN INTERESTS AND THE NATURAL WORLD

Is 'human nature', as we use the term in accounts of human rights, part of the natural world? Can claims about human interests be correct and incorrect, true and false, in the way that claims of fact can be?

Claims about human interests based on biological needs can be correct and incorrect. One plain human interest connected closely to pain and survival is in nourishment: without it we suffer or die. Another plain interest is in certain kinds of human contact: if a baby is fed but denied other forms of nurture, it will suffer great psychological damage and might die. There are clear criteria for judgements that nourishment and other forms of nurture are human interests: namely, that they avoid egregious disvalues: ailment, pain, and malfunction. These plain disvalues are part of the framework necessary for the intelligibility of language.

Now look at values not in that framework. One of them would be the example I used earlier, accomplishment. If I accomplish nothing in my life, I shall suffer; my life will lack point or weight. But it is an altogether less experiential sort of suffering than the gross ailment and malfunction of a baby deprived of nurturing.

Still, these values outside the framework of intelligibility are both continuous with the values in it and, like them, firmly embedded in human nature. Particularly deeply embedded in us are certain biological aims—for food, health, protection of our capabilities—and certain psycho-biological aims—for example, for companionship, affection, reproduction. But we are not only intentional animals; we are also reflective animals. It does not take us much reflection to see that goods differ in degree, and that many are good only as means, often remote means, to other things that are good as ends. We come to see that the goods we aim at day in and day out are mostly trivial or mere means. It is natural for intentional, reflective beings to form second-order desires. We want something more than the satisfaction of trivial wants or wants for mere means. We want the whole activity, the unstopping succession of desire and fulfilment, to be itself sometimes leading to what is neither trivial nor a mere means. That is, I think, the characteristic aim of reflective, intentional beings. It is characteristic even though often not an especially conscious aim. But we form a desire to get out of the 'rat race', or we wonder whether we would not be better off sacrificing some income for a better quality of life. And it takes only a whiff of our own mortality for just about any of us, reflective types or not, to wonder whether we have wasted our lives. These large-scale, course-of-life desires emerged at the time of the evolutionary transition from a merely biological being to a reflective, intentional one. Non-biological interests, such as accomplishment, are as deeply embedded in human nature as biological ones are. To put it briefly, we are rational animals; biological interests are embedded in our animal nature, and non-biological ones in our rational nature.

The shift from biological to non-biological interests brings with it other changes that we should note: for instance, the move from predominantly experiential forms of harm such as pain and ailment, which are fairly easily identified, to non-experiential sorts of harm. How do I know that lack of food is harmful? Well, obvious physical symptoms appear. How do I know that lack of accomplishment is harmful? Well, because life is empty in a certain way—namely (and here circularity threatens), it lacks meaning or point.

Are there criteria for those non-experiential sorts of harm that would allow judgements about them to be correct or incorrect? The only plausible account of how we identify something that is in our interest, such as accomplishment, gives a role to both recognition and reaction, but without separating them nearly as sharply as the taste model does. The taste model says that value judgement involves, first, recognizing certain features of the natural world and then, second, reacting to them with approval or disapproval. But, as we saw, to explain value, we need not mere reaction but *appropriate* reaction. And to explain the appropriateness of a reaction, we need more than just a description of the object in purely natural or factual terms—that is, where the words 'natural' and 'factual' have the boundaries given them by seventeenth-century science or eighteenth-century philosophy, say, in the form of David Hume's sharp distinction between 'fact' and 'value'. For example, we bring what I am calling 'accomplishment' into focus only by resorting to such terms as 'fulfils life', and such language is not value-neutral but already organizes our experience by selecting what we see favourably. Being 'fulfilled', in the sense needed, is not a psychological matter of having a feeling of fulfilment; it is a matter of life's not being empty or futile or wasted. Of course, a notion such as 'wasted' is itself evaluative, so a value is already built into our notion of 'life-fulfilling', a value that makes itself felt in not just any object's being a possible object of fulfilment. Approval is not left free to fix on one object or another; its direction is already fixed in, and manifested by, what we see favourably. Reaction here is nothing as simple as a sentiment of approval; certain standards of appropriateness are essential to its being the reaction that it is. And recognition is not itself fully describable without the introduction of some reactive elements.

There is Aristotle's question, Are things valuable because desired, or desired because valuable?[6] The taste model answers: the first. The perception model, on certain well-established interpretations, answers: the second. But there is a third answer: neither; there is no priority. I want to recommend the third answer. I shall regard it as a variation on the perception model, but one could, if one preferred, give it a name of its own.

So the notion of recognition is best understood as something not entirely reaction-free, and vice versa. 'Recognition', in this appropriately impure sense, is meant to be a kind of sensitivity to something in the world. But one is not entitled to talk in terms of a sensitivity unless one can explain what it is for the sensitivity to work well and what to work badly. We have a clear, well-established account of the working of the physical senses. A theory of what goes on in the world includes an explanation of what goes on in human perception. We rely on our perceptions to justify the theory, and the theory to justify our reliance on our perceptions. But the theory explains, among other things, why perceptions in certain conditions are as a body reliable, how they fail, and how we can sometimes detect and correct their failure. Is anything approaching this possible for value judgements? Unless it is, why should we think that we have got a sensitivity *to* anything in the world?

Now, one might see hope of developing an account of the notions of 'correct' and 'incorrect' applied to *moral* judgements if one thought (as I do) that these judgements are grounded in some way, not necessarily a consequentialist way, in (largely human) interests. But we are now concerned with judgements about human interests themselves, and they seem, as value judgements go, to be ground-floor. Still, although ground-floor, the sensitivity I mean is complex in its workings and rich in its connections. We can say a fair amount about what it is for it to work well. One needs, first of all, a lot of knowledge of the familiar, undisputed factual sort about the world.

One has also to have sufficient human capacities to know how enjoyment, say, figures in human life. In this way, one can build up an account of the conditions for the successful workings of our sensitivity to prudential values, akin to conditions such as good light, good eyes, and good position for successful seeing. The account of failure in the sensitivity is independent of most judgements that the sensitivity should deliver. To show that it failed, one would have to show that the person concerned lacked the concept, or information, or certain human capacities, and the test for lacking any of them is fairly well removed from the deliverances of the supposed sensitivity. For instance, to show that I lack certain capacities for feeling, you would have to go to empirical psychology or to biology to show how the difference from a normal human psyche came about. One ought to be able to build up an account of the conditions in which, if all are met, the sensitivity succeeds. If so, this sensitivity will differ from a sensitivity such as sight, not in there being no account of its working, but in the greater difficulty of knowing when the conditions for its working are met. It is not that we never get evidence that they are all met. A full account of deliberating about human interests suggests that in the right conditions we are sensitive to certain things' making life go better. There are, of course, other explanations of what is going on besides the existence of such a sensitivity, but there are examples that make them seem implausible. For instance, we aim at some things simply because of deep, largely invisible social pressures. But there are also persons who come up with new (to them, at least) value notions, such as accomplishment, that have never been taught to them and the ethos of whose society is live-for-the-moment. In the end the best explanation of such changes is that the person has hit upon, has become sensitive to, something valuable, and that its being valuable is to some extent independent of the process of coming to regard it as such. A sensitivity to values would also be a good explanation of convergence of belief between persons, especially if the convergence emerged when the conditions of reliability were present, but most else—social ethos, psychological bent, economic class—were all very different. One could hope for simpler, more direct evidence, but this evidence is neither out of reach nor negligible.

So I think that we may conclude that judgements about human interests can be correct or incorrect. They report deliverances of a sensitivity to certain things going on in the world: namely, interests being met or not met. These interests are part of *human* nature, and not just human nature as seen by society. These judgements seem to be correct or incorrect, not, say, in the way that conclusions in mathematics can be, but rather true or false in the way that statements of natural fact can be.

The notion of 'meeting an interest' is rather like the notion 'soothes': something is relieved. We think of something's being soothing and something's meeting an interest as both being, to put it in rough, intuitive language, not properties *in* objects but properties *of* objects, properties that relate to the objects' interaction with other things. Of course, there is a rich, well-understood causal base for a judgement about something's being soothing. If we want some enlightenment about the authority that our ethical beliefs have, we must know somewhat more about the kind of truth they have—for instance, whether we may regard statements about human interests as statements of natural fact.

Well, a statement about being soothing and a statement about meeting interests must be much like one another because, on closer look, the first statement *is* an instance of the second. An ointment, say, soothes an irritation, and an irritation is in the general class of pains and discomforts, which are cases of disvalues. Compare 'That ointment soothes my irritation' with 'That accomplishment makes my life fulfilled'. In the second judgement, too, a value enters to explain why people are in certain respects as they are—namely, with interests met or unmet. It explains why some people suffer from a sense of emptiness or futility, especially at the end of life, whereas others do not. The value can be at work on us even without our being conscious of it—even, indeed, without our having the concept of 'accomplishment'. The absence of the value can explain the vague, unfocused dissatisfaction with life that can come before we are able to explain it.

Now, advocates of the taste model will, of course, resist my current line of thought. One does not have to cite a *value* (as if one were talking about something in the world), they are likely to reply, in order to explain this sense of emptiness; all that one needs to cite is a *belief* that one's life is empty, and all that one needs to cite to explain the vague, unfocused sense of emptiness is a vague, unfocused belief. But this reply falls short at two points. First, it goes no way towards explaining why the emptiness in question occupies much the same sort of place in our life as does an irritation that some ointment might soothe. Both are lacks that are part of human nature. It also ignores where the belief that one's life is empty itself comes from. The best explanation of why so many people form the deathbed belief that their life has been empty may well be that there has been a characteristic human interest often unmet.

6.3 THE TEST OF THE BEST EXPLANATION

I suggested earlier that it seems best to think in terms of our possessing a sensitivity to certain values in which recognition and reaction are merged—that is, the perception model, so adumbrated. We recognize a lack, an interest; furthermore, we recognize that certain things fill the lack or meet the interest. That is, we recognize a value by recognizing certain things that characteristically go on in human life. The best explanation of certain people's belief that something or other is to our advantage is that there are features of human life that they recognize. The best explanation of, say, someone's coming up with a new (to him or her) value notion such as accomplishment is that the person has become sensitive in this way to an interest to be met, to a value.

Then there is, as I mentioned briefly earlier, the phenomenon of convergence of beliefs between several persons. Most facts about convergence and divergence in normative beliefs are neutral as between the taste model and the perception model. What matters to the choice between these two views, however, is what *explains* the convergence or divergence. This is a complicated empirical issue. But if, when certain knowledge and sensitivity and conceptual equipment are all in place, convergence in belief occurs, and if that happens when other causal influences on the formation of belief, such as social pressures, are different, then the best explanation may turn out to be the workings of the recognition that I was just referring to. Certainly, if the explanation I suggested earlier in the case of one person's coming to recognize the value of accomplishment is plausible, it will be a likely candidate in the many-person case.

I have been employing the test of the best explanation. We conceive of a belief-independent world of empirical fact as playing a role in affecting our concepts, our beliefs, and our sometimes converging on the same beliefs. We attribute existence in the world of empirical fact to a kind of thing—any kind of thing, including values—in assigning a certain sort of explanatory role to it. One sort of explanatory role that would seem to have these existential implications—sufficient for them, but perhaps not necessary—is causal. This gives us a test of empirical existence in terms of the best causal explanation: a kind of thing has empirical existence if things of that kind must appear in the best account of what happens in the empirical world. If entities such as electrons or properties such as electrical charge must appear in the best account of what happens in the world, then there are such entities and such properties. The same would be true of human interests and of events such as these interests' being met or unmet.

The test of the best explanation is often taken to be a test of realism about a thing. What realism claims, including realism about values, is very difficult to settle. Much of language has meaning only within the context of natural human concerns, desires, interests, sense of importance, and so on—Wittgenstein's idea of a 'form of life'. This raises the possibility that the embeddedness of our concepts in the human point of view is so deep and inescapable that it makes no sense to speak of a belief-independent reality. There may be a case, for all that I have said, for a wide irrealism that would carry a narrower irrealism about values along with it. But I have not here used the test of the best explanation as a test of the all-things-considered reality of values, but only of their factuality. What I have been after is some fuller understanding of the way in which judgements about human interests can be true, and I am content to conclude no more than that they can be true in the way that judgements about 'soothing' can be.

So my proposal is this. A judgement about some accomplishment's being life-fulfilling and a judgement about an ointment's being soothing are both judgements about what goes on in the world of (human) nature. They are true in virtue of that part of the natural world. That the concepts 'soothing' and 'life-fulfilling' are deeply embedded in the human perspective, that recognizing their occurrence necessarily involves a human response, that the world of (human) nature may not be entirely mind-independent, does not undermine the possibility of their having a truth-value. A typical human response goes into making something 'soothing' and also 'life-fulfilling', rather than being (as the taste model represents it) a truth-destroying part of the criteria for judging it actually to be soothing or life-fulfilling. And nature consists of objects, properties, and events that are independent of our ideas and beliefs about them in the following sense. Our ideas are shaped by what they are ideas of; we can alter an idea, or even drop some ideas and invent new ones, as we discover more about nature or just reflect more deeply on what we already know. And we confirm our beliefs against nature—that is the truistic version of the correspondence theory of truth. We look more closely; we collect evidence; we find counter-examples. These are the ordinary ways in which we established the truth of a claim that a certain ointment soothes a certain irritation.

What I propose is that whether certain human interests are met is also a matter of fact. It is *also* a matter of value. So my suggestions run contrary to the sharp separation of fact and value present in the taste model.

That I am in pain is a matter of fact; to that everyone agrees. Now, pains have both a phenomenological side to them (the internal feel of our experiences of pain), and, equally important, an active side (reactions of avoidance, alleviation, and so on). One learns the word 'pain' both by having certain experiences and by understanding where pain fits into human life—that 'pains' are characteristically (though not, necessarily universally) to be avoided or alleviated. This reactive element cannot be sharply separated from the recognitional element. And this is so not because, with pain, recognitional elements and reactive elements, though separable in principle, are difficult to disentangle, but because the distinction between these two kinds of elements ceases to hold here. And that is because our standard of sameness in the sensations that we bring together under the concept 'pain' is partly that they are characteristically what are to be avoided, alleviated, and so on. With pains, we do not recognize something to which we also, independently, react. Our reaction is a constituent of our recognition. The way in which pain fits into human life is part of the criterion for its being pain.[7] And it is not that, as a matter of fact, we just find ourselves desiring to avoid pain or to have it alleviated. What is going on is more complex: we have these desires *because* we find pain undesirable. We have an attitude towards it; we find it bad, and for obvious reasons. Some basic values are part of the framework necessary for language, and the disvalue of pain must be one of them. The distinction between fact and value, as we find it in Hume and more generally in the taste model, becomes difficult to sustain at this point.

Cases of interests' being met and unmet, I think, earn their way into the world of facts. We can place them in our everyday natural world, and do not need to resort to anything remotely like a detached 'value realm'. That conclusion brings out what seems to me immensely plausible about ethical naturalism. In talking about human interests we are not talking about entities in such an other-worldly realm—detectable, say, by intuition—but, rather, about certain things that happen in the only realm that values need: mainly, what goes on in human lives, that *this* or *that* meets an interest, and so makes a life go better. It makes sense to ask how these sorts of happenings relate to other, fairly well-defined levels of explanation: say, the psychological. But I doubt that there is any point in asking how such happenings relate to a level so grossly defined as the 'natural' or the 'empirical' or the 'factual', because the boundaries that we use to delineate the 'natural' or the 'empirical' or the 'factual' are not just fuzzy, but so central to what we must settle as to make assumptions about where they are located question-begging. We do not start our investigations with these boundaries satisfactorily drawn. We have only a common, extremely vague intuition about the 'natural' or 'empirical' world, one that is full of contentious ontological assumptions. So we should not start by asking how values relate to 'fact', as if we really knew the territory inhabited by 'fact' and were wondering only about its foreign relations. That procedure makes their relation more puzzling than it needs to be. I suggest that our notion of the 'factual' is wide enough to include events of meeting and failing to meet interests. The right position, therefore, is, after all, a kind of naturalism. But it is not the usual kind of reductive naturalism, in which the boundaries of the 'natural' or the 'factual' are kept relatively tight: that is, roughly in the position that they have long had in the fact/value split in Hume's view that values cannot be derived from facts. What seems attractive, however, is an expansive naturalism, in which the boundaries of the 'natural' or the 'factual' are pushed outward a bit, in a duly motivated way, with the effect that they now encompass human interests.

6.4 THE METAPHYSICS OF HUMAN RIGHTS

How much of the epistemic and metaphysical standing of human interests carries over to the human rights derived from them? In turning now from human interests to human rights, we move from prudence to morality.

Here is an example of a relatively easy such move. 'That's cruel' is a judgement about action, but is short of commanding action, as 'ought' and 'must' judgements do; so it avoids some of the further complexities that arise with them. All the same, 'That's cruel' already encapsulates a standard of behaviour. How does this moral standard arise? The full answer to that question will draw on evolutionary biology, anthropology, psychology, decision theory, as well as on the patterns of justification that especially concern ethics. My partial answer will draw primarily on the last.

A person who acts cruelly intends to make another suffer without compensating good. That intention is both necessary and sufficient. If I do something just to hurt you (say, twist your arm) but, by a fluke, save you greater pain (say, by replacing your dislocated shoulder), what I do is none the less cruel.

If I try to help you (say, by replacing your dislocated shoulder) but cause you greater pain (say, by breaking your arm), I am clumsy or oafish but not cruel.

But, then, is 'That's cruel' not, after all, a moral judgement, but a factual one about intent? John Mackie thinks so. 'What is the connection', he asks, 'between the natural fact that an action is a piece of deliberate cruelty—say, causing pain just for fun—and the moral fact that it is wrong?'[8] Mackie accepts the taste model: we delineate the action through the factual description 'cruel' and then respond to it with disapproval. But the notion 'cruel', I think, leaves no space for disapproval to be an independent step. To understand 'pain' already involves regarding it as a disvalue. We typically respond to pain negatively, and its having that standing in our life often gives me a reason to avoid causing you pain, and so to avoid being cruel to you.[9]

There are prudential values and disvalues so basic, so centrally embedded in our conceptual framework—pain, for instance—that the idea of deliberation to reach the conclusion that it is a value or a disvalue does not fit the case. One cannot make sense of those looming presences in our life, other people, without understanding how, with their vulnerable bodies and psyches, they fit into the world—not least, their being able to be hurt by it. Deliberation about the value of pain is left no space to get going. When we move on to moral deliberation, we find much the same thing. A moral notion such as 'cruel', being conceptually so close to 'pain', inherits much of its obviousness. How would one establish that I had a reason not to be cruel to you? My reason comes partly from inevitable features of our conceptual framework: my seeing you as a person involves my accepting that there are certain basic values at stake in your life, and my seeing them as values produces a reason for me to respect them. Again, deliberation has no space to get going.

The obviousness of the judgement 'That's cruel' comes also from its generally being made well within certain motivational limits. It is well within the capacities of the human will not to torture cats for fun; the most ordinary people manage it. And it costs us nothing, at least nearly all of us, not to torture cats for fun. The judgement 'That's cruel' generally operates within an area in which the human frame can easily manage the required action, so the condemnation built into the word 'cruel' is apt.

The same is true of many norms. Sometimes the standard for behaviour they set is well within human capacity. If we are willing to make the judgement 'That's cruel', with its condemnatory force, we should be willing to accept the norm 'Don't be cruel'.

The moral judgement 'That's cruel' does not go much beyond claims about pain and, importantly, intention. The property 'cruel', being a combination of pain, causes, and intentions, has whatever metaphysical standing they have—standing as natural facts, I should say.

Some philosophers would insist that 'cruel' has prescriptive force, which my analysis solely in terms of natural facts about intention, cause, and pain fails to capture. One should concede to the objectors that 'cruel' does indeed have prescriptive force, if that means merely that it gives a reason for action. The explanation of its reason-giving status, I have suggested, is roughly the same as the one for 'pain'. 'It hurts' can generate a reason for me to avoid the thing myself and also a reason for me not to visit it on you. The reason-generating force of 'cruel' derives from, and has the same explanation as, the reason-generating force of 'pain'. There is no residual force that needs further explanation of a natural-fact-undermining sort.

But let us now turn to an example of the second kind of transition from prudence to morality: not smooth, hardly irresistible, and perhaps involving considerable change in epistemic and metaphysical standing. Recall the earlier discussion of the norm 'Don't deliberately kill the innocent'.[10] Human life is of especially high value. From that we derive an especially strict norm, 'Don't deliberately kill the innocent'. Part of the content of the right to life—indeed, in the seventeenth century much of it—is not killing another person without due process, though as far back as Locke, philosophers were including certain further protections—for example, aiding the desperately needy.[11] But, as I said earlier, when we make the move from human interests to moral norms, certain limitations of human agents enter the picture, especially limitations in will and understanding.[12] There are limits to what may be demanded by human agents, and those limits help to shape the content of the human right to life—for example, the matter of how much aid for the needy may be demanded of one. And the limits of understanding limit what is available to us to decide the content of human rights. Sometimes we can calculate reliably enough—that is, to a degree of probability on which we should be prepared to act—the consequences of large-scale, long-term social arrangements. We can, if the changes in question are extreme enough. But in less extreme cases, often in just the cases we regard as live options, we cannot—cases such as deliberately killing non-combatants in war, using terrorism as a political instrument, killing one patient to save five others, and so on. Here too we often cannot do the calculation of consequences to a reliable degree of probability. And there is no obvious remedy for this failure.

In the absence of a remedy, we find some other way to conduct our moral life. Or rather, in many cases a sufficiently reliable, all-encompassing calculation of consequences has never been available to us, so we have simply carried on with our moral life pretty much in the piecemeal, not fully systematic way that mankind has always done. We have at times raised our standards and broadened the considerations that concern us, but we have not convincingly risen to an overarching system. Instead, we long ago developed a different approach to ethical decision making. The very great value of human life has led to our having very great respect for it; we allow that there can be exceptions to the norm 'Don't deliberately kill the innocent', but out of our great respect for human life we demand that the case for any exception be especially convincing. That is, we respect life: we do not try to promote it, for example, by maximizing it. There is an element of policy in this approach, and we can see that another society might adopt a somewhat different policy. As this norm constitutes a large part of the content of the human right to life, there is therefore an element of policy in the human right as well.

The policies I refer to are not, at least typically, consciously chosen. It is not that we become aware of our limitations of will and understanding and then, in conjunction with others, decide in light of these limitations to adopt a certain policy. We do not discover our limitations, because it never seemed to us that our will and understanding were unlimited. Instead, such policies usually emerge in a society without anything so deliberate as a group decision. Nor are these policies arbitrary; they are shaped in large part by, and are largely a response to, the great value that we attach to human life. And the policies can be criticized. They can be too strict or too lenient, too demanding or too undemanding, too limited as to object or too unlimited, and so on. For example, not long ago the policy in our society that 'charity begins at home' was often interpreted to allow charity to end there too; but now we think that our duties of help can sometimes be worldwide. Our actual, present-day ethical policies may, no doubt, be inadequate, but we are able to improve them. Because of our limitations of understanding and will, moral philosophy cannot realistically aspire ultimately to abolish this element of policy; its more realistic, but still ambitious, aim is to arrive at the best policy.

This element of policy is not peculiar to the right to life. One of the two grounds for human rights is practicalities.[13] The content of most human rights becomes sufficiently determinate only by considering certain practicalities. The personhood ground tells us, for example, that we have a right to security of person; without it there would be no security of agency. But the personhood ground, on its own, does not yield a line nearly determinate enough to tell us what in practice is prohibited. For that we need to consider human psychology and the ways in which societies function, and decide whether we need a safety margin, and roughly how generous it should be. And here too an element of policy enters. The line we have plumped for may not be quite the same as the line another society has plumped for—and not necessarily because of a difference in our societies but because of a difference in the policies that our two societies have happened to plump for.

If this element of policy is a necessary determinant of the content of many human rights, what does this mean for their metaphysical standing? The norm 'Don't deliberately kill the innocent' expresses a policy. An expression of a policy is not true or false in the way that a statement that a human interest is or is not met is; it is not a matter of natural fact. Of course, one difference is that a moral policy is often expressed in imperative mood. Still, even if we were to translate the norm 'Don't deliberately kill the innocent' from imperative to declarative mood, and to express it in a form more amenable to assessment in terms of truth and falsehood—say, 'Deliberately killing the innocent is wrong'—nothing important would have changed. The best understanding of the latter form of words would still be, in part, an utterance of a policy, and policies attract assessment not in terms of truth and falsity, but in terms of how well they perform their function. That might tempt one to think that the statement 'Deliberately killing the innocent is wrong' reduces to the claim 'The policy of prohibiting deliberately killing of the innocent is a good one', and that statement may in turn be reducible to the claim that the policy performs its function well—as the claim 'That is a good pen' may be reduced to the claim that it performs the functions of a pen well, which *may* itself be a statement of natural fact. But, of course, one should not be tempted. Expressing a policy is not assessing it. We are not asserting that it is a good policy, though we should not adopt a policy if we knew that it were on balance a bad one, or that there were a substantially better one. But at a fairly early point in assessing policies such as 'Don't deliberately kill the innocent', we reach a point where we can no longer tell that one policy is better than another.

7

The Relativity and Ethnocentricity of Human Rights

7.1 ETHICAL RELATIVITY

Ethical relativism, as I shall understand it, makes two claims: first, that ethical judgements are made within a framework of basic evaluations, which may take the form of beliefs, preferences, sentiments, and so on; and, second, that there are divergent frameworks for judgements on the same matter, no one framework being most authoritative.[1] We can then specify the framework further case by case—the basic evaluations of individual persons, of social groups, of cultures, and so on.

Ethical relativism, as most commonly expressed, is universal: *all* ethical judgements are relative to a framework. Its contradictory is therefore particular negative: some are not. I argued in the last chapter that some ethical judgements—namely, judgements about basic human interests—are objective, where 'objective' means dependent not upon a person's subjective states but upon considerations that would lead all successfully rational persons to the same conclusion. So universal ethical relativism is, I conclude, false. But philosophers tend to treat values as if they were uniform: all are objective, or none is; all are a matter of knowledge, or none is; all are relative to a framework, or none is. But in the last chapter I also questioned this assumption of uniformity. Some complex moral norms, such as 'Don't deliberately kill the innocent', have an element of policy to them, and so lack empirical truth-value, whereas the judgements that a particular human interest is or is not met have one.

Relativism need not take a universal form. Consider relativity to the evaluative framework of individuals, based on their different desires and sentiments. Value beliefs can be subjected to criticism by facts[2] and by logic.[3] Many ethical beliefs are shaped by a person's understanding, often misunderstanding, of the empirical world: of the consequences of our acts, of what the objects of our desires are really like, and so on. Once one's desires and attitudes have been corrected, one may come to change them; over time they may increasingly converge with the desires and attitudes of others. What a relativist must maintain, however, is that some divergent beliefs will remain, and remain for the reasons relativists give. In any case, our interest here is human rights. Are *they* relative to a framework?

How can one make a case for ethical relativism? The commonest way is to cite, with little in the way of argument, certain examples of particularly stubborn ethical disagreement, which are meant to leave one thinking that the best explanation of the disagreement is the relativist's. This is, of course, an extremely weak form of argument. Establishing the best explanation of stubborn ethical disagreements requires understanding all the possible origins of these conflicting beliefs and all the possible resources that might resolve the conflict—no quick or easy job. That the job is so difficult leaves many relativists, despite its inadequacy, doing no more than citing examples. Let me give a brief sampler of the examples that they have offered.

Some societies regard theft as a serious crime; others do not even have the concept of private property, on which the idea of 'theft' depends.[4] It is hardly obvious that relativism provides the best explanation of this difference. If one lives where food is plentiful without cultivation, there may be no pressure to develop an institution of private property. But if one's survival depends upon clearing land and shouldering the burdens of growing one's own food, some form of control over the land and the crop is highly likely to emerge. The best explanation may be difference not in ethical framework but in material conditions.

Some societies have tolerated infanticide; others condemn it.[5] But consider the extreme case of life-threatening poverty. Tolerance of infanticide is an adaptation that most of us would make if forced to it by the direst poverty: say, if one were faced with the awful choice between the survival of one's newborn baby or one's young child. A plausible explanation of the disagreement over infanticide between a society of such abject poverty and one better off may not be a difference in evaluative frameworks but, again, a difference in material conditions.

Many people are committed to preserving the environment; others see no objection to exploiting it.[6] This is a conflict that does indeed look irresolvable. To my mind, we can coherently talk about the value of the environment not just when changes in the environment affect human beings, say our health or enjoyment, but also apart from any effect on sentient life. The environment has a value in itself. The idea of the environment's being intrinsically valuable rests, I believe, on an idea of appropriateness of attitude. The only appropriate response to, say, the enormous age, biological complexity, and beauty of the Great Barrier Reef is wonder and awe. And wonder and awe prompt respect. There is something lacking in a person who does not have some such response. The wanton destruction of the Great Barrier Reef would be a monstrous act. Ethics, I should say, is broad enough to encompass standards not just of *right* and *wrong* but also of *appropriate* and *inappropriate*. Now, if the natives on an island in the Great Barrier Reef decide to improve their quality of life by mining, and thereby destroying, the Reef, the apparent rational resolution of the conflict between the preservationists and the exploiters would be to weigh the costs and benefits to sentient creatures against the intrinsic value of the Reef. But that, I suspect, is a piece of weighing we cannot do. We must remember that some values may be incommensurable, in this sense of the term: two values are incommensurable if and only if they cannot be ranked against one another as 'greater than', 'less than', 'equal to', or 'roughly equal to'.[7] For a pair of values to be commensurable in this sense, there must be a bridging notion in terms of which the comparison between them can be made. For example, most, perhaps all, human interests, I should say, lend themselves to comparison. They do, not because there is a substantive super-value behind them, but because there is a formal value notion in terms of which we can, and regularly do, compare them: for example, 'prudential value', 'quality of life', or 'human interest' itself. We thus have the conceptual materials to judge that 'this would enhance the quality of my life more than that', 'this is a more major human interest than that', and so on. But sometimes—not often, I believe—two competing values are so different in nature from one another that there is no bridging notion available. In this conflict over the environment, for example, there is no bridging notion; comparison breaks down. This is indeed an intractable difference, but it does not derive from difference in ethical framework but from incommensurably different values. There is even a possible resolution of this disagreement: bringing both parties to see that the values they purport to commensurate are incommensurable.

A last example. Many of us think that abortion is prohibited; many others think that it is permitted.[8] Most often a person who holds that abortion is forbidden also holds background religious beliefs. But then is this, after all, an example of ethical relativity? Virtually all of us would accept that abortion is prohibited if we believed that an all-good, all-wise God had told us so. But with such a background, this intractable disagreement seems to have arisen not from different ethical frameworks but from different metaphysical beliefs. Perhaps, though, this just means that we should reconsider our definition of ethical relativism as relativity to a framework of basic *evaluations*. Evaluations cannot be sharply divided from empirical and metaphysical beliefs; our basic evaluations are what they are in part because of non-ethical beliefs. But if this truth is to support the relativity of a belief about the morality of abortion, it must be because of the further relativity of facts or of metaphysical conceptual schemes. Ethical relativity would then not stand alone. Although these further relativities seem much shakier than ethical relativity, perhaps that impression is mistaken.

Still, not all ethical disagreements about abortion arise from differences over religion. When they do not, what best explains the stubbornness of the divergence? No doubt, many different things. But one explanation that is hard to make plausible is that there are two different frameworks of fairly well-articulated and well-defined ethical beliefs producing this disagreement. That would make thought at this level far clearer and more inferential than it is. What might these ethical beliefs be? Nor is it plausible that these divergent beliefs about abortion are themselves basic ethical beliefs. They do not have quite that depth; they need justification themselves. What is more plausible, I should say, is that the framework for each of these conflicting views is a complex mix of ethical beliefs, factual beliefs, and sentiments. They might be beliefs such as 'A foetus is already a fully biologically formed potential person, as much so as a new-born baby' or 'An early foetus is too biologically primitive to be a person'. Or they might be sentiments such as revulsion at the very thought of killing a foetus or, on the contrary, equanimity in the face of it. But these beliefs are vague, and their implications for action by no means clear. And we should have to decide what weight to attach to these sentiments of revulsion or equanimity. What authority do they have?

My discussion of each of the four examples I have given is, I admit, inconclusive—neither decisively for nor against their relativity. But that is my point. One would have to dig much deeper before one could reach a satisfactory conclusion. Merely citing an example is no case at all. Let me now try to dig somewhat deeper in the example that primarily concerns us: human rights.

7.2 THE RELATIVITY OF HUMAN RIGHTS

Human rights are suspected—by Westerners as much as by Easterners—of being relative to Western culture. Human rights are undoubtedly a Western product: introduced by Christians in the late Middle Ages and further developed there in the early modern period and in the seventeenth and eighteenth centuries.[9] They were part of the growth in individualism in that particular time and place; they were part of a new sense in Europe and the Americas of 'the dignity of man' and the great value of human autonomy and liberty.

But why think that human rights are, as well as a product of the West, also relative to the values of the West? One argument might be that the values from which human rights are derived—most prominently autonomy and liberty—are themselves peculiarly Western values. Some societies, it is true, value autonomy highly, seeing in it the peculiar dignity of the human person, while other societies value autonomy much less, seeing in it the threat of social atomism and the loss of solidarity and fraternity and of the harmony that comes from our all serving the same values. But anyone who thinks seriously about the value of our status as normative agents and the benefits of living in a cohesive fraternal community will recognize that both are highly important. And they will recognize the same about both others' having to respect our individuality and our having duties of concern and care for others. It may be that realizing certain of the values of individualism is incompatible with realizing certain of the values of community. But incompatibility of values is not their relativity. Besides, the frequency of the incompatibility is exaggerated. Not all forms of autonomy are the autonomy to which we attach great value.[10] I would display more autonomy, in one correct use of the word, if I calculated my own income tax each year and decided for myself the plausibility of the Big Bang, instead of relying on the expertise of others. But neither of those is the autonomy to which we attach great value. What we attach great value to is the autonomy that is a constituent of normative agency, and relying on a tax accountant or an astrophysicist does not derogate in the least from one's normative agency. And the form of solidarity to which we attach such great value does not require surrendering our normative agency, though it may require greater trust in one another and greater convergence in public standards. The form of solidarity that is of great value is a joint commitment to the members of one's community and to the community's successful working. The plausible explanation of the fact that different societies rank autonomy and solidarity differently is not that they are rankings of the relativist sort. Everyone, on pain of mistake, has to admit that autonomy and solidarity are both highly valuable. No one would maintain that any loss in autonomy is worse than any loss in solidarity, or vice versa. And the more specific a choice between the two becomes—a certain loss of autonomy, say, to achieve a certain gain in solidarity—the more convergence in choice one will expect there to be. We do seem able, if only roughly, to compare these competing values.

A second argument for the relativity of human rights—indeed, an argument arising from my own account—is this. In the last chapter we saw how certain moral judgements—for example, 'That's cruel'—could be derived from judgements about human interests—for example, 'That's painful'.[11] The judgement 'That's cruel' goes so little beyond claims about pain, cause, and intention that it inherits the metaphysical and epistemic standing they have—standing as natural facts, I proposed. This suggests—merely suggests—that a human right (a moral standard) might similarly be derived from a certain human interest (a prudential value), again inheriting from it a sort of objectivity that would defeat the claim of relativity. Take the derivation of autonomy (the human right) from autonomy (the prudential value). But I also admitted that the derivation of still other human rights from human interests was less simple—for example, the right to life, which has an element of policy to it. The norm 'Don't deliberately kill the innocent', which is one of the correlative duties of the right to life, in part expresses a policy, and different societies might adopt different policies. Some human rights thus have a clear conventional element. Do they thereby have an element of relativity?

Take the right to autonomy. Once one recognizes the value of autonomy, one recognizes also a reason to be autonomous oneself and a reason not to deny other people their autonomy. Human rights are protections of one's personhood, and so protections of, among other things, one's capacity for and exercise of autonomy. Is the objective epistemic status of the judgement that autonomy is prudentially valuable transferred to the judgement that autonomy is a human right? We should ask: What more comes into the second judgement than is already present in the first? The obvious answer is: the first is a prudential judgement, the second a moral judgement. I find it very hard to understand the nature of the transition from prudence to morality, but, despite my uncertainty, I think that at least there is a kind of rationality to it. It is tempting to treat the reason-generating consideration that moves me when my autonomy is at stake as different from the one that moves me when yours is at stake. The obvious difference between these two cases is that in the one it is *my* autonomy, and in the other it is *yours*. But the most plausible understanding of the engine of these two judgements is *autonomy: because a person's quality of life is importantly at stake*. The *my* and *your* are not part of the reason-generating consideration. The clause *because a person's quality of life is importantly at stake* lacks reference to me or to you, but it lacks nothing of what we understand the reason to be. To try to deny 'autonomy' its status as a reason for action unless it is attached to 'my' would mean giving up our grasp on how 'autonomy' works as a reason for action.

Return now to my question: What more is present in the second judgement than is already contained in the first? There is, of course, whatever is added by calling autonomy a 'human right'. Many philosophers say that the judgement that something is a human right carries with it a claim that it has a particular moral importance: for example, it has the status of a 'trump' or a 'side-constraint'. But I have already argued several times against this characterization of human rights. They are neither trumps nor side-constraints. They are not even the most important of rights. Autonomy—or, more generally, personhood—is not necessarily the most important human interest. Human rights make only an overrideable claim that a person's autonomy be given due respect—that is, the respect due to the sort of autonomy at stake in any particular case. And that much follows simply from autonomy's being a prudential value. It is true that to know that autonomy is a prudential value is also to know how valuable it is: that it is generally highly valuable to us, valuable enough to attract, as it has, special protection, but of varying value from case to case, and overrideable by other important values.

When I speak here of the 'derivation' of the human right to autonomy, I do not mean an entailment. I mean only that a reasonable person who recognizes the prudential value of autonomy will also recognize the respect that it is due. And the reasonableness of that transition is enough to deny a relativist a foothold here.

Another important qualification. The transition from prudence to morality is, of course, too complicated a matter to be dealt with as briskly as I have just done—so complicated that there is no point in my embarking on a few more brisk comments. I have discussed the subject more fully elsewhere, and will fall back on that.[12] So let me leave my brief sketch of the kind of rationality involved in the transition from prudence to morality as a kind of marker: I need a fuller argument at this point, but so too would a relativist who wants to resist the objective tendency of my line of thought.

Let me turn to the second example I mentioned: the human right to life. Does a relativist find a foothold at least here? There is, I said, an element of policy in this right. Such policies are, it is true, social artefacts. All that we can say, though, is that a different society might choose a *somewhat* different policy. There are strong constraints on the policies that can be chosen. The non-arbitrary determinants of the content of the policy are the prudential value of human life, facts about human nature, and facts about how societies work. The great value of life would lead nearly all societies to adopt severe restrictions on deliberately taking an innocent person's life, the severity manifesting itself in reluctance to recognize many exceptions, especially, given what people are like, exceptions that cannot themselves be clearly enough limited or that have to rely on agent's being capable of highly subtle distinctions. Some societies may, even so, turn out to be relatively liberal about the restrictions, while others are relatively conservative. But that fact offers no appreciable support for relativity. If the convention adopted by one society could be seen to be working rather better than the convention of another, then there is strong rational ground for the second to adopt the convention of the first. If, as is common, we cannot tell whether any one convention is working better than the others, then no society would have good reason to resist an obvious solution to the divergence: agreement on a common convention. This sort of difference between societies represents not a different framework of basic evaluations but merely a highly constrained difference in arational opting.

What may we conclude? I have carried my discussion both of the metaphysics of human rights (in the last chapter) and of their relativity (in this chapter) only so far. In the last chapter I did not argue for the reality of prudential values, but only for their factuality: judgements about human interests, I concluded, can be true or false in the way that judgements about an ointment's being soothing can be. In this chapter, I want to conclude that judgements about human interests and about human rights do not offer appreciably more scope for relativism than do judgements about natural facts. But I have already acknowledged[13] that one can be a relativist about natural facts—for example, the sort of comprehensive relativism that Wittgenstein is sometimes thought to hold: relativity to a form of life. The assessment of this radical form of relativism I again leave to others.[14]

7.3 WHAT IS THE PROBLEM OF ETHNOCENTRICITY?

There are those who maintain that, even if ethical relativism were false, the problem of ethnocentricity would remain.[15]

What exactly *is* the problem of ethnocentricity? Perhaps this.[16] Human rights are, or are widely held to be, universally applicable. But if the only available justification for them is in Western terms, then they are not universally authoritative. If this were the problem, it would be overcome by establishing an objective justification of human rights authoritative for all rational beings. An objective justification of this sort would be sufficient, but perhaps not necessary. Certain forms of intersubjective justification might also do.

Still, if such an objective or intersubjective justification were forthcoming, a problem of ethnocentricity might even then remain. Such justification may be a long way off, or may take some societies a long time to come around to, and the language of human rights is something that we use now and have reason to go on wanting to use now. Perhaps we need a case for human rights, or even a variety of cases, not made in what for many are alien Western terms. Perhaps we must still aim to avoid ethnocentricity.

But this does not follow. Hundreds of thousands of Westerners have adopted Asian religions, and not because they have managed to find Western metaphysical and ethical counterparts for these often culturally remote Asian beliefs, but, on the contrary, because they have looked into these religions on their own terms and been attracted by what they found. No one regards their Eastern origin as, in itself, an unscalable barrier. The alien can be baffling, but if this problem can be overcome by Westerners in the case of Eastern religions, why not Easterners in the case of the much more accessible Western human rights?

Full, definitive rational justification aside, there seem to me, as I said earlier,[17] to be two ways to bring about unforced agreement on human rights. One would be to put the case for human rights as best we can construct it from resources of the Western tradition, and hope that non-Westerners will look into the case and be attracted by what they find. The other would be to search the ethical beliefs of various non-Western societies for indigenous ideas that might provide a local case for human rights, or for something not unlike them. This search is a valuable component of the current debate about Asian values, and many writers have helpfully explored the conceptual resources of Islam, Buddhism, Confucianism, and so on to that end. At first glance it will seem that this second approach (let me call it the less ethnocentric approach) is clearly the better one simply because less ethnocentric. But on a longer look the first approach (let me call it the more ethnocentric approach) is, I want to propose, on balance, preferable.

We now, in these cosmopolitan times, tend to exaggerate the differences between societies; societies change faster than foreigners' pictures of them.[18] It is true that different parts of the world have sometimes had radically different histories, which still exert an influence on their vocabularies, their ways of thinking, their religions, their values. But the influences on the members of virtually all societies are now much more a mix of local and global than they were even a hundred years ago. Since then there has been a massive increase in global communication, convergence on economic structures, homogenization of ways of life due to growing prosperity, and widespread travel and study abroad precisely by the persons most likely to be influential in their society. Too many contemporary writers merely echo Rawls's belief that a pervasive and ineradicable feature of international life is a radical inter-society pluralism of conceptions of justice and the good. But Rawls's reasons for regarding these differences as ineradicable are difficult to find. We exaggerate, in particular, the disagreement between societies over human rights. Several Asian governments emphatically affirmed human rights in the Bangkok Declaration of 1993, though, it is true, also insisting that 'while human rights are universal in nature, they must be considered in the context of a dynamic and evolving process of international norm-setting, bearing in mind the significance of national and regional particularities and various historic, cultural and religious backgrounds'.[19] To declare that human rights are 'universal' but qualified by 'particularities' makes one alarmed about what that qualification will be used to justify. Still, there are loopholes in human rights themselves; no human right is absolute. Westerners themselves often contribute to the exaggeration of differences between East and West by exaggerating the strictness of the Western conception of human rights. Much of the flexibility and qualification in the Eastern conception is there, too, in the Western conception, on an accurate account of it. There is a wide variety of conditions that outweigh or qualify human rights: for example, if the very survival of a good government is at stake, or if a large number of lives can be saved from terrorist attack.[20] And there is a great difference between possessing a freedom and its possession's being of value. This raises the question, also prompted by the Bangkok Declaration, whether social and economic rights have priority over civil and political rights. I myself think that the arguments go heavily against such a priority,[21] but these are all legitimate questions, as the United Nations Universal Declaration (1948) perhaps too amply acknowledged,[22] and they deserve serious answers. Still, these legitimate questions are raised by the 'particularities' not of Asian societies but of any society in certain circumstances of emergency, or at certain stages of development, or in facing certain ethical choices that we all face (e.g. between the values of individualism and the values of community).

How might the less ethnocentric approach go today? An obvious move would be for members of each society to look for their own local understanding of what, according to the United Nations, is the ground of human rights—'the dignity of the human person'. One's local explanation of that idea need not repeat my explanation: namely, autonomy, liberty, and minimum provision. It might also include, for example, forms of justice and fairness and well-being that my account does not.[23] But there is a problem for this whole strategy for reducing ethnocentricity. The less ethnocentric approach, on the present interpretation, would come down to finding local values similar to the Enlightenment values of autonomy, liberty, justice, fairness, and so on. It would look for local counterparts of whatever Western values back human rights. It would then have to rely on the indigenous population's seeing how valuable these values or close counterparts of them are, and how they can serve as the ground of human rights. But this is virtually what the more ethnocentric approach does.

The less ethnocentric approach might, of course, aim for greater independence of the Western approach to human rights. It might look, not for local counterparts of Enlightenment values, but for possibly non-equivalent indigenous values that can serve as that society's own peculiar ground for human rights. The Western ground and various non-Western grounds might turn out to support pretty much the same list of human rights. The advantage, it might be thought, in indigenous societies' aiming for independence of Western ideas, would be that they would then accept human rights discourse more readily. Global conversation in terms of human rights could start straightaway. The drawback, however, is that the conversation would be likely to break down early. A useful human rights discourse is not made possible just by agreeing on the *names* of the various rights, which is all that agreement on the list secures. We need also to be able to determine a fair amount of their content to know how to settle some of the conflicts between them. Think of how the international law of human rights would be constrained if it knew only their names. To know their content and ways to resolve their conflicts requires knowing what the values are that ground human rights and to reach some measure of agreement on them. That is, international law requires such knowledge if, as I shall argue later, international law aspires, and should aspire, to incorporate basic human rights with ethical weight. It is hard to tell how well the international community could scrape along agreeing only on the names of human rights; perhaps we are not far from that position now, and the discourse of human rights has, none the less, had some undeniably good results. But we should be much better off if we could agree on the contents of human rights and how to resolve their conflicts. And that constitutes a strong case for favouring the more ethnocentric approach, if it were found feasible.

And it is feasible. The deepest cultural divide in history is not between the West and China (e.g. Confucianism, leaving Buddhism aside as an Indian import), and certainly not the West and Islam (Islam is an Abrahamic religion), but the West and India (Hinduism and Buddhism). The West aims at progress, at the growing achievement of the goods of human life; Hinduism at timeless, changeless being. Westerners see understanding as largely analytic—breaking things down into parts and discovering their interaction; for Hindu metaphysicians knowledge is an intuition of an indivisible whole, and differences between things are illusory. Westerners regard knowledge, in large part, as knowledge of the behaviour of external objects, as in paradigmatically that largely Western achievement, the natural sciences; in contrast, Hindus regard reality as a distinctionless, entirely static *nirvana*. And so on.[24]

But this deep cultural difference is not evidence of a serious current 'problem of ethnocentricity'. It is perfectly proper to use the word 'culture' in this context. The differences between the West and India go far back: the European idea of human rights goes back to the late Middle Ages, and the idea that human beings are made in God's image goes back to Genesis 1: 27. The Buddha was born about 563 BC; Hinduism emerged centuries before that. Each of these religions developed at a time when Europe and India were sufficiently isolated for there to be criteria of identity for their 'cultures'. But that was millennia ago. To address *our* problem of ethnocentricity, we must take account of where each of us is *now*.

Also, the ultimate religious ideals are usually considerably different from, and far less influential in ordinary life than, the rules for everyday conduct that they also teach. Buddhism tells us to extinguish the self, but it also has rules for the whole pack of squabbling, thieving, lying ordinary people. Buddhism has its Five Precepts: do not kill, do not steal, do not lie, do not be unchaste, do not drink intoxicants. Jesus set unattainable standards: be ye therefore perfect; love thy neighbour as thyself. But Christianity never abandoned the down-to-earth Jewish Ten Commandments: thou shalt not steal, nor commit adultery, etc. So, though Indians may have heard occasionally about ultimate goals and ultimate reality, most of them, like most of the rest of humanity, lived their lives well this side of the 'ultimate'.

The picture of India as spiritual, mystical, anti-rational, in sharp contrast to a West of science, rationality, and progress, is a gross oversimplification. It became, none the less, the dominant European picture of India, not least because it was a self-serving picture for European colonists in need of a justification for their presumptuous civilizing mission. But, as Amartya Sen and others have shown, India has a long tradition of secular rationality, scientific investigation, and freedom of thought. It goes back at least to Ashoka, Buddhist Emperor of India in the third century BC, and to the late medieval and early modern period—a striking example given by Sen is the liberal thought of Akbar, the late sixteenth-century Mughal emperor of India.[25] And these rational, liberal ideas spread widely among a middle-class elite during the nineteenth and twentieth centuries.

When Indians came in contact with the development of the natural sciences of the West, they had no trouble whatever, despite reality's being unchanging, understanding and contributing to the laws of its change. Similarly, when Indians campaigned for their independence from Britain, they had no trouble at all, despite autonomy's and liberty's being illusions, articulating what their aims were. When they were told by the British that they were not yet ready for self-government, that they would make mistakes, Gandhi replied: 'Freedom is not worth having if it does not include the freedom to make mistakes.'[26] It may well be the case that the Hindu tradition, with its caste structure as the source of rights and privileges, contains no concept of the rights one has simply in virtue of being human.[27] It may also be the case that the Buddhist tradition, with its focus on perfecting the individual through meditation and insight rather than on improving society, also lacks the concept.[28] But this does not matter. The Hindus (and Muslims) who made up India at Independence seem to have had no trouble grasping the values of liberty and autonomy, and their Constitution (1950) puts beyond doubt that they had no trouble handling the language of human rights.[29] And Aung San Suu Kyi, the determined human rights advocate in next-door Burma, regards human rights as consistent with and as developing Buddhist teaching.[30]

The case of India and the West reveals no serious, present-day divergence in understanding what human rights are and why they are important.[31]

7.4 TOLERANCE

I have already discussed John Rawls's views on human rights.[32] I want now to look at what he says about tolerance between peoples. There may be 'decent' peoples, as Rawls calls them,[33] who reject some of the items on the Enlightenment list of human rights. Some rights may be contrary to deep, sincerely held commitments of theirs—religious beliefs, say, about the role of women. So long as a people counts as 'decent', however, it deserves our tolerance. 'To tolerate', Rawls says, 'means not only to refrain from exercising political sanctions ... to make a people change its ways', but also 'to recognise these non-liberal societies as equal participating members in good standing of the Society of Peoples.'[34] Granting decent, non-liberal peoples this form of respect may encourage them to reform themselves, or at least not discourage reform, while denying them respect might well do so.[35] But there is also a non-instrumental reason to grant them respect: it is their due.

Rawls takes as his example of a decent, non-liberal people an imaginary hierarchical Islamic society, Kazanistan.[36] He attributes the difference in political structure between Kazanistan and a Western liberal country largely to their cultural, particularly religious, differences. For the reasons just given, this seems to me highly doubtful. Rawls's question about tolerance, though, need not be motivated by cultural differences. A decent hierarchical people, according to Rawls, has two defining properties. One is that such a people does not have aggressive aims. The other is that its system of law secures human rights for all, imposes genuine moral obligations upon its members, and its legal officials sincerely and not unreasonably believe that the law is guided by a common good conception of justice.[37] Recall, though, that Rawls substantially shortens the list of human rights and reduces their function.[38] His list omits such typical human rights as freedom of expression, freedom of association (except for the limited form needed for freedom of conscience and religious observance), the right to democratic political participation, and any economic rights that go beyond mere subsistence. And he reduces human rights to two functions: fixing both the rules of war and the grounds for international intervention.

A great obstacle to our accepting Rawls's shortened list of human rights—especially if, like Rawls, we want a list with a realistic chance of being adopted—is that it would never be accepted by the international community. The United Nations' list of human rights is too deeply entrenched for it to be changed quite so greatly. It could no doubt be amended here and there, but not subjected to Rawls's radical surgery at its very heart. The international community would firmly resist the reduction of the discourse of human rights to Rawls's two functions only; it would carry on using human rights to assess the behaviour of a single nation and institutions within a nation; and many of us, I believe, would go on using them to assess even the conduct of individual persons. Rawls, it is true, does not deny that the rights he drops from the list could appear among a people's 'fundamental' or 'international' rights. They are not, though, human rights proper, he says; they are merely 'liberal aspirations'.[39] But this is a radical demotion in their status, and it is this demotion that would be resisted. That raises a question about a strong, unexamined assumption of Rawls's. 'I leave aside', he says, 'the many difficulties of interpreting ... rights and limits, and take their general meaning and tendency as clear enough.'[40] There is, of course, some clarity to them; they are not nonsense. But my first chapter was devoted to arguing that there is an intolerable degree of indeterminacy of sense in what a human right is—an indeterminacy that leaves unclear the criteria both for what should be on the list of human rights and, even more worryingly, what the contents of the individual rights are. This applies also to all the rights on Rawls's own shortened list: for example, the rights to life, liberty, health, and welfare, each of which I shall come to later.[41] We can make our understanding of these rights adequate for our own thought only with the addition of some further substantive value. It need not be my addition, only *some* addition. Once the value is added, however, it will determine which human rights there are, and they cannot then be restricted in the arbitrary way that Rawls chooses to do.

There is another worry. There are grounds for intervention that are not violations of human rights. I argued earlier that the domains of human rights and of justice overlap, but are not congruent.[42] Some matters of justice—for

example, certain forms of retributive and distributive justice—are not matters
of human rights. Imagine, for instance, a country structured socially so that
nearly all of its great prosperity goes to a small white colonial elite, leaving
the mass of the black native population just at subsistence level. If this gross
injustice were also likely to persist for some time, diplomatic or economic
sanctions might well be justified. Think of a country somewhat like South
Africa under apartheid, but with a decent consultation hierarchy that works
well enough to raise the poor to subsistence level but not higher. So far
as his theory goes, Rawls is free to amend it to say that serious violation
of human rights is sufficient, but not necessary, to justify intervention, and
that certain violations of justice (and perhaps yet more) are also sufficient.
Actually, Rawls treats observance of human rights as definitive of a decent
hierarchical society, without mention of retributive or distributive justice.[43]
Admittedly, he does mention as also definitive the possession of 'a common
good conception of justice',[44] but it is doubtful that this requires acceptance
of a principle for distribution of welfare at fairly high levels.[45] Rawls cannot
believe that a common good conception requires a society to raise its members
above subsistence level, because a decent hierarchical society need not do
more than that. My example of the South Africa-like country raises doubts
that subsistence level is high enough. A satisfactory case that the level must
be higher than subsistence is likely to make appeal to something especially
valuable about human status that will not be protected by mere subsistence,
and once that special value starts generating rights, no arbitrary stopping
points are allowable.

The serious weakness in Rawls's functional explanation of human rights
is that it leaves the content of his shortened list—the content both of the
list itself and of each individual right—unworkably obscure. How do we
determine, for example, the minimum of welfare required by human rights?
If one has a further substantive value to appeal to—say, the value attaching
to normative agency—then the minimum would be the somewhat more
generous provision of what is necessary to function effectively as a normative
agent. But it looks as if Rawls could, if he wanted, avail himself of an
altogether different approach to fix the minimum. He could ask: at what
level of welfare would its neglect start to provide prima facie justification for
intervention by other peoples? But confronted with that question, we would
not know how to answer. We should need help from some further substantive
ethical thought. We might, for instance, appeal to the idea of 'the dignity of
the human person', but that suffers badly from vagueness. We should lose the

dignity of our normative agency, for instance, before we sank as low as mere subsistence. Subsistence that forced us to labour all our waking hours just to scratch out an existence from the earth, without leisure, reflection, or hope, brutalized by our conditions, would lack the dignity of normative agency. So, if this were our line of thought, we should still need to determine what sort of 'dignity' is at work in human rights. In any case, Rawls does not seem to avail himself of this approach. Instead, as we have just seen, he assumes that 'the general meaning and tendency' of human rights are already 'clear enough'. But, as I have argued, they are not.

I am not trying here to make a contribution of my own to the understanding of tolerance, important though that matter is. My interest now is human rights, and my conclusion negative. We should not follow Rawls's lead in commandeering the language of human rights to explain intervention. The language that he can provide is too indeterminate in sense to do so, and, once its sense is made more satisfactorily determinate, it will contain what is needed to justify the ampler list of human rights that, for so long, the tradition has championed.

PART II

HIGHEST-LEVEL HUMAN RIGHTS

8

Autonomy

8.1 THE THREE HIGHEST-LEVEL HUMAN RIGHTS

Human rights are protections of our normative agency, the personhood account holds. Normative agency has stages. The first stage consists in our assessing options and thereby forming a conception of a worthwhile life, where, as I said earlier,[1] the sort of 'conception' I have in mind is not a map of the whole of a good life, which is of doubtful value, but characteristically piecemeal and incomplete ideas about what makes life better or worse. That is what I have been calling 'autonomy'. To form and then to pursue that conception, we need various kinds of support: life itself of course, a certain level of health, certain physical and mental capacities, a certain amount of education, and so on. I have been calling these 'minimum provision'. And these are not enough for agency if others then stop us; we must also be free to pursue that conception. I have been calling this 'liberty'. All human rights will then come under one or other of these three overarching headings: autonomy, welfare, and liberty. And those three can be seen as constituting a trio of highest-level human rights.

some degree of well-being

8.2 THE DISTINCTION BETWEEN AUTONOMY AND LIBERTY

This way of distinguishing between autonomy and liberty is not particularly new, but it is not at all common, either. More commonly philosophers use the words 'freedom' or 'liberty' to cover both autonomy and liberty, as I shall use the terms, though in recent decades many have then gone on to distinguish usually two, but sometimes more, 'concepts' of freedom or liberty. Isaiah Berlin's much-discussed distinction between two 'concepts' of liberty is not at all the distinction I want to draw between autonomy and liberty.[2] My distinction comes about this way. The explanation of why normative agency is so valuable to us falls into two parts: we have here, I think, two distinct values.

What I want to identify is not 'autonomy' as it is used in correct, ordinary speech or 'autonomy' in all its varied philosophical employments. My interest is much narrower: namely, autonomy, the particular moral and political value that is the basis of a human right. My interest is, more specifically, the distinction between autonomy and liberty that I have proposed, why this sort of autonomy is valuable, how this value supports a human right, and what the content of that right is.

In the late Middle Ages a gradual but great transformation of ethics began. Previously, mankind had largely been seen as separated from God by an unbridgeable gulf in both knowledge and power. But God, in his goodness, had laid down laws that mapped our road to salvation; our role was to obey them, to submit to God's will. By the late Middle Ages, however, we began to see ourselves as having a more elevated status—indeed, as having been made in God's image. The thought that we are made in God's image first appeared in Genesis (1: 26), but it took time before the Church was ready to draw certain radical moral conclusions from it. We are like God in being normative agents, creators, although we are creators on a limited front; we create ourselves and, to some extent, our personal relations and the world about us. And we are all equal, because equally made in God's image.

This new egalitarian spirit, this new confidence in human capacities, this new expectation of a more active and independent humankind, reset the moral stage. Our moral role changed from obedience to God-given law to compliance with self-given law.[3] This change, which culminated in the eighteenth century, was the working out of an egalitarian and individualist tendency long latent in Christianity, and its completion made possible the unintended consequence of an ethics without God.

The idea of autonomy that emerged in this transition was just the idea I am concerned with here—self-decision. Not every human decision is autonomous. Many decisions are effectively determined by outside influences: by unconscious drives largely shaped by others, by genetic abnormalities such as males with two Y-chromosomes, and so on. What is meant is a decision that results from one's exercising one's capacity to distinguish true values from false, good reasons from bad—in short, the decisions of a normative agent.

Normative agency consists not only in deciding for oneself what is worth doing, but also in doing it. We attach great value not only to the autonomy

---

[margin notes]

*liberty - what are the things that could function as legit/ not legit choices you choose to persue (previous page)

* political - what we do politically has respect for the autonomy of people (you should have say in how you/com. is controlled) polis→city

of our decisions but also to our accomplishing something with our lives by carrying out our decisions—by actually reducing someone's pain, say, or raising a child well, or treating people justly. That is, we also value our liberty.

Autonomy and liberty are different values.[4] And their enemies are different. The enemies of autonomy are indoctrination, brain-washing, domination, manipulation, conformity, conventionality, false consciousness, certain forms of immaturity. The enemies of liberty are compulsion, constraint, impoverishment of options in life. An example will bring out the difference. One can be at liberty but not autonomous—say, so conventionally raised that, without thought, one falls in with society's values, but is still free to pursue them as one wishes. One can be at liberty and autonomous—having chosen one's values, after deliberation, and being free to pursue them as one wishes. The second is a better life. The value of autonomy is separate from the value of liberty.

Autonomy, in our sense, is a particularly ubiquitous value. People adopt different lists of the things that make an individual life go well, though the lists usually have a common core: for example, accomplishing something with one's life, deep personal relations, understanding certain moral and metaphysical matters, and living autonomously and at liberty. But nothing counts as an accomplishment (where this is a term of art used here of a particular prudential value) unless it is one's own choosing. One's deep personal relations are valuable only if the love or affection they involve is based on one's recognition of the other person's value. Understanding, in the relevant sense, can only be autonomous. And obviously one does not live autonomously without autonomy.

8.3 THE VALUE OF AUTONOMY

What is so valuable about autonomy? Is not autonomy, in our sense, the root of a socially fragmenting individualism? Is it not the enemy of fraternity, of solidarity, of homogeneous moral community? But this familiar doubt is a doubt about autonomy's being an unalloyed good, not about its being good. Its value, on my account, is related to its being a constituent of the dignity of the human person. The sense of 'human dignity' that I am invoking must also be specified, because there are several acceptable uses of 'dignity' not relevant to human rights: for example, the dignity that quite properly should be accorded to a person deep in dementia or even to a person's dead body.

The sort of dignity relevant to human rights, however, is that of a highly prized status: that we are normative agents.

These remarks do not constitute an argument for the value of autonomy. To adopt the personhood account of human rights is to adopt normative agency as the interpretation of 'the dignity of the human person' when that phrase is used of the ground of human rights. It is not at all an eccentric interpretation; it is Pico della Mirandola's interpretation in his influential work *The Dignity of Man*, and it is the most common interpretation in the tradition.[5] If normative agency is valuable, it is intrinsically valuable. One can only try to make it sufficiently clear what normative agency is and expect others then to see that it is valuable.[6] Nor have I come near to showing that we really are normative agents, or what would be the consequence for the existence of human rights if we were not, though I shall return to that last matter shortly.

8.4 THE CONTENT OF THE RIGHT TO AUTONOMY

The decisions relevant to autonomy, the specific moral and political value that I want to explain, are decisions about the life to pursue, and of course not all decisions are about that. An adult son whose mother still orders his meals in a restaurant, though he would rather do it himself, has less autonomy, in one established sense of the word, but the mother does not infringe her son's autonomy, in our sense. Restaurant meals are not important enough for that. They could be for some quite unusual persons, but they are not so for most of us. If the son let others take his investment decisions for him or decisions about what to believe in science and mathematics, he might not lose any autonomy, in our sense, either. He might not, even if his letting others take these decisions was not itself an autonomous decision of his. Decisions about investments are not, for most people, part of their thinking about or pursuing a worthwhile life. It can even sometimes be highly desirable—prudent, say, or particularly responsible—to abandon some forms of autonomy. If one were hopeless at science, one's best way to form scientific beliefs might be to trust the authorities. If, however, the son let his mother decide what he should do with his life, he clearly would lose autonomy, in our sense. He would lose it even if he voluntarily delegated his life decisions to her. Then there are cases where it is less clear what to say. He might be totally wrapped up in his career—novel writing, say—and on election day merely asks his mother to tell him how to vote. Sometimes, I should say, this would involve no sacrifice of autonomy in our sense, but sometimes it would. When the issues in an election are especially important, one can have an obligation to make up one's own mind, and then not to do so would considerably derogate from one's autonomy, in our sense.

These cases show that there are senses of 'autonomy' in which it is false that the more autonomous we are, the better. Exaggerating the desirability of autonomy can undermine justified deference to authority or trust in others.[7] It can be rational to abnegate autonomy, though none of these rational abnegations will be abnegations of autonomy, in our sense, because they do not abnegate dignity-conferring autonomy—that is, the dignity of being a normative agent. Nor does the person whose surrender of autonomy, in our sense, is itself a paradigm of an autonomous act, also in our sense—say, a monk's surrendering his autonomy to his abbot—lose this sort of dignity.

How demanding are the standards for autonomy, in our sense? In medical practice nowadays, 'patient autonomy' often comes down to 'informed consent', which in turn often comes down to a doctor's explaining to the patient what the proposed treatment involves, its risks and its alternatives, and the patient's then signing a consent form. But this standard is clearly too low. The patient may well be under too much stress to think straight. The doctor's explanation may be too brief or too technical for the patient sufficiently to understand. And the doctor describing the options is likely to be the person who, in the first place, chose the recommended option.

In reaction to this, it is then easy to make the standard for autonomy too high. For example, one might now say that a decision is autonomous if, and only if, the person deciding appreciates fully the weight of all the relevant reasons, all of whose inferences are faultless, and whose decision is not influenced in a decisive way by anything but these reasons and inferences. But this standard is so high that it may rule out autonomous wrongdoing. If an action is autonomous only if it follows from an autonomous decision, and if a decision is autonomous only if all the reasons have been properly weighed and the decision is the correct one, then actions flowing from the incorrect decision are not autonomous, and so not blameworthy. This is an objection often made against Kant. If, as Kant thinks, an autonomous action must rise above the causal network and be determined by no feelings or attitudes or desires or pleasures or pains, all of which are heteronomous, then autonomous doing, it seems, can only be right doing. Many Kantians have tried to rebut this objection,[8] but none to my mind successfully. But even if it is rebuttable,

Kant's sort of autonomy requires a purity of rationality that is unattainable. We exercise our rationality through thought; thought of any complexity requires complex language; and language is a cultural artefact, and thus part of the causal network. It is what the cultural community devised to satisfy various human needs and to reflect its sense of importance. Each language has its own accidents of development, some happy and some unhappy. It is hard for us to know what the accidents of development in our own language have been, so it is hard to know how much one's thought is affected, for good or ill, by them. We have, from time to time, reformed and improved our language in response to distortions we come to detect in it; for example, we stopped talking about 'humours' and developed instead the modern language of physiology and psychology. But at any one time there remain distortions in our language of which we are unaware. These distortions matter less if one has to focus only on blatant failures in rationality, such as contradictions, as Kant does. But Kant needs to appeal to not only contradictions in formulation but also contradictions in the will, and at least our judgements about the latter are likely to be affected by distortions in our language.

Let us therefore look in the logical space between the first, apparently too low standard and the second, apparently too high standard. Think of the common phenomenon of one's shifting one's position in a chair, without at all attending to it, to relieve the growing discomfort of remaining too long in one position. There is usually no conscious registering of the discomfort nor a conscious decision to act to relieve it; we just do it. Cats and dogs do the same, and the human mental process involved may be much like the feline or canine mental process. But does this fact (if it is a fact) make a human being's shifting position in this way heteronomous? Does its cause lie outside a purely rational, conscious centre, the workings of which are undetermined by feelings, dispositions, genetic make-up, and so on. Kant agreed with Hume that feelings, dispositions, and so on exclude reason. Kant was, like Hume, a subjectivist, or intersubjectivist, on judgements about prudential values but, unlike Hume, an objectivist about moral norms. But, to my mind, there are good reasons to think that rationality enters importantly also into the identification of human ends or interests, that judgements about them are subject to standards of correctness and incorrectness, that they can be objective. These are large subjects, but I have discussed them above and in other writings.[9]

If the identification of human interests is indeed a matter of rational decision, then the following would be a paradigm case of an autonomous decision: I come to understand that one's accomplishing something with one's life, other things being equal, makes one's life better, certainly better than, say, the aimless life I have been living up till now. And if certain conditions obtain, I may, as a result of this understanding, change my approach to life. This paradigm example has the form: registering a value or disvalue and then taking action appropriate to it. And if judgements about what makes an individual better off or what satisfies certain characteristic human desires is subject to standards of correctness and incorrectness, then perhaps such judgements can be autonomous. There is a sense in which my feelings, desires, dispositions, and reactions, as well as my consciously recognized reasons, can be my own. The fact that, as in the case of my shifting in my chair, my feelings, desires, and so on are like those in virtually all other people, and sometimes overlap with those in cats and dogs, and are often genetically based, does not remove all senses in which they are *mine*. They are my perfectly sensible reactions. They display the same form as what I just proposed as a paradigm case of autonomous action: registering a value or disvalue (accomplishment in the one case, discomfort in the other) and responding appropriately to it. Now think of cases much like shifting in one's chair but with increasing elements of consciousness and thought: pulling one's hand away from the tap when the water turns out to be scalding; or closing one's eyes when they tire in the light; or, if one finds that closing one's eyes is not enough, also turning off the light. In all of these cases there is a registering of a disvalue, more or less consciously, and an acting in response to it, more or less deliberately. Are these actions autonomous or heteronomous?

I think that if we employed Kant's way of distinguishing the categories of 'autonomous' and 'heteronomous', we should be hard put to say. But those are not the categories for us to appeal to here. We are interested in autonomy, the moral and political value that is the ground for the human right. There is, on the personhood account, a material constraint on autonomy: we are interested in the autonomy involved in forming a conception of a worthwhile life. The autonomy involved in what I called the paradigm case is certainly the kind we are interested in, while the other examples are not, if only because discomfort in one's lower back or pain in one's hand from the scalding water are on too particular a level. Forming a conception of a worthwhile life typically operates on a more general level—the level of concepts such as 'pain' or 'discomfort'. When natural rights were embedded in a Christian metaphysics, what mattered to our possession of the rights was that we were created in God's image, that we were ourselves creators of our own lives. The cat's capacity to register discomfort and consequently to shift position falls well short of this God-like capacity. Indeed, no known species but *Homo sapiens* has the capacity that carries autonomy, in our sense. The registering of value and disvalue that contributes the sort of autonomy that supports a human right involves complex language: at the least, the language of prudential values (many of which words involve long-term, even whole-life evaluations) and the language needed for weighing values against one another and for arriving at an all-things-considered judgement about them. If some non-human species have what might count as a rudimentary language, there is not a scrap of evidence that they have language of the complexity needed for normative agency.[10] It is not that the uniqueness of human beings in this regard is important to establish. There may, for all we know, be rational aliens elsewhere in the universe with equally complex languages.[11] But the uniqueness of human beings among known species is enough to justify the ground of human rights that the United Nations has adopted: the dignity of the human person. There is no problem in showing that the autonomy that we are after is highly valuable. It is not the autonomy that we are after unless it *is* highly valuable.

It is common for writers on autonomy to reach for a brief phrase that, they think, summarizes the idea. I earlier called autonomy 'self-decision'. To my mind, we could also, in the sterner spirit of Kant and Rousseau, call it 'self-rule' or 'self-legislation'. But, once autonomy is distinguished from liberty, certain phrases are misleading. The term 'self-determination' suggests not only forming a conception of a worthwhile life but also, to some extent, realizing it. And the phrases 'self-definition' and 'authorship of one's own life' can mislead in the same way.

So the picture of the sort of autonomy that we are after is this: a capacity to recognize good-making features of human life, both prudential and moral, which can lead to the appropriate motivation and action. This autonomy is a threshold notion, with a fairly low threshold. Most adult human beings have this capacity to the degree that confers 'dignity' and 'worth'. It seems to me clear that above the threshold different persons will have different capacities to recognize good-making features; it is just that these further differences no longer matter to the 'dignity' or 'worth' in question.[12] And on this conception there is the possibility of autonomous wrongdoing. A person can have the capacity that constitutes autonomy, yet not exercise it. I might have the capacity to appreciate vividly the value of accomplishing something with my life but, for one of various possible reasons, not appreciate it vividly enough to stop me from sinking back into frittering my life away. The capacity in question is a capacity not for doing right but for understanding and imagination, which may of course, if exercised, lead to doing right. I should be likely to kick myself for not seeing vividly enough the benefits of accomplishing something with my life, though, as it may seem to me, I clearly could have. And if I had, the conditions may have been such that I would have, in response, changed the direction of my life.

8.5 AUTONOMY AND FREE WILL: WHAT IF WE ARE NOT AUTONOMOUS?

If normative agency is not valuable, or we can never rise to it, the personhood case for human rights collapses. It is not that there would then be no reason to protect our capacity for, and exercise of, our deliberation and action; it is, rather, that human rights, on my account, would not be it.

There is nothing in my picture of autonomous action to explain why I failed to understand the value of accomplishment vividly enough, or why in the same situation I failed and you did not. The explanation might be that I am depressed and in some deep recess of my mind harbour the potent thought that I do not deserve a good life. Or it might be that talk of accomplishment reminds me of long-past lectures from my parents about pulling my socks up, and I quickly switch off. There are many explanations that might rightly undermine my belief that, though I failed to, I could have. Perhaps I never could have done otherwise.

There is a way of maintaining the value of autonomy no matter how the free-will dispute comes out. One could claim that personhood in general, and autonomy in particular, are only instrumentally valuable.[13] If so, could we not continue to derive human rights from them as protections of their great (instrumental) value? Indeed, some may find this a pleasingly deflationary account of the value of autonomy. All that one need claim is that it is good for people to have their interests and desires met, and that they are more likely to be met if people take their own decisions, on a less rigorous standard of self-decision than I have hitherto suggested. Still, this deflationary move has its problems. It will eventually require extraordinarily large-scale calculations of consequences, which may be beyond our powers.

Think back to the familiar challenge to freedom of the will. It seems to me that often—perhaps because of depression or a deafness to anything reminiscent of a parental lecture—a person could not have acted otherwise. What is doubtful is that one never can. Suppose that a friend tells me how important accomplishment is to a good life, that I understand what he means by 'accomplishment' and see why it is so valuable, and that this understanding is the dominant cause of my subsequent change in direction. Whatever the truth about freedom of the will is, though, it is too much to try to establish it in this book. I think that the non-instrumental conception of autonomy is the right one to use in an account of human rights, and no doubt enough other people do too for me to go on following this line of thought.

liberty:
- freedom to act w/out constraint
- cannot infringe on others liberty

9

Liberty

9.1 HIGHEST-LEVEL RIGHTS

I have proposed that we explain personhood in terms of autonomy, liberty, and minimum provision. All more specific human rights can then be seen as falling under one or other of these three abstract headings. Under liberty, for example, fall several well-known freedoms, such as freedom of expression, of religion, of assembly, and so on. My interest here is not any of these specific freedoms, but liberty in general — liberty, the high-level right.

9.2 BROAD AND NARROW INTERPRETATIONS
OF LIBERTY

There is a broad conception of liberty in circulation — Thomas Hobbes, John Locke, Jeremy Bentham, John Stuart Mill, and Isaiah Berlin, among many others, have used it[1] — that regards any restriction on my doing what I want as a restriction, no doubt often justified, on my liberty. If, for instance, I want to drive the wrong way down a one-way street, then, on the broad conception, the traffic restriction infringes my liberty — though probably justifiably.

There is nothing wrong with this broad use. It is well established both in ordinary speech and in philosophical discourse. But it is not the use relevant to the human right to liberty. There is a material constraint on the human right to liberty. The considerable values that human rights protect do not include our being able to satisfy any wish, even whim, that happens to cross our minds. Rather, they protect our being able to form our own conception of a worthwhile life, piecemeal and incomplete as our ideas will be, and then to pursue it. So liberty protects only what is part of our personhood, and our being free to drive the wrong way down a one-way street is certainly not that. I describe, of course, the material constraint arising from the personhood account. If a different substantive account were thought better, there would be a different material constraint, but still such a constraint.

There is, as well, a formal constraint on liberty. The case for my having a right to liberty is equally a case for other persons' also having one. At most, each of us has a right to liberty compatible with equal liberty for all. So, to take an obvious example, no one's freedom of religion extends to Thuggee, ritual robbery and murder, practised by the Thugs, a Hindu sect, worshippers of the goddess Kali, which the British quite rightly suppressed in the early nineteenth century. A less extreme case is present-day religious sects that deny women human rights. This constraint, too, considerably narrows the content of the right to liberty.

These arguments for the use of the narrow interpretation of liberty seem to me all right so far as they go, but they do not yet go far enough. We must return to them.

9.3 'PURSUIT'

Liberty guarantees not the realization of one's conception of a worthwhile life, but only its *pursuit*. Here is another word that needs explanation. What does society commit itself to in accepting the duty to protect freedom of pursuit?

One can be denied liberty in many ways. One can be constrained—physically by another person, or by a law with swingeing penalties, or by the threatening presence of an absolute ruler, or by severe social disapproval. Or one can be compelled to live in a way that one does not want to—by a state or a church or a family, each with its own idea about how one should live. Or one can find oneself placed in conditions that themselves allow only a very few ways of life, one's own rationally chosen way not among them.

Constraint and compulsion are familiar enemies of liberty, although the forms they take are not always easy to recognize. Denial of liberty need not take the form of active intervention. The mere presence of a powerful agency able to intervene can be enough to cow people into self-censorship. And liberty is not fully satisfied simply by non-interference in the way of life that one has in fact chosen; it requires also that one would not have been interfered with had one chosen another way of life—indeed, any way of life in the protected domain of liberty. However, the third enemy of liberty, paucity of options, is less familiar, and more needs to be said about it.

A person's right to liberty can be infringed only by another agent. If our options are narrowed by acts of nature or by large-scale economic or social events not under human control, no one's liberty is infringed. A young male Inuit living in an igloo in the Arctic a few centuries ago had little choice of ways of life; his and his family's survival depended upon his devoting most of his waking hours to hunting for food. His way of life was determined for him by an extraordinarily exigent nature. But nature cannot be accused of violating his liberty.

Then consider a case at the other extreme. When the Taliban took power, they left Afghan women still able to choose autonomously among available options and freely to pursue the option chosen. The Taliban had simply grossly narrowed the choice, leaving only the options that accorded with their own conception of an Islamic woman's life, and leaving many Afghan women with no option that they themselves considered choice-worthy. The Taliban were, of course, gross violators of liberty; their deliberate reduction of options was coercion.

The same form of coercion can happen on a small scale too. Parents may, for the salvation of their children's souls, settle far from all corrupting society, without modern technology and with no books but the Bible. Here their children's cramped circumstances are deliberately created by their parents. Here, too, the children can still autonomously choose and freely pursue one of the remaining ways of life. It is just that they can not realistically choose to be a research scientist or a philosopher or a painter or a poet or a composer; the resources, tradition, training, and stimulus that one would need would be missing. And if one's own desired choice lies outside what one's parents have left available, one's liberty has clearly been violated.

Most commonly, the restrictions we face are a mix: partly nature-made, partly human-made. One's long-established culture might itself limit one's options, without intentional action on the part of anyone now living. Children might find themselves born into an isolated, technology-free, Bible-dominated society merely because their distant ancestors chose to live that way. Still, a culture typically includes prohibitions and requirements that, if not imposed by the present generation, could still be eased or abolished by it. If a child in the society managed to come up with an informed desire to rejoin the larger society and become, say, a philosopher, and the parents, or the elders of the community, prevented it, that too would be a violation of the child's liberty.

What the *pursuit* of a conception of a worthwhile life largely requires, and what a society might sometimes have some obligation to help provide, are the all-purpose means to pursue any plausible conception of a worthwhile life: that is, education, basic health, minimum material provision, help to overcome lack of key capacities, a fairly rich array of options, and so on. To what level of all-purpose means? To the level needed to live as a normative agent.

Compare the following two forms of impoverishment of options. Suppose all professional football teams went bankrupt, denying to many a major form of enjoyment and to some especially fanatical fans the source of their major interest in life and their primary sense of belonging. In contrast, suppose all firms involved in the circulation of information and ideas went bankrupt. Society, I should say, would have a duty, correlative to human rights, to remedy the second bankruptcy but not the first. That is not to say that there are not other sorts of reasons why society might think it ought also to remedy the first. But without the circulation of information and ideas, one cannot either properly form a conception of a worthwhile life, or effectively pursue it, or satisfactorily live it.

Society does not have an obligation even to ensure equal opportunity in the realization of one's conception. First of all, the job of equalizing opportunity is far beyond its capacity. Every conception of a worthwhile life has its own degree of difficulty of realization. One might have one's heart set on a career as a philosopher, but there may not be many jobs available—many fewer, for example, than in law. It would be within society's power to create more jobs for philosophers, even as many as in law proportionate to aspirants, but the aim of making every conception of a worthwhile life that might crop up equally realizable is as impossible for governments to bring off as it would be economically damaging for them to try to do so. Besides, there are conceptions—say, achieving a mountaineering feat that only a half-dozen persons in the world are physically capable of—in which the low chance of success may lie in an aspirant's physique, which society has scant power to change.

Not only can society not bring about such equality of opportunity, there is also no human right to it. What human rights guarantee is that one be able to live the life of a normative agent. In a society with an ample range of options, if one cannot realize one conception, there are others: other lives that one can also value and that can become fully worthwhile lives for one to live. Some good things in life—for example, enjoyment—characteristically have many sources; enjoyment can be found in many different directions. And generally one can find fulfilment in various sorts of lives. For the many of whom that is true, there is equality of opportunity on a more general level: not equal opportunity to achieve any particular conception of a worthwhile life that one might choose, but equal opportunity to make a good life for oneself. So long as the various ground floors guaranteed by human rights are in place, the obstacles to making a good life are likely to be deep inside oneself, beyond the reach of others.

In general, we must simply accept, and build our lives from, the range of options with which fortune has endowed us. Society cannot do much to alter it, and the life of a normative agent does not require more than this.

But of course there are exceptions. I have been emphasizing what society cannot do. But it can and should sometimes enlarge the range of options, even in a society with a large choice already. The elders of the isolated Christian fundamentalist community that I imagined above can allow the child who wants to become a philosopher to move to the larger society. Otherwise, they would violate the child's liberty. Even in our own much larger and more varied society, we have to be sensitive to similar violations of liberty: that is, restrictions imposed by our culture so familiar to us that we scarcely even notice them, but well within society's capacity to remove. Our culture is not any of our doing, nor all of our doing; it has evolved over millennia. But if there are same-sex couples who want to form some sort of union and raise children—who want, that is, to have the rich, stable, recognized, respected relations that are at the heart of most people's conceptions of a worthwhile life—and, because of our ethical traditions, there are no social institutions to allow it, then we should create one or other form of them. This too, I believe, is an issue of liberty. No matter how many options there are already, this one, because of its centrality to characteristic human conceptions of a worthwhile life, must be added.

But if, when jobs for philosophers run out, we may ask the aspiring philosopher to choose an alternative career, why may we not ask the same-sex couple to live without legal recognition of their union? Indeed, why can we not, as some today would like to, return to the social conditions of a century ago: criminalization of sexual relations between members of the same sex, prohibition of their begetting children, and so on? Homosexuals could still find celibate alternatives that would allow them to have fulfilled lives and to preserve their normative agency.

To my mind, our answer should be this. What is at stake for same-sex couples are several of the most important components of a good life available to human beings. Most same-sex couples could not have rich and deep personal relations in the conditions of a hundred years ago. Their affection would be stifled. They would not have, or raise, children, which for most of us, homosexual or not, is our best chance of accomplishing something important with our lives. Unless one is exceptionally talented, unless one is a Rembrandt or a Mozart, or at least a David Hockney or a Cole Porter, raising one's children well is probably the only great accomplishment available to us. Some persons could no doubt rise gloriously above the restrictions of a hundred years ago; some persons do not want deep personal relations or to raise children. But the great majority of us do, and the restrictions of a hundred years ago would deny same-sex couples some of the greatest, most widely distributed, most deeply embedded—sometimes even genetically embedded—least easily substituted ends of human life that there are. And although these claims about the conditions a hundred years ago apply less strongly to same-sex couples today, they apply strongly enough to support the same conclusions.

The case of my parents' moving me to a simple, Bible-dominated society to prevent me from becoming a philosopher is in crucial ways different from society's telling an aspiring philosopher, in the absence of jobs for philosophers, to choose a different career. If liberty were to demand that a job as a philosopher be created for the aspiring philosopher, it would demand that the same be done for everyone else in relevantly similar conditions. This would turn into an enormous and costly social programme; the opportunity costs for society would be heavy. My parents intended to thwart my philosophical ambitions, though there were jobs for philosophers available in the larger society. But autonomy requires that an individual normative agent be the final arbiter of his or her conception of a worthwhile life. When we think of agency, we have a tendency to think primarily of autonomy (using the term in my way) and to underestimate the importance of liberty—that is, of being able, with normal chances of success, to pursue one's conception of a worthwhile life. Some restrictions on the pursuit are necessary: for example, to ensure equal liberty for all, to accommodate demands of justice, to prevent wasteful, inefficient use of public funds. But restrictions beyond those, and perhaps one or two others, are unjustified. That is why my parents violate my liberty in moving me to the Bible-dominated community, but why society does not violate the liberty of the aspiring philosopher when jobs in philosophy run out and the aspirant must choose another career.

Liberty has a wide application, but one must keep it within sensible bounds.[2] For example, parents rightly take it as their duty to acquaint their children with the world, to give them sound values. Much of the education they give their children is beyond controversy: the seven-times table, looking both ways before crossing a road. The truth or usefulness of those lessons cannot be gainsaid. But when it comes to passing on a religion or a set of values or good taste, that is not always so. Children are then at risk of indoctrination. Indeed, it sometimes seems that parents cannot help but infringe their child's liberty to some degree; their job, after all, is to encourage certain inclinations and suppress others. On my account, of course, very young children do not yet have any human rights to be infringed. But a parent's influence can be long-term, and the values they inculcate may in time close off certain kinds of life for their mature child.

When that happens, have the parents infringed their child's liberty? If what the parents have done amounts to indoctrination or brain-washing, then yes. If, on the contrary, the parents were only trying to equip the child properly for life and the closing off of options was an unintended consequence, then it is harder to say. Respect for one's children's liberty requires that parents also teach them open-mindedness, high intellectual standards, and proper scepticism. It is not that the parent's intention is decisive; a well-intentioned parent might still have been heavy-handed and should have known better. What is decisive, I should say, is that at a certain point moral criticism of parental education becomes inappropriate. Such education generally aims at the good of the child; if the child's liberty is at stake, it is not all that is at stake. We should have, at the least, to weigh the gains from the education against the possible losses of liberty. And children's education is a complex and poorly understood process. Moral criticism, even mild moral criticism, is appropriate only if agents have a greater degree of control over outcomes than is present here. Contrast the case of education with this case: when a government justifiably detains suspected terrorists without trial, it does not *violate* the liberty of the innocent persons unintentionally detained among them, though it does clearly *infringe* it. That is the distinction that these two words have come to mark. But cases of responsible education of children are different from these cases of detention. A government knows perfectly well how to avoid infringing people's liberty: charge and try suspects and release whomever it cannot prove to be guilty. But beyond a certain point parents do not know how to educate their children without risk of permanently closing off options for them. Parents do not now, and may never, understand the processes of education well enough for that. If the term 'infringe' implies any moral disapproval, it is then inappropriate. The same applies to criticism, blame, punishment, psychotherapy, and so on; if well done, they do not infringe liberty.

9.4 NEGATIVE AND POSITIVE SIDES OF LIBERTY

Liberty is often said to be a negative right, and thus easily complied with. One can respect the liberty of the whole of humanity at a stroke, it has been said, simply by minding one's own business.[3] But the picture is not so simple when one recalls paucity of options. Then liberty may also include positive duties.

Does liberty really have a positive side?[4] I am sure it does, for the following reasons. Suppose my family had blocked my wish to become a philosopher by the crudest means imaginable: they locked me in my room at the first sign of my wish. This is what I called 'constraint'. But suppose that my parents were less crass and, with the same end in mind, moved the family when I was young away from all society, leaving me only the Bible to read. This is what I called 'paucity of options'. Both the constraint and the deliberate impoverishment of options would have been merely different ways of achieving the same end: stopping me from becoming a philosopher. My parents, I should say, should no more have deliberately impoverished my options than they should have locked me in my room. Now suppose that I grew up in a similarly impoverished setting but that it was not shaped by any recent generation. My parents, say, were content to live in it because its restrictions happened to fit the simple pious life they sought. Suppose, also, that I had somehow developed an informed wish to become a philosopher and already felt deeply alienated from the few ways of life possible in my society. My parents, let us say, could meet my wish (they had money to send me away to university) but for my own good, as they saw it, chose not to. Here too, I should say, my parents would have violated my liberty. Unlike the previous case, they do not have to reverse an earlier illiberal act of their own; here they have a positive duty to make the options wider. This example throws doubt on the sharpness of the distinction between positive and negative rights.

There is also a more general argument, which I used earlier, that does the same.[5] The content of a right defines the content of its correlative duties: to put it roughly, what one person has a right to demand, some other agent has a duty to supply. I called these the primary duties correlative to rights. But there are also secondary duties: duties to promote human rights, duties to monitor their observance, and duties to ensure compliance with them, when that is indeed feasible. Certain of these secondary duties are so close to their related primary duties as to be treatable, for all practical purposes, as one. The primary duty to follow fair procedures in taking decisions about people's life, liberty, and property is, in our actual circumstances, indistinguishable from the secondary duty to create and maintain a fair judicial system. My conclusion earlier was that it would be artificial to regard a right to procedural justice and a right to the social institutions needed for any realistic hope of procedural justice as other than the same human right. Similarly, the primary duty to respect people's liberty is, in our circumstances, indistinguishable from the secondary duty to protect people's liberty. That some secondary duties merge in this way with their primary duty undermines the belief that there are purely negative rights.

9.5 HOW DEMANDING IS THE RIGHT?

How demanding is the positive side of liberty? To answer, let me begin by listing the constraints to which its correlative duties would be subject.

First, the formal and material constraints mentioned earlier in connection with the negative side of liberty apply as well to its positive side. The formal constraint would say here: one person cannot claim a broader range of options than is compatible with an equally broad range for others. If my conception of a worthwhile life turns out, even for the best of reasons, to be so expensive that its being made available to me would close down options equally important to you, then the positive side of liberty gives me no right to it.

Second, the material constraint would say here: liberty applies to the final stage of agency, namely to the pursuit of one's conception of a worthwhile life. By no means everything we aim at matters to that. Therefore, society will accept a person's claim to the protection of liberty only if the claim meets the material constraint that what is at stake is indeed conceivable as mattering to whether or not we function as normative agents. The obvious danger with this constraint is that society might find conceivable only what it finds congenial. Still, a group of people who, citing liberty, insisted on being allowed to have sexual intercourse in public would rightly be met with scepticism. Is that really an issue of liberty? Is public nudity? Are even some practices that one might think society should allow, such as public suckling of babies?

Third, liberty may not require broadening options restricted entirely by nature. Remember the Inuit. Besides, no agents in that case were able to change what so limited their options—the Arctic climate—and *ought* implies *can*. Even in the case of an isolated, narrowly pious community, it is not easy, and often not possible, for someone single-handedly, or even with others, to ease a deeply embedded cultural prohibition or requirement, let alone abolish it.

Fourth, liberty is not a right to a worthwhile life itself, but merely a right to pursue it with no more impediments than those imposed by mother nature, including, prominently, human nature.

Fifth, liberty seldom requires the availability of the very particular form of option that a person has settled on. Most individual conceptions of a worthwhile life have alternatives, as good or nearly as good, and a person may reasonably be asked to find an alternative, if the form first chosen is costly and reduces options for others.

Finally, there is an important general constraint. Our options are provided by nature and culture and economic growth and scientific and technological advance. Human beings are then given to restricting them. A positive duty that liberty imposes is that some of us sometimes do something to remove some of these restrictions. But many think (I among them) that there is a sizeable area in which partiality to one's own family and chosen institutions and aims is permitted. That there is an area of permitted partiality restricts the impartial claims that can be made on us, including even the claims of human rights.

In the light of these constraints, how demanding is liberty likely to prove? One can easily satisfy the negative side of liberty by not poking one's nose into other people's business.

The demands of the positive side, of course, are not so easily met. In a deliberately severely restricted society, such as Taliban-run Afghanistan, the duty that falls on those Afghans capable of effective resistance will be heavy but, in compensation, their natural motivation to resist is also likely to be great. Still, self-interest and permitted partiality impose powerful limits on the duty even then.

At the other extreme, in a liberal society like ours with quite a rich array of options, the demand would be light. It is not that liberal societies do not fail in the positive duties of liberty. Remember same-sex marriage. But do I, then, as things stand now, have a duty to work for the introduction of same-sex marriage? I can improve my society in many different ways, and I have leeway as to whom I choose to benefit. I also have my permitted domain of partiality. What is needed is for *some* people to work for the introduction of same-sex marriage; not all are needed. And some of the most directly interested parties are, in the form of gay-rights organizations, already at work to that end. It is natural to leave much of the job, if they will do it, to those with the greatest motivation.

It is ironic that the potentially most demanding side to liberty was originally thought of as purely negative: non-interference. If our primary duty of non-interference is best treated as absorbing our secondary duty to protect one another from interference, then liberty may require police, lawyers, courts, armies, navies, and nuclear deterrents. In any case, the defence of our liberty would require at least some of that costly protection. To know how much, we should have to decide the actual ends that this massive defensive shield serves: it clearly serves more ends than just the liberty of individual citizens.

9.6 MILL'S 'ONE VERY SIMPLE PRINCIPLE' OF LIBERTY

Most anglophone philosophers believe that John Stuart Mill has given us a near definitive account of liberty.[6] Mill's principle of liberty, what he calls his 'one very simple principle', is that society (i.e. not just the government with its legal sanctions, but also churches and other powerful shapers of public opinion with their social sanctions) may forcefully control public (other-affecting) actions, but not private (self-affecting) actions.[7] What I suggest as the protected area is not the *private* sphere, but the sphere of *personhood*, and they are not the same. Whether or not I wear a necktie now and then will have no effect on my choosing and pursuing my idea of a worthwhile life. It is too trivial for that. So I should say that necktie wearing falls outside the protected area of liberty. My college requires everyone, willy-nilly, to wear academic gowns at certain dinners in Hall, but on my account of human rights it is not thereby infringing anyone's liberty, even a very minor one. Yet, whether or not I wear a gown falls within my private sphere: I do not harm others by dressing, within limits, as I please. So it seems to me implausible to take 'privacy' as definitive of liberty. We do not attach value to the private as such. If I could not care less whether I wear a gown at dinner but in fact do not do so, my being made to by my college is an intrusion into my private sphere, but it is hard to see any ground for my minding. The grounds that one might plausibly advance for minding, Mill's own perhaps, are really covert appeals to personhood. Stopping me from wearing the clothes I want, as inessential as any particular set of clothes may be to my human standing, will, if it goes far enough, touch my self-respect. To deny me freedom to express my own taste may eventually threaten my status as a self-determiner. Exactly which clothes I choose may be trivial, but my status as an individual centre of taste and choice is not. This is beginning to sound like something valuable in a way that might just attract the protection of liberty because it is getting close to an appeal to personhood.

Consider this example. Our legislators are debating a ban on smoking in all indoor public eating places. Previous legislation had already required smokers to eat at some remove from non-smokers, but now the swell of opinion is for an outright ban. The smokers protest, invoking Mill. They are not harming anyone, they say, so a ban will violate their liberty. Now suppose they do indeed harm no one. The smokers are already kept far enough apart that there is no risk to the health of the rest by passive smoking. It is just that the rest dislike the smell. Still, dislike is not harm, the smokers are quick to point out. But Mill's harm test imposes much too stiff a burden of proof on the rest. Why can they not just say that smoking makes them enjoy themselves less? After all, what is at stake for the smokers is usually that smoking allows them to enjoy themselves more. Exceptional circumstances aside, this is a clash between the enjoyment of some and the enjoyment of others. Why not just settle it by finding out where the balance of enjoyment lies? Why introduce liberty? It just erects a powerful protective barrier around the enjoyments of the one group at the expense of the enjoyments of the other (possibly larger) group. Mill's harm test wrongly turns these cases into issues of liberty, while the personhood test does not.

Mill and I are, admittedly, looking for different things in a principle of liberty. I am looking for an account of liberty, the human right, that fits all cases, large social scale and small interpersonal scale. Mill is looking for something narrower: the limits on social institutions in exercising their power to restrict individuals' behaviour.[8] Still, as what I say about liberty is also meant to apply to social action, the conflict between Mill and me remains.

This conflict brings me back to the choice between broad and narrow interpretations of liberty. My earlier remarks left a problem about the choice unsolved, which arises like this. Liberty, indeed any human right, not being basic in the whole moral structure, needs grounds; it needs sufficiently determinate existence conditions by reference to which we can tell whether the term is used correctly or incorrectly. But once there are existence conditions (e.g. as specified by the personhood account), there follow material constraints on the content of the right. In order to decide what is and is not an issue of liberty, society must decide, according to the personhood account, what can and cannot conceivably matter to whether we function as normative agents. But, as I noted earlier, that seems altogether too dangerous a decision to leave in society's hands. And Mill's account of liberty seems to have the great virtue of avoiding that danger.

So should we, after all, return to the broad interpretation of liberty centred on human desires? What human beings desire has the advantage of being a matter of fact, often quite a plain matter of fact. Even my personhood account may lead me to abandon my earlier allegiance to the narrow interpretation. There is the second ground for human rights: practicalities. Perhaps when we start thinking about formulating a principle of liberty suitable for actual social circumstances, we shall be drawn to simplify in the way in which the broad interpretation simplifies.

I think not. The broad interpretation of liberty, too, cannot be without constraints. It cannot plausibly treat literally any restriction on one's doing what one wants as an infringement of liberty—for example, the murderous desires of someone gone berserk, or the imprudent desire of an infant to touch a hot kettle, or the desire of a colonist to enslave the native population. The third desire would violate the formal constraint: liberty compatible with equal liberty for all.[9] The first two desires are not the desires of responsible agents. The broad interpretation would have to be supplemented by some requirement of rationality and some requirement of respect for the interests of others.

Mill meets both requirements: the first by limiting the application of his principle to persons 'open to rational persuasion', and the second by applying it only to actions that do not 'harm' others. This is, of course, merely Mill's particular way of meeting the two requirements, but every broad interpretation of liberty would have to be accompanied by some such restrictions. For instance, James Fitzjames Stephen, a prominent Victorian jurisprudent and utilitarian critic of Mill of a distinctly conservative bent, also employed the broad interpretation of liberty and also imposed his own, rather different restrictions on it.[10] If liberty is broad, and so a kind of licence, Stephen reasonably asks, what is so good about it? Surely, whether it is good or bad to be free to pursue what one wants all depends upon what one wants.[11] In place of Mill's harm principle, and in order to get a domain of liberty more restricted than Mill's, Stephen imposed a three-point utilitarian test for permitted coercion: coercion is permitted if 'the object aimed at is good, if the compulsion employed such as to attain it, and if the good obtained overbalances the inconvenience of the compulsion itself'.[12] At a time when utilitarianism was a radical doctrine, Stephen used it, along with pessimistic assumptions about human nature, to churn out conclusions 'much more akin to the tenets of Hobbes, Burke, or Carlyle than those maintained by Jeremy Bentham and the two Mills'.[13] A central argument of his went like this: as most of us require 'both the spur of hope and the bridle of fear', and as religion is perhaps the most effective device for spurring and bridling us, it is no infringement of liberty for society forcefully to inculcate religion.[14]

Consider again Mill's principle of liberty. Would one want to allow society to decide what counts as 'harm'? And who is really 'open to rational persuasion'? Society's record on just these decisions is alarming. Just by being permissive (but by no means ridiculously so) about what counts as a 'harm' and strict (but not ridiculously so) about who is 'open to rational persuasion', one can make most of the illiberal regimes of the twentieth century—the dictatorship of the proletariat, to take a chilling example—compatible with Mill's principle of liberty. Now consider Stephen's principle of liberty. Who is going to decide whether contraception, abortion, suicide, euthanasia, homosexual acts, and women's seeking a role outside the home are gross evils, the prevention of which would be 'good obtained'? Stephen's principle is yet more vulnerable to distortion than Mill's; he has no way of meeting perfectly realistic worries about government by moral authoritarians. The Taliban government of Afghanistan could sincerely have cited Stephen's test to show the world that they too were British liberals.[15]

What I am offering here is a *tu quoque* argument. It suggests that every proposed principle of liberty will have to leave some potentially dangerous decisions in the hands of society. Of course, the degree of danger matters, but the broad and narrow interpretations of liberty do not seem to be appreciably different in this respect. Liberal societies will establish liberal standards of 'harm' and 'openness to rational persuasion'; illiberal societies will adopt illiberal ones. Similarly, liberal societies will establish liberal standards for what can be seen as mattering to a worthwhile life; illiberal societies will adopt illiberal ones. One cannot make a formula fool-proof or villain-proof just by adding more words. In the end one is bound to some extent to rely on an interpreter's good sense and good will.

The broad conception of liberty is such a familiar instrument in our modern intellectual tool-box that, despite anything I can say, it will go on being used. And that seems to me perfectly justified. I would not want to deny that the broad interpretation may be the one we need elsewhere in our political thought, only not, I should still wish to say, in explaining the human right to liberty. Indeed, it might seem that I am overlooking an obvious value attaching to Mill's private sphere as such. The private is defined as the non-harmful (to others), and as harm is a plain disvalue, privacy, or non-harm, is a plain value. But I do not think that this identifies a role for the broad conception of liberty. The private sphere, as defined, contains a large value-neutral area: namely, the area between, on the one hand, the class of my actions essential to my personhood and, on the other hand, the class of my actions harmful to others. An example would be whether or not I wear a gown at dinner. It is more promising to consider whether the best policy for a society to adopt, on practical grounds, is to start with the broadest liberty possible and to impose the burden of argument on anyone who wants to restrict it. Still, however good a policy this may be will not alter the fact that much that is thereby protected is likely to be without positive value or of such slight value that it doubtfully merits the powerful restrictive role that principles of liberty would give it.

There is a difference between broad liberty and narrow liberty worth noting. Broad liberty, just because of its great breadth, has to be limited. Both Mill and Stephen limit it by imposing external constraints upon it. Narrow liberty is narrower because it already has internal constraints—the formal and material constraints I mentioned earlier—which define what this particular intrinsically valuable form of liberty is. At any point in political theory at which we wish to introduce an idea of liberty, we should ask which of these two conceptions yields the more plausible consequences.

Take an influential example. A prominent theme of Isaiah Berlin's writing is the incompatibility of certain 'ultimate values'.

Liberty ... is an eternal human ideal, whether individual or social. So is equality. But perfect liberty ... is not compatible with perfect equality. If a man is free to do anything he chooses, then the strong will crush the weak, the wolves will eat the sheep, and this puts an end to equality.[16]

Here Berlin just assumes broad liberty. On narrow liberty, however, the strong are not free to crush the weak. Admittedly, on narrow liberty, the strong may still come out in the end rather better off than the weak, but it is a good deal less clear that one person's turning out better off than another is as morally objectionable as one person's crushing the other, if indeed objectionable at all. It is true that some writers believe that the mere fact of two persons' turning out unequal is prima facie a bad thing. But what is the content of the principle of equality that they would be appealing to here? There are very many different principles of equality, as many as there are different forms of morally weighty forms of equality: for instance, equal regard (i.e., the moral point of view itself), equal rights, equal opportunity, equal well-being, and so on. To give the name 'equality' its necessary content, we must be able to answer the question, Equality of what? It is clear that Berlin means something like equality of well-being, or of various components of well-being, such as wealth, social status, and accomplishment. But this is a form of equality the moral weightiness of which is also much in question. Is the mere fact of difference of level of well-being, if all are well above the minimum acceptable level, morally objectionable? Once we raise the question of content, Berlin's case becomes doubtful.[17]

9.7 GENERALIZING THE RESULTS

The form of my remarks about liberty can be repeated for all other human rights. One starts with a demand for a fuller account of the existence conditions of a human right than we have so far established. Because it is *human* rights that we are interested in, not rights generally, it is likely that the account we need will be, at least in part, evaluatively substantive; we must explain what being 'human' in this context means. This demand for a fuller account is, I think, impossible to resist. But once we have such an account—the personhood account is only one form it might take—it will imply a material constraint on the content of each human right. In understanding human rights, a name is not enough; it is not enough to know merely that we have a right to *liberty*, to *life*, to *health*, and so on. We also need to know the contents of these rights. It is the formal and material constraints that determine their contents. Once determined, their contents will usually turn out to surprise us. It is not just the twentieth-century inflation in the number of rights that has to be challenged: the inflation of the content of individual rights does too. The implications of this are wider than just the case of liberty.

10

Welfare

10.1 THE HISTORICAL GROWTH OF RIGHTS

Contrary to widespread belief, welfare rights are not a twentieth-century innovation, but are among the first human rights ever to be claimed. When in the twelfth and thirteenth centuries our modern conception of a right first appeared, one of the earliest examples offered was the right of those in dire need to receive aid from those in surplus.[1] This right was used to articulate the attractive view of property prevalent in the medieval Church. God has given all things to us in common, but as goods will not be cared for and usefully developed unless assigned to particular individuals, we creatures have instituted systems of property. In these systems, however, an owner is no more than a custodian. We all thus have a right, if we should fall into great need, to receive necessary goods or, failing that, to take them from those in surplus.

One finds, very occasionally, what seem to be human rights to welfare asserted in the Enlightenment, for example, by John Locke, Tom Paine, and William Cobbett.[2] Following the Enlightenment, rights to welfare have often appeared in national constitutions: for example, the French constitutions of the 1790s, the Prussian Civil Code (1794), the constitutions of Sweden (1809), Norway (1814), The Netherlands (1814), Denmark (1849), and, skipping to the twentieth century, the Soviet Union (1936)—though it is not always clear that the drafters of these various documents thought of these fundamental civil rights as also human rights. By the end of the nineteenth century, political theorists were beginning to make a case that welfare rights are basic in much the sense that civil and political rights are.[3] But it was Franklin Roosevelt who did most to bring welfare rights into public life. The Atlantic Charter (1941), signed by Roosevelt and Churchill but in this respect primarily Roosevelt's initiative, declared that in addition to the classical civil and political freedoms there were also freedoms from want and fear. In his State of the Union message of 1944, Roosevelt averred:

We have come to a clear realization of the fact that true individual freedom cannot exist without economic security and independence. 'Necessitous men are not free men' ...

In our day these economic truths have become accepted as self-evident. We have accepted, so to speak, a second Bill of Rights ...

Among these are: The right to a useful and remunerative job. ... The right to earn enough to provide adequate food and clothing and recreation ...

The United Nations committee charged with drafting the Universal Declaration of Human Rights (1948), chaired by Eleanor Roosevelt, included most of the now standard welfare rights: rights to social security, to work, to rest and leisure, to medical care, to education, and 'to enjoy the arts and to share in scientific advancements and its benefits'. The Universal Declaration is a good example of how extensive—some would say lavish—proposed welfare rights have become.

Virtually all of the classical rights of the seventeenth and eighteenth centuries (what are sometimes called 'first-generation' rights) are, on the face of it, negative—with the possible exception of the rights to life and property (more about them later). The welfare rights of the mid-twentieth century ('second generation' rights), being positive, seem to increase not only the number of rights but also their kinds.[4] And if, as many philosophers think, duties not to harm are generally more stringent than duties to aid, welfare rights may constitute a less demanding kind of right—second rank as well as second generation. Many writers doubt that welfare rights can even aspire to the status of *human* rights.

10.2 WELFARE: A CIVIL, NOT A HUMAN, RIGHT?

A human right is a claim of all human agents against all other human agents. It is, as I said earlier, doubly universal.[5] At least, that is the way liberty rights have been thought to work: all of us have a right not to be dominated or blocked, and the correlative duty falls on every other individual and group and government—in short, upon all agents. But this is not the way most of us think of welfare rights. We think that only members of a particular community may claim welfare, and may claim it from only their own community. This implies that welfare rights are, at most, ethical rights that one has as a citizen—civil rights, not human rights.[6]

The strongest argument for this view comes from what I have called the Kantian schema: the division of obligations into perfect universal, perfect non-universal, and imperfect.[7] On this schema, obligations to help the needy are imperfect, to which there are no correlative natural rights. This is taken to explain various features of supposed rights to welfare: for example, the unspecifiability of the duty-bearers. I discussed these matters earlier.[8]

The next strongest argument runs along these lines. The ground for the right to welfare is membership of a community, in particular the co-operation and reciprocity that such membership typically involves. Think of a small frontier community. Everyone benefits from being in the community—mutual protection, some division of labour, social life, and so on. Everyone typically contributes to these benefits. If one year a certain family's crops are hit by a blight, the others help out, partly owing to the sympathy that naturally grows up in a small community, but also out of a sense of being part of a co-operative group, each benefiting the others and being benefited in return. This special relationship justifies claims to a certain mutual concern and help.

This special relationship carries over into large modern societies. It may seem that financial support for, say, a single mother in a modern urban slum is pure charity and has nothing to do with reciprocity, but that is not so. It matters to a society whether children in it grow up alienated and hostile or co-operative and productive, and mothers matter greatly to the outcome. So single mothers should be seen as contributing to society in return for the assistance they receive.[9] Most of us think that it is vital to preserve the model of reciprocity. That is why we invent new names for various kinds of welfare, such as 'job-seeker's allowance' and 'workfare'. This insistence on reciprocity leaves the undeserving poor out in the cold, but we shall consider their fate later.

One of the few other potentially weighty objections to regarding welfare as a human right, I should say, is the charge that a right to welfare would undermine liberty. It would, the objection goes, reward the unsuccessful and penalize the successful; it would penalize them by compelling a redistribution of their resources to the needy, and such compulsion would violate their liberty. That is a general point, to which Robert Nozick has given a well-known particular twist.[10] I have two kidneys and can survive on one: in that sense one of my kidneys is surplus to my minimum requirement. Yet most of us would regard it as a gross violation of my human rights if the government were to demand one of my kidneys for transplant. I may offer it, but it cannot be demanded. Much the same is true, Nozick thinks, of my property. Part of me is in it: my thought, my effort, are all bound up with it. I may choose to give some of it to the needy, but if the government confiscates it, even for the same purpose, it violates my human right to liberty. To force redistribution of one's income, even for a worthy cause, is, in effect, to force me to work for a certain time for the state. It is forced labour; the government arrogates to itself partial ownership in my person. It thereby violates my human right to liberty, in the way that slavery does. It is, therefore, ruled out on moral grounds. But then the supposed human right to welfare is ruled out on the same grounds.

Nozick's particular version of the liberty objection has been replied to often and, to my mind, successfully.[11] I should myself wish to enter an objection to it at a very early stage. Nozick misunderstands what the political value of liberty is. Not every interference with what one wants to do is a violation of liberty.[12] One violates someone's liberty only by stopping that person from pursuing what that person sees as a valuable life. For a government to tax someone's income, especially someone comfortably above the minimum level, does not stop that person from pursuing, or even living, a valuable life. My income's being taxed for redistributive purposes does not destroy my liberty, properly conceived, any more than my recognizing a moral obligation to give to charity does. Both are demanded of me—though in different ways—yet neither destroys my liberty. Neither is a form of, or tantamount to, slavery. If a slave manages to live a good life, on the slave's own conception of a good life, it is merely by lucky chance. But to have, say, one-third of an ample income taken in tax does not stop one from pursuing, and having reasonable hopes of achieving, a worthwhile life. This reply to Nozick is also a reply to other versions of the liberty objection.

10.3 A CASE FOR A HUMAN RIGHT TO WELFARE

The intuitive case for a *human* right to welfare goes something like this. Human rights are protections of human standing. We attach a high value to our living as normative agents—our autonomously choosing and freely pursuing our conception of a worthwhile life. Then it is not surprising that we should include among human rights, as indeed the tradition did from the start, not only a right to liberty but also a right to life. If human rights are protections of a form of life that is autonomous and free, they should protect life as well as that form of it. But if they protect life, must they not also ensure the wherewithal to keep body and soul together—that is, some minimum material provision? And as mere subsistence—that is, keeping body and soul together—is too meagre to ensure normative agency, must not human rights guarantee also whatever leisure and education and access to the thought of others that are also necessary to being a normative agent?

That is the heart of the case. It appeals to our picture of human agency and argues that both life and certain supporting goods are integral to it. Life and certain supporting goods are necessary conditions of being autonomous and free.[13] Many philosophers employ this necessary-condition argument to establish a human right to welfare—or, at least, to establish the right's being as basic as any other right.[14]

Of course, not every necessary condition for one's having autonomy and liberty—for example, that one was conceived—comes into the class of human rights. We can stop the chain of necessary conditions that are rights from getting ridiculously out of control by restricting them to 'proximate' necessary conditions, though that leaves us in need of a criterion for 'proximate'. No doubt, the early advocates of natural rights were trying to get some ethical purchase on characteristic human agents; it is a hard enough job to do that without adding the difficult cases, such as potential human agents, non-human agents, foetuses, new-born babies, and so on. So as a start on a criterion, we can take necessary conditions of agency as 'proximate' only if they are necessary for the agency of human agents as already going concerns.

I too want to invoke the necessary-conditions argument; I should only want to strengthen it. It is now common to say that liberty rights and welfare rights are 'indivisible'.[15] But that, also, is too weak. It asserts that one cannot enjoy the benefits of liberty rights without enjoying the benefits of welfare rights, and vice versa. But something stronger still may be said. There are forms of welfare that are empirically necessary conditions of a person's being autonomous and free, but there are also forms that are logically necessary—part of what we mean in saying that a person has these rights. The value in which human rights are grounded is the value attaching to normative agency. The norm arising from this value, of course, prohibits persons from attacking another's autonomy and liberty. But it prohibits more. The value concerned is *being* a normative agent, a self-creator, made in God's image. The value resides not simply in one's having the undeveloped, unused capacities for autonomy and liberty but also in exercising them—not just in being able to be autonomous but also in actually being so. The norm associated with this more complex value would address other ways of failing to be an agent. It would require protecting another person from losing agency, at least if one can do this without great cost to oneself; it would require helping to restore another's agency if it has already been lost, say through giving mobility to the crippled or guidance to the blind, again with the same proviso. All of this is involved simply in *having* a right to autonomy or to liberty. Welfare claims are already part of the content of these rights. What, then, should we think of the common division of basic rights into 'classical' liberty rights and welfare rights? Into which of these two classes does the right to autonomy or to liberty go? Into which of the two classes do the difficult, apparently borderline cases go, such as rights to life, to property, to the pursuit of happiness, to security of person, and to privacy? The sensible response would be to drop the distinction.

What is more, a right to welfare *is* a human right. Recall my earlier discussion about identifying the duty-bearers correlative to human rights.[16] I said then that ability to help played an important, but not the exclusive, role in determining the duty-bearer, and that ability to help shifted from one agency to another as circumstances changed—in England, for example, from the Church (in the Middle Ages) to local government (after the dissolution of the monasteries), then fitfully to central government (especially during the nineteenth and the first half of the twentieth centuries), and now, in the AIDS crisis in the Third World, to rich countries. Ability to help is not the only determinant of the duty-bearer; the domain of permitted partiality, for example, also limits both duties and duty-bearers.

The history of help for the needy suggests two conclusions. First, ability to help undoubtedly plays a major role in determining who bears the duty. And, second, the right does not restrict the duty-bearer to the government, nor the right-bearer to a citizen. The most plausible interpretation of the right to welfare universalizes both right-holder and duty-bearer; it is a right that each of us has against all the rest. There are indeed severe restrictions on the right-holders and duty-bearers in this case, but they are best seen as arising, above all, from ability to help and the domain of permitted partiality.

This universalization helps to explain why governments in practice do not treat welfare rights merely as civil rights. For instance, the State of

California has, in recent years, tried to deny various welfare services to illegal immigrants—that is, to people who are, in this particularly egregious way, non-citizens. In August 1996 the Governor, Peter Wilson, signed an executive order ending their access to a wide range of welfare benefits, including pre-natal care, long-term health care, and public housing.[17] But his order stopped short of denying them emergency health care. The Governor acted under a provision of a federal law that makes illegal immigrants ineligible for all state and federal benefits, though with similar exceptions; the federal law also excludes services such as emergency medical care and disaster relief. And there is an obvious justification for those exceptions: there are some forms of aid that anyone well able to give them owes to anyone in great need of them—whether or not the two agents are related as government and citizen.[18]

Many writers have insisted (this is Isaiah Berlin's version) that 'Liberty is one thing and the conditions for it are another'.[19] Interpreted literally, this is too obvious to need saying; of course, there is a difference between a thing and a necessary condition for the thing. But I take it that the point is that, in the case of liberty, this distinction is often ignored. Too much, these writers suggest, is being smuggled into the notion of liberty in order to trade on liberty's undeniable rhetorical appeal. But I am not smuggling a right to welfare into the right to liberty. They are two distinct rights. But the earlier discussion of the distinction between negative and positive rights[20] shows that to restrict human rights to purely negative concerns would not provide an adequate explanation even of the values in which human rights are grounded. Liberty already has positive elements.

10.4 IS THE PROPOSED RIGHT TOO DEMANDING?

Does this account of a human right to welfare fail by making it too demanding? I have several times employed the common proviso 'so long as the cost to oneself is small', but surely the cost to oneself can be somewhat greater than small and one still have to pay it. And surely the benefit to the other person can be somewhat less great than life itself and one still have to provide it. Where are the two cut-off points?

I said a moment ago that mere ability is only one reason-generating consideration in cases of aid, that a limit on the demands on us comes from the domain of permitted partiality. This limit still leaves open the possibility of hefty claims on governments and, through taxation, on citizens to help the needy, as well as claims directly on individuals to be charitable.

There is a second limit, this one deriving from the content of the right. How much may the needy claim by human right? The United Nations,[21] along with several philosophers,[22] says that the claim is to a 'satisfactory' standard of living, but the obvious trouble with relying on the word 'satisfactory' is its tendency to change with time and place. What seems 'satisfactory' is too likely to be relative to the wealth of a society. What we need is some stable, non-arbitrary, normatively based criterion. On the personhood account, of course, there is one: the cut-off point is when the proximate necessary conditions for normative agency are met. That point will be higher than mere subsistence but lower than levels of well-being characteristic of rich contemporary societies. That, admittedly, leaves a large middle ground, and there will be hard interpretative work to be done on the idea of 'proximate necessary conditions for normative agency' to make it sharper-edged. Still, this idea gives us less meagre starting conceptual materials than society often has to work with.

Major indeterminacies remain, the most important, to my mind, being this: we have good empirical evidence to believe that in a famine there is usually enough food in the stricken country to keep all the population alive; it is just that the starving have no effective way of getting at it.[23] We also have reason to believe that liberal democracies are less likely than countries with other forms of government to suffer serious famine.[24] And we have reason to believe that rushing food to an area of famine is often only a short-term palliative. What is needed in these countries for long-term improvement is often deep political change. Is bringing about that change one of the duties correlative to the right to welfare? Must better-off countries therefore intervene in the internal affairs of other countries? There will be a long list of good reasons why one should not, or need not, intervene: the effects of intervention can be highly uncertain; the means can be very costly; and so on. But our interest now is only in the content of the right to welfare: does it include a prima facie claim on others to their help in bringing about, where necessary, radical political change?

To answer, we must go back to the role of human rights, which is to protect normative agency, both our capacity for it and our exercise of it. Take an extreme (but by no means exceptional) case: think of someone very poor in an area of recurrent famine whose whole family suffers from chronic malnutrition. Food aid during one famine may do little to change that person's life. It may merely keep the person alive until the next famine, probably suffering from chronic malnutrition all the while. It is most unlikely that a person could rise to normative agency in such circumstances: no education, no leisure, no hope, no ambition, no long view. What such a person would need for normative agency is a remedy for these lacks. And in many cases a necessary condition for their remedy will be radical political change. If human rights protect not just our capacity for agency but also our exercise of it, then the prima facie duties correlative to the right to welfare will sometimes include political intervention in the affairs of another country. By parity of reasoning, it may also include bringing about radical political change in our own country. Of course, weighing against this prima facie duty will be all the good reasons for restraint on the long list I started compiling.

Is the right to welfare implausibly demanding? To my mind, no. The long list of counter-reasons is the appropriate counterweight to it.

10.5 THE UNDESERVING POOR

Many politicians and many theorists insist that welfare aid be restricted to the deserving needy. ('Deserving needy' is a better term than 'deserving poor'; a multi-millionaire might need a liver transplant from the National Health Service, the only source.) Indeed, some philosophers write the restriction to the deserving needy into the definition of the right.[25] If they are correct, welfare cannot, after all, be a human right. The restriction is incompatible with the necessary universality of the class of right-bearers. If welfare is a human right, we are not, it seems, allowed to introduce desert into the statement of the right.

But there is a way in which we can introduce it, without abandoning the requirement of universality. Although a restriction to the deserving cannot be written into the human right itself, desert is still an action-guiding consideration that may be weighed, in case of conflict, against the right. The potentially undeserving are a mixed lot: a teenage girl who deliberately gets pregnant in order to claim welfare support, a gambler who loses all his money, a heavy smoker or drinker who needs a transplant, an AIDS victim who ignored the warnings about unsafe sex, a work-shy welfare exploiter when jobs are available. A concessive modern view is that smoking, drinking, and gambling are addictions; that the work-shy welfare exploiter is alienated from society, and so on. On this view, we are all victims, and the class of undeserving needy is empty. But unsafe sex is not an addiction; nor are all those who practise it alienated from society. And the level of addiction of some regular smokers is probably low enough to be controllable.

If so, then we have conflicts between desert and the right to welfare. How can we weigh them against one another? Both the individual and society are likely to be better off if the work-shy welfare exploiter is forced to be self-supporting; so one may, in certain circumstances—for example, once the welfare exploiter is informed of a suitable job—deem the duties correlative to the right to be discharged. The practice of teenage girls deliberately getting pregnant in order to claim welfare support is something that society might also want to discourage, but in this case it is much harder to see how to do it and *faute de mieux* the government may have to continue the support.

The plainest case of a conflict between welfare and desert would be a clearly undeserving smoker who will die without a lung transplant. But why is the smoker undeserving of help? Because the need is the smoker's own fault. So the deeper question is: what weight are we to attach to its being a person's own fault? Well, fault must have weight at least as a tie-breaker. If I am clearly undeserving and you thoroughly deserving, but we are regarded by the hospital as having equal claim on the next lung available for transplant, you may properly protest that the way the hospital decides priorities is unfair. So fairness also enters, at least to affect priority, and with it, as its inevitable counterweight, will come beneficence. If with the transplant I would have another thirty years of vigorous life and you, despite your desert, only one year of much impaired life, that too should carry weight. What then are the relative moral weights of the right to welfare, a person's desert, and the amount of benefit conferrable?

This question has never yet been satisfactorily answered, but fortunately it is not our question. Ours, rather, is this: is desert an independent consideration to be weighed against the right to welfare, or is it already incorporated as a restriction in the right itself? On the personhood account, the great value of the capacity for and exercise of normative agency sets up claims on us not to destroy them, and within limits, to protect and promote them. The value they have does not rest at all on an agent's desert. And the limits referred to in the qualification 'within limits' are not, at least not usually, incorporated into the statement of the right itself (think, for instance, of the limit to our welfare duties arising from the amount of benefit that can be produced or from the domain of permitted partiality). And the reason is plain: the values that ground the right to welfare do not ground these particular limits. Their grounds lie elsewhere in the moral domain. So too do the grounds of desert.

10.6 HUMAN RIGHTS, LEGAL RIGHTS, AND RIGHTS IN THE UNITED NATIONS

Let us look again at the welfare rights in the Universal Declaration, this time, let us hope, with a more critical eye. The Universal Declaration was merely hortatory. The rights it declared acquired legal force only when the two Covenants of 1966, the International Covenant on Economic, Social, and Cultural Rights and the International Covenant on Civil and Political Rights, were ratified, and then they acquired it only within the ratifying countries. But are all of these rights, in the light of the personhood account, really human rights? To show that they are, it is not enough to show that there is a successful moral case for granting people the right; rich societies have often found good reason to give legal entitlement to rather higher levels of welfare than human rights demand. There can be (legal) rights to welfare, even important ones, that are not also human rights.

There is a regrettable, and often remarked, tendency in the Universal Declaration to an uncritical generosity, which in general gets worse in later rights documents. Article 25.1 asserts a person's right to 'a standard of living adequate for ... the well-being of himself and his family'. It does not say 'a certain minimum level of well-being', and the term 'well-being' on its own is too generous: 'well-being' covers all levels of quality of life from the lowest to the highest. Article 24 plausibly announces that there is 'a right to rest and leisure', but then implausibly includes in it 'periodic holidays with pay'. Although some leisure is necessary for normative agency, paid holidays certainly are not. (Incidentally, Article 25.1, in a rare act of ungenerosity, restricts welfare rights to the deserving poor; a person's needs, it states, must be due to 'circumstances beyond his control', thereby entangling the United Nations in the inconsistency mentioned a moment ago.)

Also dubious is the Universal Declaration's wholesale inclusion of justice among human rights—though this, I should say, is less over-generosity than confusion. The Universal Declaration includes not only procedural justice, but also distributive justice and fairness. It is not only the United Nations that does this; many philosophers do so too.[26] But this is an assumption I sought to challenge earlier.[27] Both the tradition and firm ethical intuitions, I argued then, regard procedural justice as a human right (e.g. a right to a fair trial), but do not admit all the other departments of justice. Our present subject, welfare rights, tends to reinforce that view. Article 23.2 declares a right to equal pay for equal work—a matter of fairness. Article 23.3 adds a right to 'just and favourable remuneration'.[28] But imagine two highly paid executives of a large multinational firm who are receiving the same remuneration, though one of them has both more work and more responsibilities than the other and resents not being more rewarded. There is a genuine issue of fairness here, but most of us would be reluctant to accept that either of these extremely well-paid executives has thereby had any human rights violated. The personhood account has an explanation for this: human rights have to do with a certain minimum—the minimum proximately necessary for normative agency. While the demands of human rights to material resources have a cut-off point, the demands of justice do not; or, if issues of justice lapse at high levels of affluence, the two cut-off points are at least not the same.

Suppose that I am right that there are several dubious items in the Universal Declaration. That leaves a question, which I turn to next: What, if anything, should be done about them?

PART III

APPLICATIONS

11

Human Rights: Discrepancies Between Philosophy and International Law

11.1 APPLICATIONS OF THE PERSONHOOD ACCOUNT

In Part I, I proposed a personhood account of human rights. In Part II, I described the three highest-level rights: to autonomy, liberty, and minimum provision. Now, in Part III, I want to work out the implications of the account for a selection of lower-level human rights.

11.2 BRINGING PHILOSOPHICAL THEORY AND LEGAL PRACTICE TOGETHER

We should be neither surprised nor especially troubled by some discrepancy between the list of human rights that emerges from a theorist's deliberations and the lists that are enshrined in law. If the discrepancy were very great, it is true, we might start doubting either the theory or the law. If it were less great, we should still want to explain it, still want to decide whether the theory or the law is in better order, or whether, perhaps because of their different functions, both are in good enough order.

I want, in particular, to reflect on discrepancies between two lists of human rights—the one from the best philosophical account and the other from the most authoritative declarations in international law. For obvious reasons, I cannot but take the personhood account as the best one.

The international law of human rights has been deeply influenced by both the natural law tradition and the Enlightenment. But there are only the slightest traces of theory explicit in the important twentieth-century declarations of human rights. The Preambles of the International Covenant on Economic, Social and Cultural Rights and the International Covenant on

[margin handwritten note: make it possible to make choices that have impact on our life; essential for attaining personhood]

Civil and Political Rights, adopted by the General Assembly of the United Nations in 1966 in order to give legal force to the merely hortatory Universal Declaration of 1948, both contain the clause, 'Recognizing that these rights derive from the inherent dignity of the human person'.[1] So, here too the ground of these rights is said to be personhood, though the exact significance of the idea is not at all spelt out. This clause is, indeed, the only gesture at theory in the two documents. It is a feature of the international declarations in general that they pay little attention to reasons or justifications.[2]

That is not a criticism. It is common in law not to dwell on justification; different groups, particularly different cultures, might agree that there is such a thing as the dignity of the person, and largely agree on the rights that follow from it, but differ in their understanding of quite what that 'dignity' is. So silence on the subject is often simple wisdom, and the personhood account, even if it is indeed the best substantive account, should stay quietly in the background. But that sensible thought is in tension with the sensible driving thought of this book: namely, that, in order to avoid nearly criterionless claims about human rights, we must develop, and be guided by, a fuller substantive account of what they are. These are not contradictory beliefs, but we have to discover how to hold both, despite the tension between them.

11.3 THE LIST OF HUMAN RIGHTS THAT EMERGES FROM THE PERSONHOOD ACCOUNT

According to my account, there are two grounds for human rights: personhood and practicalities. Personhood initially generates the rights; practicalities give them, where needed, a sufficiently determinate shape.

From a well-developed form of the idea of personhood, we should be able to derive all human rights. We have a right to autonomy. In private life, this means that, once we are capable of taking major decisions for ourselves, parents and teachers—in general, those in authority—must not make us, or keep us, submissive to their wills. In public life, this yields a right to some form of equal say in political decisions. Even a skilled benevolent dictator would be likely to infringe our autonomy; nowadays it is rare to encounter circumstances in which authoritarian rule is justified. So there would be a large range of human rights protecting our autonomy, because autonomy is one of the two essential components of agency.

We have a right to life and to some form of security of person. We have a right not to be tortured. There will be a large range of rights to certain necessary conditions of agency.

Then, we must be free from interference in the pursuit of our major ends. We must be free to worship, to enjoy ourselves, to form the personal relations we want, to try to arrive at certain basic forms of understanding, to create works of art. We must also be free to inform others of what we believe, to display our works of art. Freedom of expression is doubly protected. It is protected because we need it in order effectively to decide our ends in life. But though art may help us in this way, it does not always, yet it would be protected even then. It may be a part, not just of deliberating about, but also simply of having a good life. So there must be a large range of liberty rights, because liberty is the other essential component of agency.

Then, it is hardly surprising that there are rights that cut across these three major categories: autonomy rights, welfare rights, and liberty rights. We have a right to some degree of privacy, because without it we should not be secure or comfortable enough either autonomously to decide our own ends or to pursue some of them. We have a right to asylum, if exile is necessary to protect our lives or our status as agents.

This, of course, is only the start of a list. There are many more human rights, and even those that I have mentioned need to be brought into sharper focus. And there is the familiar problem of whether, once they are brought into sharper focus, one person's rights will be compatible with another's. But this brief account is enough to give some sense of the range of rights that would appear on my list, and why they would.

11.4 CURRENT LEGAL LISTS: CIVIL AND POLITICAL RIGHTS

The other lists I want to look at are, for the most part, the ones in the three major United Nations documents on human rights: the Universal Declaration of Human Rights (1948), the International Covenant on Civil and Political Rights (1966), and the International Covenant on Economic, Social and Cultural Rights (1966), and the lists in the three regional documents, the European Convention on Human Rights (1950), the American Convention on Human Rights (1969), and the African Charter on Human and People's

Rights (1981). But now and then I shall introduce an example from other international documents.

Let me first take claims to civil and political rights. There are striking discrepancies between my list and the lists in these documents. Seen through the lens of my account, the majority of items on the other lists are acceptable, but there are some that are not, and several that are at least debatable.

(a) *Unacceptable cases.*

The International Covenant on Civil and Political Rights asserts: 'Any propaganda for war shall be prohibited by law' (Article 20.1). It is not clear that this even has the form of a right. It is the denial of a freedom: namely, the freedom to propagandize for war. There seem to be no issues of personhood here to justify the prohibition. And on any account of human rights, this is an almost incredible claim. Should one be prohibited from advocating even a just war? The African Charter makes a related claim that all people have 'the right to national and international peace and security' (Article 23.1).[3] It is plausible that there should be a collective right to security; such a right can be seen as grounded in individual rights to security of person. But a right to peace? Would a country that decides to defend itself against invasion violate its citizens' rights? These scarcely credible claims to rights are a manifestation of an often remarked propensity of the drafters to tack on to these international declarations of rights what are really just aspirations. Even worthy aspirations such as peace are not, thereby, human rights. They would not be rights on my account, and it is hard to think of any sensible account on which they would be.

The International Convention on the Elimination of All Forms of Racial Discrimination, adopted by the United Nations General Assembly in 1965, in the course of rehearsing what are for the most part standard, uncontentious civil rights, introduces 'the right to inherit' (Article 5. D. vi). This is not a right to bequeath goods, which one might or might not choose to exercise, but a right to be left them. But this too is scarcely credible. Would a multi-millionaire who knows that his children can look after themselves and leaves his money to charity violate their human rights? Even if this right is interpreted not as a claim-right of the potential heirs, but as a liberty-right of the testator, it is still highly dubious. Suppose a government decided not to allow transfer of goods between generations but to have each generation make its own way. Would this, if there were also adequate welfare provisions in place, violate anyone's human rights? Not on my account and intuitively not as well. It might be less efficient socially, but that is different. And it would not violate a human right to property, if there is one, but merely restrict one kind of transfer.

The Universal Declaration, though relatively restrained, still has its highly dubious items. It asserts that there is a right to protection against attacks on one's honour and reputation (Article 12), which is repeated in various later documents.[4] But could there be such a general right? An author cannot have a right not to receive reputation-shaking reviews, and a dishonourable person cannot expect protection against exposure. At most there could be a rather different right—a right to redress against libel and slander. But although in most countries there is such a legal right, even that rather different right is doubtfully a *human* right. Its concern is a matter of fairness, not of human rights, and, as I argued earlier, they are not the same.[5]

The Universal Declaration also claims that we have freedom of movement and residence within the borders of our own country (Article 13.1).[6] Is there a freedom of residence? One's personhood would not be threatened if one were required to live in a particular place, so long as the basic amenities were provided: a decent education, adequate material provision, access to art, and so on. Of course, some people prefer living by the sea and others in the mountains, some in cities and others in the country, and where one lives can be an important component of the quality of one's life, and so should be restricted only for the strongest reasons. But many things affect the quality of one's life; that they do hardly thereby makes them a matter of a human right. Imagine a slightly fictionalized Brazil of about fifty years ago. The coastal areas, especially the cities, are heavily populated, but the rich, beautiful interior is largely empty. The Brazilian government decides to open up the interior to settlement, and as a first step creates a new capital city, Brasilia, deep inland. But the citizens on the seaboard are reluctant to move, and the government is reluctant to force them because forced removal would be likely to break up families and friendships, upset settled expectations, and so on. But a boatload of new citizens, immigrants to the country, arrives in Rio, and they are informed that they must settle in the interior. Brasilia, let us assume, already has all of the amenities that I just desiderated. The immigrants, let us assume, would be able to choose between living in Brasilia itself or the country around it. The area has great natural beauty; life would be comfortable, and a free shuttle to Rio and São Paolo, let us add for the sake of the argument, would be laid on. Of course, some of the immigrants may have a general preference for coasts over interiors, and they will not therefore have everything they want. But then life seldom provides everything one wants, and there is certainly no human right to the greatest possible satisfaction of one's preferences.

Would this policy violate a human right? The right that it would be most likely to violate would be liberty. But not every compulsion that stops one from getting what one wants—for example, parking restrictions—violates liberty. Living where one wants is much more central to a worthwhile life than parking where one wants. But if one is denied a choice between two options that offer equal prospects of a worthwhile life, then it is hard to see any case for claiming a violation of a human right.

The Brazil case, as I say, is fiction. But there are real compulsions, economic ones, to live in a particular place that may violate, or at least come close to violating, a human right. There have been such cases for thousands of years. But the most interesting examples are ones that are likely to arise in the near future, because they will be the result of deliberate political choice. With the introduction of a common currency in the European Union, and with the harmonization of various tax rates, the major tool for managing the economy left to the nations that have adopted the currency will be levels of unemployment. If welfare rates are fixed so as to force a migration of labour, then a Greek worker, say, may have to migrate to Germany. In Germany, because of the difference in language and hostile attitudes in the local society, the Greek worker might well have little effective voice in political decisions. The worker will therefore be subject to laws without having an equal voice in making them. This *begins* to make the sort of case—much more needs to be said—that would support a claim that a human right has been violated. The case would be very different if the worker had merely to migrate from the Greek countryside to Athens. And it is very different from my fictional case of the immigrants to Brazil having to settle inland rather than on the coast. So this example does not support the right, in all its generality, claimed by the Universal Declaration.

(b) *Debatable cases.*

Of all the putative civil and political rights in the major international documents, the most challenging to my account are the ones that come under the general heading 'equality before the law'.[7] This is how they appear in the Universal Declaration:

Article 7.   All are equal before the law and are entitled without any
            discrimination to equal protection of the law. ...

Article 8.   Everyone has the right to an effective remedy by the competent national tribunals for acts violating the fundamental rights granted him by the constitution or by law.

Article 9.   No one shall be subjected to arbitrary arrest, detention or exile.

Article 10.   Everyone is entitled in full equality to a fair and public hearing by an independent and impartial tribunal ...

Article 11.   (1) Everyone charged with a penal offence has the right to be presumed innocent until proved guilty ...

(2) No one shall be held guilty of any penal offence on account of any act or omission which did not constitute a penal offence ... at the time when it was committed.

These articles are spelt out in more practical terms in the International Covenant on Civil and Political Rights, for example in Article 14:

3. In the determination of any criminal charge against him, everyone shall be entitled to the following minimum guarantees, in full equality:

   (*a*) To be informed promptly and in detail in a language which he understands of the nature and cause of the charge against him;

   (*b*) To have adequate time and facilities for the preparation of his defence and to communicate with counsel of his own choosing;

   (*c*) To be tried without undue delay;

   (*d*) To be tried in his presence, and to defend himself in person or through legal assistance of his own choosing ...;

   (*e*) To examine, or have examined, the witnesses against him and to obtain the attendance and examination of witnesses on his behalf under the same conditions as witnesses against him;

   (*f*) To have the free assistance of an interpreter if he cannot understand or speak the language used in court;

   (*g*) Not to be compelled to testify against himself or to confess guilt ...

6. ... the person who has suffered punishment as a result of such conviction [namely, a miscarriage of justice] shall be compensated.

Most of these are, according to my account, clear human rights, but I am inclined to say that some are not, though the case for saying so is not nearly as simple as in what I earlier labelled 'unacceptable' cases.

It is entirely plausible that we have a second-order human right to remedy for violations of our human rights. Human rights are meant to be protections of our personhood, so we should be able to claim not only that others not violate our personhood but also that society in some way help in its protection. It is plausible, too, that we have a human right not to be subjected to arbitrary arrest, detention, or exile; those are extreme violations of our liberty, in the sense of the term that comes out of the personhood account. And everyone has a (human) right to be presumed innocent until proved guilty; if one's guilt were presumed, and action appropriate to that presumption then followed, such as serious loss of liberty or property, then one's capacity to live one's chosen life would be seriously impaired. It is true that not all cases of presumption of guilt need result in diminished personhood, but the line between those that do and those that do not would be hard to draw, and the sort of simplicity needed by both moral norms and civil laws is likely to result in a blanket presumption of innocence.

However, there is a general point that should be recalled here. There is no inference from something's being a matter of justice or fairness to its being a matter of human rights. This is a major point of conflict between my account and certain international law. Some international lawyers write as if the domains of justice and of human rights are identical.[8] But they are clearly not. Human rights do not exhaust the whole domain of justice or fairness. Recall the examples I used earlier.[9] If you free-ride on the bus because you know that no harm will come, as the rest of us are paying our fares, you do not violate my rights, though you do, clearly, act unfairly. If when we play our occasional game of poker, you use a marked deck of cards, you are again acting unfairly, but you are not violating my human rights. This explains why the tradition regards procedural justice as a matter of human rights, but not several forms of distributive justice. Procedural justice protects our liberties. Distributive justice, for all its importance, often does not bear on our personhood—so long, that is, as the human right to minimum provision is respected. In fact, as most people in most societies never attract the attention of police or courts, their interests are likely to be affected far more by matters of distributive justice than of procedural justice. But matters of justice can be highly important in our lives without being matters of human rights.

If, therefore, we want to say that some human rights are grounded in justice, we have to explain which considerations of justice ground human rights and which do not. One possible answer would be mine: the considerations that ground human rights are those of personhood, understood as I have explained it. But not all of the putative rights that I have just quoted can be found a rationale in personhood. For instance, the right to compensation following a miscarriage of justice cannot be. In a society with proper welfare provisions, not to be compensated will not undermine the *personhood* of the victim of a miscarriage of justice. There is, all the same, a different but perfectly strong reason to compensate the victim: justice demands it. But the case for it is based in the victim's desert, not in the protection of the victim's personhood.

On the face of it, there is a similar case for rejecting several other of these proposed rights to fair procedure: for example, rights to be informed of the charge against one promptly and in detail, to have adequate time to prepare one's defence, not to be compelled to testify against oneself, and so on. There is, of course, a very strong justification for these guarantees—namely, in justice or fairness. It is true that when one is being tried for an offence, one's liberty or some other component of personhood might be at stake, and then these procedural guarantees could be seen as protections of one's personhood. But not all charges carry the risk of loss of liberty—the worst penalty might be a fine that one can easily afford or a suspended sentence. But justice and fairness would still be very much at stake, so these guarantees would retain their rationale even if no component of personhood were in the slightest jeopardy. Their rationale, this line of thought goes, is justice itself, not the more specific matter of human rights. And accepting this line of thought need not bring with it any loss of expressive power. We do not have to speak in terms of human rights, or even of rights, in order to specify fair legal procedure, and generations of philosophers and jurists have managed to say all that must be said on the subject without them. And there need be no loss in moral power either. The case for these procedures is that they are quite plainly matters of justice. What more powerful backing would one want? Human rights have been proliferating at such a suspect rate because we all want to cash in on the power of the language of rights. But why not instead recover and protect the power of the language of justice? It is a great mistake to think that, because we see rights as especially important in morality, we must make everything especially important in morality into a right.

Still, this line of thought succeeds only very occasionally. To my mind, it succeeds in threatening the supposed right to compensation for a miscarriage of justice. But it does not threaten these other rights to fair legal procedures. These other rights were originally introduced as protections of liberty, autonomy, and the material basis of life as an agent. They were seen as defences against the arbitrary behaviour of governments. They were meant as defences against death, imprisonment, and confiscation of property without due process. The right to be informed of the charges against one promptly and to have adequate time to prepare one's defence are obvious protections against arbitrary denials of liberty. The right not to be compelled to testify against oneself is protection against threats and torture, which undermine autonomy. It does not matter that the penalties for some offences do not involve loss of liberty or damaging confiscation of property. One has to expect a certain simplicity in norms, both legal and moral. The historical motive for the introduction of these rights was to protect personhood.[10] But, to repeat, not all of the rights to fair legal procedures claimed in the International Covenant can be defended in this way. The supposed right to compensation for unjust punishment, for example, cannot be.

There is this objection to my conclusion. The drafters of these international covenants might say, as I do, that the considerations of justice that ground rights are those of 'personhood'. But they might want to employ a rather more generous interpretation of 'personhood' than I do. We should concentrate, as most of these documents do, on the notion of the *dignity* of the person. If one is accused of a crime and then subjected to unfair treatment by a court, even to a failure in compensation after unjust punishment, one's dignity as a person, the drafters might say, is not respected. And thus one's human rights, not just one's legal rights, are violated. These procedural guarantees, including the right to compensation, are meant to define what it is, in the legal context, to treat someone with the basic dignity due to a person. For that reason, the drafters might say, they are properly regarded as *human* rights. Free-riding and cheating at cards are real enough cases of unfairness, but they differ from not getting a fair hearing in court. The latter unfairness is so fundamental to our life that protection against it is part of what it is to accord us our dignity as persons, while protection against trivial free-riding and cheating at cards is not.

The proposal that I attribute here to the drafters is like mine, in that we both ground rights in the dignity of persons. But my account puts its stress on *persons*, whom it understands as normative agents. The dignity is then to be seen as deriving from the value we attach to our normative agency. That is why my account is more restrictive: human rights have to be protections of one or other component of agency. The drafters' account—at least as I have just imagined it—puts its stress on *dignity*. It leaves *person* a more intuitive notion: our dignity as a person may encompass more than just the components of agency. But the very elasticity of this notion of dignity causes problems. If dignity is not to be understood in my way, how is it to be understood? One promising place to start is with the closely connected notion of *respect* for persons. On everyone's understanding of it, the moral point of view consists in having equal respect for all persons. This need not be the same as treating them all equally, one's own children no differently from a stranger's. It is, rather, giving them all some form, still to be spelt out, of equal weight in our deliberation. One prominent way of spelling out the idea of respect for persons is Kant's: everyone must be treated as an end, and never merely as a means. But this whole approach, no matter how it is spelt out, will not help us. It is spelling out a notion of the dignity of persons that underlies moral obligation as a whole. If we adopted this understanding, human rights would expand to fill that whole domain, which is so counter-intuitive a consequence that we must avoid it.

Taking a cue from the examples of free-riding and cheating at cards, which we want to keep out of the class of infringements of human rights, we might amend this last proposal. We might introduce the distinction between minor or trivial violations of respect for persons, which these examples might be taken to represent, and major or serious violations. But, as we have already seen, this does not help either. We should not let human rights expand to fill the whole domain of major or serious affronts to respect for persons either. A husband might have been cold and unpleasant to his wife throughout their marriage, causing her great unhappiness. He might thereby have done her a gross moral wrong, but he would not have infringed her human rights. A plutocracy might perpetuate an unjust distribution of goods, thereby denying a majority of the population of substantial benefits. But if everyone in the population has at least the minimum provision for life as an agent, the government does not infringe anyone's human rights. It is deeply counter-intuitive to regard all serious moral wrongs, even all substantial injustices, as infringements of human rights.

The distinction we need is not between major and minor violations of respect for persons, but something along the line of fundamental and non-fundamental ones. But apart from my way of spelling out the 'fundamental' features of the dignity of persons, what kind of well-motivated, workable account is there? And we cannot leave the notion of 'dignity' as elastic and intuitive as it is now because, unless we have tolerably clear criteria for whether the term 'human rights' is being correctly or incorrectly used, the term will remain as seriously degraded as it is now.[11]

(c) *Acceptable cases.*

Despite the unacceptable and the debatable cases, most of the claims to human rights that one finds in the Universal Declaration come out on my account, as I have said, as entirely acceptable. That is partly because the Universal Declaration is brief, does not go into fine detail, and is relatively restrained in the claims it makes to economic, cultural, and collective rights. My own list, which I made a start on earlier, contained only the most obvious rights, and much more needs to be added to it. Many of the items in these international documents I should want to add to my list. I shall mention just one. Article 15.1 of the Universal Declaration says: 'Everyone has the right to a nationality.' There is a powerful case for this. Everyone must live within the boundaries of one country or an other. If one cannot vote, one lacks the only form of autonomy that political life within those boundaries allows. And states are the main agents of security of person. And so on. It is true that in some states one can vote and enjoy the protection of the police and army without being a citizen, but only citizenship makes their possession secure. The case for saying that there is a human right to a nationality is powerful.

11.5 INTERLUDE ON THE AIMS AND STATUS OF INTERNATIONAL LAW

The exercise I have just been through—examining discrepancies between my list and the lists in major international documents—might be thought to be in various ways misconceived. Do the drafters of these documents and I not have different aims? I am trying to understand what a human right is; I am trying to make the sense of the term determinate enough for it to be a clear and helpful addition to our moral and political reflection. The drafters of these documents were trying, in the aftermath of two devastating World Wars, to establish a basic code of conduct for the behaviour of states towards those subject to their power, in the belief that the promotion of human rights contributes to the promotion of peace.[12] There is not the slightest doubt which is the more important, more noble ambition. My aim is, at best, a contribution to their much larger aim. But then the drafters were not interested in arriving at a narrow list of human rights with impeccable semantic credentials. They were interested in an ampler list, in a way the ampler the better, with some claim to being, or decent prospects of becoming, a standard that crossed cultures, religions, borders, and power blocs. And so they made use, without too much worry, of a deeply obscure, largely undefined notion of 'the dignity of the human person'.[13] But in an important way its obscurity does not matter—indeed, is an advantage—because different cultures can understand different things by it. Their lists have succeeded in crossing at least some borders, and they have been, all things considered, a substantial force for the good. The rights on their lists, even if it turned out that they were not all strictly speaking *human* rights, have become, once embodied in treaties, basic international *legal* rights. That is a status hardly to be scorned.

What is more, does not international law have its own perfectly coherent conception of a human right? I have said that we badly need criteria for deciding when the term 'human right' is used correctly and when incorrectly. But does not international law in a way supply them? It does not supply them as I do, by putting more normative substance into the notion of personhood. It supplies them, rather, with something more in the nature of a rule of recognition. There are various procedures which, if carried far enough, establish a human right in international law. For instance, an international group alarmed at the degradation of nature might declare there to be a fundamental right to live in a healthy environment. Other groups, say regional organizations of nations, sensing the same threats, might include a similar right in their charters or conventions. In this way, a fair measure of consensus may develop. Next a committee of the United Nations—say the United Nations Sub-Commission on Human Rights—may define the right more fully and embody it in a set of draft principles. If matters had proceeded only so far (as, in fact, as I write, they have), then one might say that a human right to a healthy environment has begun to emerge in international law, though it is not yet clearly established. It is a matter of judgement and convention when the right *is* established. If, say, the General Assembly were to adopt in some hortatory form the draft principles from its Sub-Commission, then the case for the existence of the right would be strengthened. If it were to embody the right in a legally binding international convention, which was then widely ratified, the case, one might say, would be conclusive.[14]

Still, my project in this book should not be underestimated. Many persons have still to be convinced of the case for human rights. There is cynicism about the whole discourse, which, being so fatally malleable, is exploited as a weapon in power politics. Some governments maintain that economic and social rights are prior to classic civil and political rights. Some say that the rights of certain groups—a people, a nation, a culture—limit the human rights of individuals. And there are doubts, not always groundless, about how firmly based some of the claims to human rights are. One way to join in advancing the cause of human rights is to make the case for them as intellectually compelling as one can.

It is not that the job can be left to international law. It is not that over the last fifty years or so the body of treaties and decisions of international courts has grown large enough for those courts now to be able to tell us definitively whether a certain human right exists and what, fairly precisely, its content is. The most authoritative sources for the courts' decisions are the treaties, and we must be able to ask whether the lists of rights in the treaties are themselves correct. And the treaties supply the terms of the argument on that subject: an item on the list is acceptable if, and only if, it can be derived from the idea of 'the dignity of the human person'. But that is precisely the idea that cries out for clarification. Has the reasoning that has gone on at the various stages in the emergence of a supposed human right been persuasive? Widespread doubts about certain reputed civil rights, objections to the lavishness of some welfare rights, scepticism about the whole class of group rights, have a rational force that cannot be countered simply by showing that these rights appear in international treaties. Part of the ambition of international law is to incorporate rights that exist independently of positive law. So international lawyers need a grasp of the existence conditions of these rights. In 2004 a group of Inuit, seal-hunting people of the Arctic, announced their intention to seek a ruling from the Inter-American Commission on Human Rights that the United States, by being a substantial contributor to global warming, is threatening their existence.[15] They and other groups (some inhabitants of tropical atolls and of the Himalayan slopes, for example) claim that the issue is not just about prudent environmental policy but about violation of human rights. These testingly difficult cases may eventually go to the international courts. What materials will the judges have to decide them? Our hope is that international law will help overcome the indeterminateness of sense of the term 'human right' by being part of the process of establishing a settled use for it. But the judges in international courts will not bring this about by deciding a case like the Inuit's by fiat; no one is going to follow that sort of lead. Their decision will have to be backed by sound reasons.

In any case, treaties are not the only source of international law. The Statute of the International Court of Justice announces (Article 38. 1) that, in settling disputes submitted to it, it shall apply (1) treaties, (2) customary law in the international sphere, (3) general principles of law recognized by civilized nations, and, as 'subsidiary means', (4) judicial decisions, and (5) the teaching of the most highly qualified publicists (i.e. experts). Some legal scholars go on to add (6) considerations of humanity (e.g. especially basic principles that appear in the preambles to conventions, prominent among which would be 'the dignity of the human person'), (7) *ius cogens* (i.e. basic principles that do not rest on the consent of nations, a notion reminiscent of 'natural law'), and (8) legitimate interests.[16] These sources overlap. Some may even collapse into others; it may be possible, for instance, to regard any *ius cogens* as an especially basic customary law.[17] None the less, an international court willing to heed expert opinion or considerations of humanity or *ius cogens* is driven to take seriously basic considerations of justice, the meaning of 'the dignity of the human person', and how justice and rights are related. The decisions of international courts are not an alternative to answering my questions; they require it.

They require, crucially, fuller understanding of the notion of 'the dignity of the human person'. I have already said that it would be a mistake to interpret it so broadly—say, as respect for persons, when that idea is meant to capture the moral point of view itself—that human rights expand to fill the whole moral domain. And if one wants something in between this overly broad account and my narrower account, then one must identify and justify it. Looking for the best understanding of 'the dignity of the human person' is precisely my project, which is why I say that it should not be underestimated.

Now, all of this seems obvious to me, but not to many international lawyers. Some writers see international law as depending at points on ethics (the incorporation of human rights would be an obvious such point), and they therefore see its bindingness as deriving, at these points, from ethics.[18] But other writers see international law as entirely independent of ethics, as occupying its own autonomous domain.[19] They could say that its bindingness, when it has it, derives from, say, the national self-interest of the participating nations.[20] They could also repudiate my concern about the indeterminateness of the sense of the term 'human right'. Our culture, our tradition, has given us the discourse of 'human rights', they could say, and whether the term has a determinate sense does not matter; we put it to use, and generally to good effect.

But the price one pays for taking this second, reductivist line is high. Human rights become largely devoid of content, except for what the tradition has already supplied or, say, national self-interest might add. But to what do we appeal to decide how much the right to welfare, or to health, is actually a right to? How would an international court go about adjudicating the Inuits' claim against the United States? I have already said that deciding these questions by fiat would drastically reduce the influence of the decisions; and so would deciding them by appeal to the self-interest of various nations. This reductivist line of thought would purge international law not only of ethics but also of explanatory capacity and action-guiding authority. It would gratuitously trivialize international law.

11.6 CURRENT LEGAL LISTS: ECONOMIC, SOCIAL, AND CULTURAL RIGHTS

I just remarked in passing that some writers are deeply sceptical about the whole class of welfare rights.[21] They see them as often admirable social goals, but without the peremptory force or universal scope of human rights. Welfare rights are, they think, for each society to decide for itself in light of its resources and its own scale of values. None of them is a human right. But that seems to me not so. What seems to me undeniable is that there is a human right to the minimum resources needed to live as a normative agent.[22] That is more than the resources needed simply to keep body and soul together, but it is a good deal less than the lavish provision that many of the international documents have in mind.

So I think that there are acceptable claims to (human) welfare rights in the major international documents. But, on my account, there are also a large number of unacceptable and debatable claims, many more than in the case of civil and political rights, and that great discrepancy also needs explaining.

(a) *Unacceptable cases.*

Some of the claims to welfare rights are hardly credible. Article 7c of the Additional Protocol to the American Convention asserts that there is a right of every worker to promotion or upward mobility in his employment. But some perfectly good jobs have no career structure. It was common a few decades ago in Oxford to be appointed to a tutorial fellowship as one's first job, and virtually everyone expected, and was content, to finish up in the same job. There are, perhaps, drawbacks in having no change of duties or responsibilities in the course of a whole career, but it is incredible that these jobs violate a human right. Nor would it be credible of a lawyer whose career is passed in a one-person practice doing much the same work, nor a GP in a similar position. Nor would a right be violated if the salary in these jobs never changed over the career. There are many issues of justice or fairness about jobs (unattractive or dangerous jobs should perhaps be shared or highly compensated, promotion should be on merit, and so on), but these issues are not addressed by this proposed right to promotion. It is hard to think of any plausible account of human rights that would justify it.

Take now a more important and more plausible claim. In his State of the Union message in 1944, which I have quoted earlier,[23] President F. D. Roosevelt spoke of 'a second Bill of Rights':

> Among these are:
> The right to a useful and remunerative job in the industries, or shops, or farms, or mines of the Nation.
> The right to earn enough to provide adequate food and clothing and recreation ...

The Universal Declaration of 1948 proclaims, in the spirit of Roosevelt's address, a right to work (Article 23.1), and many subsequent international documents have repeated the claim.[24] Yet, on my account, there is no right to work. There is certainly a right to the resources needed to live as an agent, but those resources do not have to come from work. If in an advanced technological society there were not enough work for everyone, and those without it were adequately provided for, then, on the face of it, no one's human rights would be violated. Work is valuable to us, it is true, in more than one way. The most obvious way is as a means to an end, as Roosevelt clearly acknowledges; what, ultimately, we need, as he puts it, is adequate food and clothing and (even) recreation. We need them, he says, in order to live as 'free men'. All of this seems to me exactly right. Still, for most people on the face of the earth, work is the expected, and sometimes the only, means to that end. Roosevelt and the drafters of the Universal Declaration, and of all the other documents that claim a right to work, reasonably enough wanted to state the right they had in mind in a form relevant to the social reality of their time. What their post-Depression societies had to do to ensure adequate provision was to ensure the availability of jobs.[25] And most societies today still have to do the same. But some societies are nearing conditions in which a job will not be, even for a large proportion of the population, the necessary means to the end.

But the value of work is far more complex than this means–end story makes out. Most people want the dignity of earning their own keep. They want to contribute something to their society. Their enjoyment of life depends upon their having something absorbing, demanding, and useful to do. One of the most important components of the quality of life is one's accomplishing something of substance in the course of it. Idleness is a close cousin of boredom; absorption in projects is a close cousin of enjoyment. So if there are not enough jobs of the old sort to go around (butcher, baker, candlestick maker ...), then a community must discover, for those who cannot discover them for themselves, jobs of a new sort (there is still plenty of scope, for example, to improve our present communities). But the advocates of a right to work meant jobs of the old sort, and that seems wrong. Strictly speaking, the right is to adequate material provision—adequate for life as an agent—and to options to live one's life in a productive, interesting, enjoyable way. But I think that the discrepancy between that right, which is what follows from my account, and the right to work, which appears in these international documents, can be reconciled. They are formulated at different levels of abstraction, the one in universal form and the other when the universal form is applied to a particular time and place.[26]

I want to mention only one more dubious welfare right—an example of a particularly lavish right that I mentioned earlier.[27] The International Covenant on Economic, Social and Cultural Rights, followed by other documents, claims that we have a right to 'the highest attainable standard of physical and mental health'.[28] On my account, there is no such right. Societies *could* mount crash programmes in the case of illnesses for which cures are attainable, but they often regard themselves as free to decide when they have spent enough on health, even if they are still short of the highest attainable standards, and may devote their inevitably limited resources to education, preservation of the environment, and other important social goods. On my account, we also have a right to life, because life is a necessary condition of agency, and to the health care necessary for our functioning effectively as normative agents. This statement of the right to life and the right to health is still very loose, and work would have to be put into making these two rights determinate enough for political life. But there is nothing in my explanation of the ground of those rights that implies that life must be extended as long as possible or that health must be as rude as possible. And that seems right.

(b) *Debatable cases.*

I have the same doubts about the inference from justice to rights in the case of welfare rights that I had before in the case of civil and political rights. Equal pay for equal work is only fair.[29] Just conditions of work are, obviously, a requirement of justice.[30] And promotion on merit is, equally, a matter of simple fairness.[31] But they are not thereby also matters of human rights. I should put all of these claims to rights in the class of the debatable, merely because the relation of justice and rights is not easy to settle. But, as I said before, I think that in the end the argument goes against their being human rights.

11.7 THE FUTURE OF INTERNATIONAL LISTS OF HUMAN RIGHTS

Suppose that I am right. What should we do about the debatable and unacceptable items on the lists in international law?

Not much, at least on a grand scale. A solitary author, especially a solitary philosopher, is most unlikely to be able to bring about a rethinking of the whole of the international law of human rights. International law is too well established, too widely institutionalized, too much in the middle of its important business, has altogether too much momentum, for that to be feasible. In any case, the law has its own ways of dealing with its errors. It can turn a cold shoulder to laws or sections of treaties that it thinks deeply flawed; it can sometimes eventually make dead letters of them. Or it can wait for courts to remedy ambiguity and confusion in the law. The cold shoulder is probably what is needed for the widely rejected 'right' to periodic holidays with pay. Many rights can be, and already are, demoted to the status of mere aspirations rather than rights proper (e.g. the 'right' to peace); a pejorative term has been coined for them: 'manifesto rights'. No doubt, some other 'rights' should be subject to demotion: for instance, the 'right' to the highest attainable standard of physical and mental health (though that will need redrafting before it can be accepted even as a reasonable aspiration) and perhaps the 'right' to freedom of residence within the borders of one's country (though that is a more debatable case). Many 'rights' are so badly drawn that they need interpretation tantamount to redrafting: for example, the 'right' to inherit and the 'right' to protection against attacks on one's honour and reputation. To this gradual critical process, even single authors can make a contribution.

After those exercises in downgrading and re-defining have been completed, there would still remain what most of us in any case regard as the core of the list. But even at the core are rights that I earlier labelled 'debatable': for example, the right to compensation for a miscarriage of justice. What should we do with those cases?

The sensible answer, I think, is this: accept them as human rights. Their defect, such as it is, is that they cannot be seen as defending personhood. They cannot be brought under what I am proposing as the canonical heading 'protection of a component of normative agency'. But very few words in our language are governed wholly by a canonical formula; very few can be defined in terms of essential properties. Many geometrical terms, such as 'triangle', can be. But the word 'game', to take Wittgenstein's example,[32] cannot be. Most words in a natural language cover some of the ground they do for reasons of utility and historical accident. Their lack of essential properties does not matter; their having a settled use is enough for there to be criteria for determining whether or not they are used correctly.

It is not hard to see how a 'right' to compensation for a miscarriage of justice should have come to be included in a list spelling out procedural justice in the law. The original impetus for these rights seems indeed to have been the urgent need to protect liberty, autonomy, and property against arbitrary government. But if society decides to entrench these protections by listing them in especially solemn form—in, say, a United Nations Covenant—it is understandable that it will aim at a certain measure of completeness. And if those who compile the list have only a vague sense of a 'human right' in mind at the time, one would not expect to find any sharply bounded set of defining properties running through all the items included on the list.

But why, then, not simply accept all the claims of human rights that appear on these lists in international law, even the ones I called 'unacceptable'? But the term 'human right' is not like the word 'game'. It does not have nearly as well settled a use as 'game' has. It is a theorist's term; it was, as words go, introduced relatively recently. It succeeded to the position of an earlier term, 'natural right', but the metaphysical background of the successor was radically different from that of its predecessor, and this meant that new criteria of use were needed. And because it is the introduction of philosophers and political theorists, they have the responsibility, not yet discharged, of giving it a satisfactorily determinate sense. And a canonical formula is, for that reason, going to play a large, if not sole, part in the way they do discharge it. It is precisely our further understanding, which a substantive account of human rights will supply, that will carry our use of the term 'human right' from indeterminateness to sufficient determinateness of sense. It may be that what carries members of the Western European Enlightenment tradition to sufficiently determinate sense may be non-trivially different from what carries members of the Hindu or Bushman traditions. It may be that, despite our different routes, we all arrive at more or less the same destination. But there has to be something that carries each of us to it. That is why we need a substantive account of human rights.

Once we have such an account, should we keep it dark? This brings us back to the thought that a substantive account should be self-effacing. If there really is a non-trivial difference in substantive accounts between members of different countries, we should hardly insist that our own particular account should be preferred by incorporation in international documents. Those documents at least can remain silent on the subject. But in deliberating about what is and what is not a human right, one cannot do anything but appeal to one's own understanding of human dignity. And we need more, not less, such deliberation. In present conditions, there is likely to be conflict when the drafters of an international document listing a new category of human rights come to decide what belongs on the list. That would be no bad thing. The conflict would provide a good test of the adequacy of the competing substantive accounts. With time, we might find greater convergence between them.

12

A Right to Life, a Right to Death

12.1 THE SCOPE OF THE RIGHT TO LIFE

On the face of it, the right to life is the least problematic of rights. Of Locke's trinity—life, liberty, and property—it was the least discussed. In the debates at the end of the eighteenth century about the ratification of the US Constitution the right to life was often cited, but without comment, as if it were too obvious to need it.[1] But when the parties to the debate turned to liberty and property, they had much to say. Their relative silence about the right to life was probably connected to another belief of theirs; they seemed to conceive of it largely negatively—as a right not to be deprived of life without due process. A prohibition of murder hardly needed comment.[2]

Still, once one reflects on the grounds for a right to life, even the grounds accepted in the seventeenth and eighteenth centuries, the scope of the right seems irresistibly to expand. The grounds tend to a generality that justifies more than just a prohibition of murder. If living at liberty is of great value (to take an indisputable human right), then *living*, as well as living in that *way*, is valuable, and that seems to justify a claim to some broader preservation of life. It would seem to justify a wider negative right than just the prohibition of murder—say, a prohibition of gratuitously endangering other people's lives or of destroying their rationality. What is more, it would seem to justify some positive rights.[3] If you are drowning, and all that I have to do to save you is to toss you the life-belt next to me, and I wantonly disregard your plight, do I not violate your right to life? Does the right not include a positive right to rescue, at least if the cost to the rescuer is not great? And if it includes a right to be tossed a life-belt if one were drowning, would it not include a right to food if one were starving, or to medicine if one were dangerously ill? And if it includes those, does it also include a right to conditions, such as clean water and female literacy, the absence of which drastically shortens a child's life? This ballooning of the content of the right to life is not just a theoretical possibility; it is just what has happened. The putative right has grown from a right against the arbitrary termination of the normal life of someone already living (murder), to a right against other forms of termination of life (abortion, suicide, euthanasia), to a right against the prevention of the formation of life (contraception, sterilization), to a right to basic welfare provision, to a right to a fully flourishing life. That last extension, no doubt, goes too far. The right to life cannot even be a right to have life preserved in *any* circumstances. That would be impossibly demanding. So, what is, and what is not, demanded by the right to life?

This line of thought leaves the right without a clear boundary. What starts off as the least problematic of rights becomes, on reflection, distinctly problematic.

12.2 LOCKE ON THE SCOPE OF THE RIGHT

What *is* the scope of the right to life? We might start by asking what the natural or human rights tradition makes of its scope. And when it comes to the trinity—life, liberty, and property—Locke is the towering figure in the tradition. Many think that on Locke's view, and on the classical natural rights view generally, natural rights are all negative.[4] But Locke's view is more complicated and better than that.

Locke's ground for natural rights is a natural law that asserts some form of equality of human beings. But it is not a sort of political equality that he has in mind (e.g., equality of distribution of goods or equality of opportunity in their acquisition, or the difference principle), but that morally fundamental notion of equal respect; what he has in mind is equal standing as moral agents. In the *Second Treatise* Locke quotes this passage from the philosopher he refers to as 'the judicious Hooker':

… those things which are equal, must needs all have one measure; if I cannot but wish to receive good, even as much at every man's hands, as any man can wish unto his own soul, how should I look to have any part of my desire herein satisfied, unless my self be careful to satisfy the like desire, which is undoubtedly in other men, being of one and the same nature?[5]

So, Locke says, no one ought to harm another 'in his life, health, liberty, or possession'.[6] We find in the state of nature none of the subordination between persons, as we do between persons and animals, that would authorize one person to destroy another.[7] But notice how Locke generalizes as he concludes:

… so by the like reason when his own preservation comes not in competition, ought he, as much as he can, *to preserve the rest of mankind*, and may not unless it be to do justice on the offender, take away or impair the life, or what tends to the preservation of the life, liberty, health, limb, or goods of another.[8]

When Locke says that one must, to the extent that one can, *preserve the rest of mankind*, he seems to include the positive as well as the negative. If one is to preserve mankind, one must rescue and bring aid—provided, as Locke puts it, that one's own survival is not in competition. It is true, however, that Locke then goes on to list a number of specific duties, all of which, being duties not to harm, seem negative.

It never becomes fully clear what Locke's view of the right to life is. The distinction between positive and negative rights was, I expect, not in his mind. And the same unclarity, the same alternation between positive-sounding and negative-sounding proposals, runs through other passages in the *Second Treatise*.[9] Still, it is also not clear for that reason, contrary to a common view, that Locke saw the right to life as purely negative. And Hooker's, and Locke's, ground for the right has echoes of 'Do unto others as you would be done by'. All of us would want to be rescued or aided if we were ourselves in great danger. And, as we saw earlier,[10] Locke is not one of those writers who thought that all genuine natural rights are negative; he recognized a natural right to 'meat and drink' when in need.

In any case, I do not think that Locke's ground for human rights—the principle of equal respect—is really what we should see, in the end, as grounding them. According to Locke, Hooker has shown how equality serves as a foundation of duties of justice and charity.[11] And that seems entirely right: the principle of equal respect is the foundation of far more than just human rights. Being the moral point of view itself, it is, in that sense, the foundation of all morality. But then Locke has not provided us with the ground for human rights in particular. If we were to accept that whatever the moral point of view itself generates are rights, then rights would spread to fill the whole moral domain. Then our account of human rights would fail a reasonable redundancy test: we already have a perfectly satisfactory way of speaking about moral demands in general. It would be a waste of the special language of human rights to let it become so inflated.

12.3 PERSONHOOD AS THE GROUND OF THE RIGHT

If personhood were, as I propose, indeed the ground of the right to life, the intuitive case for it would go like this. We attach a high value to our autonomously choosing and freely pursuing our conception of a worthwhile life. Then it is not surprising that we should include among human rights, as the tradition always did, not only a right to liberty but also a right to life. Can we value living in a characteristically human way without valuing the *living* as well as the autonomy and liberty that make it characteristically human? If human rights are protections of that form of life, they should protect life as well as that form. This intuitive case, which we have met earlier,[12] leads to a right to life with positive as well as negative elements.

If we accept that the right to life implies positive duties, then we face several problems. How great will the demands be? One limit on them is that the right is not to a fully flourishing life, but only to that more austere state, the life of a normative agent. And there are limits, which I also mentioned earlier,[13] deriving from the principle that *ought* implies *can*. There are limits to human powers of calculation. There are limits to human motivation, especially to the motivation of the sorts of persons we should want there to be. There is a domain of permitted partiality, which limits the extent to which ethics may demand that we sacrifice ourselves, or those especially close to us, for the benefit of strangers.

Still, the protection even of that relatively austere state, the life of a normative agent, can be highly demanding. Here the right to life, with its positive elements, substantially overlaps a right to health. The right to health is not, strictly speaking, a right to health itself. Health is only partly within human control. I have no right not to be struck down by an incurable disease. Nor is it a right merely to health care. Much more is relevant to our health than health care, narrowly conceived: for instance, safe roads, female literacy, good sewage, clean water, and so on. Our right is to health care, broadly conceived. But then it is a right only to *basic* health care, also broadly conceived, where what is 'basic' is decided by what is necessary for life as a normative agent, and no more. There are many forms of ill health that have no bearing on normative agency. For example, there are the mild neurotic hang-ups that afflict us all. They are pathological, but they usually do not stop us from being normative agents. We have no human right, therefore, to their treatment. It is easy to imagine very many physical ailments of the same sort. We should not be disturbed by this consequence. There are perfectly good reasons, even moral reasons, to treat minor illnesses besides a human right's requiring it.

The combined effect of these limits makes the demands on us arising from the positive side of the right to life much more manageable than they may seem at first sight.

12.4 FROM A RIGHT TO LIFE TO A RIGHT TO DEATH

There are groups that invoke the right to life to justify banning abortion, suicide, and euthanasia. The right to life, so interpreted, not only protects our freedom to live, but can also oblige, even condemn, us to go on living.

It may seem an odd interpretation of a human right that would have these consequences—a welcome entitlement that turns into an unwelcome prohibition—but there are several other rights much like this. No doubt in most of what are called 'entrapped cases' (e.g. a person with advanced motor neurone disease with a perfectly good mind in a non-functioning body), the patient would wish to waive the sort of right to life that these groups have in mind. But not all rights are waivable. I cannot waive my autonomy or liberty. If I freely ask you to take all my central decisions in life for me, you may not do it, except in rare circumstances. If I voluntarily offer to be your slave, you may not accept. In general, I may not waive my dignity as a human person. I am often obliged, even condemned, to maintain it. Nor is there any conceptual error in linking a human right of mine, which is often a freedom, with an obligation upon me, which is a kind of restriction on my freedom. One has, for instance, both a human right to education and an obligation to exercise it. Similarly, one has, as well as a right, an obligation to be autonomous and at liberty.

How are we to distinguish human rights that are waivable from those that are not? On the personhood account, one looks at whether normative agency would thereby be seriously diminished; if so, the right in question is unwaivable. That is why, though one cannot waive one's rights to autonomy and liberty, one probably can, in certain circumstances, waive one's human right to privacy. Most of us need certain forms of privacy to function at all effectively as agents, but especially self-confident persons, or shameless exhibitionists, may not. And for most of us the loss of certain minor privacies would not seriously compromise our normative agency.

To whom could I owe these sometimes unwelcome obligations? In a secular ethics, my obligation to maintain my status as a normative agent is one that I owe, it seems, in the first instance, to myself. On the face of it, my obligation to be educated is more complex; I owe it not only to myself but also, if I have political power in a society, to my fellow citizens. The relative clarity of the case of education might then lead us to accept that, in the same social circumstances, I owe it also to my fellow citizens to maintain my normative agency generally. These conclusions depend upon there being obligations to oneself. I shall here simply suppose that there are.

Do I, by parity of reason, then have an obligation as well as a right to go on living?[14] If I have an obligation to maintain my normative agency, do I not therefore have an obligation, to myself, to maintain myself in being so long as I remain a normative agent? I think that, by parity of reason, I do. The crucial question, of course, is: how strong a one? There need be no element here of an obligation to others. If I have certain powers of decision in society, then my correlative obligation to others is that I exercise them responsibly, but that obligation has no clear implications about my committing suicide. One's obligation to maintain oneself in being would often be an obligation only to oneself, grounded in the dignity of living as a normative agent. Respect for personhood would require respect for its very existence. But respect for personhood would require respect also for its exercise—for example, in reaching a judgement that suicide in certain conditions is rational. There is no reason why the first form of respect should always outweigh the second. It would, most of us would think, be outweighed by one's life's holding nothing but intolerable pain, as judged by oneself, as a normative agent, for oneself. It would be outweighed, many of us would say, even by a person's deciding to commit suicide on certain semi-aesthetic grounds: say, on the ground that one had no obligations to others, that one had reached a certain perfection in life, and that what lay ahead was only pitiful decline. It could be outweighed, however, if I were a quite exceptional person upon whom depended the avoidance of some great social disaster, or if I were a perfectly ordinary person who had dependants who would suffer greatly without me. Then I might have to soldier on. The obligation to soldier on could fall on one quite apart from responsibilities to others, if, though my pain were great, it was not so great as to outweigh the often underestimated value of living as a normative agent. There is truth in the criticism that suicide can be 'the easy way out'. Some suicide is cowardly or shows a bad sense of values. A person who kills himself because he is about to be charged with fraud may act from narcissism, or a wish to hurt others, or ignorance of the forms of dignity still left him.

We have now identified three kinds of value of human life. Hitherto I have concentrated on what is good for the person whose life it is and how that life can be good or bad for others. But just now I have added the value of the life itself—not value *for* anyone, the person concerned or others, but an intrinsic value. And this intrinsic value, many say, is generally overlooked by secular accounts of the value of life. I think that is so. And I have just tried to describe this third sort of value and how it manifests itself. But many would also think I am still underestimating it, that I recognize the category but not its true weight. It manifests itself, they will say, in a right to life that prohibits, or at least more severely restricts than I understand, suicide and euthanasia. Still, I would respond that the way I have described the intrinsic value of life at least makes it comprehensible and plausible. The accounts that make it still weightier—weighty enough for it to manifest itself in these much more restrictive ways—are extraordinarily hard to make intelligible. Is there an account of this weightier value that is both comprehensible and plausible?

Many think that there is. Many, like Locke, derive it from God's will:

Men being all the workmanship of one omnipotent, and infinitely wise maker; all the servants of one sovereign master, sent into the world by his order and about his business, they are his property, whose workmanship they are, made to last during his, not one another's pleasure ... Every one ... is *bound to preserve himself*, and not quit his station wilfully ...[15]

It is sometimes said that Locke saw human life as a gift from God, but the word 'gift' does not begin to capture Locke's thought. If my life were a gift, I should now own it and could do with it as I please. But Locke's idea is that God retains ownership and gives me only a loan of it, and so restricted use.[16] This makes an especially weighty, highly restrictive intrinsic value of life entirely comprehensible; whether it is also plausible, we can leave aside, because we are looking for a secular account. Indeed, even theists may reject Locke's view if, for instance, they think, as many do, that the loan conception of human life is theologically and scripturally under-motivated.[17]

In *Cruzan* v. *Missouri* (1990), Chief Justice Rehnquist, for the majority, asserted that the state has an interest in protecting human life itself, even when it is contrary to the interests of the person concerned (the person concerned in this case being Nancy Cruzan, who had by then spent more than seven years in a persistent vegetative state, and whose parents had petitioned for her to be allowed to die). A possible state interest in restricting suicide and euthanasia could arise from a more permissive policy's creating an atmosphere in which suicide and euthanasia become too psychologically easy, to the detriment of the many who then killed themselves without sufficient justification. That, I think, cannot be gainsaid; nor, I think, can the claim that human life has intrinsic value. The crucial question, however, is how weighty its intrinsic value is, measured in the strength of the restrictions it implies.

The most powerful secular case for strong restrictions is, to my mind, Kant's. Mere things, he says, have *price*: they have equivalents, so substitutes. But persons have *dignity*; they have no equivalents or substitutes. The dignity that one has as a person is a value one has *in* oneself, not *for* oneself nor *for* others. Persons require respect; they must be treated as ends in themselves and never merely as means. To kill oneself because one's life is no longer worth living, or even worse, is to treat one's rational nature, one's personhood, as a means of controlling what is good *for* one and not as an end in itself. And the same would be true for the same reason of an act of euthanasia.[18]

This is too brief to stand as an account of Kant's views, but my concern here is not the ethics of suicide and euthanasia in general, but the content of the right to life. Well, one might think, what could be more appropriate as a role (not necessarily the only one) for the human right to life than to protect the intrinsic value of life? Once one admits that there is such an intrinsic value, does one not have to accept that there is a right to its protection? All that I want to claim here is that the human right to life does not protect the intrinsic value of life on Kant's strong interpretation of it. I have argued this earlier.[19] Kant derives what he calls 'natural rights' from his idea of respect for persons, and that results in a far broader set of rights than we have from the Enlightenment tradition or in present international law. Kant's 'natural rights' rest on the a priori 'Universal Principle of Right', which says, 'Any action is *right* if it can co-exist with everyone's freedom in accordance with a universal law, or if on its maxim the freedom of choice of each can co-exist with everyone's freedom in accordance with a universal law.'[20] As I explained earlier, his term 'natural right' therefore covers much of morality, far more of it than our term 'human rights' now covers.[21] Why not then go over to Kant's way of speaking? There are three good reasons not to. First, we should no longer be explaining what we set out to explain: human rights with roughly their current extension. Second, we should be shifting from a limited basis for human rights that is likely to be widely accepted to a basis in a comprehensive moral view that is widely disputed. And, finally, the distinction between the value of life *for* the person living it and the value of the life *in itself*, as Kant uses the second notion, is far too sharp: the dignity of having a rational nature includes exercising it in making rational judgements, and one cannot respect a rational nature and therefore its exercise without respecting those judgements, which may well concern what is good *for* persons.

There are different ways of understanding Kant's views on the value of human life. There are also Kantian accounts of the value of life that do not aim to be interpretations of Kant's own. And there are entirely non-Kantian accounts—say, a non-theistic teleological account. Each of them might come up with a weighty intrinsic value of life that justifies strong restrictions on suicide and euthanasia, but I shall stop with this subject here. I know of no account that yields a weighty value that is both comprehensible and plausible. I know some that are comprehensible but not plausible, and some that may be plausible but are scarcely comprehensible, and some whose restrictive consequences are announced, but the value that is supposed to support them is left unspecified. Of course, someone may come up with an account that is both comprehensible and plausible. We should then have to revisit these matters.

Let me return to the current ballooning of the content of the right to life. There is, I conclude, an intrinsic value of a human life as well as a value for the person living it. Does the human right to life severely restrict suicide and euthanasia? No; the right protects the intrinsic value of human life in protecting our personhood generally, but there is nothing in the intrinsic value that makes it incommensurable with the other two values, the values for oneself and for others, nor anything that makes it resistant to frequently being outweighed by the value of the life for the person who lives it. Does the right to life include a right to a flourishing life? No, as I have already argued;[22] it is a right only to that more austere state, the life of a normative agent. Does it imply a prohibition of abortion? No; as I have already argued,[23] embryos and foetuses do not have human rights, though there may be moral considerations other than human rights that serve to prohibit abortions. Does a human right imply a prohibition of contraception? No; the pre-conception forms of life that can produce a human person do not have human rights, though again it is an open question whether there are other moral reasons for a prohibition.

12.5 IS THERE A RIGHT TO DEATH?

Most of us think that the right to life does not severely restrict suicide and euthanasia. Indeed, is there not, as well as a right to life, a closely related right to death?

There is an answer to that question that is tempting in its simplicity: a right to death is the obverse of the right to life.[24] But that is too simple. Rights to autonomy and liberty are needed to justify the right to death. A free, informed, and competent person will choose a valuable life, but may not choose a valueless life or, all the more, a life in which the bad irreversibly overwhelms the good. Both of those choices, for life and for death, are manifestations of the same highly valued thing, one's status as a person. If the first choice is protected by rights—the right autonomously to choose what one judges to be a worthwhile life and freedom to pursue it—so must the second be—the right not to live a valueless or a thoroughly bad life. The second right is just a special case of the autonomy and liberty that are the ground of the first. Whether dignity-destroying pain or deterioration is to be endured is one of the most momentous decisions that one can take about what one sees as a life worth living.[25] If one is denied that momentous decision, or the possibility of implementing it, then one's right to autonomy and liberty are hollow shams. If one has a right to anything, one has a right to death.[26] The right to life enters this argument only in the obvious way that it enters any appeal to autonomy or to liberty: the rights are to *living* autonomously and *living* at liberty.

Like all human rights, the right to death is borne only by normative agents. In the case of the right to death, however, there is the special problem that suicide is often the act of a disturbed mind. Then, others may intervene to stop a person bent on suicide at least long enough to ensure that the suicide is indeed the act of a normative agent—free, informed, and competent. Freedom is perhaps the hardest of the three conditions to establish. The old and ill often feel themselves to be an unwelcome burden on their children, and if suicide becomes more widely accepted, if children see their infirm parent as resisting the sensible way out, the pressure on the parent to commit suicide could become hard to resist. And if one's doctor encourages suicide, as it has been said some Dutch doctors have done to free scarce hospital or hospice resources,[27] then the pressure could become overwhelming. Sometimes suicide is rational, given the state of one's society, or given one's position in it. If one is poor, and adequate medical treatment is beyond one's means, it may be rational to kill oneself. But, in those circumstances, what most urgently ought to be done is not to make suicide easier but to improve the inadequate medical care that can drive people to it. We have a secondary obligation to protect vulnerable agents from such coercion.

Still, a human right can be outweighed. The right to suicide seems especially vulnerable to being overridden. Take the simplest case available: that of rational, unassisted suicide. Perhaps a policy of blanket prohibition would have better consequences overall, even for the would-be suicides themselves, than the rather vague, permissive policy that we might eventually be able to formulate. These are not idle speculations. About 25 per cent of terminally ill patients die in pain.[28] Despite this, the class of doctors most opposed to euthanasia are experts in pain management.[29] They believe that few need die in pain, and that many who do are the victims of ignorance, usually their own general practitioner's ignorance. Would a society not therefore be better off prohibiting suicide while, at the same time, ensuring that as few as possible die in pain?

But few societies have the resources to provide the best medical treatment, or even adequate pain management, for all its members. And in those circumstances, a society can hardly prohibit suicide on the ground that it would be better for it to provide effective pain management instead, if it is not actually going to do so. Even if it is going to do so, it is reckoned that 15 per cent of the dying suffer extreme pain beyond the reach of present pain-killers.[30] Anyway, not all conditions that make suicide rational involve physical pain. Some are untreatable and intolerable mental illnesses. Yet others are forms of gross physical and mental deterioration. It is true that one could deeply sedate all such patients. But this would merely consign them to a form of living death.

In any case, how heavily could the fact that a policy of blanket prohibition of suicide had better consequences overall than a more permissive policy, if indeed it were a fact, weigh against a right to suicide? A right to suicide is an instance of the general anti-paternalist rights to autonomy and liberty. In general, to respect a person's autonomy and liberty is to let the person decide and then carry out the decision. One may try to dissuade the person, but one may not intervene. It is true that these rights can be outweighed, but only in extreme circumstances. There are many cases of suicide in which the agent is, in fact, free, informed, and competent. And if there is any substantial doubt about it, our rights to autonomy and liberty demand, at the minimum, that an agent be given the benefit of the doubt. And there is very substantial doubt about the claim that blanket prohibition of suicide would have better consequences overall than more permissive policies. We simply do not know with much reliability, and probably not with sufficient reliability for action, how the calculations of the long-term, large-scale consequences of these competing policies come out. It would be thoroughly perverse to deny a very large number of people a highly important right on the basis of a thoroughly shaky guess about cases in which the exercise of the right might turn out to be a mistake.[31]

12.6 IS IT A POSITIVE OR A NEGATIVE RIGHT?

What is a right to death a right to? The right clearly entails a duty on others, in certain circumstances, not to stop one from killing oneself. But does it also entail a duty on some others to help one?

This is, of course, a subject of hot dispute. As I mentioned earlier, there are many who think that human rights should be kept purely negative. I doubt that there is a sharp enough divide between positive and negative elements in most human rights for that strategy to be feasible, and, anyway, it is a myth that the classical human rights of the seventeenth and eighteenth centuries were purely negative.

What, then, might be the positive element in a right to death? Perhaps the most common circumstance in which one would want to commit suicide is when one is terminally ill and the value of life is low. One would want to determine the time and manner of one's death. But one would also not want to die before one needs to. So the chances are not negligible that, when the need arises, one's own physical capacities will have diminished. One may be bedridden and weak. One may be in hospital and subject to its rules. If one's right to suicide were merely a right not to be stopped, then the right would often, in the circumstances most relevant to rational suicide, amount to little. One cannot slit one's wrists if one has not got a knife, or take an overdose of drugs if doctors and nurses have no duty to supply them, or even a duty not to do so. Here the moral significance of the line between non-prevention and assistance becomes difficult to defend. In these circumstances, there is no question of stopping one from committing suicide; one cannot even get started. One has become much like an entrapped case. The right to liberty does not impose a duty on others actually to supply one a valuable life, but merely not to stop one from pursuing it. But what if, as in this case, one does not even have the capacity for the pursuit? Is what we value in liberty merely non-denial of the pursuit or, somewhat more fully, ability to pursue? For the same reasons as apply to other apparently negative rights that turn out partly positive, I think that the more plausible account of what we value in liberty is the more generous one. We value not merely the capacities of agency, but their exercise. The right to vote, for instance, includes its exercise, and its exercise can require special ballots for the illiterate, absentee ballots for the infirm, and, for everyone, widespread publication of the issues, police to prevent intimidation, and other expensive forms of assistance. More generally, the right to liberty requires supplying prosthetic aids to the crippled and guide dogs to the blind. The right is not satisfied just by non-interference in one's attending a political meeting; it requires one's being able to attend it. So it requires some sort of restoration, if they are lost, of the capacities necessary for agency. Entrapped cases present special problems here, but still come under all the same principles. Prosthetic aids are of no help to them. At present, the only equivalent help is for someone else to act as the patient's arms and legs, even if the patient's intention in moving the limbs would be to commit suicide.

There remains the question of whether it is possible to draft a law permitting euthanasia and assisted suicide that does more good than ill. Who may assist? What are the standards for a patient's being free, informed, and competent? Who is to decide whether a patient meets the standards? No answer to those questions is without its troubles. The practical problems in formulating an acceptable principle may be so intractable that we must give up the project.

That conclusion seems to me too despairing,[32] but at this point the question comes down largely to matters of fact about which I am not competent to judge. In any case, my questions here have been of a more theoretical sort: Is there a right to life? Is there a right to death? What are their grounds? What is their content?

13

Privacy

13.1 PERSONHOOD AND THE CONTENT OF A HUMAN RIGHT TO PRIVACY

With the resources of the personhood account to hand, we can make the following case for a human right to privacy.[1] Without privacy, autonomy is threatened. Most of us fear disapproval, ridicule, ostracizing, and attack. We are social animals; we seek acceptance by the group; we are severe self-censors, often unconsciously. It takes rare strength to swim against strong social currents. If our deliberation and decisions about how to live were open to public scrutiny, our imperative for self-censorship and self-defence would come feverishly into action. Of course, there are, so far, no mind-reading machines outside science fiction, but there are alternatives: seizing one's diaries or papers, strapping one to a polygraph, administering truth drugs, or magnetic resonance imaging of the brain that, it is claimed, can distinguish truth-telling from lying with 99 per cent accuracy.[2]

All of these threats are possible in the case of one person's solitary thoughts. But a lot of our most fruitful deliberation takes place in communication with others. Frank communication extends our vision, corrects or confirms our ideas, gives us confidence to go on thinking boldly. Frank communication, too, needs the shield of privacy; it needs the restraint of peeping Toms and eavesdroppers, of phone taps and bugging devices in one's house, of tampering with one's mail or seizure of one's correspondence. This is only a start, but we must also guard against padding the list. Too often the form of argument for a human right, or a right of any kind, is to identify a value (say, a valuable form of privacy) and then conclude that there is a right that protects it. But that is a blatant non sequitur. Not all values support human rights, or indeed rights of other kinds. For example, relaxation is valuable to us; without a certain kind of privacy, one cannot fully relax. But this hardly shows that there is a human right to relaxation. Without relaxation, one might be a rather stressed agent, but if the stress is not great, one would be an agent all the same.

So much for autonomy. Think now of liberty. Autonomy is a feature of deliberation and decision; it has to do with deciding for oneself. Liberty is a feature of action; it concerns pursuing one's aims without interference. Only with frank, private communication, can I discover that you and I have certain of the same unpopular beliefs and so be confident enough to act singly or discover the opportunity to act jointly. One would be inhibited from sexual experimentation, especially the kind that invites shock and disapproval, unless there were no fear of peeping Toms or hidden cameras. The richness of personal relations depends upon our emerging from our shells, but few of us would risk emerging without privacy. What is more, we need not only the fact but also the assurance of privacy, and for assurance we need well-established principles of behaviour, deep dispositions, strong social conventions, and laws effectively enforced.[3]

The issue about a human right to privacy is whether certain forms of privacy are necessary conditions of normative agency. What sort of necessity of condition is at issue? In this case, not conceptual necessity;[4] one can conceive of a person's functioning as a normative agent despite a plague of peeping Toms, listening devices, and magazines devoted to photographs of intimate moments. The strongest form of necessity that could be meant here is empirical necessity: that *Homo sapiens* will not in fact function as a normative agent in the absence of these forms of privacy. But that is implausible too. There are a few people courageous enough or self-confident enough, or just exhibitionist enough, to thrive in full public gaze. It is just that the rest of us cannot. But as long as these familiar weaknesses are characteristic of humanity widely, they are enough to provide a ground for a human right. Normative agency constitutes what we call 'human dignity'. Human rights are meant to protect the dignity of perfectly ordinary human beings. It would distort the existence conditions for human rights to limit them to what is necessary for the normative agency of supermen or exhibitionists. It would equally distort them, in the opposite direction, to include what is necessary for the normative agency of even the most pusillanimous among us; it would be likely to result in too great a loss in other values, such as vigorous expression of opinion.

This, then, is the narrow, agency-focused right to privacy derivable from the personhood account. How much would it protect? It is what several recent writers have labelled 'informational privacy': certain of my acts and thoughts and utterances should not be accessed by others and, if known to them, should not be further spread. Which ones? Ones that, if public, would typically threaten normative agency. 'Informational privacy' is not the ideal name; it suggests data—financial, medical, educational records, and the like—while it must be understood also to include certain correspondence, conversations, actions, even works of art if they are self-revealing and deliberately kept under wraps. A peeping Tom's mere observation must count, for our purposes, as a violation of informational privacy. So long as we realize just how much the name 'informational privacy' is meant to cover, it will do.

A question for us is whether this right to informational privacy is too narrow to constitute *the* human right to privacy. Over the last fifty years, lawyers in several jurisdictions have appealed to a right to privacy in order to protect all of the following as well: the sale and use of contraceptives, abortion, sodomy, miscegenation, same-sex marriage, access to pornography, use of drugs in one's own home, refusal to incriminate oneself, euthanasia, freedom from loud noises and foul smells that penetrate the home, not to have one's reputation attacked, a father's participation in the birth of his child, and much more. No doubt, current appeals to the right to privacy are too broad. But would we be willing to see them shrunk solely to informational privacy?

13.2 LEGAL APPROACHES TO THE RIGHT TO PRIVACY

Several national constitutions promise protection of 'privacy'.[5] The United States Bill of Rights never uses the word, but proclaims:

The right of the people to be secure in their persons, houses, papers, and effects, against unreasonable searches and seizures ...

The Universal Declaration of Human Rights (1948), Article 12, says:

No one shall be subjected to arbitrary interference with his privacy, family, home or correspondence, nor to attacks on his honour and reputation.

This is repeated almost verbatim in the International Covenant on Civil and Political Rights (1966), Article 17. The European Convention on Human Rights (1950), Article 8, says:

Everyone has the right to respect for private and family life, his home and his correspondence.

What one finds many times repeated in national and international documents are requirements of respect for or, more strongly, assertions of the sanctity of one's person (security of person), private life, family life, home, and correspondence, with not infrequent mentions as well of protection against attacks on one's honour and reputation. On the face of it, this is a heterogeneous list. One can see how married and family life, home, and correspondence might all be collected under the rubric 'privacy'. But what about attacks on one's honour and reputation? They seem a matter either of justified interest or of libel and slander, and their links with privacy are unclear.

Our immediate interest in looking at the law is in what it suggests to us about the content of the human right to privacy, particularly what more it suggests than simply informational privacy. The extreme brevity of what national constitutions and international declarations say about privacy, at which we have just had a glance, is not much help here. It is more helpful to consult case law. I want to look at the particularly rich case law on privacy that has grown up in recent decades around the United States Supreme Court. Of course, the ultimate aims of deliberation of a judge, a legislator, and a moral philosopher need not be identical. The constraints on a judge to interpret a constitution or a law and to build, where possible, on precedent, and the constraints on a legislator to find solutions to actual social problems and to stay within the bounds of what can feasibly be treated by law, are not as strong for a philosopher seeking to formulate a human right. But I shall not be trying to interpret either United States law or Supreme Court decisions, but rather, to use them simply as prompts to thought.

The first explicit, though unsuccessful, claim to a constitutional right to privacy appeared in Justice Louis Brandeis's dissent in *Olmstead* v. *United States* (1928). The case concerned wire-tapping. But Brandeis's worry about such intrusions went back a long while—to an article that he and Samuel D. Warren published in the *Harvard Law Review* in 1890.[6] As Brandeis wrote in his dissent in *Olmstead*, echoing the article:

The progress in science in furnishing the government with means of espionage is not likely to stop with wire-tapping. Ways may some day be developed by which the government, without moving papers from secret drawers, can reproduce them in court .... Advances in the psychic and related sciences may bring means of exploring unexpressed belief, thoughts and emotions.

The privacy that exercises Brandeis here is informational privacy. But he claims further that the constitutional right to privacy, deriving, he thinks, from the

Fourth and Fifth Amendments,[7] provides protection against 'invasion of "the sanctities of a man's home and the privacies of life"'. This looks like the right to the protection of some sort of private space and private side of life, with the value attaching to these forms of privacy serving as the ground of the right. Call this the privacy of space and life. The right to informational privacy protects us against people's access to certain knowledge about us. The right to the privacy of space and life protects us against intrusions into that space and into that part of our life—say, into our married or family life. These two rights overlap in their protections, but, on the face of it, are different.

Brandeis next takes a step that increases the range of the proposed right to privacy still further:

The protection guaranteed by the amendments [viz. the Fourth and Fifth] is much broader in scope. The makers of our Constitution undertook to secure conditions favourable to the pursuit of happiness ... .They conferred, as against the government, the right to be let alone—the most comprehensive of rights and the right most valued by civilized men.

This seems to be something else again: a general right to liberty. Brandeis, though, overstates it. There is only, as doubtless he knew, a right to be let alone *unless* there is an overriding public interest. Several well-known principles of liberty take this form: *freedom of action unless an overriding public interest*. For instance, it is the form of J. S. Mill's principle of liberty: *freedom of action unless harm to others*.[8] It is also the form of the principle of liberty much employed by the Supreme Court itself in the second half of the twentieth century: *freedom of action unless certain forms of immorality*, which may well include harm to others. In *Bowers* v. *Hardwick* (1986) the Court announces that people are generally to be let alone, but that the government is justified in forbidding acts as repellent to American sensibilities as oral and anal sex.[9]

Why did Brandeis move so easily and so without remark from informational privacy to the relatively narrow privacy of space and life and, finally, to the broad privacy of liberty? He moved so easily because he took these principles to be the same. So did many subsequent writers, including many of his brother Supreme Court Justices.[10] Brandeis's inferences suffer from his using different senses of the word 'private'. Any principle of liberty defines an area into which authorities may not intrude: that is, an area not of legitimate public interest, that is, a private area. Call this, as I did a moment ago, the privacy of liberty. An enormous number of actions exhibiting the privacy of liberty are what we would ordinarily call 'public'. It would fall within our private sphere of liberty, for example, at least on Mill's account of it, for two homosexuals to kiss very publicly. The sense in which the intimacies of the locked diary and the marital bed are private is not the same as the technical sense, derived from a general principle of liberty, in which a public kiss is private. And it does not seem that the right to private space and private life is just a specific form of a general right to liberty. The claim made by the Supreme Court, and by many others, seems to be that private space and private life are themselves valuable to us, indeed 'sacred', and that the right to them is derived from those values. A general right to liberty, on the other hand, is derived from the value of our being able to pursue our conception of a worthwhile life; the values of private space and private life play no role in the derivation here. A general right to liberty is a right to *do* various things: to pursue the life one values, and perhaps also to use contraceptives, to have an abortion, and to commit suicide. Liberty says nothing explicit about whether, when I *do* use contraceptive devices in the marital bed, you may not spy on me. That is a further protection, needing a further rationale.

This puzzling shift from informational privacy to the privacy of space and life and then to the privacy of liberty recurs often in subsequent Supreme Court thinking. Four years before the famous *Griswold* v. *Connecticut* decision, which concerned Connecticut's ban on the sale and use of contraceptive devices, the Court was invited to consider the very same ban in *Poe* v. *Ullman* (1961), but declined on the ground that there were no controversies raised requiring the adjudication of a constitutional issue, with Justice Harlan dissenting. Harlan insisted that, on the contrary, there were constitutional issues to be adjudicated, and to be adjudicated thus:

Precisely what is involved here is this: the State is asserting the right to enforce its moral judgement by intruding upon the most intimate details of the married relation. ... In sum, the statute allows the State [intolerably] to ... punish married people for the private use of their marital intimacy.

This looks like an invocation of the right to private space and life, but only a few lines later Harlan's identification of 'precisely what is involved here' changes:

This enactment involves what, by common understanding throughout the English-speaking world, must be granted to be a most fundamental aspect of 'liberty' ...

Indeed, Harlan says, the liberty involved here is Brandeis's liberty in *Olmstead*, the right to be let alone, which Harlan extols as 'perhaps the most comprehensive statement of the principle of liberty underlying these aspects of the Constitution'. When Harlan observes that the State of Connecticut is enforcing its own moral judgements, he might be thought to suggest that this in itself is wrong. But he does not mean that. The liberty involved is not absolute, he says; states may enforce morality. So this is not Mill's liberty, *freedom of action unless harm to others*. It is the formally similar but materially different liberty: *freedom of action unless certain forms of immorality*. Hence Harlan's concentration on married couples. He leaves it open that, as far as the Constitution goes, fornicators, adulterers, homosexuals, and the incestuous may be denied contraceptives.

Only four years later, in *Griswold* v. *Connecticut* (1965), Harlan's dissent became, in almost all major particulars, the Court's view. For the first time the Court itself declared a right of privacy, 'the right of marital privacy':

> The present case ... concerns a relationship lying within the zone of privacy created by several fundamental constitutional guarantees. Would we allow the police to search the sacred precincts of marital bedrooms ...? The very idea is repulsive to the notions of privacy surrounding the marriage relationship.

This seems clearly to be the right to private space ('the sacred precincts of marital bedrooms') and to private relations ('the marriage relationship'), and it is the 'sacredness' of the space and of the relationship that seems to be offered as the ground for the right. But then, once again, comes the now familiar shift. What Justice Goldberg, concurring, cites as the ground of the right to privacy is Brandeis's general liberty—and, once again, not the liberty of *freedom unless harm to others* but *freedom unless certain forms of immorality*. On Goldberg's conception of liberty too, fornicators, adulterers, and homosexuals, no matter how private their acts, are not necessarily protected by the right.

The Court's opinion in *Roe* v. *Wade* (1973), which ruled unconstitutional a comprehensive ban on abortion, stretched the idea of 'privacy' yet further. The majority opinion, written by Justice Blackmun,[11] starts with an idea of privacy we have met before:

> ... the Court has [hitherto] recognized that a right of personal privacy, or a guarantee of certain areas or zones of privacy, does exist under the Constitution. ... the right has some extension to activities relating to marriage ... procreation ... contraception ... family relationships ... and child rearing and education.

This again looks like the right to private space ('areas or zones of privacy') and private life ('marriage', 'procreation', 'family relationships'). But is an abortion private in either of these ways? It does not always take place within private space (the home, the marital bedroom) but often in clinics or hospitals with doctors and nurses in attendance. Nor is an abortion a matter of a personal relationship; it is in part a matter of a professional relationship. Soon the same shift from the privacy of space and life to the privacy of general liberty occurs in *Roe* v. *Wade*. Justice Stewart, in concurring, explains a person's right to privacy as 'his right to be let alone by other people'—that is, a general liberty. The principles of liberty that we have so far canvassed are of the form *freedom of action unless an overriding public interest*. Suppose liberty is, as Mill said, *freedom of action unless harm to others*. Abortion of—death to—a foetus can, I think, often be regarded, without intolerable conceptual strain, as a 'harm' to the potential person denied life. But that is not enough to settle the moral question. If the phrase 'harm to others' is best glossed as 'harm to other persons', then we have to decide whether a foetus, or a foetus at a late stage of gestation, is a 'person' in the morally freighted sense intended. Suppose, on the other hand, that liberty is *freedom of action unless certain forms of immorality*. Then we have to decide the question of the morality of abortion. On either conception of liberty, we have to settle the major questions about the morality of abortion independently of the notion of privacy.

The reasoning in the Court's opinion in *Roe* v. *Wade* is, to my mind (and hardly just to my mind), seriously flawed (though flawed reasoning, of course, does not imply wrong conclusion). Conceptions of privacy that seem, prima facie, to fit other cases do not seem, even prima facie, to apply to abortion. Liberty, however, does seem to apply, but various principles of liberty come with an unless-clause that can hardly be ignored. The Court, though, ignores it—and understandably so. To confront it, the Court would have had to take a stand on just the issues that then deeply divided, and still divide, the country and the Court itself: for example, whether the foetus is a person, whether death harms the foetus, and whether, more generally, there is serious immorality in abortion. So it is not surprising that the Court, in its majority opinion, while appealing also to liberty, chose not to stress it but took refuge in ideas of private space and private relationships. Once we endow private space or private relationships with 'sanctity', we are off the hook: what then takes place in that space or in those relationships, whether moral or not, may not be regulated. The disturbing trouble, though, is that the ideas of private space and private relationship do not fit abortion.

What deserves our attention in *Bowers* v. *Hardwick* (1986), in which the Court declared Georgia's criminalization of sodomy to be constitutional, is

Justice Blackmun's dissent. The crux, he says, is the right to be let alone, and that right protects the practice of sodomy. By now we are familiar with how interpretations of Brandeis's principle of liberty shift around. But Blackmun goes on in his dissent to give a rationale for the right to general liberty different from any we have met before in Supreme Court deliberation, and a rationale, I should say, of great power:

> We protect those rights [he refers here to certain rights associated with the family] ... because they form so central a part of an individual's life ... We protect the decision whether to have a child because parenthood alters so dramatically an individual's self-definition ... The Court recognized in *Roberts*, 468 U.S. at 619, that the 'ability independently to define one's identity that is central to any concept of liberty' cannot truly be expressed in a vacuum; we all depend on the 'emotional enrichment from close ties with others'.

This important passage does two things worth our attention. It offers a defence of informational privacy. And it introduces a new conception of liberty. It does both of these by putting great weight on the idea of personhood. Our capacity as normative agents constitutes what the tradition has called 'human dignity'. As Blackmun puts it, we are capable of self-definition. As the Court in the earlier *Roberts* decision put it, one has the 'ability independently to define one's identity', and that, it adds, 'is central to any concept of liberty'. Normative agency cannot successfully be exercised in a vacuum. We need to read and talk and assemble without pressures on us to conform, and that requires, among other things, the absence of various kinds of monitoring—that is, it requires informational privacy. Blackmun's appeal to a personhood conception of liberty was not unique. A few years later, in *Planned Parenthood of Southeastern Pennsylvania* v. *Casey* (1992), Justices O'Connor, Kennedy, and Souter also rejected the view of the earlier Courts and averred that 'at the heart of liberty' is personhood.[12]

This new personhood conception of liberty can be explained like this. As I pointed out earlier, there are narrow and wide conceptions of liberty.[13] On the wide conception, any restriction on what one wishes to do is a restriction on one's liberty, probably often justified. This is what I have been calling here 'freedom unless': that is, blanket freedom unless there is a justification for a restriction. On this conception, the one-way restriction on the road that I should love to nip down when I am late for work infringes my liberty, but no doubt justifiably. The personhood account, however, yields a narrow conception of liberty. What liberty protects, it says, is our pursuit of our conception of a worthwhile life. And my nipping the wrong way down a one-way street is certainly no part of my conception of a worthwhile life; it is too trivial for that. On the narrow conception, the traffic restriction does not violate my liberty, even a very minor liberty. It is a narrow conception because there are material constraints on it. On the wide conception, the domain of liberty is everything left after the unless-clause has made its exclusions; it is the large residue. On the narrow conception, however, the domain of liberty is limited to what is major enough to count as part of the pursuit of a worthwhile life. There is also, on the narrow conception, a formal constraint on the content of liberty: one is at liberty to do only what is compatible with equal liberty for all. We shall come back to these two conceptions shortly.

So much for my selective survey of Supreme Court decisions. I do not pretend that it is a contribution to United States constitutional jurisprudence. I am not expert enough. Rather, I want to use it to advance my project. What does it tell us about the content of the human right to privacy?

13.3 HOW BROAD IS THE RIGHT? : (I) PRIVACY OF INFORMATION, (II) PRIVACY OF SPACE AND LIFE, AND (III) THE PRIVACY OF LIBERTY

We come away from the survey with three forms of privacy for our consideration: informational privacy, the privacy of space and life, and the privacy of liberty. We have thereby identified various understandings of the right to privacy, one for each of these three forms of privacy and four for their possible combinations, so seven altogether. And we have encountered two different understandings of liberty: a broad or residual liberty and a relatively narrow liberty derived from personhood. And we have encountered two different examples of residual liberty: *freedom unless harm to others* and *freedom unless certain forms of immorality*, though in principle there are more.

What solid ground is there in all of this? There are, it seems to me, two pieces of solid ground. One is the right to informational privacy. We have seen the solid enough ground for considering at least *that* to be a human right. The second piece of solid ground is the right to liberty. The question of whether the broad or narrow interpretation of liberty is to be adopted is still with us, but nobody doubts that there is a general right to liberty, on one or other of the understandings.

We must now try to make some of the rest of the ground firmer. Let me start with the relation of privacy and liberty. Should we, in the cases that have concerned us, forget about the right to privacy and appeal solely to the right to liberty? Does liberty do all the work? No, I should say. What Justice Stevens meant by 'liberty' in his opinion in *Bowers* v. *Hardwick* is what I mean by 'liberty' as distinct from 'autonomy'. The various principles of liberty we have identified all concern 'liberty' in my distinct sense. But informational privacy, which constitutes certainly at least part of a right to privacy, rests not only on liberty but also on autonomy. As I said earlier, we need certain forms of privacy to develop the confidence and capacity to overcome the enormous barriers to autonomous decision.

I explained earlier still, in discussing practicalities,[14] why, though the value of normative agency constitutes much of the value attaching to human rights, the rights cannot be fully reduced to it. There is also a looser pragmatic sense of reducibility in which human rights are irreducible. We could not discard specific rights and appeal only to the overarching right to normative agency without *practical* loss. It is hardly enough to give police the instruction: 'Do not violate normative agency.' There is a lot of work and judgement, usually not at all obvious, involved in a strict derivation of a specific right, such as privacy, from the overarching interest, normative agency. A society would not successfully protect human rights if it appealed only to the one overarching value. We need to spell out far more specific rules such as respect for a person's privacy of information: that is, a person's correspondence, diaries, beliefs, associations, and so on.[15]

Let me now turn to the key question: Is there more to privacy than informational privacy? I want to suggest that we say, No. The Supreme Court, of course, has repeatedly said, Yes.

I have two reasons for doubting the existence of a right to privacy of space and of life as the Supreme Court has conceived it. First, not only is it not needed to settle the Court's questions about contraception, abortion, and many others; it is also not what actually does settle them. Justice Stevens is right: the issue they raise is liberty. The government may not interfere with my using contraceptives, or with my partner's having an abortion, or with my watching pornographic films, and much else besides, unless there is a substantial enough public interest to outweigh my liberty, and in all of these cases there is none. That, anyway, is what I am willing to argue, and it is, at any rate, the real issue.

My second reason for scepticism is the difficulty of finding any plausible explanation of why private space and private life should have the sort of considerable value that supports a human right. It is easy to explain it in the case of informational privacy; that sort of privacy is a necessary condition of normative agency, and so is instrumentally valuable. But why should we care about, say, a private space? There is an ancient saying that still exerts an influence on our modern thought about private space: 'An Englishman's home is his castle.' For a long while, a man (the gender is essential) was accepted as an absolute sovereign in his own house. This sentiment originated in an age when a man had his goods and chattels, with his animals included among his chattels and his wife and children often not a big step above them. But now we think that society has urgent and still insufficiently recognized duties to regulate what goes on inside the private space, even in the marital bed. Society now rightly exerts control over marital rape, violence against a spouse, a parent's physical or sexual abuse of a child, the parents' neglect of their child's health or education, and a family's cruelty to its animals. Justice Blackmun avers that what is particularly protected against state regulation is 'intimate behaviour that occurs in intimate places',[16] but that is doubtful. The ancient idea of an Englishman's home, with a privacy that was a near-absolute bar to outsiders, has given way to a much more permeable modern privacy. These remarks bring out the force of the feminist attack on privacy; but feminists have an objection not to the true human right to privacy but merely to a patriarchal distortion of it.[17]

Our question is not whether private space is of *some* value. Of course it is. One needs private space the better to relax, and the better to be creative—Virginia Woolf's 'room of one's own'.[18] But though Virginia Woolf's point might be good reason for my family's aspiration to, say, our each having a room of our own, it is most implausible that it gives us a human right to one. There are levels of health and education, as well as kinds of privacy, that are highly desirable, but beyond what is required by human rights. But what of other cases? We are often concerned for the privacy of non-agents—for example, patients with advanced dementia in a nursing home. Their privacy is not only morally important, but it is also, we say, a matter of the dignity to be accorded to the human person. Why does not this non-agency value therefore, contrary to what the personhood account says, support a human right? But one cannot conclude merely from the fact that we speak here of 'human dignity' that a human right is involved; the expression 'human dignity' is far too widely used for that inference to be valid. Is not the more plausible explanation instead this: that those sunk in dementia still deserve deep respect for the full persons they once were, traces of whom may still survive, and anyone who lacks that respect has grossly defective feelings?

The same is true, though to a somewhat lesser degree, of someone who lacks deep feelings of respect for the dead body of a beloved parent. But in neither case does the respect seem to be best explained in terms of possession of a human right. Appropriate behaviour does not always have to be determined by rights.

Does an undetected peeping Tom with a blissfully ignorant victim, then, not violate his victim's right to privacy? After all, he does not actually inhibit his victim's agency. But a human right is a right that one has simply in virtue of being human; one does not actually have to be a victim. What grounds the right to privacy is that certain forms of publicity typically inhibit human agency. The right is borne universally by human beings simply because of this typical vulnerability. So the right would be violated even by an undetected peeping Tom. Besides, the second ground of human rights, practicalities, which is also universal in scope, will lead to an easily grasped and widely drawn private domain: one that will foster the levels of assurance that agency needs, as well, perhaps, as supplying a reassuring buffer zone. There are the demands of the human right to privacy in any society, but the exact levels concerned may vary in time and place. To employ an earlier distinction,[19] basic human rights are universal in the class of persons. But derived human rights, ones that arise from applying a basic human right to a particular time and place, may vary in content from society to society. In our present society it might require, at least for a while longer, protection of our nakedness and certain other culturally determined forms of modesty, which we know not all other human societies, or groups within our own society, need.[20]

What we have been looking for is a value attaching to private space besides, on the one hand, one that though undoubtedly a value is insufficient to support a human right and, on the other, a value that supports a human right but only because of its instrumental connection to informational privacy. At a certain point one must just either produce such a value or confess that one cannot find any. I confess that I cannot find any.

I believe, none the less, that we should retain a form of the right to privacy of space—only much more restricted than, and differently based from, the one that the Supreme Court employed. There is this instrumental argument. It is doubtful that society would be successful in keeping my correspondence and beliefs and sexual practices private if its officials were free to walk into my house whenever they liked. Also laws, even moral laws, need to work with fairly clear, easily understood boundaries, and the walls of one's house form a far clearer boundary than the line between one's beliefs and practices that are relevant to informational privacy and those that are not. And around what is especially valuable to us, we like, for good practical reasons, to have an ample buffer zone. So perhaps for reasons such as these, the right to privacy will include a private space. But, even if so, the value of a private space would, on this explanation, depend on the value of informational privacy. So this gives us no reason to treat privacy of space as an independent addition to informational privacy.

What holds of private space holds too of private life. 'Private life' covers, among other things, certain personal relationships. They are a major component of a good life and, indeed, central enough in most people's conception of a good life to help support a human right, usually liberty. Liberty is being free to pursue one's conception of a worthwhile life, and society can improperly interfere with its pursuit both by erecting a barrier between one and one's ends, say by legal prohibition, and by undermining the necessary conditions of the end itself, say by destroying the privacy that personal relations need. But the privacy that they need is informational privacy, as a necessary condition for autonomy and liberty. The privacy of space and of relationships is playing no further, independent role.

13.4 A PROPOSAL ABOUT THE RIGHT TO PRIVACY

My proposal is that we reduce the human rights that we appeal to in settling the cases we have had before us to two: the fairly circumscribed right to informational privacy and the long-established right to liberty.

Early on I listed some of the heterogeneous issues claimed to be settled by the right to privacy. If my proposal is accepted, the list will have to be considerably trimmed. On my proposal, the following issues are to be settled, not by appeal to privacy, but by appeal to liberty: contraception, abortion, homosexual acts, pornography, interracial marriage, same-sex marriage, and euthanasia.

The following issues, however, *are* to be settled by appeal to privacy: wire-tapping, planting listening devices in a person's house, unauthorized photographs of or other forms of information about one's sexual life or intimate personal relations, publishing membership lists of political organizations, disseminating information about one's sexual life or personal relations unless there is an overriding public interest, and, if practicalities do indeed counsel extending the exclusion zone to the walls of the house, then a derived right to the privacy of that space.

Then there are what are claimed to be issues of privacy that are in fact issues neither of privacy nor of liberty: nuisance noises and smells that penetrate the house (is this an issue of human rights at all? is it not a matter for some other part of tort law that has no bearing on human rights?), attacks on one's honour and reputation (again, is this an issue of human rights? should it too not be left to another part of tort law?), and two closely related matters—rights to security of person and to bodily integrity. Each of these two rights is derivable from normative agency. One would have no security of agency without certain kinds of security of person or of body. So these rights do not seem to be a matter of either liberty or privacy. There is also the supposed right to determine what happens in and to one's body. One interpretation of this further right is that it asserts that one's body is a private space, within which one is sovereign or near sovereign. It has prominently been cited to defend a woman's right to abortion.[21] In this use, it echoes the ancient claim of male domination: an Englishman's home is his castle. It becomes the modern claim of female domination: a woman's body is her castle. And it is equally suspect. Would it protect a woman's taking drugs likely seriously to deform her foetus, or having as many children as she wants? Would it protect a woman's, or a man's, refusal to be safely inoculated against a disease that seriously endangers public health, or to supply a breath or blood or urine or DNA sample? Would it make mandatory drugs tests for airline pilots an infringement of their rights? Would it give us a human right to sell our body parts? I suspect that there is nothing to this supposed right except what is already included in the right to liberty or in the right to security of person. In any case, it seems not a matter of privacy.[22]

13.5 PRIVACY VERSUS FREEDOM OF EXPRESSION AND THE RIGHT TO INFORMATION

There is a worry. Will one person's right to privacy not constantly be in conflict with other persons' freedom of expression? And if the right is specifically to *informational* privacy, will it not often be in conflict with other people's right to information?[23] I think not.

To decide whether two rights really conflict, it is not enough to know their names. One must know their content. Freedom of expression is freedom to state, discuss, and debate anything relevant to our functioning as normative agents: religion, ethics, learning, art, and whatever goes on in society or government that bears on our thinking and deciding autonomously and being free to pursue our conception of a worthwhile life. If I stop a friend from mischievously shouting 'Fire' in a crowded theatre, or simply from boring us with stories about his holiday, I do not infringe his freedom of expression, even in a small way. Similarly, the right to information is a right to the information needed to function as a normative agent: access to the relevant thoughts of others, to the arts, to exchange of ideas, and, in a democracy, to information about the issues before the public, certain of the government's acts and intentions, and so on. If the government of my country does not reveal certain of its acts and intentions, my right to information may be infringed. If the newspapers in London fail to publish the results of my favourite baseball team in Cape Cod, I may be maddeningly frustrated, but my right to information will not be infringed.

With an adequate understanding of the public–private distinction in place, society could then demand much finer-grained arguments for the existence of a public interest than anything we are offered now.[24] The argument that adopting a public life forfeits a private life is ridiculous. So too is the argument that, it is reported, many journalists use to establish a public interest: '*anything* may be relevant to assessment of a person's character'.[25] True, anything may be relevant to a person's character, but not everything relevant to a person's character is of public interest. The odious practice of outing homosexuals, for instance, has also been defended on the ground of public interest. In 1994 Peter Tatchell, the head of the British organization Outrage!, urged ten (unnamed) Anglican bishops to admit their homosexuality, with the threat of outing hanging over their heads. Outing, he said, was justified 'when public figures abuse their power to harm other gay people'. 'Queer homophobes', he went on, 'are hypocrites, and their hypocrisy deserves to be exposed.'[26] There is an apparent public interest here: a society is the healthier for combating certain forms of hypocrisy; it is certainly better for combating injustice. But a homosexual bishop who believes, even if misguidedly, that priests should not be active homosexuals is not necessarily abusing his power. Not all persons whose appearance differs from their reality are thereby hypocrites. A homophobe, whether homosexual or not, who acts hostilely towards homosexuals solely because they are homosexual is unjust. The injustice deserves exposure. *That* is the public interest. But if the homophobe is himself also homosexual, to publicize that further fact is protected neither by the outer's freedom of expression nor the public's right to information. On the contrary, it is an outrageous infringement of the homophobe's right to privacy.[27] It is not that a person's sex life is never of public interest,[28] but that usually it is not.[29]

We are easily confused on these matters because, with human rights, we have been content merely to know their name. But we have also to know their content. And to know their content, we have to know their existence conditions.

14

Do Human Rights Require Democracy?

14.1 TWO PLAUSIBLE LINES OF THOUGHT

Can only a democratic government respect the full range of our human rights? Seventeenth- and eighteenth-century writers generally thought not; they believed that the monarchies of their day could respect them. The power of monarchies then, and even more so in the Middle Ages, did not reach nearly as far into the countryside, or into as many pockets of human life, as do modern governments. Sometimes a monarch lacked control over parts of the countryside. Sometimes a monarch understood that if he tried to take too much power, coalitions would form capable of resisting him.

But nearly everyone accepts that human rights protect our dignity as human persons, on some interpretation of that widely invoked idea, and the heart, though perhaps not the whole body, of our dignity is our autonomy and liberty. Does one not, therefore, have a right to an effective say in decisions that importantly affect one? And, at least in modern conditions of highly pervasive government, do not most decisions of government importantly affect one? If so, and if only a democracy ensures an effective say, then do not human rights require democracy? The United Nations thinks so. The Universal Declaration of Human Rights (1948), Article 21, asserts:

Everyone has the right to take part in the government of his country, directly or through freely chosen representatives ... The will of the people shall be the basis of the authority of government; this will shall be expressed in periodic and genuine elections which shall be by universal and equal suffrage and shall be held by secret vote or by equivalent free voting procedures.[1]

And many contemporary writers agree; they say, variously, that there is a right 'to participate in the government and ... to control the nation's public acts',[2] 'to democratic participation',[3] 'to democratic institutions',[4] 'to a voice in public affairs and to exercise control over government'.[5] If there is such a human right, then of course human rights require democracy.

14.2 AUTONOMY AND LIBERTY

Many human rights are necessary conditions both of normative agency and of democracy: freedom of expression, of assembly, the right to privacy, to information, and so on. But this shows that democracy requires certain human rights, and we are wondering about the converse. The human rights that are most likely to serve as the moral grounds for democracy are not those, but the two abstract rights at the centre of normative agency: autonomy and liberty. Autonomy is self-legislation, deciding one's own goals in life, choosing one's own conception of a worthwhile life; liberty is being free to pursue that conception.

In deciding whether human rights require democracy, one must keep in mind just how much ground the rights to autonomy and liberty cover. It may seem obvious that rights to the necessary conditions of normative agency could not possibly support a right to democratic participation. Can one not be a normative agent in far less than ideal political conditions—even, say, in a tyranny? But, as we just saw, autonomy requires rights to privacy, assembly, information, free expression, and so on; to be assured of them requires in turn very many elements of a liberal society. And liberty, as we saw earlier,[6] requires freedom to pursue one's own conception of a worthwhile life, and that in turn requires a society that promotes a decent array of options, and certainly does not unnecessarily limit them, which in turn requires a society that does not undermine various kinds of liberty and prosperity.

14.3 DEMOCRACY

The term 'democracy' has been, and is still, used promiscuously: for example, of certain Communist dictatorships. For our purposes, we must narrow the extension. I shall not try to define 'democracy' in terms of necessary and sufficient conditions; I do not think that one can. Instead, I shall appeal to some paradigms—the democracies of Western Europe, North America, India, the Antipodes, and a few other places—and note some of their characteristic features.

One can start with an apparently factual explanation of democracy. It is one possible answer to the question, Who rules? One person rules (a

monarchy). The rich rule (a plutocracy). The people rule (a democracy).
And so on. But the idea of 'ruling' involves semantic standards, standards
that, when sufficiently spelt out, become evaluative. It is not just a matter
of the people's having a say, because a say can be ignored. It is not just
a matter of the say's being effective, because an effect can be partial; the
rich could have two votes and the rest only one, resulting in a hybrid
plutocracy-democracy. For a government to be democratic, all must have
an equal say. But many a past government widely accepted as 'democratic'
excluded huge proportions of their adult population from the franchise: slaves
(even freed slaves), the propertyless, the original natives, and women. Robert
Dahl writes that in some governments considered democratic, 'a substantial
number of free *men*—on some estimates about 40 percent—were denied
the vote'.[7] These exclusions were supported by largely factual beliefs: that
certain races were of lower intelligence, that they were child-like, that women
were not interested in politics, that they were already adequately represented
by their husbands, and so on. Once the falsity or irrelevance of these beliefs
was recognized, these excluded groups had to be admitted into the class of
'people' referred to in the defining formula 'the people rule'. *All* the people
must have a say, without further restriction, except perhaps to sane adults
and to exclude certain special groups (peers in Britain, convicts in the United
States). How big a say? It is commonly thought that, when populations are
large, representative democracy works better than direct democracy. But if
the people chose a representative form of government for themselves in the
past, and if the people in the present are content with it, then the say that
one has in the decisions that importantly affect one, though in contrast to
direct democracy considerably limited, is none the less to some extent fair. In
contrast, if the people had not chosen the representative form of government
that they find themselves living under and think that direct democracy
would serve them better, then we should be reluctant to call the government
'democratic'. And what matters to being a 'democracy' is not only how one
has a say, but also about what. The people must control the agenda; they
must themselves decide what is important enough to have to be decided
by them. And they must decide the content of all laws. Admittedly, the
legislative and judicial functions are not always easy to keep apart; sometimes
a small group of judges may, in effect, make law. But if this judicial role
becomes common, and if the people or their representatives do not ultimately
control the appointment of judges, then we should withdraw, or qualify, the
description 'democratic'.

By now evaluative elements have emerged. A democracy is a form of government in which the people rule; only the people decide, with each person having a fair say—that is, equal in accordance with freely accepted decision procedures and with control over what is important enough to be decided by them. So I conclude that fairness must appear in an adequate account of what 'democracy' means, in the sense we want to understand.

Let me pursue this thought a little further. 'Democracy' is not to be equated with majority rule. Majority rule is merely a decision procedure—a fairly crude one at that, and not at all deep evaluatively. There are other decision procedures that are also democratic, and perhaps better. For example, one might aim at consensus, arrived at through discussion and a series of compromises.[8] Or one might sometimes be able to devise a tolerably reliable measure of how important a certain proposal is to the different parties involved, and so be able to use weighted votes. In a democracy the choice of a decision procedure will, of course, be influenced by the size of the group. But the choice should be based largely on which procedure is fairest in the circumstances. And many countries have adopted a mixed system of simple majority for some issues and a qualified majority for others, a decision also based on fairness. So are the attempts to solve the still largely unsolved problem of the tyranny of the majority, which is at its worst when the majority and the minority are fixed, hostile communities. The minority might then have almost no effective say in political decisions. The closer the minority is, in effect, to being disenfranchised, the further away the system of government is to being democratic. It is widely, but I think wrongly, thought that having a bill of rights solves this problem. Of course, whether it does depends upon the scope of human rights. I have already argued that the domain of human rights and the domain of justice appreciably overlap, but are not congruent.[9] On the personhood account, human rights protect only one's status as a normative agent. The minority, therefore, could not by right be allowed to sink below the minimum acceptable level of welfare, where that is understood as the level needed for normative agency; but the society could be, none the less, and in these cases often is, structured in a way that unjustly directs the lion's share of the wealth to an already well-off majority. A society with democratic aspirations might, for that reason, limit the operation of majority rule in various ways—say, by reserving a certain number of seats in the legislature for members of the minority. The society could again be considered 'democratic' if its various changes to the political structure gave the members of the minority a sufficiently fair say.

These thoughts are also useful in showing us something about what it is for a government to be legitimate.[10] Governments come in many kinds and sizes: governments of a town, a state or district or department, a sovereign country, a college or a university, and so on. My primary interest here is in the government of a sovereign country. And the word 'government' sometimes refers to the particular group of persons who hold the major political offices, and at other times to the political institutions themselves, the form or structure of government.[11] The notion of 'legitimacy' that I am looking at here applies to 'government' in both senses. Particular office-holders constituting a government in the first sense may fail the test of legitimacy because they abuse the political institutions that they are supposed to uphold. Or the political institutions themselves may be so unjust that they fail the test of legitimacy no matter who holds the offices. So, as a first attempt, we might say that 'legitimacy', in the sense in which we are interested, has to do with whether the government, in either sense, is morally justified to exercise power over those subject to it. But the group exercising the power might be so ruthless that rebellion would turn out to be so bloody as to be morally unjustifiable. We should, none the less, want to insist that, though in these special circumstances rebellion would not be morally justified, the government is still illegitimate. There must be certain kinds of evils that alone are sufficient to deny a government its legitimacy: for instance, substantial injustice or substantial failure to perform the important duties and functions of government, such as security, public order, and the promotion of prosperity. The qualifier 'substantial' is essential. All governments have shortcomings; all of them do things that are morally objectionable. What matters for legitimacy cannot be whether each exercise of the government's power is morally impeccable, but whether its exercise of power, in general, and making due allowances, is justified.

A government's respecting (where that includes protecting) its citizens' human rights is often taken to constitute the necessary and sufficient condition of legitimacy. But a government must do much more than respect human rights in order to be legitimate. A democratic government, for instance, has also to give all of its citizens a fair say in order to be either democratic or legitimate. It must also meet minimum standards of justice in the distribution of wealth—minimum though still above the minimum standard of welfare that human rights demand. For instance, if a government unjustly directed most wealth to the privileged majority, while keeping the poor minority *just* above the minimum level required by human rights, it would still be likely to lose its legitimacy.

14.4 DO HUMAN RIGHTS REQUIRE DEMOCRACY?

We might expect a strong form of requirement here: for example, that a right to democratic participation is already contained in the content of the basic, universal human rights already on our list, that the former is implied by the latter without further premises—say, without empirical information about a particular time or place. When we look more closely, though, the gap between autonomy and democratic participation seems sizeable. Think of the distance between deciding one's own conception of a worthwhile life, on the one hand, and jointly making laws for everyone, on the other. Perhaps this considerable gap could be closed in the following way. Autonomy is self-legislation, and public legislation can stymie one's following one's self-legislation. Indeed, one's society might prohibit the very life that one decides is most worth living. So, in order to be a successful self-legislator, one must, at the least, also be a public legislator.

But that does not follow. There is the familiar point that to have one vote among millions does practically nothing to protect one's being able to pursue one's chosen ends. And public legislation could frustrate self-legislation only if they both sought to legislate in the same domain. If public legislation stayed out of the domain of one's pursuit of one's own personal goals, there would be no conflict. It is the human right to liberty, not to autonomy, that is the more relevant to democratic participation. Each of us has a domain of personhood over which, with rare exceptions, society may not exercise control. But democratic participation does not seem to be a necessary condition of liberty, either. One vote among millions will not protect one's actions from being stymied by public legislation. It may be that a democracy is more likely than any other form of government to respect the domain of personhood; but to appeal to that fact is to introduce a further, and a non-universal and empirical, premiss, which we are now trying to do without.

I can discover no inferential route from human rights to democracy without adding some non-universal empirical premisses. So let us change our question. Human rights may require democracy in a weaker sense of 'require'. Is it empirically possible for there to be a society of human beings that both does not violate human rights and is not democratic? If so, is it also empirically possible for a society in typical modern conditions of highly pervasive government, large population, advanced technology, concentration of coercive power at the centre, ethnic diversity, educated citizenry, the sort of social cohesion necessary for a tolerably successful democracy, and so on, to respect all human rights, yet not be democratic? The answer to the first question, I shall propose, is Yes, and to the second, No.

As to the first question, I said earlier that one does not have liberty unless one is free to live the continually evolving life that comes as one's values mature and unless one's society provides a reasonable array of options, given the level of its economic and technical development.[12] One is free only if one could also have lived any sort of life chosen from the morally permitted and feasible range. Nor is it enough if one could have lived any sort of life in the morally permitted and feasible range though only by chance—say, the government has not yet clamped down, but might do so at any moment. We need some sort of assurance that the lives in the relevant range are actually permitted to us. Without such assurance most persons would be inhibited to the point of self-censorship. Would it be enough for such assurance that we had a monarch whose control of the inaccessible countryside, where we live, was tenuous indeed? In these conditions, let us say, we are able to live any life in the relevant range, and are assured of that fact because of the natural limits to the monarch's power. I think that, in those conditions, we could say that we have liberty (though we might not be able to say that our right to liberty was *respected* by the monarch). Would it be enough, then, if we were ruled by a trusted benevolent dictator who respected our human rights? It is true that dictatorships are, on the whole, much less stable than democracies; but let us suppose that a rebellion against this particular dictator would be most unlikely to succeed. There would remain, of course, uncertainties about what would succeed this dictator. But a democracy too can be overthrown, and no matter what succeeds it, we might still have been at liberty before the change. It will also be extremely rare for there to be a person in one's society whom all the people could reasonably trust enough to feel secure in their rights. But it is possible, especially in a small society. Perhaps in ancient Athens or in modern Monaco the people could know a potential dictator well enough to be able reasonably to gain the necessary confidence. They need not even have chosen the dictator; they could just have found themselves subject to his authority. If all of this is true, then human rights do not *require* democracy, in this sense: it is possible, in certain realistic, perhaps even actual historic, though not necessarily common, conditions, for there to be forms of government that do not violate any human right but are not democratic.

One can see why. Human rights and democracy have grown up to meet quite different needs. Human rights grew up to protect what we see as constituting human dignity: the life, autonomy, and liberty of the individual. Democratic institutions grew up in our need for a decision procedure for groups—a procedure that is stable, manages transfer of power well, appropriate to a society whose members are more or less equal in power or worth, reconciles losers in social decisions to the basic structures of the society, and tends to promote the commonweal—that is, order, justice, security, and prosperity. Much more comes into democracy, both into the idea itself and into its major duties and functions, than can be got out of human rights. It is unsurprising that fairness should enter into what can count as a democracy, and also that the promotion of a large variety of social ends should enter into its major duties and functions. One cannot derive a requirement of fair political procedures from human rights alone, though one may be able to derive it from morality as a whole.

My use of the word 'fair' here needs more explanation. 'Fair' and its related notion 'equal' qualify many different kinds of thing, some involving respect for human rights and some, in fact many, not. So I have to identify the kind of fairness that concerns democracy but is not the concern of, nor can be derived from, human rights. If a society recognizes and respects men's human rights, but not women's, then women are being denied their equal rights. A person is a bearer of human rights in virtue of being a normative agent, so equal in these rights. Their denial of them would be unfair. Another kind of fairness that is the concern of human rights is a fair trial; though some forms of justice fall outside the domain of human rights, procedural justice in courts is one that does not. But, as I have argued earlier, there are also forms of fairness, and of justice, that are not the concern of human rights: for example, the unfairness of free-riding and of cheating at games.[13] Another example, I want to propose now, is the form of fairness central to democracy: a fair say in political decision. A fair say is a say for everyone who meets fair criteria of membership, a say about what subjects are to be decided by the people, a say through a social decision procedure (majority rule, or a modification of it, or something else altogether) that is as fair as we can reasonably make it or at least fair enough for us to be willing to go along with it. My point here is that the form of fairness relevant to democracy, a fair say, cannot be derived from the various forms of fairness that are encompassed by human rights.

Might there be, none the less, a weaker human right: a right not to democratic participation but merely to political participation, where that is understood as a say about politics that rulers will listen to? It would be something close to what John Rawls meant by a 'consultation hierarchy'.[14] But we must know not just the name of the supposed right—a right to political participation—but also its content. As we saw, its content cannot just be to have a political say—merely freedom of speech—because a say can be ignored. It cannot be merely to have a ruler who listens with understanding and sympathy. Such a ruler could still be a well-meaning catastrophe. Why should there be a human right to that? To get a plausible content for a human right, the ruler would have to make some form of fair assessment of each individual's desires and to combine in some sort of fair way the individual views into a social view and in some way be guided to action by the result. Anything less than this, and we lack a plausible content for a human right. My objection is not that the right to political participation might not actually protect something valuable; no human right, even the stronger right to democratic participation, need actually protect what it declares should be protected. My objection is that, even if it is fully complied with, the supposed right to political participation need not protect anything valuable. A biased ruler who listens sympathetically to all expressions of opinion but simply cannot see the point of many of them fully respects the supposed right. But a true human right must be in some way grounded in our human dignity—the dignity due to our personhood—and an entitlement merely to be listened to by a ruler who may be dismissive of one's views is hard to see in that light.

Nor can one derive satisfactory standards for the legitimacy of governments from human rights. It is often said, quite to the contrary, that the main function of human rights is to test legitimacy.[15] But if a government seriously fails to discharge its most important duties, if it fails to bring about certain forms of distributive justice or to meet certain of the demands of retributive justice or to promote the general prosperity, it can lose its legitimacy. Yet all of these functions can fall outside the demands of human rights. For example, human rights require only that everyone be at least at the minimum acceptable level of welfare, which is the level necessary for life as a normative agent, whereas a government's duties to promote prosperity, though not endless, certainly extend well above this minimum. Because human rights do not demand an equal voice in social decisions, they fall short of demanding democracy. Because they do not demand certain highly important forms of justice and the promotion of general prosperity, they fall short of being the test of legitimacy. I have not strictly defined 'political legitimacy', the requirements of which can vary in stringency. I have, however, stated a few necessary conditions for it that nearly all of us accept. And they are not necessary conditions of respecting human rights.

My conclusions here depend upon my belief that human rights do not encompass certain requirements of justice, fairness, and well-being. Though many persons believe that justice and fairness, at least, fall within the domain of human rights, few persons regard the promotion of prosperity above the minimum as a demand of human rights. So it is worth noting that even if human rights were to encompass all of justice and fairness, they still would not constitute the test of legitimacy.

My conclusion leaves the lively possibility that, though human rights in particular do not require democracy, morality as a whole does—especially forms of respect for persons not already included in human rights. And though human rights do not require democracy in the first conditions I described earlier, they might require it in the second conditions. Some human rights are not basic, but arise by applying basic rights to particular circumstances.

14.5 IN MODERN CONDITIONS?

What about our actual situation? Though there is no basic universal human right to democratic participation, might there be a derived right to it in modern conditions? By 'modern conditions' I mean the conditions I listed earlier; I do not mean any kind of society to be met with in modern times—for instance, an Islamic theocracy populated by adherents.

Would we, if governed by a benevolent dictator in typical modern conditions, have the assurance that liberty requires? I think not. We could not have the depth of acquaintance with the dictator that we might have in a small society, and without deep acquaintance we should lack the necessary rational assurance of the dictator's benevolence or understanding. We might in time, it is true, learn more about the dictator's character, but we should still not know, even roughly, when the dictator will die and what will follow. That, in itself, could inhibit certain of our choices in life. We might, in such conditions, have a span of time in the middle of a dictator's rule during which we had such rational assurance, but there would also be times before and after when we did not. And the two limitations that could reassure the people in an early monarchy about their monarch's power—that it was neither ubiquitous nor irresistible—does not hold true of a modern government's power.

Most of the other non-democratic forms of government are also likely, in typical modern conditions, to violate the same human rights. If the few rule (oligarchy) or the rich (plutocracy), and even if the government eventually proves benevolent and competent, the citizens are unlikely initially to have the assurance that liberty needs. They are also highly likely not to know what will succeed their current form of government, with the inhibiting effects of this uncertainty.

This is true of most non-democratic forms of government. But of absolutely all? What about a modern aristocracy of the talents, composed of the best available judges, philosophers, economists, and public servants that the society has to offer? We must keep in mind that we are now thinking of a citizenry educated and cohesive enough to be able to form a democracy.

A society of this sort, having just come under the rule of such an aristocracy of the talents, would still have to wait to see what its political complexion turned out to be—much as the citizens of the United States would have to wait a while to gauge the orientation of a newly constituted Supreme Court. It would be highly likely that the persons chosen for this aristocracy of the talents would be Establishment figures with a track record for soundness, and that they would tend to be rather old and rather conventional. And if this aristocracy were self-perpetuating, a conservative majority would be likely to produce as its successor an even greater conservative majority. And an aged aristocracy is likely to be in some respects out of harmony with the younger generation. For example, if the society faced our own current problems, the young and the old might well differ over pornography, or same-sex marriage, or adoption of children by homosexuals—each being a case in which human rights are highly likely to be at stake.

Of course, this line of thought shows only that an aristocracy of the talents would have a tendency, of some not yet determined strength, to violate certain human rights. And I am asking whether it is empirically possible for a society in typical modern conditions to respect all human rights yet not be democratic. The answer to that question must be, Yes. The members chosen for the new aristocracy may have reputations that are so reassuring that the citizens are not inhibited to live as they choose. And the new aristocracy may contain a mixture of conservative and liberal, old and young, thus avoiding any serious intergenerational conflict of values. Such a happy outcome may not be at all likely, but surely it is empirically possible.

This answer strongly suggests, though, that there is another question that is more important for us to attend to. We live not just in modern conditions but also in the real world, subject to all the vagaries of human nature and the nature of human societies. We should be concerned, therefore, not only with the possible but also with the probable. We should be duly sceptical about the judgement and benevolence of both governors and governed. We should be worried by the concentration at the centre of coercive power and of information, especially secret information the source of which, we may be told, cannot be revealed without compromising it. We should not be willing to rely on good luck. For instance, we should want not to have to depend upon our governors' turning out actually to *be* benevolent; we should want to constrain them in ways that would be most likely to lead them, whatever their inclination, to *act* benevolently. And we should look largely to political institutions to achieve that.

So we should also want to ask: What form of government is most likely to respect human rights? At first sight, this seems *not* to be our question. Even if a democracy is the most likely to respect human rights, that leaves it possible that other forms of government could also respect them, in which case human rights would not *require* democracy. But it is no easy or quick matter for a society to establish a form of government. And once it has established a form of government, it is not easy to change it. Any group establishing a form of government must be concerned with the long run, and the long run will bring governors of very different moral and intellectual endowments. What is more, the obligations arising from human rights are not fully discharged just by one's not oneself violating them. I have discussed this earlier.[16] The obligation (of a strength still to be determined) extends to some persons' having somehow (who and how still to be determined) to promulgate human rights, enforce them, protect others from their violation, and, if not yet done, create the institutions that will aid in this. So the obligation that human rights lay upon us is to do what is most likely to minimize their violation—for example, to choose the form of government that is most likely to bring about this result. And minimize not just the government's violation of its citizens' rights, but also one citizen's violation of another's rights.

Would the form of government, then, have to be democratic? Well, what are the most effective ways to constrain governors to act for the common good? We should want to constrain any tendency they had not only to act solely out of self-interest or sectional interest but also to lose sight of or to discount the common good—for example, through the infamously dangerous pursuit of what they saw as an altogether higher goal than the common good. We should want them to know about, and take seriously, the aims of other generations or groups than their own. In both cases, the threat of being thrown out in the next election would be a powerful incentive. Some economists have shown a striking correlation between democratic government and avoidance of famine.[17] India, under a democratic government since Independence, has had no serious famines; China, under Mao, had a devastating and entirely unnecessary famine in the course of the upheavals of the Cultural Revolution. The problem in virtually all famines is not lack of enough food to go around, but the lack of power or entitlement of the vulnerable to get some of it to go to them. The most effective protection of the human rights to life and to minimum material provision, it would seem, is democratic participation in social decision; it seems to be the surest way to force our governors to heed our interests.

At this point I shall stop trying to answer our question. The answer involves highly complex, empirical matters about individual and group psychology and about the behaviour of political institutions, about which philosophers have no special expertise. At any rate, I do not. And as there are many forms of democratic government,[18] our present question subsumes the immensely complicated question: What form of *democratic* government is most likely to respect human rights? But as important as these empirical issues are, my primary interest lies elsewhere. I am inclined to think, despite my inexpertise, that, in modern conditions, human rights do indeed require democracy. That is why I think the United Nations was justified in declaring a human right to democratic participation. However, that right, I want to say, is not a fundamental, universal one. It is, at best, a derived one, arising from the application of fundamental human rights to particular conditions. There are two kinds of derived rights: rights derived solely from fundamental ones, thus retaining universality, and rights derived by applying universal rights to particular conditions, not therefore universal. The human right to democratic participation, I want to say, is an applied right. The United Nations rightly ignores these nice distinctions of kinds of rights. Their job is to promulgate rights, not taxonomize them. These distinctions are of concern, though, to anyone trying to understand the path from the grounds of human rights in general to a particular putative human right—that is, to anyone trying to understand what really are human rights.

So, the answer to our original question, Do human rights require democracy?, is, I should say: Yes and No, depending upon circumstances.   ? ? ?

15

Group Rights

15.1 THREE GENERATIONS OF RIGHTS

Writers sometimes refer to different generations of rights. The first generation consists of the classic liberty rights of the seventeenth and eighteenth centuries—freedom of expression, of assembly, of worship, and the like. The second generation is made up of the welfare rights widely supposed to be of the mid-twentieth century though actually first asserted in the late Middle Ages—positive rights to aid, in contrast, it is thought, to the purely negative rights of the first generation. The third generation, the rights of our time, of the last twenty-five years or so, consists of 'solidarity' rights, including, most prominently, group rights.[1] A people, a nation, a race, an ethnic or cultural or linguistic or religious group, are now often said to have rights. Group rights—at least the most interesting form of them, and the form in which I am interested—are supposed not to be reducible to the individual rights of their members. They are supposed to be rights that certain groups have simply in virtue of being those groups.

Why, then, discuss this sort of group rights if my subject is individual human rights? For one thing, it is hard to see how group rights and human rights are related. Despite what is claimed for them, are group rights, or many of them, reducible to human rights? To the extent that group rights seem to have the status of rights, is it because they are reducible to human rights? I think so. The fairly recent appearance of group rights is part of a widespread modern movement to make the discourse of rights do most of the important work in ethics, which it neither was designed to do nor, to my mind, should now be made to do.

15.2 NO QUICK WAY OF DISMISSING GROUP RIGHTS

It is not that there is a simple flaw in the very idea of a group right, although some think that there is. They think that only persons (or agents) can have rights (I am not talking about human rights here, but rights in general), and that this fact alone rules out animals, trees, and most human groups from bearing rights. For instance, some say that one can have rights only if one can also have duties,[2] because they think that the ability to bear rights is necessarily part of a package that includes the capacity to discharge duties. Others say that most rights should themselves be seen as packages, that many of them can be analysed into, among other things, liberties and powers[3] (Hohfeldian components). Therefore, both groups conclude, only persons can bear rights, because only persons can have duties or exercise liberties or powers. The word 'person', they concede, must be understood here to include 'artificial persons'—for example, legal persons such as corporations, schools, and clubs. These legal persons are person-like in the necessary sense, because they too can decide, act, accept responsibility for their actions, have duties, make amends, and so on.

Groups, then, are said to be person-like only if they have the kind of fairly complex internal organization that allows them to decide, act, and so on. Corporations, schools, and clubs can have it. Parliament has it, which is why it made sense for the English Declaration of Rights of 1689 to assert the rights of Parliament against the Crown. But it is striking that nowadays many groups for which group rights are often claimed lack it.[4] Recent Hispanic immigrants to the United States, blacks, women, and the elderly all lack the requisite internal organization. It is true that occasionally a non-agent-like group acts collectively. A mob might spontaneously collect in the streets and, united by strong common grievance, act as one and, say, storm the Bastille or the Winter Palace. It is doubtful, though, that having this sort of ephemeral unity would be enough, on this conception, to have rights, but recent Hispanic immigrants, blacks, women, and the elderly lack even ephemeral unity. So they clearly do not (or do not as such) have rights. Or so this attack on group rights goes.

It is an attack which, to repeat, seems to me to fail. Many people have already extended the use of the word 'rights' beyond persons—for instance, to foetuses, animals, and eco-systems. They have already abandoned the requirement that rights-holders be agents. And why not? The use of words changes. The question is whether this change gives us a more helpful moral vocabulary. And the answer to that question cannot be quick. We have to look at what sort of case there is for introducing group rights, and whether it yields a tolerably clear and useful term.

There is a further point. Agency does not seem crucial to a group's having rights. Agency is indeed a necessary condition of being a holder of individual human rights. I would myself put it still more strongly: the defence of agency is what individual human rights are meant for. But what is crucial to a group's having rights is a different feature of human rights: that the right-holder have the kind of weighty interest that attracts the protection of rights. As we shall see shortly, that is the form taken by the strongest arguments for group rights, and the groups concerned in these arguments—peoples, nations (as in 'the Navaho nation'), ethnic and cultural groups—need not, and often do not, have anything approaching agency.

15.3 A CASE FOR GROUP RIGHTS: THE GOOD-BASED ARGUMENT

What seems to me the best case for *individual* human rights takes this form: it finds a class of goods (in the case of human rights, the goods comprising normative agency) with the sort of importance that attracts the protection afforded by rights. One case for group rights mimics this case for rights of individuals; it claims to find goods that can be attributed only to certain groups, then tries to show that this new kind of good attracts the protection of a new kind of right: namely, a group right.

If this form of argument is successfully to yield rights not reducible to rights of individuals, then we need group goods of a quite special kind. They cannot, for instance, be merely what economists call *public goods*. The term 'public good' lacks sharp boundaries, but three important features that contribute to a good's being 'public' are that it is non-excludable (i.e. it cannot be designed so that it benefits some people but not others), non-rivalrous (i.e. its enjoyment by some does not compete with its enjoyment by others), and jointly produced (or, at least, produced by many). Clean air and effective defence are standard examples. Although the entities to which we should most naturally attribute clean air and effective defence are fairly large groups, the values involved in public goods are individual in both their enjoyment and conception. The benefits of clean air and secure defence are enjoyed by each member of the group individually. And to the extent that public goods support rights, they seem to support only familiar individual rights—in the case of clean air, a right to basic health; in the case of secure defence, a right to security of person or to liberty.

Are there group goods of the special kind we need? Consider this example. Some dinner parties are good because they generate an atmosphere of conviviality.[5] Conviviality seems to be public, not just in the sense of non-excludable, non-rivalrous, and jointly produced, but in a more thoroughgoing way. Conviviality is a property of the party, not of each individual guest. That a group is involved is part of the very concept of conviviality: Jack enjoys himself partly because Jill is enjoying herself, and Jill is enjoying herself partly because Jack—or some other guest—is enjoying himself, and so on.[6] Conviviality is enjoyment together and interactively. Admittedly, the word 'conviviality' is not always used in this narrow sense, but there is such a phenomenon of joint and interactive enjoyment, and 'convivial' is a good way to describe it. And that a group is involved is also part of the felt character of conviviality: one is partly—though not necessarily especially consciously—enjoying others enjoying themselves.[7] We must concede, of course, that the only experiences that constitute this enjoyment take place entirely inside the minds of individuals.[8] But we might still think that the other features of conviviality already noted are enough to mark it off as different from mere public goods. One might put it like this. An account that reduced the value of conviviality to the values of the individual experiences of enjoyment of which, admittedly, it is composed

... would be an unsatisfactory account since, as we have seen, each of these experiences refers beyond itself to the wider group ... An account, then, of the value of these things that was sensitive to what it was like to enjoy them would have to focus on their communal character.[9]

And 'no account of their *worth* to anyone can be given except by concentrating on everyone together'.[10]

It does not matter that our example, the conviviality of a party, is of negligible ethical interest. There are heavyweight group goods that are thought also to have this special character: for example, fraternity, solidarity, mutual tolerance, and the value of a society with a common culture.[11]

The next step in the argument is an inference from these special group goods to group rights. In much recent writing[12] the inference is made using a particularly influential account of a right, which we owe to Joseph Raz and have met earlier.[13] Let me quickly remind you. To say that a person has a right, his account goes, is to say that, other things being equal, an aspect of that person's well-being is a sufficient reason for holding some other person, or persons, to be under a duty. Given that definition, it seems clear that I, as only one person, do not have a right to, say, fraternity, because the benefit to me alone is insufficient to justify holding the rest of you to be under the considerable burden of a duty to produce a fraternal society.[14] One might, then, add the individual benefit to me to the individual benefit to you, and so on, until, if we eventually include enough individuals, our reason for imposing the duty on others becomes sufficient.[15]

I shall come back to Raz's account of rights shortly. For now, I want to make only two comments.

First, there does not seem to be any general inference from a group good of the special type so far isolated to a right to it. For instance, it is thoroughly counter-intuitive to think that from the claim *conviviality is a good of a party*, we can infer *a party has a right to conviviality*. That is not because of the lightweight nature of the example; we do not think so in the case of the heavyweight examples either. From the claim *fraternity is a good of a community*, we cannot infer *a community has a right to fraternity*. Fraternity, solidarity, and tolerance are highly desirable qualities in a society, and we members of it should, no doubt, be willing to work hard to bring them about. But what seems deeply counter-intuitive is to think that they are a society's by right. What we need is not just a good that is special in some way or other, but one that is special in a particular way: that it is the sort of good that attracts the protection of a right.[16]

My second comment is this. What is special about these supposedly strong group goods is merely that their description refers to several individuals together as interacting parts of a functioning whole. It is not that their value cannot be reduced to individual values. The value of conviviality resides in the enjoyment that each individual experiences singly. The specialness in these goods is something conceptual. The point seems to be that we do not properly describe conviviality without introducing how the enjoyment of one person works to enhance the enjoyment of another, and so on. That, it is said, is an important part of what conviviality is. Similarly, we do not properly describe fraternity without acknowledging that Jack's benevolent concern for Jill is strengthened by his recognition of Jill's benevolent concern for him, and so on through much of the group.

That conceptual point seems to me correct. But exactly the same is true of many individual goods and of the individual rights to which they give rise. Autonomy and liberty are two of the classic goods of first-generation rights. Part of what is meant by autonomy is not being dominated or controlled by others; much of what we mean by liberty is not being blocked by others.

The same conceptual point applies in their case: one will have no grasp of these two goods unless one understands certain things about how people interact in groups. That interaction is built into the concepts. And these goods support not only basic rights to living autonomously and at liberty, but also derivative rights that are equally conceptually dependent upon group interaction: rights to minimum education, to exchange of ideas, to assembly, to democratic participation, and so on. Take the last right. In certain social circumstances I have a right to a fair say in social decisions. An obvious form for the recognition of this right to take in many modern circumstances is a derived right to vote. This social good—our having an equal say in social decisions—repeats all of the features of the supposed group goods. Any social structure for fair influence on decision is non-excludable: all agents in the group may avail themselves of it. It is non-rivalrous: your voting does not stop me from voting. It is jointly produced: it is because we all (or most of us) play by the rules that it exists. And it has that additional feature that group goods, in this further special sense, are supposed to have: that the only accurate description of the good must bring in the good to members of the group considered not just as individuals, or even as an aggregation, but as individuals considered together as interacting parts of a functioning whole. The description would have to include how one person accepts the weight given to the views of a second *because* the second person accepts the weight given to the views of the first, and so on.

So we have not yet managed to identify the kind of group good that will underpin a group right. To that end, let me now return to Raz's account of a right: in particular, to how he elaborates it into the conditions for the existence of a group right—just what we need but have not yet found.

To the core of his explanation of rights in general, he adds this further condition.[17] In the case of a group right, he says,

> the interests in question are the interests of individuals as members of a group in a public good and the right is a right to that public good because it serves their interests as members of the group.

For instance, a 'nation' can, in certain circumstances, have a right to self-determination. Each member of the nation may have an interest, as an individual, in its self-determination, because its self-determination may be bound up with the flourishing of its culture on which the individual's sense of identity depends.[18] The individual alone, however, does not have a right to the group's self-determination, because that single person's interest is not sufficient to justify imposing such a considerable burden upon others. The interest of the whole group, however, might be. And the interests of the individuals that might build up sufficiently to justify imposing that burden upon others would be, Raz thinks, not individual goods that accrue to them as individuals, but more diffuse group goods that accrue to them only in virtue of their being members of the community. Membership of certain groups, especially cultural groups, is of great importance to their members. A good life depends importantly upon the successful pursuit of worthwhile goals and relationships, and they, in turn, are culturally determined.[19] So the 'pragmatic' and 'instrumental' case, as Raz describes it, for the existence of a group's right to self-determination would go along these lines.[20] The 'prosperity and self-respect' of what Raz calls 'encompassing groups'—say, cultural groups membership in which has a large role in one's self-identification and one's sense of possibilities—are of enormous value to us.[21] An encompassing group does not necessarily have to be self-determining in order to prosper; it may prosper as part of a liberal multinational state. But in less favourable historical circumstances, the only, or much the most satisfactory, way of ensuring its prosperity may be through its being self-governing. Then one has all that one needs for the existence of a group right to self-determination. [22]

That, I think, is Raz's well-wrought argument. It has the great merit of seeing the kind of thing that is needed in order to establish the existence of a group right. Still, I have my doubts about it.

First, are Raz's existence conditions sufficient? Why do they not prove too much? According to Raz, we have a claim, in certain historical circumstances, to self-determination because we have a more general interest in 'the prosperity and self-respect' of our encompassing group, and we have that interest because each of us has a major interest in having a healthy sense of identity and a satisfactorily large array of ways of life open to us. This suggests that standing behind the proposed right to self-determination, in those special circumstances in which such a right arises, is a broader right that one has to the prosperity and self-respect provided by one's encompassing group. And that broader right seems, indeed, to qualify as a group right on Raz's list of existence conditions. Our interests in a healthy sense of identity and in having a good array of options from which to choose seem to justify imposing on certain agents (viz. those political entities with the power to allow or deny our group a political setting in which it can prosper) the burden of allowing it. And the interests involved are our interests as members of the group in a public good. And the interest of a single member would not be sufficient on its own to justify imposing that heavy burden on others. The trouble with this is that it seems to justify a right to even quite high levels of 'prosperity'. It seems to justify any level, no matter how high, in which the benefits are great enough to justify imposing the burden. Now, the word 'prosperity' here does not mean just material wealth, although that must be a large part of it; it means whatever contributes to an encompassing group's prospering. Still, the benefits of a robust sense of identity and a rich array of options in life are characteristically so enormous that they are likely to justify imposing the burden on others to allow it. But this loses what seems to me an important intuitive feature of both individual human rights and, presumably, closely related categories of rights such as group rights: namely, that such rights have to do not with any increase in the satisfaction of interests capable of justifying a duty on others, but with the satisfaction of only special kinds of interests and with their satisfaction only up to a certain point. In the case of human rights, for instance, we have a claim not to any form of flourishing but to that more austere condition: what is necessary for our status as agents, which includes autonomy, liberty, and some sort of minimum material provision. That element of austerity, that reference to a minimum, must not be lost. We have a right to material and cultural resources up to a point beyond which, though more would importantly enhance our lives, they are not a matter of right. How does Raz accommodate that essential feature?

The answer, I think, must be: through his notion of a 'duty'. The interests, he says, have to be sufficient to impose a duty on others, and the sort of duty he has in mind is not merely another reason for action, able to be merged in an overall balance of reasons for action. It is, as we saw earlier, a reason of a special kind, one that excludes a certain range of reasons from consideration. Not every aspect of a person's well-being will have this exclusionary effect. A paradigm case of an exclusionary reason is a promise. But our case now is a human right to minimum provision or to the survival of one's culture. Where on the spectrum from the most modest provision of material and cultural resources to the most lavish do we pass from interests that impose a duty, in this sense, to those that do not? Raz would say, I suppose: when the interests stop supplying an exclusionary reason. But the case of material and cultural resources has none of the clarity of the case of promising; it is not, as with promises, that the whole point of the reasons present here is to exclude a certain range of other reasons. And one kind of reason can exclude others in many different senses: by totally silencing them, by outweighing them in all but the most extreme circumstances, by characteristically outweighing them, and so on. We must know which sense is relevant to rights. We do not understand what a right is until we understand roughly where along such spectra we are to make the break. The personhood account can tell us: the break comes when the material and cultural resources are no longer necessary for normative agency. But Raz's more formal existence conditions—interests justifying the imposition of exclusionary duties—leave it unclear.

My second, closely related doubt is that when Raz gives us examples of group rights, he makes them plausible as rights just to the extent that he appeals to familiar first-generation rights. Consider again his case for a right to self-determination. In certain historical circumstances, says Raz, I would have an interest in the self-determination of my encompassing group. 'At least in part', he says, 'that interest is based on a person's interest in living in a community which allows him to express in public and develop without repression those aspects of his personality which are bound up with his sense of identity as a member of his community.'[23] I have an interest in membership in a developed culture, because it supplies me with options in life, and they are protected by the right of the individual to autonomy. I have an interest in openly expressing, without fear of repression, what I am and wish to be, because that is central to my agency, which is protected by our individual right to liberty. This begins to look like a case for rights, because it stresses our being able to choose and our being free to live as we choose. But those are familiar cases of first generation rights. It is true that these rights are based on interests that we have as members of a group, but so is our right to a vote, which is also first-generation. Much the same can be said of another example that Raz gives. The British people, he says, have a right to know how Britain was led into the Falklands War.[24] That, too, we have as members of our group; the citizens of France, for instance, do not have a right to this information about Britain. But a British citizen has a right to it because a citizen of any country cannot have an effective voice in important political decisions without such knowledge. But that, too, is a first-generation right.

Let me mention a final doubt. Raz's most sustained argument for a group right is his case (made jointly with Avishai Margalit) for national self-determination.[25] But it seems to me just that: a moral case (and a good one too) for granting self-government to certain nations.[26] The further claim that it is a matter of right need not, and should not, be made. A right can be outweighed by another right or by sufficiently important considerations of the general good. But Raz's case for self-determination is not like that. It does not first establish a right, and then consider possible overriding conditions. It is, rather, an all-in moral case. According to Raz, what we must show is that, in particular historical circumstances, self-government is necessary both for the prosperity of a certain encompassing group and for its members' participation in it,[27] that the encompassing group forms a substantial majority in the territory to be governed, that the new state is likely to respect the fundamental interests of its inhabitants, that it will not gravely damage the just interests of other countries, and so on until the all-in case is made.[28] The analogy with the case for individual human rights, therefore, breaks down here; Raz makes no claim that a nation, in virtue of its nature, attracts the protection of a right (compare: a person or an agent, in virtue of what they are, attract the protection of individual human rights). It is just as well that he makes no such claim. A nation, as such, does not have a right to govern itself, even an overrideable one. A nation that is respected and flourishing as part of a liberal multinational state does not have a right to secede. If there is a right here at all, it seems to me to be a right that, as I suggested earlier, is only one element in a case for self-determination: namely, a right to the conditions necessary for the members of an encompassing group to have an acceptable array of options in life and the freedom to pursue the ones they choose. But this is just the right that reduces to various first generation rights. My final doubt, then, is this: self-determination does not seem to me to be a *right*, and the right that is indeed part of its backing does not seem to me to be a *group* right.

I wonder whether Raz is not taking as group rights what are really derived individual rights—rights derived from applying basic individual human rights to particular social circumstances.[29] In any case, his attempts to motivate his proposed examples of group rights appeal to what are no more than such derived rights.

So, to sum up my thoughts so far, the first general kind of case for group rights—their derivation from group goods—seems to me unsuccessful.

15.4 ANOTHER CASE FOR GROUP RIGHTS: THE JUSTICE-BASED ARGUMENT

Other writers arrive at group rights in a different way. They base them on considerations of justice. My view is that this second argument largely succeeds as an argument, but that it is not an argument for group rights. What this second case says is better said, I think, not forced into the language of rights.

The argument that I have primarily in mind has some claims in common with Raz's, but its direction is quite different. Will Kymlicka puts it like this.[30] The survival of a people or culture or ethnic or linguistic group is of enormous value to its members. It is the basis of their sense of identity—their sense of who they are and what they might become. The range of options open to one is determined by one's culture, by the examples and stories that it provides, from which one learns about the courses of life it is possible to follow. We all 'decide how to lead our lives by situating ourselves in these cultural narratives, by adopting roles that have struck us as worthwhile ones, as ones worth living …'.[31] 'Loss of cultural membership, therefore, is a profound harm that reduces one's ability to make meaningful choices'.[32]

For society at large to treat a minority culture as of negligible importance, for it to reflect back upon its members a demeaning picture of themselves, for it to deny the culture any concern for whether it lives or dies can, as Charles Taylor has put it, 'be a form of oppression, imprisoning someone in a false, distorted, and reduced mode of being'.[33] To be held in low esteem by society at large easily turns into holding oneself in low esteem, and persons then become compliant in their own oppression.[34] Lack of recognition for one's group can be a grave harm, which society at large should not inflict upon any of its members.

There is a constant danger that, in one way or another, a dominant culture in a society will stifle minority cultures. The markets and majority rule will usually work in its favour, and its very vitality can sap the strength of minority cultures, even to the point of their extinction. Minority cultures can unfairly, even if by no one's conscious wish, end up with many fewer resources than the majority culture. Unfair deprivation is a prima facie ground for erecting special protections around a minority group or for giving it special privileges. For instance, if its voice is unheard in the legislature, perhaps it should be given special representatives;[35] or perhaps its central government should adopt a federal structure or find some other way of devolving powers to smaller communities. Or if the market works to their disadvantage, perhaps minorities should be given special subsidies. The acknowledgement of minority rights can, in these ways, serve to prevent or correct the injustice.[36] These are just some of the possible means; the end, however, is always the same: rectificatory justice.[37]

By grounding group rights in justice, we can explain why there are also minority cultures that do *not* attract protection. When the Boers in South Africa sought, through apartheid, to protect their minority culture against being swamped by the black majority, they had no case. Apartheid itself was unfair. And that is also why a group is usually not justified in imposing certain restrictions internally on its own members, such as a ban on leaving the group, even if it promotes its own survival. Such bans are usually violations of liberty. So, as Kymlicka puts it, we 'should endorse certain external protections, where they promote fairness between groups, but should reject internal restrictions which limit the right of group members to question and revise traditional authority and practices'.[38]

This second case seems to me stronger than the first. But what is it a case *for*?

First, as it stands, the case is grossly oversimplified. The loss of cultural membership does not, in itself, reduce one's ability to make meaningful choices. All that one needs for meaningful choice is *some* culture, and if, as is often the case, a minority culture is in decline because it is being supplanted by a majority culture, one can, depending upon how much dislocation is involved in the process, still have *a* culture available to one. And the better the culture is—that is to say, the richer it is, the more examples it supplies and stories it tells, the more humane those stories are—the better off one is in that respect. It is true that there may well be things that could be said in one's original language that cannot be said in the language that supplants it. But the question is not whether there are such things, but to what extent they are central to one's being able to conceive the important choices in life. They might be; they might not be; and even if they are, one might still on balance be better off in the new language. We cannot tell in advance. All of that has to be decided case by case.

And one must not oversimplify, or sentimentalize, what it means to people to abandon an old culture for a new one. Cultures can, and must, be criticized. Some cultures are authoritarian, intolerant, sexist, distorted by false belief, dominated by unjust caste or class systems. Some people willingly emigrate, leaving behind one culture for another, as they hope, better one. They might have small sense of loss and great sense of gain. Other people—say, natives who see their culture destroyed by colonists—may have great sense of loss and small sense of gain. People's experiences are hardly uniform. And there is the important question of what sense one *should* have when one's original culture changes substantially, or becomes mixed with another, or gives way to another. One will not know what one should feel until one evaluates what is happening, and in all of these cases what is happening is likely to be immensely complex, and the proper assessment of it hard to make.

Also, it is easy to exaggerate the extent to which our deliberation about our options in life depends upon our own particular culture. What that deliberation most needs is a sense of what things in general make a human life good. I have written about this elsewhere, so I shall merely state my view.[39] There are certain things that make any characteristic human life good: accomplishing something in the course of one's life, deep personal relations, certain kinds of understanding, enjoyment, and so on. Each of the items on this list needs a lot of explanation, so much so that they become in effect terms of art. There are not always words in English, as it is now, that will quite serve to name these individual values; to some extent, one has to invent a vocabulary. And this new vocabulary applies to characteristic human life: not British or American or Chinese or Sudanese life, but human life. It is a grotesque oversimplification to say that having a sense of meaningful options in life requires access to one's original culture, when no culture or language, as it stands, has quite the vocabulary we need, and when the vocabulary that deliberation can lead us to is, with qualifications, cross-cultural.[40]

There is something worryingly passive about the agent who figures in these arguments for the importance of cultures. According to these arguments, our culture gives us our options; we merely receive them as an inheritance. But this picture leaves out our active critical life. We examine life; we criticize our inheritance. Of course, we do it in our own language. But this does not mean that we are condemned to a life either so deeply embedded in our particular culture that we have no access to views originating outside it, or so detached from any particular culture that we have critical resources too feebly abstract to settle much. We do not have to be either inside or outside a culture; that is a false dichotomy—one the wide acceptance of which is puzzling in our current cosmopolitan conditions, in which most of us would be hard put to name the culture of which we are ourselves members. A very great deal of our critical vocabulary for ethics has still to be developed, and much of it will be neither the thick terms from a particular cultural perspective nor the thin terms of the spare rational agent of much modern philosophy. What we especially need are the key terms of a successful account of human well-being, still largely unsettled, and of realistically described agents living satisfactory lives in a realistically described society, also still largely unsettled. Once this critical vocabulary has been developed and we look back on our original conceptual framework and ask whether we are inside or outside it, I think that we are likely to drop the question as ill drawn. We shall have substantially expanded our original conceptual framework; it is enough to say that. We can expect other people in other cultures to have been equally critically active. And we can, with some justification, expect points of convergence between us.[41]

So far I have been concentrating on the sources of personal identity (in the suspect, loose sense of the term found in these discussions) and capacity for choice. But there are, of course, many other reasons for protecting cultures than those. If one's culture dies, especially if records of it are few or are themselves destroyed, one loses touch with one's roots. For some people this is not felt as a great loss, but for others it is. Often one's sense of loss will depend upon how secure one's sense of self is within one's current society and how much respect the society shows one. And often one's loss of cultural roots is something that is inflicted upon one. There is a great difference ethically between one's voluntarily abandoning one's culture and a dominant group's destroying it. In general, no one should deny another autonomy—for instance, the autonomy to amend their culture, as they see fit. But the values here are not the survival of a culture, admirable or not, but autonomy and good ways of life. What we should cite here is not the right of a group that its culture survive, but one's right autonomously to choose and freely to pursue one's conception of a good life, both of which are individual human rights.

And that seems to me to be the trouble with all of these arguments. They are arguments about matters of the greatest importance, but they are not arguments for anything as general as a right of a group that its culture survive.

Without doubt, for society at large to deny a minority group proper recognition, to regard it as of little importance, inflicts a great harm upon its members. But this is not a reason to confer upon it and upon all cultural groups a general right to the survival of their culture,[42] but a reason to give it, and indeed everyone, equal respect: every human life matters and matters equally, regardless of gender, race, or ethnic group. This is a case for the irrelevance of a culture, not for society's guaranteeing its survival. It may be that in some cases the only practicable way for a society to avoid inflicting this harm on people is to ensure the survival of the identity of their group. But, as it is certainly not always so, this argument cannot be an argument for the universal right of cultural groups to the continued existence of their culture. Every individual must be granted equal respect. Individuals and groups must be granted autonomy. But cultures must be open to criticism, and therefore to constant change, even to the point of a natural death.

Indeed, a culture is alive only if it is open to any change that its members think desirable, even if what survives is no longer the 'same' culture. A society intent on preserving a minority culture is actually severely limited in its options. Once one tries to preserve a culture, one has to decide what constitutes it, and that very decision tends to fix it as it happens to be at one moment in time. Embalming is a form of preservation, but it is not a form of life.

My appeals to the politics of sameness (e.g. the *universal* human right to autonomy) run the risk, of course, of missing the point of someone, such as Charles Taylor, who is promoting, precisely, a new 'politics of difference'. '[W]ith the politics of difference', he says, 'what we are asked to realize is the unique identity of this individual or group, their distinctness from everyone else.'[43] His idea is that when this distinctness is destroyed by a dominant or majority identity, the group loses touch with the ideal of authenticity; it loses touch with its own authentic ways of being. Individuals should be accepted as what they are, and not made to conform to a model appropriate to someone else; for example, women should not be forced, on pain of failure in their careers, to adopt modes of being appropriate for men. Still, when we autonomously choose a conception of a good life, whether or not it is compatible with the models given to us by our cultures, we are hardly sacrificing our authenticity.

The second case for group rights can be summed up like this: our culture is the source of our identity; some cultures are at an unfair disadvantage to others and need protection. What is important in this argument is not best expressed in terms of the right of a group that its culture survive. To say that a group has a right to the survival of its culture is to suggest that a culture deserves the strong sort of ethical protection that overrides all but the most pressing competing ethical concerns. But the demands on a society to protect a culture are not of this nature. The story is much more complicated than that; the demands upon society are much more complex, less categorical, than that.

Nor does the fact that some cultures are at an unfair disadvantage provide a case for a general right to the survival of one's culture. Rights do not cover the whole moral domain, or even the whole domain of justice. Not all legal rights that legislators enact have corresponding moral rights. Not all moral claims that one person makes upon another, or one group upon another, involve rights. Minorities often make successful moral claims upon the majority society, but it is often better to see those claims as based on considerations of justice—usually on fair distribution—rather than on rights. These last claims raise general issues, to which I now want to turn.

15.5 EXCLUSION

One suggestion that has emerged so far is that many supposed group rights are best not seen as rights at all, and some others can be reduced to individual rights. Let me say more about these two possibilities: exclusion and reduction.

It may seem high-handed of me to dismiss many supposed minority rights as not really rights. Or it may seem that I am making only a trivial verbal point: that whereas I choose to define 'rights' so as to exclude many reputed minority rights, others choose to define 'rights' in a way that includes them. But I am not just arbitrarily choosing a definition of rights. Of course, there is an element of stipulation in anyone's proposal about what 'rights' are, but there are constraints on this stipulation. A case must be made for it—in terms of fidelity to the tradition, or of theoretical or practical pay-off, or whatever. Well-chosen stipulations are not high-handed; in the case of rights, they are sorely needed.[44]

I said before that human rights do not exhaust the whole moral domain, or even the whole domain of justice.[45] For example, human rights encompass procedural justice in courts, but not distributive justice (except for the minimum provision for the needy required by the right to welfare, which still leaves much of distributive justice untouched), or retributive justice (with similar exceptions), or many forms of fairness. Recall the case of a minority culture that is losing out in the marketplace and in the normal workings of a democratic legislature; the majority culture, say, gets a great deal of financial support, while the minority culture gets none, and its art and literature are decaying from neglect. The principle of equal distribution of resources may well require some sort of rectification, say in the form of a special subsidy. Now it seems to me that there will often be a strong case to that effect, but a case, I am suggesting, based in equality, not in rights. There is an obvious reply to me. The deprived minority, it says, has a moral claim on resources, and a natural way to express a claim is in terms of rights. After all, when Hohfeld produced his taxonomy of rights, the class of rights that he called rights 'in the strictest sense' were claim rights. The weakness in this reply, however, is that it is distinctly counter-intuitive to express *all* claims in terms of rights. If one spouse is being gratuitously nasty to the other, the latter has a (moral) claim on the former to stop. But not all moral obligations are spoken of as giving rise to rights; this one, for instance, is not.

Of course, we can use the word 'rights' so that its domain of application coincides with the whole domain of moral obligation,[46] but I think that we ought not to. It seems to me that an account of general moral rights should be able to pass a redundancy test. The word 'rights' should not just provide another way of talking about what we can already talk about perfectly adequately. 'Rights' should mark off a special domain within morality, and there should be sufficient motivation to mark it off. The pass level for the redundancy test is, of course, fuzzy.[47] It is obviously a matter of judgement when a motivation is 'sufficient'. But making the domain of rights coextensive, by definition, with the whole domain of moral obligation, for which we already have a perfectly adequate vocabulary, fails the test. True, we could use the word 'rights' to mark the contrast between obligation and supererogation. But I myself doubt that this motivation is sufficient. We already have vocabulary to mark the distinction between duty and supererogation without conscripting the word 'rights' for the job. Besides, this use would be at variance with the philosophical tradition of rights. Certainly in the mainstream of the tradition the term 'rights' has a different and more specific job.

My argument here is an appeal to linguistic intuition. Is nothing more rigorous available? I have proposed excluding many forms of distributive and retributive justice from the class of moral rights. Is not the more rigorous procedure that we need, first, to establish what 'rights' in general are, then what the more specific 'moral rights' are, and finally what the still more specific 'human rights' are?

I doubt, though, as I said in the first chapter,[48] that this more rigorous procedure is available to us. The sense of some words can be explained verbally—that is, in terms of a definition by intension or, somewhat more loosely, by certain forms of explanation, such as 'we say that a person has a "right" when …', followed by conditions other than the extension of the word. This cannot be done, though, in the case of very many terms, the members of the extension of which have nothing stronger linking them than Wittgenstein's 'family resemblances'.[49] These terms can, none the less, acquire satisfactorily determinate senses by acquiring fairly settled uses. I can find nothing more that the word 'rights' has than a fairly settled use, with many senses, varying from strict to loose. One can, of course, give a lexicographical definition of the term, but this is not what we need to settle our questions about the process of exclusion. We need a much more selective explanation of the terms 'rights' and 'moral rights'. We must take seriously that no one has yet come up with this more selective explanation, and not for lack of trying. It may not be possible, and certainly will not be easy, to give one. In the meantime, we should look for another way forward. Parts of the extension of the term 'human right' are widely agreed. The extensions of 'right', 'moral right', and 'human right' have developed in a fair degree of independence of one another. We do not say that a man who free-rides when filling out his income tax return violates his fellow citizens' human rights; he is a cheat, clearly, but not a human rights violator. Nor do we say, of a woman given an unjust prison sentence, either too little or too much, that her human rights have been violated; she has, though, not been fairly treated. What we say in ordinary speech is reinforced in this regard by the most consequential statements about human rights in our time: the Universal Declaration of 1948 and virtually all subsequent documents of national and international law of human rights. These documents include procedural justice but not all of distributive justice, or of retributive justice, or of many forms of fairness. And if these sorts of justice are excluded from the domain of human rights, would they not, by parity of reasoning, also be excluded from other forms of moral rights, such as moral group rights?

This hardly exhausts ways to resist my programme of exclusion.[50] But I cannot myself find any compelling reason, all things considered, to include claims to rectificatory justice, as such, in the class of rights. It is better—if for no other reason than so much clearer—to go on speaking of justice for deprived groups rather than of their having group rights.

15.6 REDUCTION

Other group rights, I think, can be dissolved by reduction. I shall take a quick look at just one example: the right of a state to non-intervention in its internal affairs. In international law this right is closely related to the 'sovereignty' of states. According to the United Nations Declaration of 1970, all states enjoy 'sovereign equality', which among other things includes the inviolability of their territorial integrity and political independence.[51] The Declaration also announces a 'principle concerning the duty not to intervene in matters within the domestic jurisdiction of any State', which bans 'armed intervention and all other forms of interference' in a State's 'political, economic and cultural elements'.[52] The overlap in content of the principle of sovereign equality and the duty of non-intervention is obvious.[53] Now, as individuals, each of us has various rights to non-interference: a right to autonomy (not to have our major decisions taken for us) and a right to liberty (not to be blocked from carrying out our decisions). It is an obvious thought, then, that a state's sovereignty and right to non-intervention might just be, in some way, an aggregation of these individual rights. Perhaps it is because, and only because, all of its citizens have the right that we are willing to say that a state has it.

But if the group right to non-intervention were thus reducible to these individual rights, a state would not have the right to non-intervention unless what it wanted to do expressed what its citizens wanted to do. But that is not at all the way that this particular group right has been understood. It has been thought to be unconditional. As the Declaration of 1970 puts it: 'No State or group of States has the right to intervene ..., *for any reason whatsoever*, in the internal or external affairs of any other State.'[54] If this once common understanding is correct, then the group right is not reducible to these individual rights.

I doubt, though, that it is correct, and in the last two decades it has been much qualified. One can, of course, create a legal right—say, in international law—to be understood in the manner of the Declaration of 1970, but we are interested in moral rights. And a country's prima facie moral right to non-intervention depends, I want to argue, upon its expressing the wishes of its citizens, and this prima facie right itself can be overridden by other moral considerations. I think that this is the understanding of the right that best explains our quite complex, considered beliefs on this subject and the changes of the last two decades.

It is true that we accept that we often, perhaps even generally, ought not to intervene in the affairs even of a country that does not express the wishes of its citizens. But the case for that, I think, is pragmatic. Any wish to intervene runs up against enormous problems of knowledge. We seldom know enough about the intricacies of the local situation to be reasonably confident that we can see what justice requires or, even more to the point, how to bring it about. And even if we can be tolerably assured about the short run, it is notoriously difficult in complex social and political matters to know what will happen in the long run. There is also the cold test of results. Though recent 'humanitarian interventions' have aimed at bringing relief, they have often brought more harm than benefit. Then there is the main concern of the United Nations: a firm ban on intervention makes a major contribution to world peace. These, and other considerations, mount up to a strong practical case against intervention. Indeed, they also have an important role in fixing the boundaries of the (moral) right to non-intervention.[55]

They do not, however, make the right absolute. When the genocide began between the Hutus and the Tutsis, there were calls, answered only late, for intervention. In certain cases, cases of genocide or of gross oppression or extreme disregard for the good of the people, what needs moral justification is not intervention but non-intervention. Sometimes non-intervention will be justified by the practical considerations that I just mentioned. But when one's knowledge is reasonably full, when one can help appreciably at smallish risk, then the moral case for intervening is strong. Non-intervention can then be at least as great a moral failure as a community's not intervening in the internal affairs of a family when the parents are so physically abusive as to endanger their child's life.

The view that I have sketched can be summed up like this. The moral right to non-intervention depends upon a country's wishes manifesting its individual citizens' wishes. If that is missing, then the right does not even exist. Even if it does exist, the right can still be overridden, though the practical pitfalls show that exceptions should be only in especially clear cases. This, in effect, constitutes a reduction of the group right to non-intervention to individual rights to autonomy and liberty. It is hardly the whole story about when intervention is justified, but it is the prologue.

15.7 WHAT IS LEFT?

There are accounts of human rights other than the personhood account. There are other possible conceptions of, and arguments for, group rights, than the ones I have discussed here. My conception of group rights is moral (in contrast to legal), non-reductive, and non-excludable. But other writers have stipulated other senses for the term. One might think,[56] for instance, that 'the important question' is not whether there are group rights in my sense, but whether there are 'legitimate interests which people have, emerging from their ethnocultural group membership, which are not adequately ... protected by the familiar set of liberal-democratic civil and political rights as reflected, say, in the American Bill of Rights ...'. And one might stipulate that 'group rights' are the protections of these interests, if there are such. But that is not the, or even an, important question; the answer is too obvious. Of course there are legitimate interests not adequately protected by classical eighteenth-century political rights. I have pointed that out throughout this book. Examples are certain matters of justice (distributive and retributive), of fairness, and of the quality of life, all of which are of great importance and none of which is a matter of a human right. Not all human interests ground rights. For example, one might, as a result of one's ethnocultural membership, lag behind the rest of society in income, although one's income still be comfortably above the level needed for normative agency; one would, none the less, have a legitimate interest in ending this injustice. Now, would our adopting this stipulation for 'group right' give us a better ethical vocabulary? I think not. This much broadened use would often be deeply counter-intuitive. For reasons that I gave earlier,[57] it would be better in these cases, because much clearer, to speak directly of 'justice', 'fairness', 'human well-being', and of what society should do in light of these.[58]

Clearly, though, there is at least one stipulation other than mine that cannot be gainsaid. One's question might reasonably be:[59] Are there moral grounds on which a good society should grant *legal* rights to certain groups? And of course there are: justice, fairness, well-being, and so on. And there is no threat of loss of clarity in our speaking of 'legal group rights', because the existence conditions for legal rights and for moral rights are, and are widely understood to be, different.

As it is not possible to identify all stipulations for 'group right' that authors might make, I can end only with a challenge. After the combined workings of exclusion and reduction, are there any compelling examples left in the class of moral group rights? When putative moral group rights seem to have the status of rights, is it not because they are reducible to human rights? Can we attach sufficiently clear criteria to the term 'group rights' to make it a helpful, non-redundant addition to our moral vocabulary. Are we not better off without the third generation of rights?

Notes

CHAPTER 1. HUMAN RIGHTS: THE INCOMPLETE IDEA

1. This is occasionally denied. Joshua Cohen, in 'Minimalism about Human Rights: The Most We Can Hope For?', *Journal of Political Philosophy* 12 (2004), says that their different intensions produce markedly different extensions. 'Natural rights' are 'rights that individuals would hold in pre-institutional circumstances'; 'human rights', on his 'minimalist' proposal, are 'rights implied by the most reasonable principle for global public reason' (p. 196). On that definition of 'natural right', he thinks, a right to a fair hearing or a right to take part in government are not natural rights: they presuppose the existence of institutions. On Cohen's definition, and indeed almost everyone's, they are, however, human rights. But Cohen's claim about different extensions is historically inaccurate. For example, at the end of the eighteenth century the terms 'natural rights' and 'human rights' were in use simultaneously, and their extensions did not noticeably differ. A right to a fair hearing in a court was regarded as a 'natural', i.e. 'human', right. At its most abstract, it is a right, simply, to a fair hearing, which does not presuppose the institution of laws and courts; a randomly assembled group in the wilderness can appeal to one of their number whom they respect to settle a dispute, and the settlement, as well as the way it is arrived at, be fair. In modern circumstances the best way to ensure a fair hearing is to have laws and police and courts, and in its lists of human rights the United Nations spells out the institutions we need in considerable detail. Similarly, we have our abstract right to freedom of expression; in a society with a press we have a derived right to, among other things, freedom of the press. Natural rights, it is true, are rights that we have in the institution-free state of nature, but the image of a state of nature is meant to stress that natural rights derive not from any institutions of society—that is, not from any social status—but from our human status alone. That belief does not entail that natural rights cannot have derived forms that spell out what certain social institutions should be like in varying circumstances. See below sects. 1.5 and 2.2, 2.8.

2. Thomas Aquinas, *Summa Theologica*, 1a2ae 93, a. 6 in corp.; ibid. Q. 91 a. 2 in corp.; ibid. ad 3. For exposition, see Annabel S. Brett, *Liberty, Right and Nature*

(Cambridge: Cambridge University Press, 1997), ch. 3, sect. 'Objective Right in Aquinas'.

3. Aquinas 'never uses a term translatable as "human rights"'; see John Finnis, *Aquinas* (Oxford: Oxford University Press, 1998), p. 136; also his 'Natural Law: The Classical Tradition', in Jules Coleman and Scott Shapiro (eds.), *The Oxford Handbook of Jurisprudence and Philosophy of Law* (Oxford: Oxford University Press, 2002), sect. 8. None the less, Finnis says, 'Aquinas clearly has the concept. He articulates it when he sums up the "precepts of justice" by saying that justice centrally ... concerns what is owed to "everyone in common" or "to everyone alike" ... rather than to determinate persons for reasons particular to them' (*Aquinas*, p. 136). But whether Aquinas has our modern concept of 'human rights' depends upon what that concept is. Finnis makes the domain of rights equivalent to the domain of justice, but there is good reason, to which I shall come shortly (sect. 2.6), for doubting that this is true of our modern notion of human rights. We regard the domain of human rights as overlapping that of justice, but not as congruent with it. Furthermore, 'justice' is a highly elastic term, sometimes referring to a quite limited part of morality and at other times stretched to cover all, or most, of morality. Aquinas uses it broadly. As Finnis explains it, 'Common good is the object of general justice. General justice can be specified into the forms of *particular justice*, primarily fairness in the distribution of the benefits and burdens of social life, and proper respect for others ... in any conduct that affects them' (*Aquinas*, p. 133; italics original). This, again, does not seem to give us the modern sense of 'human right'. The United Nations uses the term 'human rights' to include principles of procedural justice (e.g. in courts), but not principles of distributive justice generally ('the distribution of the benefits and burdens of social life'). And few persons nowadays use 'human right' of anything as broad as 'respect for others in any conduct that affects them'. I return to this matter later, as indicated above.

4. My interest, in this brief historical survey, is in writers with breadth of influence rather than depth of thought. Hobbes had the latter, but, given his widely unwelcome views about human motivation, not nearly the amount of the former that the writers I shall mention had.

5. Hugo Grotius, *On the Law of War and Peace*, trans. Francis W. Kelsey (Oxford: Oxford University Press, 1925), Prol. 11, p. 13.

6. Samuel Pufendorf, *On the Law of Nature and Nations*, trans. C. H. and W. A. Oldfather (Oxford: Oxford University Press, 1934), II. iii. 13, p. 201.

7. The phrase comes from Kant's essay 'Idea for a Universal History with a Cosmopolitan Purpose', Fourth Proposition: 'the unsocial sociability of men, i.e. their propensity to enter into society, bound together with a mutual opposition which constantly threatens to break up the society'. See *Kant: On History*, ed. and trans. Lewis Beck White (Indianapolis: Bobbs Merrill, 1963),

p. 15; and H. S. Reiss (ed.), *Kant: Political Writings*, 2nd edn. (Cambridge: Cambridge University Press, 1991), p. 44.

8. For a case for this dating, see Isaac Kramnick (ed.), *The Portable Enlightenment* (New York: Penguin Books, 1995), Editor's Introduction, p. x.

9. 'The state of nature has a law of nature to govern it, which obliges everyone: and reason, which is that law, teaches all mankind ... that being all equal and independent, no one ought to harm another in his life, health, liberty or possessions' (*Second Treatise of Government*, sect. 6).

10. Early in his career, however, Locke lectured at Oxford on the subject of natural law (lectures written shortly after 1660, almost thirty years before *An Essay Concerning Human Understanding*; and not published in Locke's lifetime). In the lectures he used 'natural law' to mean 'moral rule' (Essay I), and a moral rule is objective (it is 'in conformity with rational nature' and its 'binding force' is 'perpetual and universal' (Essay VII)). See John Locke, *Essays on the Law of Nature*, ed. W. von Leyden (Oxford: Clarendon Press, 1954). See also J. B. Schneewind, *The Invention of Autonomy* (Cambridge: Cambridge University Press, 1998), ch. 8 sect. 6. Locke also had much of a theoretical nature to say about morality in the *Essay Concerning Human Understanding*, III. xi. 16–18; IV. iii. 18–20.

11. Locke, *Essay Concerning Human Understanding*, II. xxi. 55.

12. e.g. Jeremy Bentham, 'Nonsense upon Stilts', in P. Schofield, C. Pease-Watkin, and C. Blamires (eds.), *Jeremy Bentham: Rights, Representation and Reform*, in *The Collected Works of Jeremy Bentham* (Oxford: Clarendon Press, 2003). 'Nonsense upon Stilts' was hitherto known as 'Anarchical Fallacies', but has been restored to Bentham's original, ruder title in this volume of his collected works.

13. The French Declaration of 1789 is a good example of the comprehensive approach. In June 1789 the National Assembly set up a committee to prepare material for a constitution. The Constitutional Committee immediately proposed that the Constitution should be preceded by a Declaration of Rights: 'In order that a constitution should be a just one it is necessary that it should be based on the rights of all men ... To prepare a constitution, therefore, it is necessary to recognize those rights which natural justice accords to each individual ... and every article of the Constitution should be the consequence of one of these principles' (quoted in Gaetano Salvemini, *The French Revolution: 1788–1792* (London: Jonathan Cape, 1954), p. 143).

14. Quoted in A. E. Dick Howard, 'Rights in Passage: English Liberties in Early America', in P. T. Conley and J. P. Kaminski (eds.), *The Bill of Rights and the States: The Colonial and Revolutionary Origins of American Liberties* (Madison: Madison House, 1992), p. 3. Other colonies that followed the Virginia Charter in claiming specifically the rights of Englishmen include Massachusetts (1629), Maryland (1632), Maine (1639), Connecticut (1662), Carolina (1663, 1665),

Rhode Island (1663), Massachusetts (1691); see ibid. p. 4. On the 'Englishness' of American colonial rights, see also John Phillip Reid, *Constitutional History of the American Revolution* (Madison: University of Wisconsin Press, 1986), vol. i, ch. i.

15. By the end of the eighteenth century the terms were used interchangeably. For example, in the Preamble to the French Declaration of the Rights of Man (i.e. human rights), the National Assembly stated its resolution 'to set forth in a solemn declaration, these natural, imprescriptable, and inalienable rights'.

16. It is not that Locke wrote the *Two Treatises* in justification of the Glorious Revolution of 1688. As Peter Laslett has shown (pp. 48, 51, 58–79), it was substantially written about ten years before the Revolution, in composition, therefore, being a justification for a possible future revolution rather than for a past one. Still, in publishing the book when he did (1st edn. dated 1690, though it appeared in 1689; p. 50), Locke hoped that it would serve as justification, as is clear from his Preface. Page references to *John Locke, Two Treatises of Government*, ed. P. Laslett (London: New English Library, 1965), Editor's Introduction.

17. See e.g. the account of the proclamations of rights by the town meetings in Boston and, subsequently, in surrounding towns in 1772 and 1773 in T. H. Breen, *The Lockean Moment: The Language of Rights on the Eve of the American Revolution* (Oxford: Oxford University Press, 2001), pp. 17–18.

18. I am grateful to James Nickel for discussion of this point.

19. See below, sects. 2.9, 10.4, 10.6. For an example of the view I want here to deny, see Charles R. Beitz, 'Human Rights and the Law of Peoples', in Deen Chatterjee (ed.), *The Ethics of Assistance: Morality and the Distant Needy* (Cambridge: Cambridge University Press, 2004), sect. 2: 'The "practical" view [which Beitz favours over the "orthodox" view] ... takes the doctrine and practice of human rights as we find them in international political practice as basic. Questions like "What are human rights?", "What human rights do we have?", and "Who has duties to act when human rights are violated?" are understood to refer to objects of the sort called "human rights" in contemporary international life ... There is no assumption of a prior or independent layer of fundamental values whose nature and content can be discovered independently of reflection about the international realm and then used to interpret and criticize international doctrine.'

20. See Lloyd Weinreb, 'Natural Law and Rights', in R. P. George (ed.), *Natural Law Theory: Contemporary Essays* (Oxford: Clarendon Press, 1992), p. 278: 'rights are not closely associated with natural law until the seventeenth and eighteenth centuries. Even then, the association is mostly verbal. The theorists are aware of the natural law tradition and refer to it to support their arguments. But the

references are little more than window-dressing.' See also J. B. Schneewind, 'Kant and Natural Law Ethics', *Ethics* 104 (1993), p. 56: 'The vocabulary of natural law was very widely used in the seventeenth and eighteenth centuries. Its terms accordingly came to be so vague that almost any outlook on the regulation of practice could be expressed in them.'

21. For instance, how are we to identify natural laws? According to early accounts, we should have to know God's intentions in shaping human dispositions. How does the inference from natural laws to natural rights work? And do natural laws exhaust duties to oneself and to other persons? Aquinas thought so (though some human duties to God may have to rest on revelation). He regarded natural laws as equivalent to basic moral principles governing this large sense of duties, accessible to all human agents, from which many more specific moral principles can easily be deduced, although there are occasional tangled cases in which moral judgements can be arrived at only with great difficulty and only by persons of rare moral sensitivity. (See Aquinas, *Summa Theologica*, 1–2, a. 91, art. 2: 'the rational creature is subject to Divine providence in the most excellent way, in so far as it partakes of a share of providence, by being provident both for itself and for others. Wherefore, it has a share of the Eternal Reason whereby it has a natural inclination to its proper act and end: and this participation of the eternal law in the rational creature is called the natural law.' See also Joseph Boyle, 'Natural Law and the Ethic of Traditions', in George (ed.), *Natural Law Theory*, pp. 11–14, 24. If we derive natural rights from natural laws, do these rights then also exhaust this range of morality? Grotius and Pufendorf seem to have thought so. Most of us today do not; we believe that they exclude the claims of charity and perhaps more. But, unlike us today, Grotius and Pufendorf drew a distinction between perfect and imperfect rights, paralleling a distinction between perfect and imperfect duties. Rights generally are moral powers derived from law. In the case of perfect rights, according to Pufendorf, we may use force to exercise our related power; in the case of imperfect rights (say, a right to bring charitable aid to the needy) we may not use force in their exercise, although someone's preventing us from exercising them might thereby be grossly inhumane. (See the discussion in Schneewind, *Invention of Autonomy*, ch. 4 sect. 8 and ch. 7 sect. 4.) If our more limited, contemporary view about the scope of rights is correct, there is then the considerable problem of distinguishing the domain of rights from this much wider domain of morality.

22. Quoted by Michael D. Baylis, 'Limits to a Right to Procreate', in O. O'Neill and W. Ruddick (eds.), *Having Children* (New York: Oxford University Press, 1979), p. 13. At the United Nations Fourth World Conference on Women (1995), Hillary Clinton claimed that it was a violation of a human right to deny women freedom to plan their own families (*The Times*, 6 Sept. 1995).

23. Judith Jarvis Thomson, 'A Defence of Abortion', repr. in R. Dworkin (ed.), *The Philosophy of Law* (Oxford: Oxford University Press, 1977).

24. John Rawls, *A Theory of Justice* (Oxford: Clarendon Press, 1972), pp. 5–11.

25. But consider: 'the eighteenth century was a period (not, perhaps, unlike our own) in which the public's penchant for asserting its rights outran its ability to analyse them and to reach a consensus about their scope and meaning' (James H. Hutson, 'The Bill of Rights and the American Revolutionary Experience', in M. J. Lacey and Knud Haakonssen (eds.), *A Culture of Rights* (Cambridge: Cambridge University Press, 1991), p. 63).

26. Thomas Paine included minimum provision of education and welfare, and also a claim to a job, in *The Rights of Man* (1791–2), and the French Declaration of 1793 (not the more famous one of 1789) included a right to education. But no welfare rights were included in the three most famous documents of the age, the American Declaration of Independence, the American Bill of Rights, and the French Declaration of the Rights of Man and of the Citizen, unless the right to property is thought to harbour welfare elements. Many governments did, in fact, make provisions for education and social security, but the provisions were made by legislation; they were merely political arrangements, not constitutional rights. Golding correctly observes that 'an explicitly recognized conception of welfare rights' existed in the nineteenth century, and in implicit form even in the Glossators' commentaries on Roman legal texts. See Martin P. Golding, 'The Primacy of Welfare Rights', *Social Philosophy and Policy* 1 (1984), p. 124. Still, welfare rights gained wide currency only fairly recently—in the early and middle twentieth century. See the Constitution (1936) of the USSR, and, most importantly, the United Nations Universal Declaration of Human Rights (1948), Arts. 22–7.

27. African Charter on Human and People's Rights, Art. 23. 1.

28. International Convention on the Elimination of All Forms of Racial Discrimination, Art. 5, D. vi.

29. Universal Declaration of Human Rights, Art. 13. 1.

30. That conclusion emerges convincingly from Wittgenstein's discussion of 'family resemblance', in Ludwig Wittgenstein, *Philosophical Investigations* (Oxford: Blackwell, 1953), sects. 64 ff.

31. The most influential being that of Joseph Raz, *The Morality of Freedom* (Oxford: Clarendon Press, 1986), ch. 7 sect. 1.

32. See below sects. 2.4, 2.5.

33. For discussion of whether ancient Greek and Roman authors had the concept of 'a right', see Richard Sorabji, *Animal Minds and Human Morals: The Origins of the Western Debate* (London: Duckworth, 1993), ch. 11; Fred D. Miller jun., *Nature, Justice, and Rights in Aristotle's* Politics (Oxford: Clarendon Press, 1995), ch. 4; Tony Honoré, *Ulpian: Pioneer of Human Rights*, 2nd edn., (Oxford: Oxford University Press, 2002), ch. 3.

34. Some writers (e.g. Jack Donnelly, *Universal Human Rights in Theory and Practice*, 2nd edn., (Ithaca, NY: Cornell University Press, 2003), pp. 38–9; and Thomas Pogge, *World Poverty and Human Rights* (Cambridge: Polity Press, 2002), p. 52), go so far as to propose the checklist of human rights as the test of the legitimacy of governments, but that, I think, for reasons that I shall come to in sect. 2.6, goes too far. Briefly, my reason is that human rights include certain departments of justice (e.g. procedural justice in courts) but not others (e.g. the full range of distributive justice). A government that saw to it that its citizens reached the minimum acceptable welfare demanded by human rights but then diverted all the rest of the nation's wealth to itself would not thereby violate human rights but would hardly be legitimate. I take a 'test' of legitimacy for governments to state necessary and sufficient conditions; widespread violation of human rights is sufficient but not necessary to fail the test. See also below Ch. 14 *passim*.
35. By Gerald Mackie, Research School of Social Sciences, Australian National University, Canberra.
36. For a much more pessimistic view about what philosophy can contribute to the public culture of human rights, see Richard Rorty, 'Human Rights, Rationality, and Sentimentality', in Stephen Shute and Susan Hurley (eds.), *On Human Rights: The Oxford Amnesty Lectures 1993* (New York: Basic Books, 1993).
37. Joel Feinberg, *Rights, Justice, and the Bounds of Liberty* (Princeton: Princeton University Press, 1980), chs. 6, 9–11. See also his earlier book, *Social Philosophy* (Englewood Cliffs, NJ: Prentice-Hall, 1973), chs. 4–6. Similar views can be found in V. Mayo, 'Symposium on "Human Rights"', *Proceedings of the Aristotelian Society*, suppl. vol. 39 (1965), and H. J. McCloskey, 'Rights', *Philosophical Quarterly*, 15 (1965).
38. Ronald Dworkin, *Taking Rights Seriously* (London: Duckworth, 1977), pp. xi–xv, 188–91.
39. In his reply to Herbert Hart's criticisms (H. L. A. Hart, 'Between Utility and Rights', in his *Essays in Jurisprudence and Philosophy* (Oxford: Clarendon Press, 1983), ch. 9), Dworkin acknowledges that the conception of the common good checked by rights need not be utilitarian: 'We need rights, as a distinct element in political theory, only when some decision that injures some people nevertheless finds prima-facie support in the claim that it will make the community as a whole better off on some plausible account of where the community's general welfare lies' ('Rights as Trumps', in J. W. Waldron, *Theories of Rights* (Oxford: Oxford University Press, 1984), p. 166). But this slight amendment does not make Dworkin's characterization of rights any less flawed.
40. Below sect. 2.6.
41. Dworkin, *Taking Rights Seriously*, pp. 191 ff.

42. Widely used because of its occurrence in the Preambles to the two United Nations International Covenants of 1966.

43. For fuller assessment of Dworkin's view of rights as trumps, see Hart, 'Between Utility and Rights', which has influenced my comments here.

44. Robert Nozick, *Anarchy, State, and Utopia* (Oxford: Blackwell, 1974), pp. 28–33.

45. John Rawls, *The Law of Peoples* (hereafter *LP*). (Cambridge, MA: Harvard University Press, 1999).

46. *LP*, sects. 8–9, esp. pp. 64–6.

47. *LP*, pp. 30–2, 78, 122–4.

48. *LP*, p. 68; see also p. 93.

49. *LP*, p. 104.

50. *LP*, pp. 68, 78–9, 81.

51. *LP*, pp. 65 no. 2, 70, 74, 79.

52. *LP*, pp. 27, 79–80.

53. *LP*, p. 70.

54. See below, this section; also sect. 7.4.

55. *LP*, pp. 78–9.

56. e.g. from Joseph Raz and Charles Beitz. For Joseph Raz's argument see this book sect. 2.9. For Charles Beitz's argument see his articles 'Human Rights and the Law of Peoples' and 'What Human Rights Mean', *Daedalus*, 132 (2003). I discuss Raz's argument in sect. 2.9; I discuss many of Beitz's points in the course of this book; see e.g. Ch. 2 *passim*.

57. See below sects. 7.2 and 7.3.

58. *Sunday Times*, 19 Oct. 2003.

59. Mary Ann Glendon, *A World Made New: Eleanor Roosevelt and the Universal Declaration of Human Rights* (New York: Random House, 2001), p. 77.

60. The philosophers surveyed also failed to agree on the ground of human rights, and the editors of the survey reported to the drafting commission that 'the philosophical problem involved in a declaration of human rights is not to achieve doctrinal consensus, but rather to achieve agreement concerning rights and also concerning action in the realization and defence of rights, which may be justified on highly divergent doctrinal grounds' (*Human Rights: Comments and Interpretation* (UNESCO and Westport, CT: Greenwood Press, 1949), p. 263; quoted in Johannes Morsink, *The Universal Declaration of Human Rights: Origins, Drafting, and Intent* (Philadelphia: University of Pennsylvania Press, 1999), p. 301).

Compare Alasdair MacIntyre: 'In the United Nations Declaration on human rights of 1949 [*sic*] what has since become the normal U.N. practice of not giving good reasons for *any* assertions whatsoever is followed with great rigour' (*After Virtue* (London: Duckworth, 1981), p. 67). MacIntyre misses the point.

61. e.g. Cohen, 'Minimialism about Human Rights', p. 213.

62. e.g. Charles Taylor, 'Conditions of an Unforced Consensus on Human Rights', in J. R. Bever and D. A. Bell (eds.), *The East Asian Challenge for Human Rights* (Cambridge: Cambridge University Press, 1999), who looks at Islam and Thai Buddhism; Norani Othman, 'Grounding Human Rights Arguments in Non-Western Culture: *Shari'a* and the Citizenship Rights of Women in a Modern Islamic State', ibid., who looks at Islam; Cohen, 'Minimalism about Human Rights', who looks at Islam and Confucianism. See also Amartya Sen, 'Human Rights and Asian Values', *The New Republic,* July 1997, and his *Development as Freedom* (Oxford: Oxford University Press, 1999), ch. 10.

63. e.g. Taylor, 'Conditions of an Unforced Consensus', on Thai Buddhism: 'the notion, central to Buddhism, that ultimately each individual must take responsibility for his or her own Enlightenment' (p. 134); 'the doctrine of non-violence, which is now seen to call for a respect for the autonomy of each person, demanding in effect a minimal use of coercion in human affairs' (ibid.), though Taylor points out that the doctrine of non-violence has consequences, e.g. far more respect for the environment, that our notion of autonomy does not have. Also, Othman, 'Grounding Human Rights Arguments', on Islam: 'The *Qur'anic* term *ibn alsabil* refers to someone who is forced to move from place to place in order to seek a more peaceful life free from oppression. That is, to endure oppression involves a double violation of divinely ordained human nature and autonomy: by the oppressor and by the victim. Implied in this is a profound affirmation of human freedom, dignity, and autonomy' (p. 189); 'The notion of *umma* refers to humankind in its entirety and diversity, and human beings are given the right of religious conscience, an entitlement to their respective religious views and commitments. This is the capacity for spirituality that all humans share' (p. 190). See Cohen, 'Minimalism about Human Rights', on Confucian-ism: the Confucian ethic includes an 'ideal of the kind of person we should aspire to be: someone whose cultivation is sufficient to understand the virtues and act on them ... According to Tu Wei-ming, Confucianism also embraces a concept of human dignity associated with the capacity for such cultivation. And, he might have added, in at least some of its formulations, Confucianism assumes this capacity to be widely distributed among human beings' (p. 204). But Cohen stresses that the conception of human rights supported by features of Confucian-ism does not rely on 'a liberal conception of persons as autonomous choosers', but draws instead on 'an ethical outlook that understands persons as embedded in social relations and subject to the obligations associated with those relations' (p. 206).

64. For fuller discussion see below sects. 7.3, 7.4.

65. I have been helped in my assessment of Rawls's *The Law of Peoples* by conversation with John Tasioulas and by his article 'From Utopia to Kazanistan: John Rawls and the Law of Peoples', *Oxford Journal of Legal Studies* 22 (2002).
66. See below sect. 3.3.

CHAPTER 2. FIRST STEPS IN AN ACCOUNT OF HUMAN RIGHTS

1. I present here what I take to be the current state of scholarship. Useful recent histories of the idea of a right are Richard Dagger, 'Rights', in T. Ball, J. Farr, and R. Hanson (eds.), *Political Innovation and Conceptual Change* (Cambridge: Cambridge University Press, 1989); James Brundage, *Medieval Canon Law* (London: Longman, 1995); Brian Tierney, *The Idea of Natural Rights* (Atlanta: Scholars Press, 1997); and A. S. Brett, *Liberty, Right and Nature* (Cambridge: Cambridge University Press, 1997).
2. See above Ch. 1 n. 3.
3. Tierney, *Idea of Natural Rights*, pp. 37–8.
4. See Pope John XXII, papal bull *Ad Conditorem* (1323), quoted in Tierney, *Idea of Natural Rights*, pp. 94 ff.
5. See Tierney, *Idea of Natural Rights*, pp. 120 ff.
6. Ibid. pp. 261–2.
7. See the sequence traced by Tierney (ibid. pp. 72–3) from *ius* (objective right) to *ius* (subjective right) that occurred about the year 1200.
8. Giovanni Pico della Mirandola, *On the Dignity of Man*, trans. Charles Glenn Wallis (Indianapolis: Hackett Publishing, 1998), p. 5.
9. See Brett, *Liberty, Right and Nature*, pp. 47–8.
10. For a modern statement of a similar point, see L. W. Sumner, *The Moral Foundation of Rights* (Oxford: Clarendon Press, 1987), ch. 4 sect. 1. 'the criterion for a natural right must itself be a natural property. A natural rights theory therefore must assign (at least some of) its rights to a class of subjects determined by their common and exclusive possession of this natural property [e.g. membership in our species]. ... what, in this context, makes a property a natural property? ... First, the property must be empirical and thus whether or not an individual possessed it must be ascertainable by ordinary empirical means' (p. 102).
11. James Griffin, *Value Judgement: Improving Our Ethical Beliefs* (Oxford: Clarendon Press, 1996), chs. 2–4.
12. Below sects. 6.1 and 6.2.
13. I. Kant, *Groundwork of the Metaphysic of Morals*, trans. H. J. Paton, in his *The Moral Law* (London: Hutchinson, 1961), pp. 95–6 (pp. 482–9 in Kant's

Gesammelte Schriften, ed. Royal Prussian Academy of the Sciences, (Berlin: Georg Reimer, subsequently Walter de Gruyter, 1900–), vol. 4i.)

14. Below Ch. 3, esp. sects. 3.1, 3.5–7.
15. For further discussion of this right, see sect. 9 below.
16. For further discussion of universality as a necessary condition of human rights, see sect. 2.8 below.
17. Sect. 2.8 below.
18. J. L. Mackie, 'Rights, Utility, and Universalization', in R. G. Frey (ed.), *Utility and Rights* (Minneapolis: University of Minnesota Press, 1984), p. 87.
19. R. Dworkin, *Taking Rights Seriously* (London: Duckworth, 1977), pp. xiv–xv; see also pp. 180, 272–4 (where one finds reference to *equal* concern and respect). Dworkin is himself aware of the problem of the vagueness of the notion (pp. 180–1).
20. For an example of someone who wants to include in human rights more of the domain of justice than I want to, and who gives a rationale for including it, see T. M. Scanlon, 'Rights, Goals, and Fairness', in S. Hampshire (ed.), *Public and Private Morality* (Cambridge: Cambridge University Press, 1978). In that article Scanlon's rationale is broadly consequentialist, and what worries me about it is the feasibility of the extraordinarily complex calculation on which it depends. Judgements about human rights have to be simpler, more manageable, than this sort of consequentialism makes them. See my discussion of consequentialism in Griffin, *Value Judgement*, ch. 7 sect. 5, esp. n. 7.
21. On the United Nations' broad definition of 'race', see its International Convention on the Elimination of All Forms of Racial Discrimination (1966), Art. 1.
22. Below sects. 11.4, 11.6.
23. See below Ch. 8.
24. See below sect.5.5.
25. See below sects. 3.3, 3.4, 10.6, 11.4, 14.4, 15.5.
26. Such worries have led some philosophers to give up on personhood accounts, e.g. Joel Feinberg; see his *Social Philosophy* (Englewood Cliffs, NJ: Prentice-Hall, 1973), ch. 6 sect. 3.
27. John Rawls makes a similar point about his notion of 'moral personality' in *A Theory of Justice* (Oxford: Clarendon Press, 1972), sect. 77.
28. Lately there have been fears that genetics, having shown that the human mind, far from being a *tabula rasa*, is stocked with the physical bases of a large array of capacities, will soon show that some persons have greater capacities than others. Will it not thereby revive the belief of many earlier periods in a natural hierarchy of ability? (Interview with Steven Pinker, *New York Times Magazine*, 15 Sept. 2002). It may, indeed, but 'agency' is a threshold notion; the only equality that human rights need is one that nearly all of us have—viz. being above the threshold. And there is no good reason to fear the existence simply of the threshold itself.

29. See below sect. 9.3.
30. I have had helpful conversation on this subject with Laura Zuckerwise.
31. Below sect. 9.3.
32. Put to me in discussion by Joseph Raz. See also Charles R. Beitz, 'Human Rights and the Law of Peoples', in Deen Chatterjee (ed.), *The Ethics of Assistance: Morality and the Distant Needy* (Cambridge: Cambridge University Press, 2004), esp. sects. 2, 3.
33. e.g. by Beitz, 'Human Rights and the Law of Peoples'.
34. See above sect. 1.5.
35. An argument advanced by Onora O'Neill, *Towards Justice and Virtue* (Cambridge: Cambridge University Press, 1991), pp. 131–4. I discuss the argument below, sect. 5.6.
36. See below sect. 3.3, Ch. 5 *passim*, Ch. 19 *passim*.
37. e.g. John Tasioulas, 'Human Rights, Universality, and the Values of Personhood: Retracing Griffin's Steps', *European Journal of Philosophy* 10 (2002). I have been helped too by conversation with Tasioulas.
38. 'The purpose of torture is to get their responses ... We must hurt them so that they respond quickly. Another purpose is to break them and make them lose their will' (Khmer Rouge Interrogator's Manual, 1986, quoted in Gill Newsham (ed.), *The A–Z of Free Expression* (London: Index, 2003), pp. 249–50).
39. For a description of modern interrogation techniques, including the use of drugs, see Mark Bowden, 'The Dark Art of Interrogation', *Atlantic Monthly*, vol. 292 no. 3 (Oct. 2003). *The Times*, 22 Sept. 2005, reports that a team at the University of Pennsylvania has developed a way of reading fMRI (functional magnetic resonance imaging) brain scans that, it is claimed, distinguishes truth-telling from lying with 99 per cent accuracy.
40. See below sect. 5.2.
41. See below sects. 13.3–4.
42. See above sect. 1.2.
43. See above Introduction and sect. 1.1.
44. See below Ch. 11.
45. See below sect. 4.6.
46. See Joseph Raz, *The Morality of Freedom* (Oxford: Clarendon Press, 1986), ch. 7, esp. pp. 166, 180–3, 208.
47. Ibid., ch. 7, esp. sects. 7–8.

CHAPTER 3. WHEN HUMAN RIGHTS CONFLICT

1. See above sect. 2.4.
2. See below Ch. 9.

3. Above sect. 2.1.

4. I. Kant, *The Metaphysics of Morals* (hereafter *MM*), in *Kant's Gesammelte Schriften*, ed. Royal Prussian Academy, of Sciences (Berlin: Georg Reimer, subsequently by Walter de Gruyter, 1900–), vol. 6 Part I ('The Doctrine of Rights'), Preface, p. 230.

5. Contemporary defenders of the co-possibility of human rights include Robert Nozick, *Anarchy, State, and Utopia* (Oxford: Blackwell, 1974), p. 166; Hillel Steiner, *An Essay on Rights* (Oxford: Blackwell, 1994), Introduction and ch. 3 sect. c.; Onora O'Neill, 'Children's Rights and Children's Lives', *Ethics* 98 (1988).

6. Abraham Lincoln, *The Collected Works of Abraham Lincoln*, ed. Roy P. Baster (New Brunswick, NJ: Rutgers University Press, 1953–5), vol. 4 p. 430; quoted in H. G. Pitt, *Abraham Lincoln* (Stroud: Sutton Publishing, 1998), ch. 6.

7. Besides the document I discuss in the text, see also European Convention on Human Rights (1950), Art. 11. 2 and Protocol 4, Art. 2. 3; Convention Relating to the Status of Refugees (1951), Art. 9; Convention Relating to the Status of Stateless Persons (1954), Art. 9; European Social Charter (1961), Art. 30 and Appendix to the Social Charter, *re* Art. 30; International Covenant on Economic, Social and Cultural Rights (1966), Art. 8. 1. a; American Convention on Human Rights (1969), Arts. 6. 3. c, 12. 3, 13. 4, 15, 16. 2, 22. 3, 27, 30; Declaration on the Elimination of All Forms of Intolerance and of Discrimination Based on Religion or Belief, Art. 1. 3.

8. See also Art. 4. 1 of the International Covenant on Civil and Political Rights (1966), which was meant to spell out and give legal force to the Universal Declaration:

> In time of public emergency which threatens the life of the nation and the existence of which is officially proclaimed, the State Parties to the present Covenant may take measures derogating from their obligations under the present Covenant to the extent strictly required by the exigencies of the situation …

Article 4. 2 goes on to spell out what is 'strictly required' by listing rights that may not be suspended: e.g. the rights to life, not to be tortured, against slavery and servitude, to equality before the law, and to freedom of thought, conscience, and religion.

9. In the Second World War the United States detained more than 120,000 Japanese-American citizens without trial. In 1988 Congress officially acknowledged that the 'actions were taken without adequate security reasons' and were largely motivated by 'racial prejudice, wartime hysteria and a failure of political leadership', and ordered that surviving detainees be compensated. Between 1939 and 1945 Britain detained without trial almost 27,000 persons, and 7,000 were deported. In the early stages of the war the threat to Britain of a German invasion was far greater than the threat to the United States of a

Japanese invasion. See Johan Steyn, 'Guantanamo Bay: The Legal Black Hole', Twenty-Seventh F. A. Mann Lecture, 25 Nov. 2003; A. W. Brian Simpson, *In the Highest Degree Odious* (Oxford: Oxford University Press, 1994).

10. There would be no conflict if the right to life were entirely negative: a right not to have one's life taken without due process, with the only correlative duty one of restraint. But the right to life is, I should say, not so restricted; it includes rights to rescue and to protection, in certain circumstances. I think that rescue and protection should be seen as parts of the original right to life, not as additional rights. The same is true of the right to security of person: a government that stood aside and witnessed constant violent assaults on its citizens would fail in its duty, a duty correlative to the right to security.

11. Nozick, *Anarchy, State, and Utopia*, p. 166.

12. See Leslie A. Mulholland, *Kant's System of Rights* (New York: Columbia University Press, 1990), p. 4.

13. *MM*, p. 237.

14. *MM*, p. 237.

15. *MM*, p. 230.

16. *MM*, pp. 390 ff.

17. *MM*, p. 237.

18. *MM*, p. 256.

19. *MM*, pp. 297, 302.

20. *MM*, p. 311.

21. *MM*, p. 337.

22. *MM*, p. 295–6.

23. *MM*, p. 278.

24. Mulholland, *Kant's System of Rights*, p. 199; see also H. S. Reiss, Introduction, in Reiss (ed.), *Kant: Political Writings*, 2nd edn. (Cambridge: Cambridge University Press, 1991), p. xx.

25. I discuss liberty below Ch. 9.

26. Above sect. 2. 6.

27. See *MM*, 'The Doctrine of Right', sect. 3.

28. Above sect. 2.9.

29. Above Ch. 1 n. 55.

30. Above Ch. 2, *passim*.

31. Above sect. 2.6.

32. For discussion of the notion *forfeitable* and its distinction from *alienable, defeasible*, and *waivable*, see Joel Feinberg, 'Voluntary Euthanasia and the Inalienable Right to Life', sect. III, in his *Rights, Justice, and the Bounds of Liberty* (Princeton: Princeton University Press, 1980).

33. e.g. obligation to the environment in conflict with welfare rights.

34. There is also the dimension of number of persons involved, which because of the complications it involves I want to set aside.

35. Below sects. 12.5–6.

36. See my *Well-Being* (Oxford: Clarendon Press, 1986), ch. V sect. 6.

37. See the discussion of bridging notions in Ruth Chang, 'Putting Together Morality and Well-Being', in P. Bauman and M. Betzler (eds.), *Practical Conflicts: New Philosophical Essays* (Cambridge, Cambridge University Press, 2004); and in her ' "All Things Considered" ', *Philosophical Perspectives* 18, (2004).

38. See my *Value Judgement: Improving Our Ethical Beliefs* (Oxford: Clarendon Press, 1996), chs. V–VII.

39. For further discussion, see ibid. ch. V.

40. See Phillip Pettit, 'Consequentialism', in P. Singer (ed.), *A Companion to Ethics* (Oxford: Blackwell, 1991), for the distinction between 'honouring' and 'promoting' values (I have substituted 'respecting' for 'honouring').

41. See my *Value Judgement*, ch. I.

42. Nozick, *Anarchy, State, and Utopia*, p. 30 n.; also see above sect. 1.4.

43. Judith Jarvis Thomson, *The Realm of Rights* (Cambridge, MA.: Harvard University Press, 1990), p. 30 n. 19.

44. T. M. Scanlon, *What We Owe to Each Other* (Cambridge, MA: Harvard University Press, 1998), p. 391 n. 21.

45. I think that the good and the right overlap: e.g. one way in which an individual life can sometimes be good for the individual living it is by its being moral. This suggests that what is good will sometimes have to be explained in terms of what is right. See my *Value Judgement*, pp. 68–79. But these complications do not make talk about the priority of the right or the good impossible.

46. See above, n. 40.

CHAPTER 4. WHOSE RIGHTS?

1. Some critics of the personhood account add to the class of those excluded from having human rights persons asleep or anaesthetized or knocked out or in a temporary coma. But although there are questions about the moral status of sleep-walkers, sleep is rightly not taken to deny one one's status as a person. Nor is short-term unconsciousness. These are transient or morally unimportant passages in what is properly treated as a conscious, intentional life.

2. This needs spelling out. As we have seen (above sect. 2.7), what matters to the possession of human rights is that one has the present capacity for normative agency; what those rights protect is both the capacity for and the exercise of normative agency.

3. John Locke, *Two Treatises of Government*, many editions, *Second Treatise*, ch. 6 sect. 55.
4. I draw this definition from the *OED*.
5. I borrow this example from Jeff McMahan, *The Ethics of Killing: Problems at the Margins of Life* (Oxford: Oxford University Press, 2002), p. 310. McMahan has a fuller discussion of the moral significance of potentiality than I give here; see ch. 4 sect. 6.
6. Preamble. So too does Amnesty International. 'The notion of special childhood rights derives from the universal recognition that children, by reason of their physical and emotional immaturity, are dependent upon their family and community and, more widely, on adult structures of political and economic power to safeguard their well-being.' See its magazine *Amnesty*, Jan./Feb. 2001.
7. Arts. 3. 2, 6. 2. Given the Covenant's definition of a 'child', it is clear that all the rights it lists apply to *some* children. 'For the purposes of the present Convention, a child means every human being below the age of eighteen years, unless under the law applicable to the child, majority is attained earlier', United Nations Convention on the Rights of the Child, adopted by the General Assembly 1989).
8. Compare the World Health Organization's also implausible definition of the right to health: physical and mental health 'to the highest attainable standard'. Drafters of human rights at the United Nations suffer from occasional mindless extravagance. On the right to health see below sects. 5.2, 11.6.
9. On the relation of justice and human rights, see above sect. 2.6; on the relation of suffering and human rights see above sect. 2.9.
10. It has been argued perhaps most prominently and most powerfully by McMahan, *Ethics of Killing*; see also his article 'Cloning, Killing, and Identity', *Journal of Medical Ethics* 25 (1999).
11. So McMahan argues; see his *Ethics of Killing*, ch. 1, where he places the start of a 'person' at approximately 28–30 weeks after fertilization.
12. McMahan would, I think, agree with this. He says that, besides identity, the degree of psychological connectedness between a person at one time and at another itself also has moral weight that contributes to the degree of moral importance of the life of this person at these different times. I myself doubt that the addition of psychological connectedness gives us a satisfactory explanation of the varying degrees of importance of a late foetus, an infant, a 3-year-old, and an adult.
13. I have already discussed an alternative to it—a more pluralist account—above in sect. 2.9.
14. I borrow these examples from a discussion of needs in my book *Well-Being* (Oxford: Clarendon Press, 1986), p. 41 (and I originally borrowed the first

example from Garrett Thomson). For a fuller development of some of the points in this section see ibid. sects. 3.2–6.

15. See, e.g., David Braybrooke, *Meeting Needs* (Princeton: Princeton University Press, 1987), p. 31: a 'criterion' of a basic need is its being something 'essential to living or to functioning normally'. Later he says more fully that the 'criterion' for inclusion on the list of basic needs and for the level of satisfaction required 'is being indispensable to mind or body in performing the tasks assigned to a given person under a combination of basic social roles, namely the roles of parent, householder, worker, and citizen. If what is thus indispensable is not supplied, the person's functioning in these tasks is deranged' (p. 48). See also Garrett Thomson, *Needs* (London: Routledge & Kegan Paul, 1987).

    'Basic need' is a technical term, and so has to be defined. Though the definitions vary, most are close to Braybrooke's. See, e.g., David Wiggins, 'Public Rationality, Needs and What Needs are Relative To', in P. Hall and D. Bannister (eds.), *Transport and Public Policy* (London: Mansall, 1981), p. 209: 'basicness is a question of the conceivability or difficulty … of arranging or re-arranging matters so that a person can dispense with x … without his life or activity being blighted'. For a more finely developed vocabulary, see David Wiggins and Sira Dermen, 'Needs, Need, and Needing', *Journal of Medical Ethics* 13 (1987), sects. 8 and 9; besides the 'basicness' of needs, they distinguish their 'gravity', 'urgency', 'entrenchment', and 'substitutability'.

16. Of course, one should not require the need account on its own to have the resources to solve all problems about morality's becoming 'implausibly lavish'. Other parts of morality might serve to keep morality from becoming too demanding or too generous: e.g. general motivational constraints on human action which limit obligations. But general constraints do not provide enough help here; they do not, e.g., explain why there comes a point where ailments and malfunctions become too trivial to create a right to a cure.

    Braybrooke discusses the problem that endless medical demands create for a basic need account in his *Meeting Needs*, ch. 8 sect. 3. He thinks these medical demands constitute 'a breakdown in the concept of needs' (p. 294). 'In the end, there is no way out of acknowledging that nothing already present in the concept of needs saves the need for medical care from becoming a bottomless pit' (p. 301). That said, Braybrooke rightly goes on to insist that this and certain other breakdowns do not weaken the case for according a dominant role to basic human needs in social decision.

    David Wiggins says that he answers this objection in sect. 17 of his 'Claims of Needs', in *Needs, Values, Truth* (Oxford: Blackwell, 1987), p. 38 n. 45. His answer is this: 'for purposes of a social morality S that is actually lived and succeeds in proposing to agents shared concerns that they can make their own, there is an *abstract claim right or entitlement to x under conditions C* just where *x is something the denial or removal of which under conditions C gives (and can be seen as giving) the person denied or deprived part or all of a reason, and a reason that is avowable and publicly sustainable within S, to reconsider his adherence to the norms of reciprocity and cooperation sustained by S.* ... A social morality cannot of course give any particular person a guaranteed title to wealth, health, happiness, or security from ordinary misfortune. But equally it must not be such as to threaten anyone who is to be bound by it that it will bring upon him or any other individual participants, as if gratuitously, the misfortune of having his vital interests simply sacrificed for the sake of some larger public good' (pp. 31–3).

Wiggins's answer goes in two different directions, in a way that makes it an uncertain guide to what we should say, e.g., about a society's not mounting a crash programme to find a cure for AIDS. AIDS victims might well see themselves as having literally 'vital' interests 'sacrificed for the sake of some larger public good' (such as keeping a few more paintings in the UK and out of the clutches of the Getty Museum), and they might well think that society's turning its back on them, as many of them see it, gives them simple reason to reconsider their 'adherence to the norms of reciprocity and cooperation sustained by S'. But then they might instead think that even such a vital interest as life gives them no 'guaranteed title to ... health'. Wiggins's emphasis seems to be more on the first line of thought. The three principles that he sees as the basis of rights (p. 34) he later describes as 'scarcely more than the preconditions of man's securing their own survival in their own way, or in the best way relative to their circumstances' (p. 39). And later still he says that '*it is pro tanto unjust* if, among vital interests actually affected by [social interventions], the greater strictly vital need of anyone is sacrificed in the name of the lesser interests of however many others' (p. 43).

17. As is said in, e.g., Joel Feinberg, *Social Philosophy* (Englewood Cliffs, NJ: Prentice-Hall, 1973), p. 111; David Miller, *Social Justice* (Oxford: Clarendon Press, 1976), ch. IV; and Wiggins, 'Claims of Need', p. 10 (the remarks in my text apply also to Wiggins's idea of a life's being 'blighted').

18. There are ways of elaborating accounts to try to meet some of these objections. For instance, one could introduce a measure for the importance or urgency of a need—say, the more the need is already met, the less important or urgent it becomes. For example, the more a society meets the demands of health, the less urgent the remaining demands of health become. T. M. Scanlon once developed this line of thought (see his 'Preference and Urgency', *Journal of Philosophy* 72 (1975)). But though this elaboration of the need account may have some plausibility as a basis of social choice (a society has devoted enough of its resources to health, and the demands of art and education are now important), it lacks plausibility as a basis for human rights. After a certain amount of investment in health,

further investment may no longer be especially important. But important for whom? Presumably, for society. But it would certainly be highly important for those people who will die because the society could, but has decided not to, mount a crash programme to find a cure for AIDS. But human rights are claims that individuals can make against others, including their society. This elaboration of the need account, though it may have its purposes, takes it away from the entitlements that reside in each individual, and so takes it away from relevance to human rights.

19. As David Braybrooke does; see n. 15.
20. Below Ch. 6.
21. Above sect. 2.9.
22. Above sect. 2.2.
23. Above sect. 1.3.
24. For helpful discussions of how they might acquire rights in stages, see David Archard, *Children: Rights and Childhood* (London: Routledge, 1993), chs. 5 and 6, and Carl Wellman, 'The Growth of Children's Rights', in his *An Approach to Rights* (Dordrecht: Kluwer, 1997).

CHAPTER 5. MY RIGHTS: BUT WHOSE DUTIES?

1. The schema is more fully expounded by Onora O'Neill, 'Children's Rights and Children's Lives', *Ethics* 98 (1988), pp. 447–9.
2. For the case, see below sects. 7.4, 8.3, 8.4, 10.8.
3. For a history of this pathological growth, see Hugo Bedau, 'The Right to Life', *Monist* 52 (1968); also see below Ch. 10.
4. See n. 2 above.
5. Above sect. 3.5.
6. For further discussion see my *Value Judgement: Improving Our Ethical Beliefs* (Oxford: Clarendon Press, 1996), ch. VI, sect. 2.
7. See below sect. 10.3.
8. Art. 12. 1. See also the African Charter on Human and People's Rights, Art. 16; Additional Protocol to the American Convention on Human Rights in the Area of Economic, Social and Cultural Rights, Art. 10. 1.
9. Twenty-second session, 25 April–12 May 2000, as reported in Draft General Comment 14.
10. See below Ch. 10.
11. I am grateful to John Watts, Corpus Christi College, Oxford, for advice on this subject.
12. UNAIDS, Table of Country-Specific HIV/AIDS Estimates and Data, June 2000; J. T. Gathii, 'Construing Intellectual Property Rights and Competition Policy Consistency with Facilitating Access to Affordable AIDS Drugs to

Low-End Consumers', *Florida Law Review* 53 (2001), p. 734; A. Tabor, 'Recent Developments: AIDS Crisis', *Harvard Journal on Legislation* 38 (2001), p. 525. For a good survey, see Sarah Joseph, 'The "Third Wave" of Corporate Human Rights Accountability: Pharmaceuticals and Human Rights', Conference, Castan Centre for Human Rights Law, Monash University, 10–11 Dec. 2001.

13. *The Guardian*, 18 May 2004.
14. See Joseph, ' "Third Wave" of Corporate Human Rights Accountability', nn. 71, 72.
15. E.g. Onora O'Neill, *Towards Justice and Virtue* (Cambridge: Cambridge University Press, 1991), ch. 5 sect. 2.
16. Ibid. pp. 131–4.
17. E.g. Carl Wellman, *Welfare Rights* (Totowa, NJ: Rowman and Allanheld, 1982), p. 181.
18. On O'Neill's claims, see John Tasioulas, 'The Moral Reality of Human Rights', in Thomas Pogge (ed.), *Freedom from Poverty as a Human Right: Who Owes What to the Very Poor?* (Oxford: Oxford University Press, 2007).
19. Above sect. 2.8.
20. This paragraph develops a thought in Tasioulas, 'Moral Reality of Human Rights', sects. 4 and 5.
21. The enforceability requirement is promulgated, e.g., by Raymond Geuss, *History and Illusion in Politics* (Cambridge: Cambridge University Press, 2001): it is 'essential to the existence of set of "rights" that there be some specifiable and more or less effective mechanism for enforcing them' (p. 143). For fuller discussion of both the enforceability requirement and the claimability requirement, see Tasioulas, 'Moral Reality of Human Rights'.

CHAPTER 6. THE METAPHYSICS OF HUMAN RIGHTS

1. I have discussed the taste model (and also the perception model, which I shall come to shortly) before in my *Value Judgement: Improving Our Ethical Beliefs* (Oxford: Clarendon Press, 1996), chs. II–IV, and I give a condensed version of the argument of those three chapters here in sects. 6.1 and 6.2.
2. Richard Brandt, *A Theory of the Good and the Right* (Oxford: Clarendon Press, 1979), p. 10.
3. John Rawls, *A Theory of Justice* (Oxford: Clarendon Press, 1972), pp. 432–3.
4. L. Wittgenstein, *Philosophical Investigations* (Oxford: Blackwell, 1953), *passim*, but esp. sects. 1–38, 136–56, 167–238. For references to 'form of life', see sects. 19, 23, 241.
5. Donald Davidson, 'Psychology as Philosophy', p. 237, and 'Mental Events', p. 222, both in his *Essays on Action and Events* (Oxford: Clarendon Press, 1980);

also his Lindley Lecture, 'Expressing Evaluations', (Lawrence: University of Kansas Press, 1982).

6. Aristotle, *Metaphysics*, 1072ª29 ff.; cf. *Nicomachean Ethics* 1175ª. For a brief discussion see David Wiggins, *Needs, Value, Truth* (Oxford: Blackwell, 1987), p. 106.

7. See Wittgenstein, *Philosophical Investigations*, sects. 243–308.

8. J. L. Mackie, *Ethics* (Harmondsworth: Penguin, 1977), p. 41.

9. For a fuller version of this argument see my *Value Judgement*, ch. V.

10. Above sect. 3.5.

11. See below sect. 11.2.

12. See above sect. 3.5.

13. See above sect. 2.5.

CHAPTER 7. THE RELATIVITY AND ETHNOCENTRICITY OF HUMAN RIGHTS

1. I have already said something about ethical relativism in discussing John Rawls' views about ethnocentrism, above sect. 1.5.

2. See David Hume, 'Of the Standard of Taste', in various collections of his essays.

3. See Richard Brandt, *A Theory of the Good and the Right* (Oxford: Clarendon Press, 1979), p. 10.

4. This is one of Gilbert Harman's examples of relativity to an ethical framework; see his 'Moral Relativism', in Gilbert Harman and Judith Jarvis Thomson, *Moral Relativism and Moral Objectivity* (Oxford: Blackwell, 1996), p. 9.

5. Also Gilbert Harman's example: ibid. pp. 8–9.

6. For the citation of incommensurable values as an example of moral relativity, see Maria Baghramian, *Relativism* (London: Routledge, 2004), ch. 9.

7. For fuller treatment, see my 'Mixing Values', *Proceedings of the Aristotelian Society* suppl. vol. 65 (1991); and my 'Incommensurability: What's the Problem?', in Ruth Chang (ed.), *Incommensurability, Incomparability, and Practical Reason* (Cambridge MA: Harvard University Press, 1997).

8. David B. Wong offers this as an example of what he would regard as ethical relativism; see his *Moral Relativity* (Berkeley: University of California Press, 1984), ch. 12, sect. 5.

9. See above sects. 1.1, 2.2.

10. See below sects. 8.2, 8.3.

11. See above sect. 6.4.

12. James Griffin, *Value Judgement: Improving Our Ethical Beliefs* (Oxford: Clarendon Press, 1996), ch. V.

13. See above sect. 6.3.

14. For a good recent assessment see Paul Boghossian, *Fear of Knowledge: Against Relativism and Constructivism* (New York: Oxford University Press, 2006).

15. For Rawls on the need to avoid ethnocentrism, see his *The Law of Peoples* (hereafter *LP*) (Cambridge, MA: Harvard University Press, 1999), sect. 17. 1, 'Law of Peoples not Ethnocentric'; also p. 68: 'To argue in these ways [i.e. largely the ways of the Enlightenment] would involve religious or philosophical doctrines that many decent hierarchical peoples might reject as liberal or democratic, or as in some way distinctive of Western political tradition and prejudicial to other cultures.'

16. John Tasioulas adopts this interpretation in his 'International Law and the Limits of Fairness', *European Journal of International Law* (2002), sect. 2.

17. Above sect. 1.5.

18. I discuss this more fully in sects. 1.5 and 13.4.

19. Bangkok Declaration (1993), Preamble and Arts. 1, 8.

20. See above sect. 3.2.

21. For reasons given by, e.g., Partha Dasgupta, *An Enquiry into Well-Being and Destitution* (Oxford: Clarendon Press, 1993), ch. 5.

22. Art. 29. 2.

23. See above sect. 2.9.

24. These contrasts are more fully drawn out by Archie J. Bahm, *Comparative Philosophy: Western, Indian and Chinese Philosophies Compared* (Albuquerque: World Books, revised 1995), esp. ch. III.

25. Amartya Sen, *The Argumentative Indian: Writings On Indian History, Culture, and Identity* (Harmondsworth: Allen Lane, The Penguin Press, 2005), esp. chs. 1, 4, 13.

26. www.quotationspage.com, *sub* Mahatma Gandhi.

27. Jack Donnelly thinks so; see his article 'Traditional Values and Universal Human Rights: Caste in India', in Claude E. Welch jun. and Virginia A. Leary (eds.), *Asian Perspective on Human Rights* (Boulder, CO: Westview Press, 1990). This question is discussed by Harold Coward, *The Hindu Tradition*, vol. 4 of William H. Brackney (series ed.), *Human Rights and the World's Major Religions* (Westport, CT: Praeger, 2005).

28. Robert E. Florida thinks so; see his book *The Buddhist Tradition*, vol. 5 of Brackney (series ed.), *Human Rights and the World's Major Religions*, see pp. 9, 205 ff.

29. Part III of the Constitution is devoted to 'fundamental rights', which include guarantees of equality before the law (Art. 14), no discrimination on grounds of religion, race, caste, sex, or place or birth (Art. 15), freedom of speech and expression, assembly, association, movement, and residence (Art. 19), freedom of religion (Arts. 25–8), and rights to life, personal liberty (Art. 21), and due process (Art. 22). What is more, the Indian drafters took Western constitutional practice as a model. See Pratap Kumar Ghosh, *The*

Constitution of India: How It Has Been Framed (Calcutta: World Press, 1966), p. 70: 'The framers of our [Indian] Constitution shared the American view [viz. Jefferson's view that a democratic constitution should include a bill of rights] and, therefore, incorporated in our Constitution a list of fundamental rights'; also M. V. Pylee, *India's Constitution* (Bombay: Asia Publishing House, 1962), p. 3: 'The makers of the Indian Constitution draw much from the American Constitution though not its brevity … Thus the Constitution of India is the result of considerable imitation and adaptation …'.

30. See Florida, *Buddhist Tradition*, p. 209.

31. Nor, I believe, does the case of Islam and the West. In cultural terms Islam is very much closer to the Jewish–Christian West than is India. Islam accepts the Old and New Testaments as among its own holy scriptures, and the prophets, including Jesus, as its prophets, too. In philosophy, Islam was deeply influenced by the writings of Classical Greece and Rome. In mathematics and the natural sciences, Islam was often well ahead of Europe during the Middle Ages. In social thought, Muhammad, by being more detailed than Jesus in his moral teaching and more specific about the desired social order, was in many ways also more explicitly egalitarian. The Koran prescribes a Poor Due, a two-and-a-half per cent tax on the rich to aid the poor. This may look meagre alongside the tithe of Jews and Christians, but the two taxes are quite different: the tithe was devoted more to the maintenance of religious institutions than, as with the Poor Due, to direct help for the poor, and the two-and-a-half per cent was levied not just on one's income but also on one's holdings. (See Huston Smith, *The World's Religions* (San Francisco: Harper, 1991), pp. 246, 250.) And there was often more freedom of religion in Islam than in the West. 'Let there be no compulsion in religion', says the Koran (2: 257; see also 5: 48). When the Catholics conquered Andalusia, where the Muslims had for long tolerated Jews and Christians, they expelled, slaughtered, or forced Muslims and Jews to convert. When the Muslims conquered Constantinople, they allowed the Eastern Catholic Church to carry on much as before, and Constantinople (Istanbul) is still today its seat. On Muslim tolerance of other religions, see Bernard Lewis, *The Crisis of Islam* (New York: Random House, 2004), pp. xxix–xxx.

    I go through this recital so quickly because the facts are familiar. One would have no more trouble discussing autonomy, liberty, and minimum provision with many modern Muslims than one would with many modern Indians. Not with all Muslims, admittedly; not clearly, e.g., with the Taliban of Afghanistan. Different Muslims draw very different lessons from the Koran. The Koran seems to teach very different lessons, from rare tolerance of non-believers, as above, to bloodthirsty intolerance, as in the famous 'verse of the sword': 'Fight and slay the pagans wherever you find them: seize them, beleaguer them, and lie in wait for them in every stratagem.' But differences within a cultural group are not, of course, differences between cultural groups. The term 'fundamentalism' acquired its present sense used of conservative Protestant evangelicals in the United States in the 1920s, and its contemporary Eastern and Western versions probably have causes in common: perhaps a desperation resulting from a fear that the modern world is inexorably leaving them behind. (See Malise Ruthven, *Fundamentalism: The Search for Meaning* (Oxford: Oxford University Press, 2004), pp. 10–15.) But there are, no doubt, causes special to Islam: a history of colonial exploitation, poverty, lack of education, the legacy of the Crusades and of the Ottoman penetration into Europe culminating in the second siege of Vienna in the late seventeenth century. And part of the explanation of the tension between the West and Muslim Middle East must be simply that they are next-door neighbours—geographical proximity rather than cultural distance. Think of the Protestants and Catholics in Ulster. The record of democracy in the Islamic world is varied, encompassing as it does North and Middle Africa, Turkey, the Middle East, the Indian sub-continent, South-East Asia, and Indonesia. But much the same political variation can be found in Latin America, where the explanation is unlikely to be cultural difference from Europe. Economic structures must play an important part in explaining the political structures of both Islam and Latin America. All that I want to deny is that cultural differences between Islam and the West are *largely* responsible for their political differences. They play a role, but so does much else.

32. See above sect. 1.5.
33. *LP,* pp. 61–7.
34. *LP,* p. 59.
35. *LP,* p. 62.
36. *LP,* pp. 5, 75–8.
37. *LP,* pp. 64–7.
38. See above sect. 1.5.
39. *LP,* p. 80 n. 23.
40. *LP,* p. 27.
41. See below, Chs. 8, 9, 11.
42. See above sect. 2.6.
43. *LP,* pp. 65–7.
44. *LP,* p. 65.
45. *LP,* p. 88.

CHAPTER 8. AUTONOMY

1. Above sect. 2.7.
2. Isaiah Berlin, 'Two Concepts of Liberty', in his *Four Essays on Liberty* (Oxford: Oxford University Press, 1969); for a more recent contribution see Quentin

Skinner, 'A Third Concept of Liberty', *London Review of Books,* 4 April 2002; Skinner is an example of someone intending to speak of yet another 'concept' of liberty when he is actually speaking of another way in which we can lose our liberty (on the central concept of liberty, which I discuss in the next chapter).

3. For histories of this development, see Brian Tierney, *The Idea of Natural Rights: Studies on Natural Rights, Natural Law and Church Law 1150–1625* (Atlanta: Scholars Press, 1997); James A. Brundage, *Medieval Canon Law* (London: Longman, 1995); J. B. Schneewind, *The Invention of Autonomy* (Cambridge: Cambridge University Press, 1998).

4. A somewhat similar distinction between autonomy and liberty is drawn by Gerald Dworkin, *The Theory and Practice of Autonomy* (Cambridge: Cambridge University Press, 1988), pp. 13–15, 18.

5. See above sect. 2.2.

6. See above sects. 6.1 and 6.2.

7. See Onora O'Neill, *Autonomy and Trust in Bioethics* (Cambridge: Cambridge University Press, 2002), ch. 1.

8. E.g. Onora O'Neill, 'Kantian Ethics', in P. Singer (ed.), *A Companion to Ethics* (Oxford: Blackwell, 1991), p. 183; see also J. P. Schneewind, 'Autonomy, Obligation, and Virtue: An Overview of Kant's Moral Philosophy', in Paul Guyer (ed.), *The Cambridge Companion to Kant* (Cambridge: Cambridge University Press, 1992), esp. sects 8–9.

9. See above sects. 3.5, 6.1, and 6.2; see also my *Value Judgement: Improving Our Ethical Beliefs* (Oxford: Clarendon Press, 1996), chs. II and IV.

10. See Ian Tattersall, *Becoming Human: Evolution and Human Uniqueness* (New York: Harcourt Brace, 1998); *idem, The Monkey in the Mirror* (Oxford: Oxford University Press, 2002), esp. ch. 6.

11. See above sect. 2.3.

12. I should, none the less, like to add as an aside that I doubt that the differences above the threshold are in fact great. The matter turns on what ethical growth is like, and so what we can reasonably expect an ethically mature person to be like. The perfectly virtuous person referred to in much modern virtue ethics is acknowledged to be a mythical figure. But so is the less extravagant figure in virtue ethics, the person who grows so much in practical wisdom as properly to be treated as an exemplar for the rest of us. If one is lucky, one has an acquaintance or two who are sound enough in certain ways for it to be a great help to ask oneself: what would A do in this situation? But A is likely to be less sound in other parts of life. We all have areas of blindness, confusion, and insecurity, which distort moral sensitivity. Perhaps thinking what B would do in another part of life would then help a lot. But one soon runs out of sound acquaintances. In any case, one has to be fairly far along ethically oneself to be able to identify soundness in one's

acquaintances; the idea of 'following an exemplar' obscures how very much of the work one must do oneself before following anyone. And on very many big questions in ethics, we are all pretty much on an equal footing. What should the rich nations be doing for the poor? How does one weigh producing good consequences against breaking important moral norms, such as 'Do no murder'? How does one temper justice with mercy? And so on and on. Even those who do not know the preliminary moves that philosophers make in answering these questions can usually be brought up to speed in a quarter of an hour. There are no experts in ethics, in contrast to the empirical, metaphysical, and linguistic matters of metaethics. In ethics, decades of study and experience count for surprisingly little. There are uneducated people with almost perfect pitch on matters of self-interest and morality, and moral philosophers who are largely tone-deaf. There is not much correlation, either, between IQ and a sense of what matters in life. There are, it is true, people with far cruder taste and judgement than others, a difference often correlated with difference in social class, but if differences in taste and judgement are the result of brutalizing deprivation, as they usually are, the overriding moral interest is not in giving them weight but in removing the deprivation. Mental defectives present difficult borderline problems here, and there is, of course, the question of when a child becomes an agent. But neither of these matters bears on the question of the rough equality of those above the threshold. Of course, the equality is only rough. But this remaining empirical inequality does not justify a corresponding ethical inequality. We should not want to award rights in proportion to each agent's deliberative and executive capacities—either on the small interpersonal scale or the large social scale. Think of a family. We neither could feasibly, nor morally would want to, assign differential rights to normal adult members of our family in response to every difference in capacity they exhibited. Nor could we, or would we want to, do so on a social scale.

13. The fullest and best-known case for the instrumental value of autonomy is John Stuart Mill, *On Liberty* (1859, many editions).

CHAPTER 9. LIBERTY

1. See Thomas Hobbes, *Leviathan* (Oxford: Oxford University Press, 1966), pp. 86 (ch. XIV para. 2), 139 (ch. XXI paras. 1 and 2); John Locke, *An Essay Concerning Human Understanding*, ed. P. H. Nidditch (Oxford: Clarendon Press, 1975), II. i. 56; Jeremy Bentham, *Of Laws in General* (London: Athlone Press, 1970), esp. p. 254 (although Bentham generally equated liberty with absence of constraint, he recognized that the term is used in various ways; e.g. many so-called political liberties are, he thought, securities against interference, and that the term is a particularly rich source of confusion); J. S. Mill, *On*

Liberty (1859, many editions), ch. I para. 9 ('In the part [of his conduct] which merely concerns himself, his independence is, of right, absolute. Over himself, over his own body and mind, ... the individual is sovereign'); Isaiah Berlin, *Four Essays on Liberty* (Oxford: Oxford University Press, 1969), pp. xxxviii–xl.

2. I am indebted to my colleagues Howard McGary and Holly Smith for discussion on this subject.

3. See Joel Feinberg, 'The Nature and Value of Rights', in his *Rights, Justice, and the Bounds of Liberty* (Princeton: Princeton University Press, 1980), pp. 154–5.

4. My distinction here between a negative and a positive side to liberty is not the same as Isaiah Berlin's often discussed distinction between negative and positive liberty. By the negative side to liberty I mean the duties it generates not to interfere; by the positive side I mean the duties it may also generate to do something that benefits others. By negative liberty Berlin means the same as I do, but by positive liberty he means self-realization—doing what realizes one's own good.

5. Above sect. 5.5.

6. e.g. John Gray, writing in the *New Statesman*, 20 Sept. 1996: 'I think myself that the last word on individual liberty and social control was uttered by John Stuart Mill, when he declared that only harm to others justified restraint of freedom'; Brian Barry, *Culture and Equality* (Cambridge: Polity Press, 2001), who explains that when, as a schoolboy, he expressed an interest in reading philosophy at university, his teacher told him to try Ayer's *Language, Truth and Logic* and Mill's *On Liberty*: 'I liked them both tremendously, but took to *On Liberty* more, and inside a week had turned in an essay arguing that Mill had got it about right—a view that ... I still retain' (p. ix).

7. Mill, *On Liberty*, ch. 1 para. 9. We often call it Mill's principle because his is probably the best, and best-known, articulation of it. But the principle long antedates Mill. See, e.g., John Locke, *A Letter Concerning Toleration*, in *Works of John Locke*, vi (London: Thomas Davison, 1823): [The state may not prohibit, e.g., killing a calf as a religious sacrifice] 'for no injury is thereby done to anyone, no prejudice to another man's goods' (p. 341); Thomas Jefferson, in William Peden (ed.), *Notes on the State of Virginia* (Chapel Hill, NC: University of North Carolina Press, 1955): 'The legitimate powers of government extend to such acts only as are injurious to others' (p. 159); Declaration of the Rights of Man and of the Citizen, Art. IV: 'Political Liberty consists in the power of doing whatever does not injure another ...'; Art. V: 'The law ought to prohibit only actions hurtful to society ...'; see also Arts. VI–XI. In his *Rights of Man* Thomas Paine gave wide circulation to these, and other, articles of the French Declaration with approval; see *Rights of Man*, ed. Henry Collins (Baltimore: Penguin Books, 1969), p. 133.

8. Mill, *On Liberty*, ch.1 para. 1.
9. This is the first of John Rawls's two principles of justice in his *A Theory of Justice* (Oxford: Clarendon Press, 1972), p. 250: 'Each person is to have an equal right to the most extensive total system of equal basic liberties compatible with a similar system of liberty for all.'
10. James Fitzjames Stephen, *Liberty, Equality, Fraternity* (Indianapolis: Liberty Fund, 1993).
11. Ibid. pp. 34–5.
12. Ibid. p. 35, see also pp. 47, 92, 96.
13. Leon Radzinowicz, *Sir James Fitzjames Stephen, 1829–1894, and His Contribution to the development of Criminal Law* (London: Bernard Quaritch, 1957), p. 16.
14. Stephen, *Liberty, Equality, Fraternity*, pp. 47–8.
15. Ibid. p. 8.
16. Isaiah Berlin, 'My Intellectual Path', in his *The First and the Last* (New York: New York Review Books, 1999), p. 75.
17. Ibid. p. 76.

CHAPTER 10. WELFARE

1. See sect. 2.2.
2. Locke thinks that 'natural reason … tells us that men, being once born, have a right to their preservation, and consequently to meat and drink, and such other things as nature affords for their subsistence'; see *Second Treatise of Government*, ch. 5 sect. 25. It is probably a human right that Paine has in mind when in *The Rights of Man* (originally published in 1792), he proposes annual payments to the children and the aged in poor families. This, he thinks, will be an adequate support for the poor in general: 'If these two classes are provided for, the remedy will so far reach to the full extent of the case, that what remains will be incidental' (p. 293). 'This support', he goes on, 'is not the nature of a charity, but of a right' (p. 296). Page references are to Thomas Paine, *The Rights of Man, Common Sense, and Other Political Writings*, ed. Mark Philp (Oxford: Oxford University Press, 1995). In *Agrarian Justice* (1797) Paine proposes a National Fund 'for ameliorating the condition of men'. 'It is not charity', he insists, 'but a right—not bounty but justice that I am pleading for' (ibid. p. 425). Paine adopts the medieval Church's conception of property. 'I have already established the principle, namely that the earth … was … the *common property of the human race* … and that the system of landed property … has absorbed the property of all those whom it dispossessed, without providing, as ought to have been done, an indemnification for that loss' (ibid. p. 420). Paine's National Fund is not, therefore, strictly a welfare scheme, because the payments are to be 'made to

every person, rich or poor'. Whether Paine regarded the right involved, based as it is on rectificatory justice, as a *human* right depends upon whether he thought that rectificatory justice can be a ground for a human right. He may have; I do not.

Cobbett claimed for the poor 'the right to have a living out of the land of our birth in exchange for our labour duly and honestly performed; the right, in case we fall into distress, to have our wants sufficiently relieved out of the produce of the land, whether that distress arose from sickness, from decrepitude, from old age, or from inability to find employment'. Quoted by E. P. Thompson, *The Making of the English Working Class* (London: Gollancz, 1963), p. 761.

3. T. H. Green, 'Liberal Legislation and Freedom of Contract', in *The Works of T. H. Green*, ed. R. L. Nettleship (London: Hutchinson, 1889); L. T. Hobhouse, *Liberalism* (New York: Henry Holt, 1911).

4. 'Third-generation' rights are the rights of the late twentieth century, rights not of individuals but of collectivities—say, of national or ethnic or linguistic groups. They are rights to national self-determination, the survival of one's culture, and so on. But my interest now is solely second-generation rights.

There is nothing surprising in the fact that welfare rights are, as far as popular acceptance goes, second-generation rights, that liberty rights were widely accepted before them. That in itself does not show that welfare rights are less central or authoritative. The natural rights doctrine was developed, especially in the seventeenth and eighteenth centuries, by middle-class European and American men. Their chief concern was resistance to absolute monarchs, freedom to pursue their (largely commercial or agricultural) interests. They were in general economically secure; their relative wealth constituted an important part of the framework for their political thought. The desperately needy had, at this time, scarcely found their voice; their poverty rendered them largely silent. The historical lateness in the general acceptance of welfare rights shows nothing about their importance, certainly not that they are dubious 'accretions' to the 'core' liberty rights. In our time, China is the main promoter of welfare rights against what they see as the one-sided advocacy of liberty rights by the United States. They argue that welfare rights have to be satisfied before liberty rights are of much value, but it would be a confusion to think, as the Chinese government seems also to think, that welfare rights must be satisfied first in time; the work of various economists (e.g. Partha Dasgupta, *An Enquiry into Well-Being and Destitution* (Oxford: Clarendon Press, 1993), ch. 5) has shown that in general the countries that most successfully avoid welfare disasters are the ones that have political liberties. Welfare rights are indeed prior to liberty rights in the sense that they are the necessary condition for liberty rights' being of value to us; but this does not show that they are prior in the sense that they must be realized first.

5. See above sects. 2.8, 5.1.

6. For examples of support for this view see Maurice Cranston, 'Human Rights: Real and Supposed', in D. D. Raphael (ed.), *Political Theory and the Rights of Man* (London: Macmillan, 1967); Rodney Peffer, 'A Defense of Rights to Well-Being', *Philosophy and Public Affairs* 8 (1978); Carl Wellman, *Welfare Rights* (Totowa, NJ: Rowman and Allanheld, 1982), p. 181.

7. Above sect. 5.1.

8. Above sect. 3.3, ch. 5 *passim*.

9. This case is made by Alan Gewirth, *The Community of Rights* (Chicago: University of Chicago Press, 1996), p. 123. Gewirth, none the less, favours the view that welfare rights are human rights.

10. Robert Nozick, *Anarchy, State, and Utopia* (Oxford: Blackwell, 1974), pp. 169–72.

11. See e.g. Jeremy Waldron, *Liberal Rights* (Cambridge: Cambridge University Press, 1993), pp. 18 ff.

12. For a defence of the narrower conception of liberty, see above ch. 7.

13. Anyone interested in the justification of a human right to welfare would be helped by looking at the writing in political theory about the case for the welfare state. The focus there is more on welfare as a necessary condition for effective citizenship in a modern liberal democracy, whereas our focus is on necessary conditions for normative agency generally, but there is overlap. See e.g. Robert Goodin, *Reasons for Welfare: The Political Theory of the Welfare State* (Princeton: Princeton University Press, 1988); Desmond S. King and Jeremy Waldron, 'Citizenship, Social Citizenship and the Defense of Welfare Provision', *British Journal of Political Science* 18 (1988).

14. E.g. Henry Shue, *Basic Rights: Subsistence, Affluence, and United States Foreign Policy*, 2nd edn. (Princeton: Princeton University Press, 1996), p. 31; Gewirth, *Community of Rights*, p. 115.

15. The indivisibility of liberty rights and welfare rights has often been claimed, e.g., by David Archard, 'Welfare Rights as Human Rights', in T. Campbell and S. Miller (eds.), *Human Rights and the Moral Responsibilities of Corporate and Public Sector Organisations* (Dordrecht: Kluwer, 2004); Mary Robinson, 'Realizing Human Rights', Romanes Lecture for 1997 (Oxford: Clarendon Press, 1998).

16. See above sects. 5.3–4.

17. *New York Times*, 27 Aug. 1996.

18. Ability also explains why we think that there may sometimes be international obligations to help. In 1996 the British Defence Secretary, Michael Portillo, told the House of Commons that Britain had a moral obligation to intervene in Bosnia to save refugees from starving, because Britain was 'one of the few nations on earth who have the military capability to help' (*Daily Telegraph*, 15 Nov. 1996).

19. Isaiah Berlin, Introduction, in *Four Essays on Liberty* (Oxford: Oxford University Press, 1969), p. liii. See also John Rawls's distinction between the *extent* of liberty and its *worth* (*A Theory of Justice* (Oxford: Clarendon Press, 1972), p. 204) and his later comments on the distinction (in 'The Basic Liberties and their Priority', in S. McMurrin (ed.), *Liberty, Equality, and Law: Selected Tanner Lectures on Moral Philosophy* (Cambridge: Cambridge University Press, 1987)).

20. See above sect. 7.4.

21. Universal Declaration of Human Rights (1948), Art. 25. 1.

22. E.g. Shue, *Basic Rights*, p. 23; Carl Wellman, 'The Right to an Adequate Standard of Living', in *Festskrit Till Stig Strömholm* (Uppsala: Justus Forlag, 1997), pp. 836–8.

23. See Amartya Sen, *Poverty and Famines: An Essay on Entitlement and Deprivation* (Oxford: Oxford University Press, 1981).

24. See Dasgupta, *Enquiry into Well-Being and Destitution*, ch. 5 sect. 3.

25. e.g. Carl Wellman and Alan Gewirth.

26. Immanuel Kant and Hillel Steiner.

27. See above sect. 2.6.

28. Fully stated, the right announced in Article 23.3 is 'to just and favourable remuneration ensuring for himself and his family an existence worthy of human dignity'. The mention of 'human dignity' may be taken to set a limit to the justice involved: perhaps we should read the clause as saying 'just remuneration, i.e. remuneration needed to ensure human dignity', an interpretation in the spirit of the personhood account. But what is needed to ensure human dignity is not justice—i.e. fair pay—but enough material resources (e.g. pay) to satisfy the necessary conditions for normative agency.

CHAPTER 11. HUMAN RIGHTS: DISCREPANCIES BETWEEN PHILOSOPHY AND INTERNATIONAL LAW

1. See also the *American Declaration of the Rights and Duties of Man* (1948): 'The American States have on repeated occasions recognized that the essential rights of man ... are based upon attributes of his human personality.' Additional Protocol to the American Convention on Human Rights in the Area of Economic, Social and Cultural Rights (1988), Preamble: 'Considering the close relationship that exists between economic, social and cultural rights, and civil and political rights, in that the different categories of rights constitute one indivisible whole based on the recognition of the dignity of the human person'; Final Act of the Helsinki Conference (1975), Principle VII: 'The participating States ... will promote and encourage the effective exercise of civil, political, economic, social, cultural and other rights and

freedoms all of which derive from the inherent dignity of the human person.

2. Henry J. Steiner and Philip Alston, *International Human Rights in Context* (Oxford: Clarendon Press, 1996), p. 127, make this observation about the two United Nations documents, the Universal Declaration of Human Rights and the International Covenant on Civil and Political Rights, but it applies generally.

3. See Ian Brownlie, *Principles of Public International Law*, 5th edn. (Oxford: Clarendon Press, 1998), pp. 582–3: 'Originating in the Algiers Declaration of 1978 a doctrine of the Rights of Peoples has appeared in the literature. A fairly typical prospectus of these rights would include the right to food, the right to a decent environment, the right to development, and the right to peace.'

4. American Declaration of the Rights and Duties of Man, Art. V; International Covenant on Civil and Political Rights, Art. 17. 1.

5. Above sect. 2.6.

6. This is repeated in the International Covenant on Civil and Political Rights, Art. 12. 1, and the African Charter, Art. 12. 1.

7. See the American Declaration of the Rights and Duties of Man, Arts. XXIV–XXVI; the European Convention, Arts. 6–7; the International Covenant on Civil and Political Rights, Arts. 14–16; the American Convention, Arts. 3, 8–10; the African Charter, Arts. 6–7.

8. See, e.g., Michael Akehurst, *A Modern Introduction to International Law*, 6th edn. (London: Allen & Unwin, 1987), p. 76, who in writing about the growth of the human rights doctrine observes that 'it was only after the United Nations Charter was signed in 1945 that any attempt was made to provide comprehensive protection for all individuals against all forms of injustice'.

9. Above sect. 2.6.

10. For the history of, e.g., the introduction of the Bill of Rights in the USA, see L. W. Levy, *Origins of the Bill of Rights* (New Haven: Yale University Press, 1999), esp. ch. 1.

11. Is there another line that the drafters of these international documents might take? An interesting phrase crops up in many of the documents. They speak of promoting observance of 'human rights *and fundamental freedoms*'. See, e.g., the Universal Declaration, Preamble, Art. 2; International Covenant on Civil and Political Rights, Preamble, Arts. 2. 3. a, 5. 1; International Covenant on Economic, Social and Cultural Rights, Preamble, Art. 5. 1; European Convention, Preamble (which links the two: 'fundamental freedoms' depend upon the observance of 'human rights' and so suggests that they are coextensive); American Convention, Art. 1; African Charter, Preamble, Arts. 1–2. Are 'fundamental freedoms' different from 'human rights'?

There is, so far as I know, no explanation of the distinction between the two. Of course, some fundamental freedoms, such as liberty, are human rights if anything is. But if some 'fundamental freedoms' fall outside the class of 'human rights', then the drafters may not be using 'human rights' as broadly as I think they are. But the most plausible interpretation of what the drafters mean by 'fundamental freedoms', it seems to me, is that they are a sub-class of 'human rights'. This makes the phrase 'and fundamental freedoms' otiose, but I am inclined to accept that consequence. (An example of a human right that is not also a fundamental freedom would be a right to welfare.)

12. See the Preamble, para. 1, of the Universal Declaration.
13. See Oscar Schachter, 'Human Dignity as a Normative Concept', *American Journal of International Law* 77 (1983). 'We do not find an explicit definition of the expression "dignity of the human person" in international instruments or (as far as I know) in national law. Its intrinsic meaning has been left to intuitive understanding, conditioned in large measure by cultural factors' (p. 848).
14. In tracing the emergence of a right to a healthy environment, I follow closely Carl Wellman's discussion in his paper 'Solidarity, the Individual and Human Rights', *Human Rights Quarterly* 22 (2000), sect. 3.
15. See *The New York Times,* 15 Dec. 2004.
16. See Akehurst, *Modern Introduction to International Law*, ch. 3; Brownlie, *Principles of Public International Law*, ch. I, sect. 2; Steiner and Alston, *International Human Rights in Context*, p. 27.
17. This is the view of Akehurst, *Modern Introduction to International Law*, p. 42.
18. For a recent example, see Allen Buchanan, *Justice, Legitimacy, and Self-Determination: Moral Foundations for International Law* (Oxford: Oxford University Press, 2004), esp. chs. 1, 5–7. 'This book is an attempt to develop moral foundations for international law. The existing international legal system...can and ought to be evaluated from the standpoint of moral principles' (p. 1). 'I am plainly rejecting the dominant view in international relations, namely, that state policy should or at least may exclusively pursue national interest' (p. 8). '...political entities are legitimate only if they achieve a reasonable approximation of minimal standards of justice, ...understood as the protection of human rights' (p. 5).
19. For a recent example, see Jack L. Goldsmith and Eric Posner, *The Limits of International Law* (New York: Oxford University Press, 2005), esp. chs. 4 and 7.
20. See ibid. On the autonomy of international law: '...international legality does not impose any moral obligations' (p. 197). 'The reason that it can exert no moral force comparable to the moral force of domestic law is that it has no democratic pedigree or epistemic authority; it reflects what states have been doing in the recent past and does not necessarily reflect the moral judgements

or interests or needs of individuals' (p. 199). 'A third category, between politics and morality, is separated out and made the subject of a special discipline, that of international law' (p. 201). On the source of the bindingness of international law: 'The more plausible view [is this:] ... efficacious international law is built up out of rational self-interest ... On this view, international law can be binding and robust, but only when it is rational for states to comply with it' (p. 202).

21. See e.g. Maurice Cranston, 'Human Rights: Real and Supposed', in D. D. Raphael (ed.), *Political Theory and the Rights of Man* (London: Macmillan, 1967); for a more conceptual doubt about welfare rights, see Carl Wellman, *Welfare Rights* (Totowa, NJ: Rowman and Allanheld, 1982), esp. p. 181.

22. See above ch. 10.

23. Above sect. 10.1.

24. See the American Declaration of the Rights and Duties of Man, Art. XIV; the International Covenant on Economic, Social and Cultural Rights, Art. 6. 1; European Social Charter, I. 1 and II. 1; the Additional Protocol to the American Convention on Human Rights in the Area of Economic, Social and Cultural Rights, Art. 6. 1.

25. See, e.g., the European Social Charter, II. 1.

26. See above sect. 2.8.

27. Above sect. 5.2.

28. Art. 12. 1. See also the African Charter on Human and People's Rights, Art. 16; Additional Protocol to the American Convention on Human Rights in the Area of Economic, Social and Cultural Rights, Art. 10. 1.

29. See the Universal Declaration, Art. 23. 2; the International Covenant on Economic, Social and Cultural Rights, Art. 7. a. i; the European Social Charter, II. 4. 3; the African Charter, Art. 15.

30. See the International Covenant on Economic, Social and Cultural Rights, Art. 7; the European Social Charter, II. 2.

31. See the International Covenant on Economic, Social and Cultural Rights, Art. 7c; Additional Protocol to the American Convention on Human Rights in the Area of Economic, Social and Cultural Rights, Art. 7c.

32. Ludwig Wittgenstein, *Philosophical Investigations* (Oxford: Blackwell, 1953), sects. 64 ff.

CHAPTER 12. A RIGHT TO LIFE, A RIGHT TO DEATH

1. The right to life was 'so far above dispute that authors [in the North American colonies] were content merely to mention it in passing' (Clinton Rossiter, *Seed Time of the Republic* (Boston: Harcourt, 1953), p. 377).

2. I do not know of anywhere in, e.g., the debate about the ratification of the US Constitution where the negative nature of the right to life is explicitly

asserted. But the general concern of the debate was the protection of individuals against the arbitrary actions of governments. Hence, the focus in the first ten amendments (1791) to the Constitution, which constituted the original Bill of Rights, was upon such matters as freedom of the press, due process, speedy trials, bans on excessive bail, the forced quartering of soldiers in private houses, and so on. This, in itself, suggests that the focus in talk about a right to life would be the prohibition of society's arbitrarily depriving anyone of life. And, although it is much later (1868), the Fourteenth Amendment says that states may not 'deprive any person of life, liberty or property, without due process of law'.

3. For a history of this growth see Hugo Bedau, 'The Right to Life', *Monist* 52 (1968). Some recent claims to the right to life have been on the modest side. The Draft Covenant on Civil and Political Rights adopted by the United Nations in November 1957 says: 'Every human being has the inherent right to life. This right shall be protected by law. No one shall be arbitrarily deprived of his life.' The Convention for the Protection of Human Rights and Fundamental Freedoms, adopted by the Council of Europe in November 1950, uses much the same terms (both quoted by Bedau, p. 552). But some late eighteenth-century claims to the right have been on the broad side. William Blackstone, in his *Commentaries on the Laws of England* (1795), says that among the 'rights of persons' are three 'absolute rights of individuals': viz. the rights of personal security, of liberty, and of private property. But he describes the first in these terms: 'The right of personal security consists in a person's legal and uninterrupted enjoyment of his life, his limbs, his body, his health, and his reputation.' Blackstone connects the absolute right to life to the following:

The law not only regards life and member, and protects every man in the enjoyment of them, but also furnishes him with everything necessary for their support. For there is no man so indigent or wretched, but he may demand a supply sufficient for all necessities of life from the more opulent part of the community ...

(also quoted by Bedau, p. 564). Joel Feinberg, in 'Voluntary Euthanasia and the Inalienable Right to Life', in his *Rights, Justice, and the Bounds of Liberty* (Princeton: Princeton University Press, 1980), strikes a balance between positive and negative interpretations:

I propose ... to interpret 'the right to life' in a relatively narrow way, so that it refers to the 'right not to be killed' and 'the right to be rescued from impending death', but not to the broader conception, favoured by many manifesto writers, of a 'right to live decently'. (p. 222)

Carl Wellman strikes much the same balance in 'The Inalienable Right to Life and the Durable Power of Attorney', in his *An Approach to Rights* (Dordrecht: Kluwer, 1997), pp. 245–7. The upshot is: there has been no agreement on the scope of the right to life for a very long while.

4. '[In the classical natural rights view], the right to life ... means the right not to be killed, whether by another individual or arbitrarily by the state. Locke's version of this right has been characterized (e.g. by D. D. Raphael, 'Human Rights, Old and New', in Raphael (ed.), *Political Theory and the Rights of Man* (Bloomington, IN: Indiana University Press, 1967)) as a ' "right to be left free to live (or, if one is unlucky, to die)" '; Susan Moller Okin, 'Liberty and Welfare: Some Issues in Human Rights Theory', in J. R. Pennock and J. W. Chapman (eds.), NOMOS XXIII: *Human Rights*, (New York: New York University Press, 1981), p. 248.

5. Richard Hooker, *Ecclesiastical Polity*, bk. II ch. VIII sect. 7; quoted by Locke, *Second Treatise*, ch. II sect. 5.

6. Locke, *Second Treatise*, ch. II sect. 6.

7. Ibid.

8. Ibid.; italics original.

9. Notice, e.g., the positive sound of what Locke says in ch. V sect. 25 about property: 'men, being once born, have a right to their preservation, and consequently to meat and drink, and such other things as nature affords for their subsistence'. This remark, being part of Locke's justification for private property, can, of course, be read as a right to the resources that would allow one to provide one's own meat and drink, rather than a claim for others to provide them when one is in need. But it could also be the latter. And it clearly is a requirement to *leave* as much and as good as the rest have, or (apparently) to *provide* it if none remains unclaimed—a positive duty.

10. See above sect. 9.1.

11. Locke, *Second Treatise*, ch. II sect. 5.

12. See above sect. 9.3.

13. See above sect. 3.5.

14. I am grateful to Laura Zuckerwise for pressing this question.

15. Locke, *Second Treatise*, ch. I sect. 6; italics original.

16. On the divine loan view, I have what could prove to be a highly unwelcome duty: not in any circumstances to take my own life. You also have a duty: never to take my life, no matter how merciful an act it would be. The divine loan view also implies that one should not put one's life at certain risks. If you lend me a book, there are limits to the risks to which I may subject it. Of course, if I am able to use it at all, I am bound to put it to *some* risk; accidents can happen. So too with my life, if it is a mere loan to me. In the *Social Contract*, in the course of a chapter entitled 'The Right to Life and Death', Rousseau offers a plausible justification for subjecting one's life to some risks. One may risk it, he says, in order to preserve it. We enter the social contract to preserve ourselves. 'He who wills the end wills the means also, and the means must involve some risks and even some losses.' The state institutes an army to protects its citizens' lives and liberties,

and one must take one's fair share of these risky offices (Jean-Jacques Rousseau, *The Social Contract*, bk. II ch. IV paras. 1–2). Still, Rousseau's justification does not justify the high risks of, say, climbing Mount Everest, and it is hard to think that climbing Everest is at variance with a right to life.

17. For a case for this conclusion, see David Hume, 'Of Suicide', many editions of his *Essays*.

18. See the discussion of Kant on the subjects of suicide and euthanasia by Jeff McMahan, *The Ethics of Killing: Problems at the Margins of Life* (Oxford: Oxford University Press, 2002), p. 478. For a good discussion of the ethics of suicide and euthanasia in general, see his ch. 5, esp. sect. 2.

19. Above sects. 3.2–3.

20. Kant, *The Metaphysics of Morals*, in *Kant's Gesammelte Schriften*, ed. Royal Prussian Acadamy of Sciences (Berlin: Georg Reimer, subsequently Walter de Gruyter, 1900–), vol. 6, Part I, Preface, p. 230.

21. Above sect. 3.3.

22. Above sect. 2.4.

23. Above sects. 4.3–5.

24. On what Joel Feinberg regards as a 'coherent and reasonably plausible' interpretation of the right to life (and the interpretation that he attributes to the Founding Fathers of the United States), 'the right to die is simply the other side of the coin of the right to live' ('Voluntary Euthanasia and the Inalienable Right to Life', pp. 249, 251). Feinberg holds that 'I *waive* my right to live in exercising my right to die', but I do not 'relinquish or effectively renounce the right, for that would be to alienate what is not properly alienable' (p. 249). But *waiving* the right to life in killing oneself or in getting a doctor to kill one is a good deal more drastic than merely not exercising the right on a particular occasion: it is ending one's life; it is ensuring that there will never be a further occasion on which to exercise the right. One may use the notion of 'waiving' in this sense, but this should not obscure the fact that what is doing the work in establishing the right to die is not the right to life but rights to autonomy and liberty.

25. This point is well made by the six philosophers who filed a brief as *amici curiae* with the Supreme Court in connection with two cases raising the question whether dying patients have a right to choose death (*State of Washington et al. v. Glucksberg et al.* and *Vacco et al. v. Quill et al.*, argued 8 Jan. 1997); see *New York Review of Books*, 27 Mar. 1997, pp. 43–5.

26. This conclusion echoes Schopenhauer's: 'it is obvious there is nothing in the world a man has a more incontestable *right* to than his own life and person'. See his essay 'On Suicide', in which he calls suicide both a 'right' and a 'mistake', in Arthur Schopenhauer, *Essays and Aphorisms*, ed. and trans. R. J. Hollingdale (London: Penguin Books, 2004), pp. 77–8.

27. E.g. Herbert Hendin, a New York psychiatrist who has spent several years study-
ing euthanasia in Holland, claims that some Dutch patients have been pressed by
their doctors to accept euthanasia rather than be given adequate palliative care.
'Euthanasia', he is quoted as saying, 'is becoming much more a habit and routine.
I even had one hospital doctor complaining to me that a doctor had killed one
of his patients because he needed the bed' (*Sunday Times*, 16 Mar. 1997).

28. This figure was cited by the Solicitor-General of the United States in oral
arguments before the Supreme Court in connection with the cases referred to
above (see n. 25); quoted by Ronald Dworkin, Introduction to 'The Brief of
the Amici Curiae', *New York Review of Books*, p. 42.

29. E.g. Dr Robert Twycross, Clinical Reader in Palliative Medicine at Oxford
University and former medical director of a hospice, threatened to resign from
the British Medical Association in protest against the pro-euthanasia stance
of its main publication, the *British Medical Journal* (*Oxford Times*, 24 Aug.
1994).

30. Reckoned by Dr Jack Morley of the Pain Research Institute, UK; quoted by
Sean Dixon-Child, correspondence, *The Times*, 16 Nov. 2002.

31. This point is put more strongly in 'The Brief of the *Amici Curiae*': 'One
cannot reasonably judge', say the *amici*, that 'the risk of "mistake" to some
persons justifies a prohibition that not only risks but insures and even aims
at what would undoubtedly be a vastly greater number of "mistakes" of the
opposite kind—preventing many competent people … from escaping … [a]
terrible injury' (p. 46). This argument assumes—what seems to me hard to
know—that the number of "mistakes" consequent upon a policy of prohibition
would exceed the number of "mistakes" upon the more permissive policy that
the *amici* favour. (The claim grows more dubious the better pain management
becomes). But one does not need such a strong claim.

32. I doubt that it is beyond our wit to formulate the right to death in a way that
would be largely beneficial. I think that it would have to be done in the same
way that is has in fact been done in most of the laws that have been passed so
far: it is the answer that the Dutch have given, and that the Northern Territory
in Australia and the State of Oregon have both given.

  In the Netherlands, euthanasia is technically illegal, carrying a penalty of
up to twelve years in jail. But in February 1993 the Dutch Parliament passed
legislation (by 91 to 45) assuring doctors immunity from prosecution if they
follow a 28-point checklist in ending a patient's life (*The Independent*, 10 Feb.
1993).

  In May 1995 the Northern Territory in Australia passed the *Rights of
the Terminally Ill Act*. By the end of 1996 two persons had committed
doctor-assisted suicide under protection of the act (*The Independent*, 7 Jan.
1997). The federal parliament in Canberra, which has power to override

the legislation of the Territory, has started the process (in December 1996 the lower house voted by 88 to 35 to overturn the law; the bill now goes to the Senate).

In November 1994 voters in Oregon approved (by 51 to 49 per cent) the 'Death with Dignity Act', a law allowing doctor-assisted suicide, but it was blocked by a court challenge on 7 Dec., the day before it would have become law. On 3 Aug. 1995 a Federal judge ruled the law unconstitutional because it violated the equal protection clause of the Fourteenth Amendment of the US Constitution (*New York Times*, 4 Aug. 1995; *The Spectator*, 19 Nov. 1994). In his decision, US District Judge Michael Hogan wrote: 'There is little assurance that only competent terminally ill persons will voluntarily die. Some "good results" cannot outweigh other lives lost due to unconstitutional errors and abuses.' The Oregon act required that at least two doctors diagnose a terminal illness and rule the patient to be competent; it required a doctor to determine the patient not to be clinically depressed; it did not put any doctor or pharmacist under compulsion to comply with a patient's request for assistance (*Boston Globe*, 4 Aug. 1995).

In thinking about these issues, we must guard against asymmetric standards of argument. Some opponents of legalizing (assisted) suicide cite reports that Dutch doctors have put pressure on certain patients to accept assisted suicide because their beds were needed. I do not know what truth there is in these rumours. But is there nothing comparable wrong with the *status quo*?

CHAPTER 13. PRIVACY

1. One finds personhood offered as the ground for a right to privacy from time to time in the literature. See, e.g., David A. J. Richards, *Toleration and the Constitution* (New York: Oxford University Press, 1986), ch. 8. esp. pp. 243–4, 252–3; Philippa Strum, *Privacy: The Debate in the United States since 1945* (Fort Worth, TX: Harcourt Brace, 1998), pp. 202–3; Lloyd Weinreb, 'The Right to Privacy', *Social Philosophy and Policy* 17 (2000), p. 25.
2. On the last, see *The Times*, 23 Sept. 2005.
3. See T. M. Scanlon, *What We Owe to Each Other* (Cambridge MA: Harvard University Press, 1998), p. 203.
4. No doubt, Charles Fried's use of 'inconceivable' is hyperbolic. See his 'Privacy', in Raymond Wacks (ed.), *Privacy*, i (Aldershot: Dartmouth, 1993): 'It is my thesis that privacy is not just one possible means among others to insure some other value, but that it is necessarily related to ends and relations of the most fundamental sort: respect, love, friendship and trust. Privacy is not merely a good technique for furthering these fundamental relations; rather without privacy they are simply inconceivable. They require a context of privacy or

the possibility of privacy for their existence' (p. 205). Despite his talk of 'inconceivability', it looks, especially from the final sentence, that Fried really has in mind empirical necessity.

At other points, though, Fried seems to return to conceptual necessity. 'To make clear the necessity of privacy as a context for respect, love, friendship and trust is to bring out also why a threat to privacy seems to threaten our very integrity as persons. To respect, love, trust, feel affection for others and to regard ourselves as the objects of love, trust and affection for others is at the heart of our notion of ourselves.' Without privacy, says Fried, there is no love, respect, etc.; without those we are, he seems to say, not persons. But a misanthrope who does not love, respect, etc. others and is not loved, respected, etc. by them does not cease to be a person. But again, Fried shifts from a conceptual to an empirical point; the passage concludes 'privacy is the necessary atmosphere for these attitudes and actions, as oxygen for combustion' (p. 205).

5. e.g. the constitutions of Argentina, Art. 19; Cuba, Art. 32; Nigeria, Art. 23; Norway, Art. 102; Poland, Art. 74; Portugal, Art. 8, USSR, Art. 128; Yugoslavia, Art. 53; all as of 1965. See Amos J. Peaslee (ed.), with revisions by Dorothy Peaslee Xydis, *Constitutions of Nations*, revised 3rd edn., i–iv (The Hague: Nijhoff, 1965–70).

6. Samuel D. Warren and Louis D. Brandeis, 'The Right to Privacy', *Harvard Law Review* 4 (1890). The article had great influence on US legal thinking. See Justice Black, dissenting in *Griswold* v. *Connecticut*, 381 U.S. 479 (1965): 'Largely as a result of this article, some states have passed statutes creating such a cause for action, and in other states courts have done the same thing by exercising their powers as courts of common law' (fn. 1).

It was Mrs Warren who was the spur; she became alarmed at how advancing technology was eroding what hitherto had been quite naturally private. Early cameras required the subject to sit still for a good while, so a photograph typically had the consent of its subject, but high-speed cameras allowed the taking and publishing of photographs of private life without consent. Whispers at the village water pump did not spread far; but then widely circulated newspapers appeared devoted largely to gossip. The result of this alarm was Warren and Brandeis's article, under the title 'The Right to Privacy'.

7. *Fourth Amendment*: 'The right of the people to be secure in their persons, houses, papers, and effects, against unreasonable searches and seizures, shall not be violated, and no Warrants shall issue, but upon probable cause, supported by Oath or affirmation, and particularly describing the place to be searched, and the persons or things to be seized.'

Fifth Amendment: 'No person shall be held to answer for a capital, or otherwise infamous crime, unless on a presentment or indictment of a Grand Jury, except in cases existing in the land or naval forces, or in the Militia, when in actual service in time of War or public danger; nor shall any person be subject for the same offence to be twice put in jeopardy of life or limb; nor shall be compelled in any criminal case to be a witness against himself, nor be deprived of life, liberty, or property, without due process of law; nor shall private property be taken for public use, without just compensation.'

All of the following Amendments have been cited in the Supreme Court at one time or an other as giving support to a right to privacy: the First, Third, Fourth, Fifth, Ninth, and Fourteenth (Due Process Clause, Equal Protection Clause).

8. J. S. Mill, *On Liberty* (1859, many editions), ch. 1.
9. The defence of these prohibitions in *Bowers* v. *Hardwick* (1986) was overturned by *Lawrence* v. *Texas* (2003) explicitly on the grounds of liberty.
10. e.g. Morris L. Ernst and Alan U. Schwartz, in their book, *Privacy: The Right to Be Let Alone* (New York: Macmillan, 1962), equate them. ' … we have chosen a subject uniquely personal in nature … : the Right of Privacy, or, as we like to call it, the Right to Be Let Alone' (p. xii).
11. For an account of the development of Blackmun's thought in drafting the opinion, see Linda Greenhouse, *Becoming Justice Blackmun: Harry Blackmun's Supreme Court Journey* (New York: Henry Holt, 2006).
12. *Planned Parenthood of Southeastern Pennsylvania* v. *Casey* (1992) concerns the constitutionality of imposing certain restrictions on abortion—not a total ban but restrictions on how it may take place: e.g. that a woman seeking an abortion must be provided with certain information twenty-four hours before the operation, and that a minor must have the informed consent of one parent. The Court ruled that some of the Pennsylvania restrictions at issue were constitutional, and some not. Though the Court's decision paid occasional lip-service to the idea of 'privacy', the crux, according to the majority of Justices, was liberty—the personal liberty conferred by the Due Process Clause of the Fourteenth Amendment. Justices O'Connor, Kennedy, and Souter emphatically rejected what had hitherto been the Court's predominant conception of liberty:

> The controlling word in the cases before us is 'liberty' … it is a promise of the constitution that there is a realm of liberty which the Government may not enter … Some of us as individuals find abortions offensive to our most basic principles of morality, but that cannot control our decision. Our obligation is to define the liberty of all, not to mandate our own moral views.

And here are what seem to me the explicitly personhood terms in which they then go on to characterize liberty:

> At the heart of liberty is the right to define one's own concept of existence, of meaning, of the universe, and of the mystery of human life. Beliefs about these matters could not define the attributes of personhood were they formed under compulsion of the State.

I point out their adoption of the personhood conception of liberty to show that Blackmun's appeal to it in *Bowers* v. *Hardwick* was not unique. Justices

O'Connor, Kennedy, and Souter justify their repudiation of the Court's earlier principle of *freedom of action unless certain forms of immorality* by appeal to epistemic modesty:

> Men and women of good conscience can disagree, and we suppose some shall always disagree, about the profound moral and spiritual implications of terminating a pregnancy ... The underlying constitutional issue is whether the state can resolve these philosophic questions in such a definitive way that a woman lacks all choice in the matter ...

This epistemic turn is, I think, unfortunate. When it comes to the limits of liberty, the law cannot abjure all non-definitive moral judgements. Our moral views about a mother's or a doctor's killing a deformed new-born baby are also not definitive, but we believe that a state may, none the less, prohibit such acts. In any case, one does not need to adopt epistemic modesty in order to reject the principle *freedom of action unless certain forms of immorality.* The idea of liberty itself gives us strong reason not to interfere with agents open to rational persuasion. One can reason with such agents, try to convince them, but often one may not, even if one knows definitively that they are wrong, decide for them. Respect for liberty alone would be enough to hold one back.

13. Above sect. 7.2.
14. Above sect. 2.5.
15. I therefore agree with Ruth Gavison that the right to privacy can always be reduced to some other interest and right; but that it can be so reduced hardly shows that it can also be jettisoned. See her paper 'Privacy', in Wacks (ed.), *Privacy*, i. I disagree with Judith Jarvis Thomson's claim that the rights to various forms of privacy are all justified by more basic property rights and rights over one's body. But the human right to privacy—a right to informational privacy—is best seen as justified by autonomy and liberty, not by property rights or Thomson's highly dubious version of rights over one's body. See her paper 'The Right to Privacy', *Philosophy and Public Affairs* 4 (1975).
16. Justice Blackmun, in *Bowers* v. *Hardwick*, 478 U.S. 186 (1986), 214.
17. C. MacKinnon, *Toward a Feminist Theory of the State* (Cambridge, MA: Harvard University Press, 1989), pp. 168–9.
18. Virginia Woolf, *A Room of One's Own* (London: Flamingo, 1994), sect. 1: 'All I could do was to offer you an opinion on one minor point—a woman must have money and a room of her own if she is to write fiction ... .'
19. Above sect. 2.8.
20. This might explain why the following is not just a violation of a legal right to privacy but a violation of our human right to privacy: 'The owner of a country house hotel rigged up a secret camera to film guests naked in a bathroom, a court was told yesterday' (*The Times*, 12 July 2003).

21. By Judith Jarvis Thomson, 'A Defence of Abortion', repr. in R. Dworkin (ed.), *The Philosophy of Law* (Oxford: Oxford University Press, 1977).

22. For completeness' sake, one should explain why various rights in the US Bill of Rights thought to imply a right to private space or private life do not really do so. In Supreme Court jurisprudence, the right against self-incrimination has been taken to rest on a right to the privacy of one's thoughts (e.g. Justice Douglas, for the majority, in *Griswold* v. *Connecticut*, 381 U.S. 479 (1965), at 485: 'Various guarantees create zones of privacy... The Fifth Amendment in its Self-Incrimination Clause enables the citizen to create a zone of privacy which the government may not force him to surrender to his detriment'). Does the right against self-incrimination assume the privacy of thought? Does it not rest, instead, on the avoidance of injustice? A confession is not, for many reasons, ideal evidence. Putting great weight on confession easily degenerates into the judicial practices of the Inquisition and the Star Chamber. It leads readily to torture, and though torture is obviously wrong for the agony it involves, it is also wrong, and a matter of a human right, because it is typically used to undermine a person's agency; it is meant to take away a person's ability to decide what to do and then to stick to the decision. Is not the right against self-incrimination based on procedural justice and the protection of normative agency? 'Our forefathers wisely inserted the Fifth Amendment in our Constitution in an attempt to prevent inquisitions of the type so common in Europe at that time and to protect accused citizens being compelled to incriminate themselves under torture' (Louis C. Byman, 'A Common Sense View of the Fifth Amendment', *Journal of Criminal Law, Criminality and Police Justice* 51 (1960–1)). McNaughton remarks that 'the policy underpinning the privilege [against self-incrimination] is anything but clear' (p. 150), but his own conclusion is that it had two purposes: first, 'to remove the right to an answer in the hard cases in instances where compulsion might lead to inhumanity, the principle inhumanity being abusive tactics by a zealous questioner', and second, 'to comply with the prevailing ethic that the individual is sovereign and ... that the individual not be bothered for less than good reason ...' (pp. 151–2) (John T. McNaughton, 'The Privilege Against Self-Incrimination: The Constitutional Appreciation, Raison d'Être and Miscellaneous Implications', *Journal of Criminal Law, Criminology and Police Science* 51 (1960–1)).

And what of the now antiquated Third Amendment right not to have troops forcibly quartered in one's house? Does that imply, as in Supreme Court jurisprudence it has been taken to imply, a right to private space? Again see Justice Douglas, in *Griswold* v. *Connecticut*, 381 U.S. 479 (1965), at 485: 'Various guarantees create zones of privacy... The Third Amendment in its prohibition against the quartering of soldiers "in any house" in time of peace without the consent of the owner is another facet of that privacy.' The American colonists had greatly resented the British Army's forcibly quartering its troops in their family houses. The Third Amendment does not guarantee that it will not happen in future, only that it will not happen in peacetime, and will happen in wartime only 'in a manner to be prescribed by law'. So does the Third Amendment define a human right (the word 'right' is never used), or merely promise to reduce and, to some extent, regulate a much-resented, though still possibly necessary, practice? If the Third Amendment has any link to privacy, it would be because the forced quartering of troops would threaten our informational privacy, just as having the police coming and going in our houses at their will would. But the comparison with frequent police intrusion is far-fetched; forced quartering of troops was fairly rare.

23. For an example, see the article 'Privacy Law Ruled Incompatible with Free Press', *The Times*, 17 June 2003.

24. It is not that the harmony between the rights to privacy, free expression, and information will be complete. Even after we have located this new line between the public and the private, the two domains can overlap. The sort of truly private discussion between a group of people about the injustices of society and their possible remedies might include decisions and plans to mount terrorist attacks that a journalist who learns of them would rightly regard as of public interest.

25. As reported by Lawrence Marks, *The Observer*, 17 Jan. 1993.

26. *The Independent*, 30 Apr. 1998.

27. There are less easy cases. Could publishing a revelatory biography violate its subject's privacy? Here the potential public interest might be precisely the subject's private life. We often benefit from a biography by having the whole of human life illuminated for us—for example, how a person's sexuality affected his or her art. I think that the right to privacy would enter consideration only if the subject were alive, because it concerns the inhibition of one's normative agency (though there is something arbitrary in this: one's normative agency can even be inhibited by fear of what will come out after one's death).

28. There was a more plausible case for a public interest (a security risk) when, in the early 1960s, John Profumo was Secretary of State for War in the British Cabinet and was enjoying the services of a prostitute also being enjoyed by the military attaché at the Soviet embassy. But even here, had there been a law prohibiting publication of a person's sex life unless there was a public interest *and* unless there were no other way of meeting that interest, the newspapers would have been forced to take their information to the police or the intelligence services, which would have been both more efficient and more humane. There are, of course, considerations on the other side to be weighed: e.g. would newspapers engage in this sort of sometimes useful investigative journalism if there were no prospect of publication?

29. There are any number of illustrations of how desperately societies need clearer and higher standards for establishing a public interest. In London, in 1992, *The*

Independent revealed that Virginia Bottomley, then Secretary of State for Health, gave birth to her first child three months before her marriage, twenty-five years earlier, to the child's father and still her husband. An invasion of privacy, her husband charged to the Press Complaints Commission. 'A legitimate public interest', *The Independent* replied, arguing in a leader that the story 'added to our understanding to discover that an able and widely respected Secretary of State for Health, drawing attention to the problems surrounding young unmarried mothers, should have gone through the difficult though in no way discreditable experience herself' (reported in *The Times*). What a sorry state of society in which *The Independent* would have the effrontery to publish such a feeble argument.

CHAPTER 14. DO HUMAN RIGHTS REQUIRE DEMOCRACY?

1. Art. 21 is repeated, in slightly different language, as Art. 25 of the International Covenant on Civil and Political Rights (1966).
2. Justice Stephen Breyer, US Supreme Court, in his book *Active Liberty: Interpreting Our Democratic Constitution* (New York: Vintage Books, 2005), p. 3.
3. Carol Gould, *Globalizing Democracy and Human Rights* (Cambridge: Cambridge University Press, 2004), p. 183.
4. Charles R. Beitz, 'Human Rights as a Common Concern', *American Political Science Review* 95 (2001), p. 269.
5. David Beetham, *Democracy and Human Rights* (Cambridge: Polity Press, 1999), p. 92.
6. Above, sect. 8.3.
7. Robert A. Dahl, *On Democracy* (New Haven: Yale University Press, 2000), p. 63.
8. This is roughly what is meant by 'deliberative democracy'. See also Jürgen Habermas, *Between Facts and Norms* (Cambridge MA: MIT Press, 1996), where he states his 'disclosure principle': 'Just those action norms are valid to which all possibly affected persons could agree as participants in national discourses' (p. 107), and his 'democratic principle': 'only those statutes may claim legitimacy that can meet with the assent of all citizens in a discursive process of legislation that in turn has been legally constituted' (p. 110).
9. Above sects. 2.6, 11. 4. I also argue it below, sect. 15.5.
10. It will be useful to me, e.g., by expanding the argument in sect. 1.5.
11. For discussion of a similar distinction, see Allen Buchanan, *Justice, Legitimacy, and Self-Determination: Moral Foundations for International Law* (Oxford: Oxford University Press, 2004), pp. 281–4.
12. Above sect. 9.3.
13. Above sect. 2.6.

14. John Rawls, *The Law of Peoples* (Cambridge, MA: Harvard University Press, 1999), sects. 8–9.
15. e.g. ibid. sect. 12.
16. In Ch. 5, esp. sect. 5.4.
17. See esp. Partha Dasgupta, *An Inquiry into Well-Being and Destitution* (Oxford: Clarendon Press, 1993), ch. 5.
18. See David Held, *Models of Democracy*, 3rd edn. (Cambridge: Polity Press, 2006).

CHAPTER 15. GROUP RIGHTS

1. See Karel Vasak, 'Pour une Troisième Génération des Droits de l'Homme', in Christophe Swinarski (ed.), *Studies and Essays on International Law and Red Cross Principles* (The Hague: Martinus Nijhoff, 1984). The fit between what Vasak says about solidarity rights and what, in recent discussion, philosophers have tended to say in definition of group rights is not perfect. But the two notions are close, and there is a virtually complete coincidence in examples. In any case, my interest is in group rights.
2. e.g. Roger Scruton, 'Groups Do Not Have Rights', *The Times*, 21 Dec. 1995.
3. Although he does not regard it as a conclusive objection to group rights, this is Carl Wellman's 'most fundamental' doubt about them in his book *The Proliferation of Rights* (Boulder, CO: Westview Press, 1999), ch. 2.
4. What sorts of groups are said to have (group) rights? Some group rights seem to be claimed simply for humanity at large (rights to peace and to the integrity of the environment). Other group rights are attributed to a 'people' or a 'nation' (Article 1 of the Universal Declaration of the Rights of Peoples says: 'Every people has the right to existence'). Yet other rights are attributed to a cultural or ethnic group—e.g. to the survival of its culture (which will be very similar to the preceding right if, as is likely, that is meant to go beyond mere physical survival to survival *as* a 'people' or a 'nation'). There are rights attributed to various deprived groups (rights to equal treatment to women, blacks, the poor, the disabled, the old). There are rights attributed to a society (a right to fraternity, tolerance, and to the conditions for achieving a certain degree of prosperity). Then sometimes rights are attributed to any group membership of which is important enough to be part of one's self-respect (a right for the group not to be defamed or reviled, not to be made the object of hate-speech).

    What is striking about the items on this short list, and what lends some force to the quick way of dismissing group rights, is that virtually none of them is, as such, agent-like. A 'society' may be an exception; it all depends upon what kind of organization is required by the concept. A 'nation' may look like another exception, but the word is not used here of anything that need have political organization, but could be applied, say, to the Apache nation, whether or not the Apaches constituted a political entity.

For an examination of how corporations and less formal associations (down to mobs) can act as groups, see Larry May, *The Morality of Groups* (Notre Dame, IN: University of Notre Dame Press, 1987), pp. 31–57.

5. I borrow this example from Jeremy Waldron, and I have an argument of his chiefly in mind in what immediately follows. See his 'Can Communal Goods Be Human Rights?', in his book *Liberal Rights* (Cambridge: Cambridge University Press, 1993), esp. sect. IV.
6. Ibid. p. 355.
7. Ibid. p. 356.
8. As Waldron does; ibid. p. 355.
9. Ibid. p. 357.
10. Ibid. pp. 358–9.
11. Ibid. pp. 357–8.
12. e.g. Denise G. Réaume, 'The Group Right to Linguistic Security: Whose Right, What Duties?', in Judith Baker (ed.), *Group Rights* (Toronto: University of Toronto Press, 1994), p. 121; Waldron, *Liberal Rights*, p. 359.
13. See, e.g., Joseph Raz, *The Morality of Freedom* (Oxford: Clarendon Press, 1986), p. 166, but also pp. 44–5, 278. We met Raz's account earlier in sect. 2.9.
14. See Waldron, *Liberal Rights*, p. 359.
15. Ibid.
16. Waldron offers further reasons for thinking that group goods give rise to group rights. One is that there is an analogy between how individuals stand to larger bodies and how groups stand to larger groups. Both of them can be oppressed, denied autonomy or liberty, be treated unequally, and so on. In these situations we reach for the language of rights in the case of individuals. Why not do the same in the case of groups? (See his *Liberal Rights*, pp. 361–6.) However, it does not seem enough to argue that, like individuals, groups can be oppressed. That ignores the large question of whether, either for individuals or groups, the remedy for all injustice is rights. I should say that not all matters of justice or fairness or equality are matters of rights. There is no inference from *there is an issue of justice here* to *there is an issue of rights here*. I return to these questions below, especially in sect. 15.5.

Waldron also offers a second, negative reason: namely, that group rights are at least not ruled out conceptually. So long as a group has a sufficiently agent-like status, as a business corporation does, then it is the kind of thing that can hold rights. But to gesture at business corporations does nothing to meet the serious doubts about the agent-like status of the groups for whom rights are usually claimed. One has either to show that they are agent-like too (a difficult job) or come up with an acceptable account of 'rights' that cuts ties with agency (another difficult job).

17. Raz, *Morality of Freedom*, p. 208. In fact, Raz has three existence conditions for a group right: (1) 'it exists because an aspect of the interest of human beings justifies holding some person(s) to be subject to a duty', (2) [as quoted in the text], (3) 'the interest of no single member of that group in that public good is sufficient by itself to justify holding another person to be subject to a duty'. The first condition is just the condition for any right. The third is an additional requirement, which I shall not ignore in the discussion that follows.

18. Ibid. p. 207.

19. Joseph Raz and Avishai Margalit, 'National Self-Determination', in Raz, *Ethics in the Public Domain* (Oxford: Clarendon Press, 1994), pp. 133–4.

20. Ibid. p. 138.

21. Ibid. pp. 129–32, 134, 141.

22. Ibid. pp. 139–41.

23. Raz, *Morality of Freedom*, p. 207.

24. Ibid. p. 209.

25. Raz and Margalit, 'National Self-Determination'.

26. According to Raz and Margalit at the start of their article, their subject is whether 'a moral case can be made in support of national self-determination' (ibid. p. 126). To my mind, it would have been better if they had not gone on to make self-determination a matter of a right.

27. Ibid. pp. 141, 143.

28. Ibid. p. 141.

29. For discussion of derived rights, see above sect. 2.8.

30. Will Kymlicka, *Multicultural Citizenship* (Oxford: Clarendon Press, 1995), ch. 3.

31. Will Kymlicka, *Liberalism, Community, and Culture* (Oxford: Oxford University Press, 1989), p. 165.

32. Will Kymlicka, 'Individual and Community Rights', in Baker (ed.), *Group Rights*, p. 25. Views like this are not uncommon: see e.g. Joseph Raz and Avishai Margalit, 'National Self-Determination', pp. 133–4; A. Buchanan, 'Liberalism and Group Rights', in J. L. Coleman and A. Buchanan (eds.), *In Harm's Way: Essays in Honor of Joel Feinberg* (Cambridge: Cambridge University Press, 1994); Charles Taylor, 'The Politics of Recognition', in his *Multiculturalism: Examining the Politics of Recognition*, ed. Amy Gutman (Princeton: Princeton University Press, 1994), pp. 32–6.

33. Taylor, 'Politics of Recognition', p. 25.

34. Ibid. p. 26.

35. I take the example from Kymlicka, *Multicultural Citizenship*, p. 36.

36. Kymlicka, 'Individual and Community Rights', pp. 23–7.

37. It is not that, according to this argument, justice is the only ground for group rights. Some (legal) rights can be grounded in historical agreement: charters, treaties, and so on.

38. Kymlicka, *Multicultural Citizenship*, p. 37.

39. See my *Well-Being* (Oxford: Clarendon Press, 1986), chs. I–IV; *Value Judgement: Improving Our Ethical Beliefs* (Oxford: Clarendon Press, 1996), ch. II.

40. Of course, one's list of good-making features of life is not independent of the world one thinks one inhabits, and world views are likely to vary from culture to culture. But they can vary within a culture too. And the variations are hardly above criticism. My own list is out of a particular tradition: modern, Western, and atheist. A cloistered monk might well have a very different list: for many of the items on my list he might have almost the opposite. Lists change with one's metaphysical views. And metaphysical views can be better or worse, acceptable or unacceptable. Variation in lists is caused by more than just different metaphysical views, but these other social differences are not immune to cross-cultural assessment either. See a somewhat longer discussion in my *Value Judgement*, p. 150.

41. See my *Value Judgement*, ch. VIII sect. 4, esp. pp. 134–5; on convergence see ch. IV sect. 2.

42. There are considerable problems about individuating cultures. It is by no means clear even that each of us is a member of *a* culture, let alone which culture it is. A culture is, roughly, a linguistic group with its own art, literature, customs, and moral attitudes, transmitted from generation to generation. I do not doubt that we can individuate *some* cultures. The clearest conditions for the use of the term are when groups develop largely independently of one another. One could apply the term to an isolated Indian tribe just discovered in the depths of the Amazon. One can properly say that Cortés destroyed Aztec culture. One can say that certain cultures are threatened today: e.g. the East Timorese Council of Priests recently described Indonesia's occupation of East Timor and its imposition of its own language as 'killing the culture' (quoted in a letter to the editor, *The Independent*, 27 Jan. 1997).

But presumably, when people claim a certain group's right to the survival of its culture, they have in mind a universal right: that everyone is a member of some culture, and that everyone equally has the right (though, no doubt, only some cultures are threatened enough for anyone to bother to claim it). But it becomes increasingly difficult to speak in those terms in modern conditions: with easy communication, travel, and trade; with the global spread of popular forms of art, of ways of life, of political ideals. (This is a point made by Jeremy Waldron in 'Minority Cultures and the Cosmopolitan Alternative', in Will Kymlicka (ed.), *The Rights of Minority Cultures* (New York: Oxford University Press, 1995), though Waldron is more sceptical about talk about 'a culture' than I am.)

One might reply that, for all the globalization of ways of life, there are still differences in ways of understanding the world, because those ways are embedded in the language. It is very easy to exaggerate on both sides of this dispute, so let me take a concrete (egocentric) example. To what culture do I belong? To the United States, where I was born and raised? Is there a single United States culture? Should I say New England? Or do I belong to the culture of Britain, where I have spent my entire adult life? Or should I say England, to exclude Scotland and Wales? Or is there now only an omnibus 'Western' culture? To what culture does a Japanese belong who listens to Mozart and reads Dostoevsky, Flaubert, and Henry James? To several? Which ones?

My point is that none of the answers to these questions is easy, and that it is not easy because the criteria for the use of the term 'a culture' do not comfortably fit very many modern conditions. It is not that one simply could not give answers to these questions, but that the answers would have to be to a high degree arbitrary. We can certainly, and comfortably, speak of the cultural side of our lives, meaning that part that has to do with literature, music, and so on. But are we any longer, for many people, able to speak of the entity—their 'culture'? Similar problems arise with the terms 'a people', 'a nation', and 'an ethnic group'.

43. Taylor, 'Politics of Recognition', p. 38.

44. See discussion of stipulation above, sect. 4.5.

45. Above sect. 2.6; see also sects. 3.3, 3.4, 10.6, 11.4.

46. As I think do, e.g., Mary Anne Warren, 'Do Potential People Have Moral Rights?', *Canadian Journal of Philosophy* 7 (1977), p. 277 n. 4; T. L. S. Sprigg, 'Metaphysics, Physicalism, and Animal Rights', *Inquiry* 22 (1979), p. 103; Thomas Auxter, 'The Right Not to Be Eaten', *Inquiry* 22 (1979), p. 222.

47. I think that we should make the pass level fairly low. Ronald Dworkin suggests that the word 'rights' marks off that special moral consideration that operates as a check on maximizing the general good. Rights play the role of 'trump' in the game of moral reasons; indeed, he often speaks as if they have no point at all except in that role (see his *Taking Rights Seriously* (London: Duckworth, 1978), pp. 139, 269). Robert Nozick thinks that they play the role of 'side-constraints' (see his *Anarchy, State, and Utopia* (Oxford: Blackwell, 1974), pp. 28–35). Both accounts more than pass the redundancy test. In fact, claims for rights can be a good deal less strong than that, I think, and still be regarded as passing the test. For instance, a broadly utilitarian account that made rights the protections of specially high-potency utilities would pass.

48. Above sects. 1.2 and 1.6.

49. Ludwig Wittgenstein, *Philosophical Investigations* (Oxford: Blackwell, 1953), sects. 320–43.

50. Much more can be said. What this sort of claim account of rights needs, in order to pass the redundancy test, is a convincing distinction between the special sort

of claim associated with rights, on the one side, and moral claims generally, on the other. This distinction will then yield a correlative distinction between kinds of duty. Now, there is an old distinction in philosophy between duties of perfect obligation and duties of imperfect obligation. In one version, it is roughly the distinction between what is morally required and what is merely supererogatory. In that version, it is no help to us here. Kant has a different version: duties of perfect obligation (e.g. to do what one promised) specify what one must do and for or to whom; duties of imperfect obligation (e.g. to help the needy) are ones that allow considerable leeway in what one does—for instance, one might be inclined to help the sick, or instead the destitute, or instead the tortured, and so on; and one might choose to help this particular sick person rather than that one, and so on. But Kant's version of the distinction does not seem to help us either. To explain summarily: there are rights the only specification of which is that the moral agents in a certain subset bear a duty of aid, but which particular agents are members of that subset is unspecifiable simply from the content of the right. Two examples are a right to minimum education and a right to life (if the latter is thought to include, as I think it must, not just a negative duty not to take life without due process but also a positive duty to assist in certain ways in its preservation). In the case of these rights, it is just that somebody should come forward to help, not necessarily everybody (some may not be in a position to help without great hardship) and not necessarily everybody in the subset of those who can help without hardship (only a few may be needed); all that is required is that a large enough number of persons (unspecified) should respond. The positive duties associated with these rights are in this respect much like duties of charity, and the class of duties of perfect obligation cannot therefore be used to isolate the sort of claims associated with rights. I discuss these matters more fully in Ch. 5.

Or one can appeal to what is called the choice account of rights. That account would distinguish the two kinds of duties like this: I have a right to something from you, it says, whenever the reasons for holding you to have a duty to me are also reasons for thinking that I have the power to release you from the duty if I so wish. This account of rights works well with promises. But, as is well known, it does not work well in many other cases. I have a right to life, a right not to be tortured, a right to minimum material provision, none of which, unlike promises, I can waive. These may be thought to be welfare rights, which some regard as doubtful claimants to rights status, but the same applies to undisputed liberty rights. I have a right to autonomy and to liberty. It is not enough to justify your denying me autonomy and liberty that I said you could. Autonomy and liberty constitute the central values of what we think of as human dignity. You may not destroy my dignity just because I am deluded, or desperate, enough to give you permission.

I doubt that we shall find the distinction we are after simply by looking at formal features: whether the duty is waivable or not, whether the particular duty-ower and beneficiary are specifiable or not, and so on. We need to put more evaluative *content* into the distinction.

51. Declaration of Principles of International Law Concerning Friendly Relations and Co-operation among States in accordance with the Charter of the United Nations, adopted by the United Nations General Assembly, 24 Oct. 1970; see the section entitled 'The principle of sovereign equality of states'. The principle of 'sovereign equality' was well established before the United Nations. It was strongly asserted by the League of Nations. Some trace it back to the Treaty of Westphalia, which ended the Thirty Years War in 1648.

     The right to non-intervention also has links in the Declaration with the right to self-determination, despite the fact that the latter right is said to be a right of 'peoples' and the former a right of 'states' (and 'peoples' and 'states' are clearly not the same). One part of the explanation of the right to non-intervention is that 'peoples' are not to be deprived of their 'national identity', which colonialism, the paradigm violation of the right to self-determination, would typically constitute. See the section entitled 'The principle concerning the duty not to intervene in matters within the domestic jurisdiction of any State, in accordance with the Charter'. The Declaration of 1970 elaborates the principles of the Charter of the United Nations (1945). The Charter says: Article 1. 2: '[The Purposes of the United Nations include] To develop friendly relations among nations based on the respect for the principle of equal rights and self-determination of peoples … .'

52. See the section entitled 'The principle concerning the duty not to intervene in matters within the domestic jurisdiction of any State, in accordance with the Charter.'

53. On certain accounts of 'sovereignty', the link with non-intervention is conceptual. 'It [a sovereign state] has undivided jurisdiction over all persons and property within its territory. … No other nation may interfere in its domestic affairs.' See article on 'Sovereignty', in *The New Columbia Encyclopaedia* (New York: Columbia University Press, 1975).

54. See the section referred to in n. 52, my italics.

55. See C. A. J. Coady, 'Nationalism and Intervention', in Brenda Almond (ed.), *Introducing Applied Ethics* (Oxford: Blackwell, 1995), for a fuller statement of the practical case. See also J. S. Mill's classic argument in the same general direction, 'A Few Words on Non-Intervention', in his *Essays on Politics and Culture*, ed. Gertrude Himmelfarb (New York: Anchor Books, 1963); and Michael Walzer, *Just and Unjust Wars* (New York: Basic Books, 1997). Coady's case seems to me the most persuasive.

56. As Will Kymlicka and Ian Shapiro do: See 'Introduction', in Ian Shapiro and Will Kymlika (eds.), *Ethnicity and Group Rights*, Nomos 39

(New York: New York University Press, 1997); for passages quoted see pp. 3–4.

57. Above sects. 2.6, 15.6.

58. Consider another stipulation. One might propose meaning by 'a theory of group rights', as Brian Barry does (see his *Culture and Equality* (Cambridge: Polity Press, 2001), ch. 4 sect. 5), a set of beliefs about how a liberal society should treat groups within it, of which some may themselves be liberal in their internal constitution and some illiberal. And one's question may therefore be: what is the best public policy for a liberal society in regulating these groups, especially the internally illiberal ones, with which the problems can become especially difficult? The question is a good one. But in what sense does the answer constitute 'a theory of group rights'? For one thing, the rights at the centre of a liberal society's treatment of groups within it are, as Barry sees it, freedom from coercion (liberty) and freedom of association, both of which are rights of individuals. So the moral thought behind the formulation of the best public policy for these groups will consist in the application of these two individual rights to particular circumstances. For another thing, the application of these two individual rights will not provide answers to questions about what ethnocultural groups, for example, may properly claim from their societies—the focus of much current discussion of group rights. Barry's group rights are reducible to individual human rights; so they are not 'group rights' in any strong sense.

59. As Thomas Pogge's is; see his 'Group Rights and Ethnicity', in Shapiro and Kymlicka (eds.), *Ethnicity and Group Rights*.

Index

abortion, 131–2, 213, 216, 230, 231–2, 239
Afghanistan, 161, 168, 172
African Charter on Human and Peoples Rights (1981), 193–4, 282 n. 27, 295 n. 8, 308 n. 6, 308 n. 7, 308 n. 11, 310 n. 28, 310 n. 29
agency, *see also* normative agency, 32–3, 44–5, 67–8, 180
AIDS, 47, 105–9, 181, 184, 294 n. 16, 295 n. 12, 295 n. 18.
Akbar, Emperor, 141
Akehurst, Michael, 308 n. 8, 309 n. 17
Algiers Declaration (1978), 308 n. 3
alienating rights, 290 n. 32
Almond, Brenda, 328 n. 55
Alston, Philip, 308 n. 2
American Convention on Human Rights (1969), 193, 289 n. 7, 308 n. 7
Additional Protocol to ∼, 206–8, 295 n. 8, 307 n. 1, 308 n. 11, 310 n. 24, 310 n. 28, 310 n. 31
American Declaration of the Rights and Duties of Man (1948), 307 n. 1, 308 n. 4, 308 n. 7, 310 n. 24
Amnesty International, 19, 104, 292 n. 6
Aquinas, Thomas, 9, 10, 11–12, 24, 30, 277 n. 1, 278 n. 3, 281 n. 21
Archard, David, 295 n. 24, 306 n. 15
Aristotle, 73, 118, 297 n. 6
Ashoka, Emperor, 141
Athens, 248
Atlantic Charter (1941), 176
Australia, 314 n. 32
autonomy, 33–7, 81, 133–5, 149–58, 159, 191, 192, 216, 226, 235, 243, 247, 260, 274–5
Auxter, Thomas, 326 n. 46
Ayer, A. J., 303 n. 6

Baghramian, Maria, 297 n. 6
Bahm, Archie, 298 n. 24

Baker, Judith, 323 n. 12, 324 n. 32
Ball, T., 286 n. 1
Bangkok Declaration (1993), 138, 139, 298 n. 19
Bannister, D., 293 n. 15
Barry, Brian, 303 n. 6, 329 n. 58
Baster, Roy P., 289 n. 6
Bauman, P. 291 n. 37
Baylis, Michael D., 281 n. 22
Bedau, Hugo, 295 n. 3, 311 n. 3
Beetham, David, 321 n. 5
Beitz, Charles, 27, 280 n. 19, 284 n. 56, 288 n. 32, 288 n. 33, 321 n. 4
Bell, D. A., 285 n. 62
Bentham, Jeremy, 18, 172, 279 n. 12, 302 n. 1
Berlin, Isaiah, 149, 159, 173–4, 182, 300 n. 2, 303 n. 1, 303 n. 4, 304 n. 16, 307 n. 19
Betzler, M., 291 n. 37
Bever, J. R., 285 n. 62
Bill of Rights, England (1689), 13, 257
Bill of Rights, US (1791), 13, 16, 227, 276, 282 n. 26, 308 n. 10, 311 n. 2, 319 n. 22
Blackmun, Harry Andrew (Justice), 231, 233, 317 n. 11, 317 n. 12, 318 n. 16
Blackstone, William, 311 n. 3
Blamires, C., 279 n. 12
Boghossian, Paul, 298 n. 14
Bologna, 30, 31
Botswana, 105
Bottomley, Virginia, 321 n. 29
Bowden, Mark, 288 n. 39
Bowers v. *Hardwick* (1986), 232–3, 235, 317 n. 9, 317 n. 12, 318 n. 16
Boyle, Joseph, 281 n. 21
Brackney, William H., 298 n. 27, 298 n. 28
Brandeis, Louis (Justice), 228–9, 230, 231, 233
Brandt, Richard, 112, 296 n. 2, 297 n. 3
Braybrooke, David, 293 nn. 15–16, 295 n. 19

Brazil, 195–6
Breen, T. H., 280 n. 17
Brett, Annabel S., 277 n. 2, 286 n. 1, 286 n. 9
Breyer, Stephen (Justice) 321 n. 2
British Medical Association, 314 n. 29
Broad Street, Oxford, 114
Brownlie, Ian, 308 n. 3
Brundage, James, 286 n. 1, 301 n. 3
Buchanan, Allen, 309 n. 18, 321 n. 11, 324 n. 32
Buddha, 140
Buddhism, 138, 140, 141, 285 n. 62, 285 n. 63
Burke, Edmund 172
Burma, 142
Bush, George W. (President), 106
Byman, Louis C., 319 n. 22

California, State of, 182
Cambell, T., 306 n. 15
Cape Cod, 240
Carlyle, Thomas, 172
Categorical Imperative, 4, 29, 62
Chadwick, Edwin, 103
Chang, Ruth, 291 n. 37, 297 n. 7
Chapman, J. W., 312 n. 4
Chatterjee, Deen, 280 n. 19, 288 n. 32
China, 25, 254, 305 n. 4
    one child policy in ~ 14
Christianity, 26, 141, 150, 155, 299 n. 31
Churchill, W. S., 176
Civil War (US), 59
claimability requirement, 107–10
Clinton, Bill (President), 108
Clinton, Hillary, 281 n. 22
Coady, C. A. J., 328 n. 55
Cobbett, William, 176, 305 n. 2
Cohen, Joshua, 277 n. 1, 285 nn. 61–3
Coleman, Jules, 278, 324 n. 32
Collins, Henry, 303 n. 7
Committee on Economic, Social and Cultural Rights, 100
compulsion, 160–1
Confucianism, 138, 140, 285 n. 62, 285 n. 63
Conley, P. T., 279 n. 14

consequentialism, 36, 59, 71–4, 80
Constantine, Emperor, 12
constitution
    ~ of Argentina, 316 n. 5
    ~ of Cuba, 316 n. 5
    ~ of Denmark, 176
    ~ of India, 142, 298 n. 29
    ~ of Netherlands, 176
    ~ of Nigeria, 316 n. 5
    ~ of Norway, 176, 316 n. 5
    ~ of Poland, 316 n. 5
    ~ of Portugal, 316 n. 5
    ~ of Soviet Union 176, 282 n. 26, 316 n. 5
    ~ of Sweden, 176
    ~ of United States, 212, 310 n. 2
    ~ of Yugoslavia, 316 n. 5
Contractualism, 78–9
constraint, 160–1
Convention for the Protection of Human Rights and Fundamental Freedoms (1950), 311 n. 3
Convention on the Rights of the Child (1989), 85, 94, 292 n. 7
Convention Relating to the Status of Refugees (1951), 289 n. 7
cost-benefit analysis, 70
Council of Europe, 311 n. 3
Coward, Harold, 298 n. 27
Cranston, Maurice, 306 n. 6, 310 n. 21
criterion of right and wrong, 72
Cruzan, Nancy, 218–9
Cruzan v. *Missouri* (1990), 218–9
culture, 142, 163, 264–5, 266–71, 325 n. 42

Dagger, Richard, 286 n. 1
Dahl, Robert, 244, 321 n. 7
Dasgupta, Partha, 298 n. 21, 305 n. 4, 307 n. 24, 322 n. 17
Davidson, Donald, 113–4, 296 n. 5
decision procedure for right and wrong, 72
Declaration of Independence, US (1776), 282 n. 26
Declaration of Principles of International Law Concerning Friendly Relations and Co-operation among States (1970), 273–4, 328 n. 51

Declaration of the Rights of Man and of the Citizen, France, (1789), 9, 13, 279 n. 13, 280 n. 15, 282 n. 26, 303 n. 7
Declaration on the Elimination of All Forms of Intolerance and of Discrimination Based on Religion or Belief, 289 n. 7
defeat of rights, 290 n. 32
definition
   possibility of ∼ of 'right', 18, 53–4
   possibility of ∼ of 'human right', 18, 54–5
democracy, 242–55
deontology, 3, 79, 82
Dermen, Sira, 293 n. 15
desert, 65, 184–6
Dick Howard, A. E., 279 n. 14
'dignity of the human person', 3, 45, 66, 133, 151–2, 192, 200–01, 203, 205, 216, 242, 309 n. 13
discontinuity, 68, 80
discrimination, 41–2
Dixon-Child, Sean, 314 n. 30
Donnelly, Jack, 283 n. 34, 298 n. 27
'Don't deliberately kill the innocent', 73–5, 80, 126–8, 129
Dostoevsky, Fyodor, 326 n. 42
Douglas, William O. (Justice), 319 n. 22
duties
   bearers of ∼, 101–10
   exclusionary ∼, 263–4
   positive/negative ∼, 215–6, 327 n. 50
   primary/secondary ∼, 104–5, 166–7
Dworkin, Gerald, 301 n. 4
Dworkin, Ronald, 20–2, 27, 39–40, 282 n. 23, 283 n. 38, 283 n. 39, 283 n. 41, 284 n. 44, 287 n. 19, 314 n. 28, 326 n. 47

Ebadi, Shirin, 25
Edict of Milan (313), 12
enforceability requirement, 109
Enlightenment, 1–2, 10–14, 16, 18, 28, 43, 61, 62, 139, 191, 211
environment, the, 130–1, 290 n. 33, 390 n. 14
equality, 173–4, 249
   ∼ as a ground for human rights, 39–44, 209

∼ before the law, 196–201
∼ of distribution, 43
∼ of opportunity, 162–3
∼ of respect, 39–40, 43
Ernst, Morris L., 317 n. 10
ethnocentricity
   ∼ of human rights, 23, 25, 27, 137–42
European Convention on Human Rights (1950), 193, 227, 289 n. 7, 308 n. 7, 308 n. 11
European Social Charter (1961), 289 n. 7, 310 n. 25, 310 nn. 29–30
euthanasia, 74, 216, 219–21, 223–4, 313 n. 18, 314 n. 27, 314 n. 32
'examined life' 45–6

fact/value, distinction between, 35–7, 117–20, 122–4
fairness, 41–4, 249–50, 251, 271
Farr, J., 286 n. 1
Feinberg, Joel, 20, 22, 27, 283 n. 37, 287 n. 26, 294 n. 17, 303 n. 3, 311 n. 3, 313 n. 24
Final Act of the Helsinki Conference (1975), 307 n. 1
Finnis, John, 278
Flaubert, Gustave, 326 n. 42
Florida, Robert E., 298 n. 28, 299 n. 30
forfeit of rights, 65–6, 290 n. 32
Francis of Assisi, 30–1
free-riders, 41, 64, 198, 201
free-will, 157–8
freedom
   ∼ from fear, 177
   ∼ from want, 177
   ∼ of assembly 159
   ∼ of association 143
   ∼ of conscience 143
   ∼ of expression, 16, 49, 142, 159, 193, 239–41, 320 n. 24
   ∼ of information, 239–41, 320 n. 24
   ∼ of movement, 195
   ∼ of press, 38, 50, 239–41
   ∼ of religion, 159
   ∼ residence, 17, 195, 209
   ∼ of worship, 16, 193
French constitutions of 1790s, 176
Frey, R. G., 287 n. 18

Fried, Charles, 315 n. 4
'fundamental freedoms', 308 n. 11

Gandhi, M. K., 141, 298 n. 26
Gates, Bill, 103
Gathii, J. T., 295 n. 12
Gavison, Ruth, 318 n. 15
generations of rights, 177, 256, 276, 305
    n. 4
Genesis, Book of, 26, 140, 150
genocide, 275
Geoffrey of Fontaines, 30
George, R. P., 280 n. 20, 281 n. 21
Germany, 196
Getty, John Paul, 103
Getty Museum, 294 n. 16
Geuss, Raymond, 296 n. 21
Gewirth, Alan, 4, 306 n. 9, 306 n. 14, 307
    n. 25
Ghosh, Pratap Kumar, 298 n. 29
Glendon, Mary Ann, 284 n. 59
Glorious Revolution, England (1688), 13
Goldberg, Arthur Joseph (Justice), 231
Golding, Martin P., 282 n. 26
Goldsmith, Jack L., 309 n. 19
Goodin, Robert, 306 n. 13
Gould, Carol, 321 n. 3
Gratian, 31
Gray, John, 303 n. 6
Great Barrier Reef, 131
Greece, 196
Green, T. H., 305 n. 3
Greenhouse, Linda, 317 n. 11
Griffin, James, 286 n. 11, 287 n. 20, 291
    n. 36, 291 nn. 38–9, 291 n. 41, 291
    n. 45, 292 n. 14, 295 n. 6, 296 n. 1,
    297 n. 7, 297 n. 9, 297 n. 12, 301 n. 9,
    325 n. 39, 325 nn. 40–1
Griswold v. *Connecticut* (1965), 230, 316
    n. 6, 319 n. 22
Grotius, Hugo, 10, 278 n. 5, 281 n. 21
group right, 204, 256–76, 308 n. 3, 322
    n. 4
    ~ to self-determination 261–2, 264–5
Gutman, Amy, 324 n. 32
Guyer, Paul, 301 n. 8

Haakonssen, Knud, 282 n. 25
habeas corpus, 59

Habermas, Jürgen, 321 n. 8
Hall, P., 293 n. 15
Hampshire, Stuart, 287 n. 20
Hanson, R., 286 n. 1
happiness
    pursuit of ~ 34
Harlan, John Marshall (Justice), 230–1
Harman, Gilbert, 297 nn. 5–6
Hart, H. L. A., 283 n. 39, 284 n. 43
Held, David, 322 n. 18
Hendin, Herbert, 314 n. 27
Himmelfarb, Gertrude, 328 n. 55
Hinduism, 140, 141, 142, 160, 211
Hobbes, Thomas, 159, 172, 278 n. 4, 302
    n. 1
Hobhouse, L. T., 305 n. 3
Hockney, David, 164
Hohfeld, Wesley N., 257, 272
Holland, 314 n. 27, 314 n. 32
Hollingdale, R. J., 313 n. 26
Hooker, Richard, 213–4, 312 n. 5
Honoré, Tony, 282 n. 33
human interests, 113–20, 122–4
human nature, 32–6 116–20, 122
human rights *see also* rights, 277, 278, 280
    n. 19
    absolute ~, 63, 68, 76–8, 80, 82
    conflict of ~, 57–82
    co-possibility of ~, 60–1
    existence conditions of ~, 44, 81, 241
    more pluralist account of ~, 51–6, 292
        n. 13
    need account of ~, 88–90, 293 n. 16
    ~ of children, 83–95, 292 nn. 6–7
    personhood account of ~, 32–9, 67, 88,
        90, 91, 100, 159–60, 183, 191,
        192–3, 291 n. 1, 291 n. 2
    top-down/bottom-up accounts of
        ~, 3–4, 29–30, 59, 69
Human Rights Watch, 19
Hume, David, 27, 35–6, 74, 111, 117,
    123–4, 154, 297 n. 2, 313 n. 17
Hurley, Susan, 382 n. 36
Hutson, James H., 282 n. 25

Ideal Contractor, 40
Ideal Observer, 40
indeterminateness of sense, 14–15, 37, 93,
    143, 211

India, 140–2, 254
infanticide, 83, 130
International Convention on the
    Elimination of All Forms of Racial
    Discrimination (1966), 194, 282
    n. 28, 287 n. 21
International Covenant on Civil and
    Political Rights (1966), 191–2, 193,
    194, 196–201, 227, 284 n. 42, 289
    n. 8, 308 n. 2, 308 n. 4. 308 n. 6, 308
    n. 7, 308 n. 11, 321 n. 1
    Draft ~ (1957) 311 n. 3
International Covenant on Economic,
    Social, and Cultural Rights (1966), 99,
    191, 193, 206–9, 284 n. 42, 289 n. 7,
    308 n. 11, 310 n. 24, 310 n. 29, 310
    n. 30, 310 n. 31
international law, 5–6, 13–14, 53–4, 104,
    191–211, 309 n. 20
Inuits, 161, 168, 204
Iran, 25
Islam, 26, 138, 140, 142, 285 n. 62, 285
    n. 63, 299 n. 31
ius, 30

James, Henry, 326 n. 42
Jefferson, Thomas (President), 299 n. 29,
    303 n. 7
Jesus, 141, 299 n. 31
Joseph, Sarah, 296 n. 12, 296 n. 14
Justice, 17, 41, 65–6, 81, 95, 186–7,
    198–201, 209, 214, 251, 278, 292 n. 9
    distributive ~, 41, 62, 64–5, 144, 187,
        198, 271, 273
    retributive ~, 41, 62, 64 ,144, 271, 273
    procedural ~, 42, 186, 198, 199–201,
        273

Kali, 160
Kaminski, J. P., 279 n. 14
Kant, Immanuel, 2–4, 24, 28, 32, 34, 36,
    57, 59, 60–3, 66, 74, 76, 78, 96,
    153–6, 178, 201, 219–20, 278 n. 7,
    286 n. 13, 289 n. 4, 290 nn. 13–24,
    290 n. 27, 307 n. 26, 313 n. 18, 313
    n. 20, 327 n. 50
Kazanistan, 142
Kelsey, Francis W., 278 n. 5

Kennedy, Anthony (Justice), 233, 317 n. 12
King, Desmond S., 306 n. 13
Kramnick, Isaac, 279 n. 8
Kymlicka, Will, 266–7, 324 nn. 30–2, 324
    nn. 35–6, 325 n. 38, 325 n. 42, 328
    n. 56, 329 n. 59

Lacey, M. J., 282 n. 25
Laslett, Peter, 280 n. 16
law of peoples, 22–7
Lawrence v. *Texas* (2003), 317 n. 9
League of Nations, 13
Leary, Virginia A., 298 n. 27
legitimacy of governments, 246–7, 250–1
Levy, L. W., 308 n. 10
Lewis, Bernard, 299 n. 31
liberty, 32, 58, 81, 149–51, 159–75,
    178–9, 191, 216, 226, 229–41, 243,
    247, 260, 274–5
    broad/narrow interpretation of
        ~, 159–60, 170–4, 381 n. 12
    demandingness of right to ~, 167–9
    formal/material constraint on
        ~, 159–60, 167–8
    negative/positive ~, 166–7
Lincoln, Abraham, 59, 289 n. 6
Locke, John, 10–11, 27, 41, 83, 126 159,
    176, 212–15, 218, 279 n. 9, 279
    n. 10, 279 n. 11, 280 n. 16, 292 n. 3,
    302 n. 1, 303 n. 7, 304 n. 2, 312 n. 4,
    312 n. 5, 312 n. 6, 312 n. 9, 312 n. 11,
    312 n. 15

MacIntyre, Alasdair, 284 n. 60
Mackie, Gerald, 283 n. 35
Mackie, J. L., 125, 287 n. 18, 297 n. 8
MacKinnon, Catherine, 318 n. 17
Magna Carta (1215), 12
majority rule, 245–6
Manhattan Project, 99
'manifesto' rights, 209
Mao, Zedong, 254
Margalit, Avishai, 264, 324 n. 19, 324
    nn. 25–6, 324 n. 32
Maritain, Jacques, 25
May, Larry, 323 n. 4
Mayo, V. 283 n. 37
McCloskey, H. J., 283 n. 37

McGary, Howard, 303 n. 2
McMahan, Jeff, 292 n. 5, 292 nn. 11–12,
      313 n. 18
McMurrin, S., 307 n. 19
McNaughton, John T., 319 n. 22
Mill, James, 172
Mill, John Stuart, 3, 28, 159, 169–74, 172,
      229–30, 231, 232, 303 n. 13, 302
      n. 1, 303 n. 6, 303 n. 7, 304 n. 8, 317
      n. 8, 350 n. 55
Miller, David, 294 n. 17
Miller, Fred D. jun., 282 n. 33
Miller, Seumas, 306 n. 15
minimum provision, *see also* welfare, 32,
      149, 159, 191, 206, 208, 327 n. 50
Monaco, 248
Morley, Jack, 314 n. 30
Morsink, Johannes, 284 n. 60
Mozart, W. A., 164, 326 n. 42
Muhammad, 299 n. 31
Mulholland, Leslie A., 290 n. 12, 290 n. 24
murder, 91, 95, 213
Murdoch, Iris, 73

natural law, 9, 10–12, 191, 279 n. 10, 280
      n. 20, 281 n. 21
natural right, 1, 9, 10–13, 18, 30, 61, 277
needs, 88
   basic ~, 88–90, 293 n. 15
need account of human rights, *see* human
      rights
Nettleship, R. L., 305 n. 3
Newsham, Gill, 288 n. 38
Newton, Isaac, 74–5
Nickel, James, 280 n. 18
Nidditch, P. H., 302 n. 1
Nobel Peace Prize, 25
normative agency, 32–3, 35, 44–8, 67–8,
      81, 92, 150–1, 180
Nozick, Robert, 21–2, 27, 60, 76, 178–9,
      289 n. 5, 290 n. 11, 291 n. 42, 306
      n. 10, 326 n. 47
nuclear holocaust, 21, 76

obligation
   perfect/imperfect ~, 96
Ockham, William of, 31
O'Connor, Sandra Day, 233, 317 n. 12

Okin, Susan Moller, 312 n. 4
Oldfather, C. H. and W. A., 278 n. 6
Olmstead v. *United States* (1928), 228, 230
O'Neill, Onora, 281 n. 22, 288 n. 35, 289
      n. 5, 295 n. 1, 295 n. 15, 296 n. 18,
      301 nn. 7–8
Oregon, State of, 314 n. 32
Othman, Norani, 285 n. 62, 285 n. 63
' "ought" implies "can" ', 72, 98

Paine, Thomas, 176, 282 n. 26, 303 n. 7,
      304 n. 2
Paton, H. J., 286 n. 13
paucity of options, 160–4
Pease-Watkin, C., 279 n. 11
Peaslee, Amos J., 316 n. 5
Peden, William, 303 n. 7
peeping Toms, 225, 227, 237
Peffer, Rodney, 306 n. 6
Pennock, J. R., 312 n. 4
personal identity, 86–7
personhood, 33–7, 44, 51–2, 80, 81,
      86–8, 97, 192, 198
personhood account of human rights, *see*
      human rights
Pettit, Philip, 291 n. 40
pharmaceutical firms, 106–7, 109
Philp, Mark, 304 n. 2
Pico della Mirandola, Giovanni, 31, 152,
      286 n. 8
Pinker, Steven, 287 n. 28
Pitt, H. G., 289 n. 6
'plan of life', 45–6
*Planned Parenthood of Southeastern
      Pennsylvania* v. *Casey* (1992), 233, 317
      n. 12
pluralist account of human rights, *see* human
      rights
Poe v. *Ullman* (1961), 230
Pogge, Thomas, 283 n. 34, 296 n. 18, 329
      n. 59
Poor Law (England, 1572), 102–3, 106
Poor Law Amendment Act (Britain, 1834),
      103
Porter, Cole, 164
Portillo, Michael, 306 n. 18
Posner, Eric, 309 n. 19
practicalities, 37–9, 44, 192, 235

principle of utility, 4, 29
privacy, 225–41, 315 n. 4
  informational ~, 226–41
  ~ of liberty, 229–38
  ~ of space and life, 229–38
Profumo, John, 320 n. 28
proliferation of rights, 17, 93, 109
promoting/respecting goods, 80
Prussian Civil Code (1794), 176
public goods, 258, 261
public interest, 239–41, 320 n. 28, 320
  n. 29
Pufendorf, Samuel, 10, 11, 278 n. 6, 281
  n. 21
punishment, 65–6
'pursuit', 160–6, 193
Pylee, M. V., 299 n. 29

Radzinowicz, Leon, 304 n. 13
Raphael, D. D., 306 n. 6, 310 n. 21, 312
  n. 4
Rawls, John, 3, 17, 22–7, 28. 50, 112, 138,
  142–5, 250, 282 n. 24, 284
  nn. 45–53, 284 n. 55, 286 n. 65, 287
  n. 27, 296 n. 3, 297 n. 1, 298 n. 15,
  300 nn. 33–45, 304 n. 9, 307 n. 19,
  322 n. 14
Raz, Joseph, 54–6, 259–60, 261–5, 266,
  282 n. 31, 284 n. 56, 288 n. 32, 288
  n. 46, 324 nn. 17–28, 324 n. 32
realism (metaphysical), 121–2
Réaume, Denise G., 323 n. 12
Red Guard, 73
redundancy test, 214, 272, 326 n. 47, 326
  n. 50
Rehnquist, William (Chief Justice), 218
Reid, John Phillip, 280 n. 14
Reiss, H. S., 279 n. 7, 290 n. 24
relativity, ethical 129–32
  ~ of human rights, 133–7
Rembrandt, Harmensz van Rijn, 164
Respect for persons, 201
Respecting goods, *see* promoting goods
revolution
  American ~, 1, 13
  French ~, 1, 13
  Glorious ~ (England), 280 n. 16
Richards, D. A. J., 315 n. 1

right, a
  choice account of ~, 326 n. 50
  infringe/violate ~, 166
  positive/negative ~, 94, 166–7, 167–9,
    182, 223–4, 290 n. 10, 310 n. 2,
    311 n. 3
  ~ to asylum, 193
  ~ to autonomy, 46–7, 64, 69, 221, 327
    n. 50
  ~ to bodily integrity, 239
  ~ to compensation for miscarriage of
    justice, 198–9, 210
  ~ to death, 216–24, 313 n. 24, 314
    n. 31, 314 n. 32
  ~ to democratic participation, 5,
    242–55, 261
  ~ to determine number of one's
    children, 17
  ~ to development, 85
  ~ to education, 52, 53, 216, 327 n. 50
  ~ to equal pay for equal work, 187
  ~ to health, 99–101, 109, 143, 174,
    208, 209
  ~ to healthy environment, 309 n. 14
  ~ to inherit, 17, 194, 209
  ~ to liberty, 41, 43, 46–7, 59–60, 63,
    65, 97, 143, 174, 180, 212–13, 221,
    327 n. 50
  ~ to life, 41, 63, 97–101, 109, 143, 174,
    180, 193, 212–21, 290 n. 10, 327
    n. 50
  ~ not to be tortured, 52–3, 193
  ~ to peace, 17, 109, 209
  ~ to periodic holidays with pay, 5, 16,
    186, 209
  ~ to privacy, 193, 216, 225–41, 320
    n. 24, 320 n. 27
  ~ to property, 41, 65, 176, 195, 212,
    213
  ~ to protection against attacks on one's
    honour and reputation, 195, 209
  ~ to rescue, 98
  ~ to security of person, 193, 239, 258
  ~ to self-defence, 63
  ~ to self-determination, 273–5, 328
    nn. 51–3,
  ~ to welfare, 5, 17, 43, 44, 144–5,
    176–87, 290 n. 33, 306 n. 13, 327
    n. 50

right, a *(cont.)*
~ to well being, 85
~ to work, 207–8
Robinson, Mary, 306 n. 15
Roe v. *Wade* (1973), 231, 232
Roman Law, 30
Roosevelt, Eleanor, 177
Roosevelt, Franklin Delano, 1, 176–7, 207
Rorty, Richard, 283 n. 36
Rossiter, Clinton, 310 n. 1
Rousseau, Jean-Jacques, 32, 156, 312 n. 16
Ruddick, William, 281 n. 22
Ruthven, Malise, 300 n. 31

same-sex couples, 163–4, 169
Salvemini, Gaetano, 279 n. 13
Scanlon, T. M., 78–9, 287 n. 20, 291 n. 44, 294 n. 18, 315 n. 3
Schachter, Oscar, 309 n. 13
Scheewind, J. B., 279 n. 10, 281 n. 20, 281 n. 21, 301 n. 3, 301 n. 8
Schofield, P., 279 n. 11
Schopenhauer, Arthur, 313 n. 26
Schwartz, Alan U., 317 n. 10
Scruton, Roger, 322 n. 2
Second World War, 1
Sen, Amartya, 141, 285 n. 62, 298 n. 25, 307 n. 23
Senegal, 19
Shapiro, Ian, 328 n. 56, 329 n. 59
Shapiro, Scott, 278
Shariah Law, 65
Shue, Henry, 306 n. 14, 307 n. 22
Shute, Stephen, 283 n. 36
Simpson, A. W. Brian, 290 n. 9
Singer, P., 291 n. 40
Skinner, Quentin, 300 n. 2
Smith, Adam, 74
Smith, Holly, 303 n. 2
Smith, Huston, 299 n. 31
Socrates, 46
sodomy, 232–3
Solicitor General (US), 314 n. 28
solidarity rights, 256
Solzhenitsyn, Alexander, 46, 47
Sorabji, Richard, 282 n. 33
Souter, David (Justice), 233, 317 n. 12
South Africa, 105, 144

sovereignty, 273–5, 328 nn. 51–3
Sprigg, T. L. S., 326 n. 46
state of nature, 50–1
State of Washington et al v. *Glucksberg et al.* (1997), 313 n. 25
Steiner, Henry J., 308 n. 2
Steiner, Hillel, 289 n. 6, 307 n. 26
Stephen, James Fitzjames, 171–3, 304 nn. 10–12, 304 n. 14
Stewart, Potter (Justice), 232
Steyn, Johan, 290 n. 9
stipulation, 91–4, 271
Strum, Philippa, 315 n. 1
Suarez, Francisco, 10
Sub-Commission on Human Rights, 203
suicide, 216, 217–24, 230, 313 n. 18
Sumner, L. W., 286 n. 10
supererogation, 327 n. 50
Supreme Court (US), 228–34, 235, 237, 313 n. 25, 314 n. 28, 317 n. 7, 319 n. 22
Swinarski, Christophe, 322 n. 1

Tabor, A., 296 n. 12
Taliban, 161, 168, 172
Tatchell, Peter, 240
Tattersall, Ian, 301 n. 10
Tasioulas, John, 286 n. 65, 288 n. 37, 296 n. 18, 296 n. 20, 296 n. 21, 298 n. 16
Taylor, Charles, 270, 285 n. 62, 285 n. 63, 324 nn. 32–4, 326 n. 43
teleology, 3, 36, 58, 73, 79–80
test of the best explanation, 121–4
theft, 130
Thompson, Garrett, 293 n. 14
Thomson, E. P., 305 n. 2
Thomson, Judith Jarvis, 78, 282 n. 23, 291 n. 43, 297 n. 4, 318 n. 15, 319 n. 21
Thuggee, 160
Tierney, Brian, 286 n. 1, 286 nn. 5–7, 301 n. 3
tolerance, 142–5, 260
torture, 33, 42, 52–3, 193
Twycross, Robert, 314 n. 29

'undeserving poor', 184–6
UNESCO, 25
United Natons, 1, 13, 14, 16, 24, 25, 27,

85, 90, 94, 99, 100, 101, 104, 109, 139, 143, 156, 177, 183, 186–7, 192, 193, 194, 196, 203, 242, 254, 275, 277, 281 n. 22, 292 n. 8
~ Charter (1945), 308 n. 8, 328 n. 51
Universal Declaration of Human Rights (1948), 5, 13, 16, 25, 60, 139, 177, 186–7, 193, 195, 196, 202, 207 227, 242, 273, 282 n. 26, 282 n. 29, 289 n. 8, 307 n. 21, 308 n. 2, 308 n. 11, 309 n. 12, 310 n. 29
universality of human rights, 48–51, 101–2, 177–8, 181–2
Utiltarianism, 24, 36, 74, 79, 80, 171, 172

Vacco et al. v. *Quill et al.* (1997), 313 n. 25
value judgement
taste model of ~, 111–21
perception model of ~, 113–21
Vasak, Karel, 322 n. 1
Virginia Charter (1606), 13
Vitoria, Francisco de, 32
von Leyden, W., 279 n. 10

Wacks, Raymond, 315 n. 4, 318 n. 15
waiving of rights, 216, 290 n. 32, 327 n. 50
Waldron, Jeremy, 283 n. 39, 306 n. 11, 306 n. 13, 323 nn. 5–11, 323 n. 12, 323 nn. 14–16, 325 n. 42

Wallis, Charles Glenn, 286 n. 8
Walzer, Michael, 328 n. 55
Warren, Mary Ann 326 n. 46
Warren, Samuel D., 228, 316 n. 6
Watts, John, 295 n. 11
Welch, Claude E. jun, 298 n. 27
Weinreb, Lloyd, 280 n. 20, 315 n. 1
welfare, 63–4, 66, 69, 79, 80, 176–87, 282 n. 26
demandingness of right to ~, 182–4
indivisibility of ~ rights and liberty rights: 180–1
Wellman, Carl, 295 n. 24, 296 n. 17, 306 n. 6, 307 n. 22, 307 n. 25, 310 n. 21, 311 n. 3, 322 n. 3
White, Lewis Beck, 278 n. 7
Wiggins, David, 293 nn 15–17, 297 n. 6
Williams, Bernard, 70
Wilson, Peter (Governor), 182
Wittgenstein, Ludwig, 113–4, 136–7, 210, 273, 282 n. 30, 296 n. 4, 297 n. 7, 310 n. 32, 326 n. 49
Wong, David B., 297 n. 8
Woolf, Virgina, 236, 318 n. 18
World Health Organization, 101, 292 n. 8

Xydis, Doris Peaslee, 316 n. 5

Zuckerwise, Laura, 288 n. 30, 312 n. 14

Lightning Source UK Ltd.
Milton Keynes UK
UKOW06f0619200716

278808UK00001B/2/P